STITCHES IN TIME

THE STORY OF THE CLOTHES WE WEAR

Lucy Adlington

BOOKS

1 3 5 7 9 10 8 6 4 2

Random House Books
20 Vauxhall Bridge Road
London SW1V 2SA

Random House Books is part of the Penguin Random House
group of companies whose addresses can be found at
global.penguinrandomhouse.com.

Penguin
Random House
UK

First published by Random House Books in 2015

www.randomhouse.co.uk

A CIP catalogue record for this book
is available from the British Library.

ISBN: 9781847947260

Typeset by Palimpsest Book Production Ltd, Falkirk, Stirlingshire
Printed and bound by Clays Ltd, St Ives plc

Penguin Random House is committed to a sustainable future
for our business, our readers and our planet. This book is
made from Forest Stewardship Council® certified paper.

MIX
Paper from
responsible sources
FSC® C018179

STITCHES IN TIME

CONTENTS

INTRODUCTION

Open your wardrobe, your closet, your bedroom drawers ...

What do you see hung, folded, strewn or crammed inside?

Clothes.

Your own unique collection of garments and accessories, waiting to be worn.

Curious or commonplace, clothes are far too often taken for granted. In *Stitches in Time* I'd like to lead you through time to explore the extraordinary stories of our most ordinary possessions. I'll be delving deep in sock drawers, shoe boxes and jumper shelves; I'll be examining what's on the coat hooks, the tie rack and the dress rail ... and even what's crawled into the darkest corner of under-the-bed storage. Because your suits, skirts, trousers, undies and boots have not been crafted out of thin air or created on a whim. They hold history like no other aspect of material culture. And clothes also hold memories – sometimes shared, sometimes secret.

Clothes are at once the most intimate things we own and the most public. *Intimate*, because they are next to our skin, soaking up secretions, absorbing perfumes, collecting dandruff, covering or revealing as custom, culture or personal taste dictates. *Public* because they are often the first thing people notice about us. Our clothes display a staggering amount of information about our gender, culture, class, profession, status, morality and creativity. Yet we usually we fling them on without a thought for the wealth of meaning they carry.

This is by no means a definitive history. No one volume could be. There are infinite permutations of how billions of individuals wear innumerable different garments across different times, cultures and continents. For relative brevity – and the sake of my sanity – I've focused on the last 200 years of clothes, while still tracing each item back as far as possible to antiquity to show how it evolved.

Stitches in Time concentrates on Western clothes. It is Eurocentric. In fact, it is rather British at times. This is by no means to disregard non-Western traditions, or to diminish the rich and varied stories of clothes from other countries and cultures – some of these are included, when they have a part to play in my chosen themes. The sari, the kaftan and the niqab are seen in the West with increasing familiarity, after all. However, my focus is so place-specific because I have naturally been drawn to relatively local sources – costume collections, letters, diaries, portraits, funeral effigies, magazines and photographs which I can personally view; also, people I can personally interview.

My research has taken me into the worlds of literature, art, politics, fashion, trade, technology, transport and exploration. Of course there's always more to know. Even as I write this introduction my mind is darting away, and fretting – *But I didn't mention this… I wonder if that.. and Has anyone ever found out why…?*

I came into the world of costume history as a child, quite by accident. I'd run out of Sellotape for fastening outfits onto my 1970s Sindy doll (Sellotape being quicker than sewing for an impatient seven-year-old) and so dived into a pile of library books instead. I found myself lost in a delightful volume called *Costume Cavalcade* – page after page of colourful clothes from history. Move forward more than a few decades, and I confess that when I add to my current collection of vintage and antique clothes I often keep an eye out for outfits reminiscent of those featured in the *Cavalcade* (which I reluctantly returned to the library, later buying my own, treasured copy).

I now run History Wardrobe – a company which offers what I hope are rather wonderful costume-in-context presentations across the UK. It's a unique opportunity to showcase everyday clothes and outfits from special occasions; to explore the sad, strange, sensational stories behind the clothes . . . and to meet thousands of people to share clothing histories.

I hope you will enjoy reading this collection of anecdotes and insights as much as I've enjoyed creating it. I also hope it gives you a renewed appreciation for each and every item in your wardrobe, from luxury labels down to the humblest sock . . .

Lucy Adlington, 2015

www.historywardrobe.com
facebook: History Wardrobe
twitter: @historywardrobe

KNICKER ELASTIC

A young woman in communist Russia was brought before a committee and asked to provide a 'voluntary' loan to help fund the Great Patriotic War. She showed her objection by bending over, lifting her skirt and saying, 'Comrade Stalin and the rest of you can kiss me just wherever you find convenient.' There was an embarrassed silence, then one committee member murmured to another, 'Did you see she wasn't wearing any knickers?'[1]

SIR RODRIC BRAITHWAITE, *MOSCOW 1941:*
A CITY AND ITS PEOPLE AT WAR, 2007

BARELY THERE

In the history of underwear, pants are conspicuous by their absence for many centuries; we have scant physical evidence of these scant garments. Relatively unvalued, pants of any variety were unlikely to be treasured family heirlooms unless they featured fine decorative details. As a result they were also less likely to be carefully stored, meaning that they would quickly fall prey to the moths, damp and general decay that can affect all natural textiles.

Art history offers us few clues: portraiture generally required the sitter to be fully dressed, while erotica or the idealised forms of Classical antiquity found underwear to be close to irrelevant.

Finally we must also suspect that modesty and even prudishness account in part for the lack of pants in the historical record.

Most early evidence concerns male underwear. Where actual

1 Being pant-less was not the norm in Soviet Russia, although some hungry peasants were known to trade underwear for food, and two women in the Russian Air Force were actually sentenced to ten years' imprisonment for 'destroying military equipment', having stolen silk from a lighting-flare parachute in order to make suitable pants, because they had only been issued with men's underclothing. One was later killed in action, and the other was heavily decorated for bravery.

textiles have survived from prehistory, it is due to their original owners also surviving in a remarkable state of preservation, still wearing them. A good example is the protective leather loincloth of the Neolithic traveller whom archaeologists, for obvious reasons, have named 'Man in the Ice'. This solitary hunter was found in an Alpine glacier, having been preserved for more than 5,000 years with his clothes as frozen as his flesh. His loincloth, blackened with age, clearly served to cover the gap between his leggings. This leather cloth was about six feet long and worn over belt and leggings – it provided a good place for keeping tinder dry in an environment where fire-making was essential for survival. It is, to date, the oldest undergarment ever discovered.

A little over 1,500 years later, in Ancient Egyptian culture, we see examples of a more intentional preservation of textiles, through burial practices aimed at fitting out the lucky deceased with a comfortable afterlife. Amongst the thousands of articles excavated in the 1920s from the tomb of Pharaoh Tutankhamen were no fewer than 145 triangular linen loin-cloths for intimate wear, known as *schenti*. These are smaller than the loincloths worn as outerwear by lower-status males, and would have been hidden beneath an elaborate kilt. As is often the case with pants, Tutankhamen's linen cloths were rather carelessly bundled up and had to be painstakingly unravelled by archaeologist Howard Carter and his team before they could be sent for conservation and display in Cairo Museum. The Egyptian boy-king was also provided with 365 magical servants called *shabtis* to wash them all. In the real world of Egyptian daily life, professional washermen saw to the linens of society's elite families, while women took care of normal household laundry.

These first loincloths offered a certain degree of protection for male genitals, as well as keeping them discreet under kilts or short outer cloths. Their descendants – underpants – were not strictly necessary for decency's sake, since outer clothes in cooler climates were more than adequate to cover private parts from view. Loincloths were therefore to remain the only kind of underwear for many more centuries, until the first appearance of what would eventually become modern boxer-shorts and briefs – *braies*.

Braies were loose shorts held up by a drawstring. They began life as male outerwear in the Saxon period. As tunics grew longer and the braies were hidden, so they began to be considered underwear. By the Middle Ages they varied in style, some having legs tied around the knee, some being as small as loincloths and others fitting like modern boxers, with a slit at the thigh for flexibility.

In medieval art such pants are added to the human form in paintings only as an incidental detail on a large canvas. For example, when Saint Sebastian is shown painfully martyred by arrows in the fifteenth-century Italian painting *Misericordia* by Piero della Francesca, the emphasis is understandably on his holy suffering rather than on his surprisingly modern-looking briefs.[2]

History is always full of surprises . . . In 2008 archaeologists uncovered tattered linen pants under the floorboards of Lengberg Castle in Austria. Carbon dating is expected to confirm their provenance as early fifteenth-century, but the really teasing question is: are they male or female?

2 Similarly, in Gaudenzio Ferrari's painting *Christ Rising from the Tomb* of c.1540, Christ wears a neat pair of brown underpants.

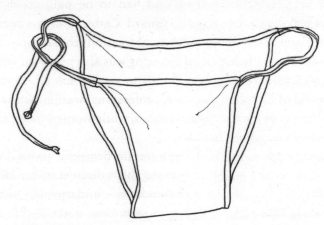

The newly discovered medieval linen pants from Lengberg.

While 'going commando' might be a modern term dating from the 1970s, it was a familiar concept for many centuries.[3] Given the lack of evidence from surviving textiles or artwork, we can only speculate as to whether it was the norm. In a charming vignette from a gorgeous early fifteenth-century painting in the *Très Riches Heures du Duc de Berry*, male peasants warming themselves in front of a fire on a snowy day lift their tunics to show their unabashedly pant-less state. As for the solitary female in the *Très Riches Heures* painting, she keeps her long tunic round her ankles – a neat symbolism for the overwhelmingly scarce evidence that we have for women's pants (or lack thereof) before the nineteenth century.

Some depictions of female pants do survive from Classical antiquity, such as on a marble statue of the goddess Venus rescued from the ruins of Roman Pompeii and now on show at Naples National Archaeological Museum. Venus bends to fasten a sandal strap while wearing a delicate filigree of gold in the pattern of a brassiere and thong. Again, there is scant evidence of the pants worn by *real* women in Ancient Greece or Rome. It seems feasible that they could have adopted the diaper-style male loincloths and we do know that, for more robust activities, Roman women sported breast-bandeaux and tight, tucked loincloths, as seen in a mosaic of female athletes uncovered at the Villa Romana del Casale in Sicily.

In the following centuries evidence for female pants improves only slightly. Eve, in medieval Christian art, is shown with only generous swathes of blonde hair and a cleverly suspended fig leaf. Prior to humanity's fall from grace in the Garden of Eden there had been no need to cover nakedness. The fig leaf – symbolic underwear – becomes a mark of shame.

The convention of covering nudity with discreet drapes, leaves or tresses continued as the Tudor dynasty was established in England, leaving historians to wonder whether nudity was the norm under one's clothes, or whether underpants were simply considered too banal to depict – particularly in devotional art.

Queen Elizabeth I's extensive wardrobe inventories do not

list pants – then known as 'drawers' – until her death in 1603, when one John Colte was paid the phenomenal sum of £10 to provide her funeral effigy with a corset and 'a paire of drawers'. That pants were worn by other elite seventeenth-century women is clear from the fact that Maria of Medici, Queen of France from 1610, owned many pairs. Elsewhere on the continent rich women clearly wore drawers on some occasions. Surviving examples of high-quality women's linen drawers from Italy reach to mid-thigh. They have a generous open gusset, lace-together waistband and silver-gilt embroidery at the leg ends. Further down the social scale, female underwear is hidden in art and – perhaps understandably – absent from historical textile collections. Why would a lower-status woman preserve her underwear? How could a poor woman afford not to wear all her clothes until they were beyond mending, and therefore beyond saving?

And so, aside from rather patrician examples, there really is a scarcity of evidence about women's drawers. As already mentioned, we can in part attribute this lack to prudery. Even as late as the 1890s, modest women were hiding underwear inside pillowcases when drying laundry outdoors; later still, municipal flats built in the 1930s had a screened balcony included in their design, because 'very poor people are sensitive about displaying their underclothes to the neighbours'.

Discretion, however, is only part of the story.

As evidence for the making, selling and wearing of female pants increases in the early nineteenth century, so we also have more opinions voiced on the etiquette of women wearing drawers. The rather negative responses suggest that they were a novelty – and an unwelcome one at that. Queens and noblewomen may have escaped censure for their drawers, but the fashion had for a long time been associated with ladies of negotiable virtue, such as Venetian courtesans. One *grande horizontale* in the early seventeenth century had her linen under-breeches embroidered with blue linen thread to spell *'voclio il core'* – 'I want his heart' – this sentiment easily pre-dating a late twentieth-century trend for slogans on underwear.

Worse, the sensibilities of the late Georgian era deplored drawers as indecent, on the grounds that they resembled male trousers. Women who wore them could be accused of breaking gender roles by masquerading as men. As if that wasn't condemnation enough, drawers were thought unhygienic, perhaps from a conviction that they were too close to parts of the body considered unclean.

Xenophobia may also account for a particular reluctance to adopt drawers in England. The English have a historical habit of blaming their on/off enemies across the Channel for both infections and fads considered shameful – hence the term 'French Disease' to refer to the scourge of syphilis, and the euphemism 'French letter' for contraceptive sheaths. French fashions were both admired for their exquisite quality and deplored for their excesses. For many centuries pants were associated if not with the French alone, then certainly with foreigners generally.

Diarist Samuel Pepys was generally far more interested in his own wardrobe than that of the women in his life, and happily confessed that he enjoyed lying around in his drawers to keep cool on hot days. However, it seems his wife Elizabeth adopted drawers too, perhaps partly on account of her French ancestry. Samuel was distracted from descriptions of daily doings in London to record his growing concerns over his wife's fidelity. He (unfairly) suspected her of having an affair with her dance master, Mr Pembleton, and so on 15th May 1663 he contrived to spy on her 'to see whether my wife did wear drawers today as she used to, and other things to raise my suspicion of her . . .' The reader is left to wonder whether it was the wearing of drawers that would signify seduction, or the lack of them.

When, in the nineteenth century, British women finally overcame their general antipathy towards pants, it was an unseen but significant revolution, leading to the modern idea that pants are an essential item in every woman's wardrobe, although they have since shrunk in size and blossomed in attractiveness.

Peerless novelist Jane Austen (1775–1817) was a contemporary of the rise of popularity in women's pants, although her letters – full of snippets about clothes and shopping – never mention them, either from motives of discretion or because this controversial garment hadn't yet reached the quiet corner of Hampshire where she generally resided.

Austen also makes no mention whatsoever of Mr Darcy's intimate apparel. When she writes in *Pride and Prejudice* that Darcy was a 'gentleman' – giving no account of his actual clothes – the curious reader is left to wonder whether he wore drawers of China silk or knitted cotton drawers with attached feet, or whether he simply tucked the generously long tails of his shirt into his breeches; all three styles were available to men at the time.

Female drawers of the Georgian age were long-legged, reaching below the knees. Pairs were advertised in 1813 at three shillings and ninepence, making them far beyond the budget of most working women. In 1817 one Mrs Morris – self-styled as 'Manufacturer of Under-Clothing to the Royal Family' – respectfully informed readers of *Ackerman's Repository* that her patent invisible drawers in best real Spanish lamb's wool were ready for the present season. Despite being fine enough to suggest invisibility, these drawers were promoted as 'a great preventive against colds', but would 'not occasion any unpleasant irritation on the skin'. For hunting, stretchy India cotton drawers were recommended, if the fair equestrienne did not care for sturdier leather models. Leaving aside these specialist garments, drawers were generally plain white and not extravagantly trimmed, often of a light cotton muslin with two separate legs attached to a drawstring waistband – hence the term *drawers*. This style was not without its perils – a private diary from America in the early nineteenth century records the humiliation of having a drawstring come loose:

4 *The Workwoman's Guide of 1838*, compiled by an anonymous 'Lady', praises *leglets* – 'they are especially advantageous for children who play a great deal out of doors, or who live in a town, they will sometimes soil one or two pair in a day'.

I lost one leg and did not deem it proper to pick it up, and so walked off leaving it in the street behind me, and the lace had cost six shillings a yard. I saw that mean Mrs Spring wearing it last week as a tucker.

Drawers remained controversial, even as they became more widely adopted. When young Princess Charlotte, outspoken daughter of the Prince Regent, took to wearing drawers in 1811, her daring met with criticism from a lady at court:

She was sitting with her legs stretched out after dinner and shewed her drawers, which it seems she and most young women now wear. Lady de Clifford said, 'My Dear Princess Charlotte, you shew your drawers.' 'I never do but where I can put myself at ease.' 'Yes my dear, when you get in or out of a carriage.' 'I don't care if I do.' 'Your drawers are much too long.' 'I do not think so; the Duchess of Bedford's are much longer, and they are bordered with Brussels lace.' 'Oh,' said Lady de Clifford in conclusion. 'If she is to wear them, she does right to make them handsome.'

Princess Charlotte was considered 'forward, dogmatical on all subjects, buckish about horses, and full of exclamations very like swearing', so her adoption of drawers could not quite be considered a seal of royal approval. That honour was conferred by the Duchess of Kent, mother of Queen Victoria, who wore generously shaped drawers in the 1820s, with a sturdy fabric waistband that could be adjusted by laces at the back, which had a wider opening than the front to allow for ease of use. Variations on this style held sway for many decades, with the added twist of detachable leglets, which were tied around the lower part of the leg only in order to keep the bottom of the drawers clean.[4]

Aside from leglets for the calves, or the longer, decorated pantalettes peeping out from under the petticoats, drawers were not usually meant to be seen in public, unless the wearer had the bravado and the frills of Lady Chesterfield, whose skirts

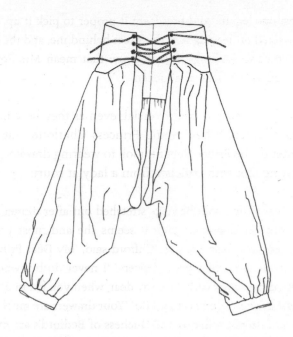

5 Deliberate 'accidental' flashes of underwear are a well-known ploy, attracting attention from press photographers. The most iconic image may well be Marilyn Monroe's pose above a New York subway grate for the 1955 film *The Seven Year Itch*; her billowing white skirt revealed prosaic untrimmed briefs.

Split drawers belonging to Queen Victoria's mother, the Duchess of Kent.

descended to one inch above her ankles and yet still showed the edges of 'those comfortable garments which we have borrowed from the other sex, and which all of us wear but none of us talk about'. The mainstream taboo against showing pants continued until the late twentieth century, which saw a short-lived trend for deliberately having knicker strings or bows visible above low-rise trousers.[5]

Though the majority of women took care not to reveal their undergarments, accidents did happen, even in the supposedly decorous decades of Queen Victoria's reign. Aristocratic ladies indulging in the craze for 'paper chase' parties – where they playfully raced along a trail of torn paper pieces, rather like hounds after foxes – faced the peril of going head-over-heels while crossing a stile. This terrible fate befell the Duchess of Manchester in 1859: 'the other ladies hardly knew whether to be thankful or not that a part of her underclothing consisted in a pair of scarlet tartan knickerbockers'.

Queen Victoria's drawers.

'VICTORIA'S 52" SECRET KNICKERS' – so screams the headline in the *Sun* newspaper of 29th April 2013.

Whenever Queen Victoria's pants appear at auction, they generate a great deal of publicity, as well as high prices and gleeful comments about their size. A pair of her drawers that were sold in 2012 fetched £360 and boasted a 39-inch waist. A buyer in Edinburgh paid almost £10,000 for a silk pair of unstated girth. And the 52-inch pair that so delighted tabloid journalists were bought by the Royal Ceremonial Dress Collection at Kensington Palace for £600. Striking though the photographs of her underwear are, while Queen Victoria was short and stout, she did not necessarily have a whale-sized waist. The prosaic truth is that, like most other examples of the style, the giant-waisted drawers were designed to be gathered to fit via a drawstring, and the excess fabric of the legs wasn't to stretch around thunderous thighs, but was simply a reflection of a preference for comfortable roominess in an age when Visible Panty Line problems were not yet an issue.

In contrast to her own ample garments, Victoria was excited to note in her diary that her husband Prince Albert inspected troops one day wearing 'cazimere pantaloons with *nothing underneath*'.

WOOL NEXT TO THE SKIN

Woollen undies may now sound hot, itchy and generally uncomfortable, but in the past they had their champions. From the

1870s onwards, German naturalist Dr Gustav Jaeger took time away from his zoological work to develop a system of healthy clothing, taking as his basic premise the idea that plant fibres were harmful to human health. His ideas were promoted in Britain in 1884 by the newly founded Dr Jaeger's Sanitary Woollen System Company, which morphed into the modern Jaeger fashion brand.[6]

Nothing but head-to-toe wool would satisfy the Jaeger school of thought, leading to decades of women and men sweating heartily – and, allegedly, healthily. Woollen undergarments were soon widespread, with many imitations of Jaeger products. The wool could be very finely spun for summer wear, or made from thicker yarns for winter. Gradually the bulk of vest or shift and

6 Jaeger published his philosophy in 1880 as *Die Normalkleidung als Gesundheitsschutz*, or *Standardized Clothing for Health Protection*. He is less well known for his pioneering work on the proof of the existence of pheromones, including one he called a 'lust compound' that was excreted through the skin. This may explain his interest in keeping the body well ventilated through animal fibres.

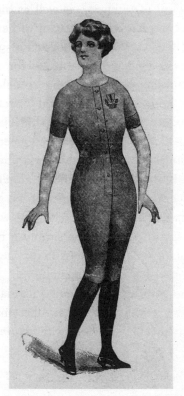

Gustav Jaeger promoted the idea of wool next to the skin, as with these combinations from the mid-1920s.

7 Damp, sweaty
fabrics were a
particular concern in
an age before
commercialised
deodorants and
universal indoor
plumbing for baths.
Advances in
knowledge of bacteria
converted the
Victorian moral
crusade for robust
health into a
twentieth-century cult
of chemical
cleanliness.

8 Some alpinists
prefer silk long johns
to wool. Sir Ranulph
Fiennes found
underwear could
chafe and cause what
is evocatively known
as 'crotch-rot'. In
Cold, his account of
his explorations, he
describes wearing
cotton boxer-shorts
under thin wickaway
long johns for his
extreme sub-zero
challenges.

drawers was simplified into the all-in-one combination suit for women and men. By the end of the nineteenth century snug-fitting combinations graced the pages of shop catalogues and fashion magazines, although the wearers were closer to cosy than coy in their poses.

Plenty of experts were eager to follow Jaeger principles, arguing that 'The adoption of woollen undergarments has resulted in a great gain in health, and the simplicity of the articles of underwear now worn contrasts agreeably with the needless complexity of those in use before.' Another agreed that the 'spoils of other creatures' were the only fit materials for human clothing, as well as arguing that cotton or linen next to the skin caused colds, but was less keen on wool, suggesting that flannel was far more sensible, particularly for sports.[7]

Jaeger's principles of aerated skin and health through under-wear were doomed to failure in the case of poverty-stricken people who had no change of clothing and little time or money for washing the undergarments they did own. And a limited budget was not the only problem. Many families stuck to the theory that it was safer and warmer not to bare the skin. Children might even be sewn into their underwear over winter, purportedly to protect them from chest infections. Hospital staff treating impoverished patients reported that many wore their underwear unwashed until it literally fell off or had to be peeled from their skin.

The ultimate endorsement for wool underclothing came with the polar expeditions of the early twentieth century. Extensive lectures, slide shows and even film clips made the public aware of the extreme conditions endured by Arctic and Antarctic teams. It was only natural, therefore, that companies such as Jaeger would be keen to kit out the teams led by Ernest Shackleton and Robert Scott, so that their woollen products would benefit from the association. Scott benefited from discounted underwear for his team from the underwear brand known as Scott, and the canny clothing company printed advertisements that read simply: GONE WITH SCOTT.[8]

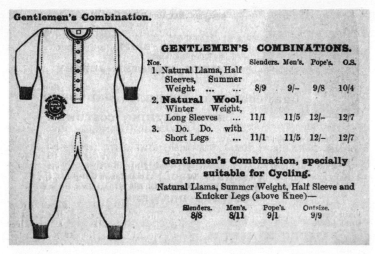

Gentlemen's Combination.

Gentlemen's Combination.

GENTLEMEN'S COMBINATIONS.

Nos.		Slenders.	Men's.	Pope's.	O.S.
1.	Natural Llama, Half Sleeves, Summer Weight	8/9	9/-	9/8	10/4
2.	Natural Wool, Winter Weight, Long Sleeves ...	11/1	11/5	12/-	12/7
3.	Do. Do. with Short Legs ...	11/1	11/5	12/-	12/7

Gentlemen's Combination, specially suitable for Cycling.

Natural Llama, Summer Weight, Half Sleeve and Knicker Legs (above Knee)—

Slenders.	Men's.	Pope's.	Outsize.
8/8	8/11	9/1	9/9

Woollen combinations, such as these from 1915, were greatly appreciated by those serving in the First World War.

From 1914 onwards, servicemen of the First World War also stocked up on woollen underwear for life in the trenches. One officer, John, 9th Duke of Rutland, sent a request for '6 prs thickest Jaeger vests and drawers (long drawers)' from the Army & Navy Stores. And aviators of the First World War had specialist underwear threaded with zigzags of wire, which could be electrically heated to combat the cold experienced in open cockpits. Early designs were temperamental, but the idea was later improved in the 1980s with the use of a more flexible knitted Terylene yarn with resistance wire incorporated, on a 28-volt direct current.

FRILLIES

On the less practical side, those with frivolous taste and the spending money to indulge it were fortunate that the final years of Queen Victoria's reign saw a flamboyant increase in frills and ribbons on all female netherwear, to combat the sturdy practicality of undyed wool or grey flannel. The orphaned young heroine of Noel Streatfeild's novel *Thursday's Child* is immensely proud of having lace on her Sunday underwear, and 'three of everything'. Conversely, Laura, the heroine of Flora Thompson's *Lark Rise* series of novelised reminiscences, was teased for having lace on her drawers, which were hand-me-downs from better-off relations. After leaving the house, Laura would take them off and hide them in a haystack.

England's first international couturier – the designer known in fashion circles as Lucile Ltd – took full credit in her memoirs for introducing the idea of making women's undergarments as pretty as the floating chiffon dresses that concealed them. 'Lucile' was the trade name of Lady Lucy Duff Gordon, who sewed her way from obscurity to fame to wealth at the end of the nineteenth century, in a real-life rags-to-riches story. She also achieved notoriety as one of those who survived the sinking of RMS *Titanic* in a woefully undercrowded lifeboat

Lucile rejected virtuous cotton *broderie anglaise* underwear: 'I was so sorry for the poor husbands, who had to see their wives looking so unattractive at night after taking off the romantic dresses I had created. So I started making underclothes as delicate as cobwebs and as beautifully tinted as flowers, and half the women in London flocked to see them, though they had not the courage to buy them at first.'

One husband was horrified to encounter some of Lucile's newest and filmiest lingerie sets at her *maison* in London:

> Picking them up he exclaimed wrathfully:
> 'No virtuous woman would be seen in such things.'
> 'I'm sorry you feel like that about it,' I told him, 'because they are just going home to your wife who has ordered them.'
> They did not come back, however, and the check for payment, although it was an unusually large one, arrived the next day.

Lucile died in April 1935, and lived long enough to see a design adaptation that, with the exception of some modern fetish wear, looks set to stay – closed-crotch pants. This innovation coincided with the energetic fight for female political and social emancipation in the early twentieth century. A stitched-up seam, as opposed to open drawers, was considered a sign of women's freedom, contrary though this may seem. It literally and symbolically rebuffed access from without. However, it also created practical lavatory issues that had been clumsily circumvented by the large gap of open drawers; now women too had to wrestle with removing pants each time they visited the smallest room. This was, perhaps, preferable to the 'hit and miss' results obtained when parting the fabric of open drawers. Men, meanwhile, had flaps at the rear of their drawers, but had to wait until 1935 for *Y-front* briefs – it was in that year that the legendary style was patented by an American hosiery firm called Coopers. Their cotton-jersey fabric and easy access gave them a reputation for being daring, but they were instantly huge bestsellers.

As the twentieth century progressed, women's pants became more recognisable as ancestors of the underwear we wear today. Since clothing was becoming lighter, shorter and looser, underwear began to shrink and shimmy more, until two styles competed for preference.

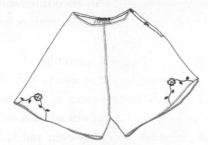

French knickers of the 1940s, with hand-embroidered decoration.

French knickers were the first style. These were pretty, loose-fitting shorts, often of silk or Celanese. They were held at the waist by elastic, then fluted out to cover the rear, sometimes reaching as far as mid-thigh. They were popular between the

1920s and 1940s, then revived in the 1980s as part of the re-feminisation of underwear, to contrast with the boxy masculinity of business boardroom 'power-dressing'.

By contrast, *Directoire knickers* – also called *tango pants* because they were secure enough to wear while cavorting Argentinean-style on the dance floor – fastened more securely round the legs with elastic bottoms, just above the knee. They could be of stretch cotton jersey, or even taffeta and cashmere for hot weather. Their leg elastic also served the function of holding a handkerchief in place, if the pants themselves did not have a handy hanky-pocket stitched on. This led to rather undignified rooting around under the skirt hem whenever a sneeze was imminent.

Directoire knickers from the mid-1920s.

The Directoire design was used in depressing shades of navy blue and bottle green for school gym knickers, greatly detested by the girls who had to wear them, both indoors and out. They came to be known as *ETB* knickers (Elastic Top and Bottom) and also earned various unflattering slang names, such as 'passion killers' and 'harvest festivals' (because, like the harvest, *all is safely gathered in*).

Crime writer Agatha Christie made special mention in her memoirs of shopping in Cork for what she termed *elephant knickers*, of unknown design. Her elderly relatives had given her the time-honoured advice, 'Always put on clean underwear when going on a railway journey, in case there should be an accident.'[9] In Christie's crime novels there is little mention of undergarments except in the case of flighty murder victims suspected of wearing lingerie of foreign origin (*4.50 from Paddington*, 1957), or when faddy vegetarian men with beards are accused of wearing patent kinds of underwear (*Body in the Library*, 1942).

French knickers, on the other hand, owing to that casual association of Gallic garments with naughtiness, became known as 'easy feelers'. The wartime 'Utility' scheme of the 1940s, which rationalised garment manufacturing, gave rise to jokes reflecting contemporary unease with the influx of well-paid, hearty American servicemen: 'Have you heard the one about the Utility knickers? One Yank and they're down . . .'

During the Second World War shop-supplies of underwear were scarce and unreliable, leading to great innovations in knicker-making. Rubber was at a premium, due to the military occupation of rubber-producing countries, as well as the huge difficulties of protecting merchant shipping from roving U-boat attacks, so rubber elastic could not be spared for lingerie. This meant that knitted pants (with matching brassieres) were a popular option. French knickers now needed a button fastening on one hip to hold them in place. One Yorkshire woman recalled dancing to a wartime band with a young man she had just met. Her button popped and her French knickers took French leave,

9 The concern over being caught in dowdy underwear continued through the twentieth century. In 2012 the *Wakefield Kinsman* reported that as relatives waited to hear how an elderly aunt was faring in hospital after being taken ill in the street, a neighbour asked anxiously, 'Was she clean underneath?'

10 In the author's costume collection are dyed parachute-nylon French knickers for a 1946 honeymoon, a slip made from cream-coloured parachute silk edged with antique Edwardian lace, and a totally transparent parachute nylon wedding dress.

11 In the author's collection is a pair of primrose-yellow camiknickers stitched by hand by a WRAF radio operator in the long hours between sending bomber crews off on their missions and waiting to hear news of their fate. Sadly, her fiancé was one of the bomber boys who did not return.

dropping down to her ankles. Her beau calmly scooped them up and stuffed them in his pocket. They were married not long afterwards.

In the fine spirit of wartime Make-Do-and-Mend, women rushed to be first on the scene if an airman was spotted parachuting down, having abandoned his plane. This wasn't because of an urgent desire to arrest enemy pilots, or to offer first-aid; the women simply wanted to steal the parachute silk, which would rapidly be transformed into trousseau items, wedding gowns and other black-market luxuries. German landmine parachutes were particularly coveted for their attractive pale-green colour.

Mid-war, the miracle fabric nylon superseded silk as parachute material. American chemical company DuPont had created nylon as we know it in 1935. It was a truly artificial, synthetic fabric. Being silky in texture, it was perfectly suited for lingerie, although it would not oust plant-based rayon until the 1950s. Towards the end of the war the British government released surplus parachutes in both silk and nylon for widespread in-store sale. Nylon was seized upon as a novel, easy-care fabric, as glamorous as silk. Helpful sewing guides were published giving techniques for cutting knickers and slips from the triangles of parachute fabric. Naturally care had to be taken to cut around printed inventory numbers or, in the case of stolen German parachutes, Nazi swastikas.[10]

During the Forties underwear items for women had proliferated, and this variety caused some concern to male CID officers investigating murders and bomb-related deaths in Britain during the Second World War. Victims were undressed in a morgue, and their clothes were tabulated as they were removed. The male officers often had trouble putting a name to the different species of undergarment, and Molly Lefebure, a morgue secretary, found she often had to provide explanations. However, she recalled, 'There was one garment they always recognised immediately, all greeting it with triumphant shouts, Camiknicks!'[11]

Camiknickers were a combination of camisole and pants, usually in a light, pretty fabric with lace or embroidery embellishments. These ones date from 1940.

BRAVE NEW WORLD

Nylon wasn't the only wonder-fabric to change the way pants were made. Lastex was the trade name for a rubber-mix fabric created by the US Rubber Company in the early twentieth century. With an elastic core covered by natural or rayon threads, it was first used in corsets and then in panty-girdles. Lycra, invented by DuPont in 1959 and also known as Elastane or Spandex, had an even more dramatic impact on the form and function of women's pants. As the flamboyant 'New Look' skirts and petticoats of the 1950s and early 1960s began to shrink to ultra-modern sheath dresses and miniskirts, there was no room for bulky layers of underwear. The new, stretchy textiles meant that female pants could not only fit closely to body contours, but could also mould the flesh they covered. Such tightly fitting female pants became one of the controlling undergarments known as 'shapewear'. In some cases they were firm enough to double up as a girdle. They were also a last bastion of decency under thigh-skimming hemlines.

Although convenient for corset-less dressing, such 'support' pants were not without their perils. More than one wearer has reported to the author their chagrin at rolls of flesh escaping from the waistline – a condition now known as the 'muffin top'. A lady who made the brave decision to cut hers lower found that the roll of flesh simply migrated south too, while a lady who yanked hers off at an RAF dance in exasperation had to coerce a bemused husband into hiding them in his uniform pocket until home-time.

On a flimsier note, paper pants enjoyed a short-lived notoriety in the 1960s, mostly used as disposables when packing for a foreign holiday. When working on Stanley Kubrick's groundbreaking 1968 film *2001: A Space Odyssey*, costume designer Hardy Amies suggested that the astronauts should wear paper-fibre-based disposable underclothes. Kubrick replied, 'Oh no, I shall have every housewife in the audience wondering if she has made a mistake in ordering a new washing machine.'

In fact, real-life astronauts wear sterilised cotton long johns. When not in a space station, MAGs are also essential – the Maximum Absorbency Garment – essentially a space nappy. These adult diaper-knickers are never featured in science-fiction films, which prefer the more aesthetically pleasing singlet and briefs, as with Sigourney Weaver's character in Ridley Scott's 1979 film *Alien*, or Sandra Bullock in Alfonso Cuarón's 2013 release *Gravity*.

Modern male underpants have remained conservative for the most part, with shorts and briefs not unlike medieval braies; Y-fronts and boxer-briefs with brand-name waistbands; and the occasional sportswear style. Novelty prints and slogans attest to male peacocking, but most male pants are of muted colours and designs – plain, plaid or striped.

However, pants today are no longer objects of shame.

Underwear is routinely advertised in home shopping catalogues, online or on bus-stop billboards. People speak of wearing 'pulling pants' when going out in search of sexual partners. Since the 1990s waistbands on jeans and shorts have dropped to a pelvic-bone low, so that pants can deliberately be seen; for male underwear this means flashing the brand name of their pants, which is intentionally woven large on the elastic waistband. Where nineteenth-century pants may have had the owner's initial inked or embroidered on, by the twenty-first century the wearer's most intimate garment is private no longer and flaunts the name of global designers.

While *magic pants* now aim to control curves, just like the shapewear mentioned above, in a bizarre twist of fashion evolution, padded pants are also now on sale, shaped with bulbous silicone inserts to enhance the shape of the buttocks. For women there are thongs, tangas, g-strings, bikini briefs, boy-shorts and Brazilians . . . the range of designs is as wide as the amount of fabric required is minimal. Where a Regency woman might have feared losing one pants leg in the street, or a Victorian lady having her long drawers exposed by a wayward crinoline cage, the modern female's greatest pant catastrophe is most likely to be tucking her skirt in her knickers on leaving the lavatory.

Men can cover up in boxers, trunks, Y-fronts, briefs and posing pouches, with fabrics ranging from plain cotton jersey to comedy prints and slogans. Nineteenth-century hand-stitched trousseau collections of twelve or twenty-four pairs of drawers have given way to economy five-packs, or three-for-two offers in supermarkets. We now have a greater array of pants to choose from than at any other time in history. No longer an anomaly, pants are a mainstay of the modern wardrobe, and a fine example of a garment that has evolved beyond prudery and practicality. More than a mere buffer between body and outer clothes, pants have a language all their own. Hidden or flaunted, they flirt, seduce, delight, compress and contain.

Very impressive for one small, stitched-together piece of fabric.

SHIRTS AND SHIFTS

My father was always one to set his own style, rather avant garde. I had had a session of dyeing a blouse a rather dark shade of pink, and this had inadvertently gone into the laundry with one of my father's white shirts. The result was a rather fetching shade of pink. He quite liked it, and decided to wear it to work the next week. At this time he commuted to London with the bowler hat brigade, and apparently this pink shirt caused quite a stir. One of the formally attired gentlemen was heard to remark, 'If THAT'S what he wears to town, WHAT does he wear in the country?'

HISTORY WARDROBE ORAL-HISTORY SURVEY,
MY LIFE IN CLOTHES

UNDERWEAR AS OUTERWEAR

Plain or patterned, fitted or outsize, mint or faded, the T-shirt finds a place in most modern clothing collections. There are T-shirts for all ages, classes, budgets and tastes. The simple cotton-jersey fabric can also act as a canvas for political causes, cultural allegiances and humour: the protest messages of Katharine Hamnett in the 1980s, the iconic print of Che Guevara or comic 'I'm With Stupid'-style messages. The T-shirt is also a billboard for designer logos and labels or, in the case of sportswear, sponsorship names. The popularity of this simple item of clothing is evidence of our current craving for comfort, informality, versatility and easy self-expression.

The T-shirt gives the impression of being a particularly

modern article of apparel. Since Marlon Brando wore a blisteringly white example in *The Wild One* in 1953, set off by his broody black biker leathers and blue denim jeans, the T-shirt has been associated with modernity, youth and rebellion.[1] Brando was followed by the equally iconic James Dean in *Rebel Without a Cause* (1955), sporting the same T-shirt, jacket and jeans combination.

In fact the modern T-shirt is only a new manifestation of ages-old T-shaped garments worn next to the body, primarily as a buffer between skin and outer clothes and, in all honesty, to soak up sweat. The T-shirt is therefore perhaps the first example of wearing underclothes as outerwear.

PRELUDE TO NUDITY

While the modern T-shirt can be fairly gender-neutral in cut, colour and design, its ancestor – the original basic T-shaped garment – had gendered features and functions.

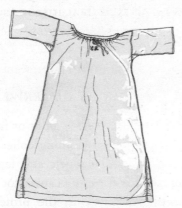

A nineteenth-century linen shift with drawstring neck and the initials C.R. worked in red cross-stitch.

For women, this intimate item was known as a 'smock' or 'shift', until linguistic fashions changed in the eighteenth century and these terms were considered too vulgar. They were replaced by the French word *chemise*. Basically a tunic in form,

1 A T-shirt produced by the combined talents of Vivienne Westwood and Malcolm McClaren in the 1970s caused them to be prosecuted under British obscenity laws, as it was 'exposing to public view an indecent exhibition' – an image of two naked cowboys. Westwood's later *Let it Rock* T-shirt collection of 1975 featured ripping, knotting, cutting and collages, with zips, studs, chains and even chicken bones.

it was the essential base layer for Western women from the Roman era onwards.

To the modern eye, the chemise is a remarkably unalluring garment. Made of linen or even hemp, it allowed few concessions to curves. Before the nineteenth century it was rarely embellished with anything other than a narrow frill at the neckline and sleeve ends. It flared down the body to knee or calf length, and was stitched with extra-strong seams to ensure it survived frequent washes. These seams had to be inspected frequently for vermin, as lice in particular liked to lay their eggs in the warm, damp fibres.

As fashion dictated, the chemise might sometimes be partially visible, showing a ruffle of white at the bosom or elbows. However, it was not intended to be seen in full beyond the privacy of the bedchamber. As far as erotic appeal goes, the chemise was more of an inevitable prelude to nudity than an enticement. That said, in Elegy XIX, 'To His Mistress Going to Bed', the seventeenth-century poet John Donne makes the distinction between ghosts who 'walk in white' and his lover in her white linen shift: 'Those set our hairs, but these our flesh upright.'

Simple and secret as it was, the chemise still played a revolutionary role in history: it helped topple a Queen of France, no less.

THE QUEEN'S SHIFT

The robing and disrobing of Marie-Antoinette – married in 1770 to the French Dauphin, and therefore Queen of France following his 1774 coronation as Louis XVI – was a very public, highly formal affair. At the morning *levee* and the evening *couchee* ladies of the court fought for the prestigious roles of women of the chamber. The Dauphine herself was not permitted to pick up so much as a stocking. While the pecking order of court was scrupulously observed and the chemise was handed from one exalted lady to another, Marie-Antoinette stood naked amongst them all, arms crossed and sometimes shivering. She had no choice in this exhibitionism, and clearly did not care for it – one lady-in-waiting wrote of her, 'Her modesty, in every particular of her private toilet, was extreme.' Marie-Antoinette even wore a long-sleeved chemise of English flannel in her bath. A chemise must have been a comfortable contrast to the highly structured prestige fabrics of formal eighteenth-century court dress that high-status ladies were compelled to wear.

Much as she revelled in buying and wearing the most expensive and sumptuous fashions, as she grew more confident, Marie-Antoinette began to experiment with a very new style of outer clothing that would inspire the iconic gowns of the Regency era. She took to wearing what became known as a 'chemise dress'. Innocent as it seemed in form and intention, the chemise dress would have catastrophic political implications for a queen whose every garment and accessory was scrutinised not only by followers of fashion, but also by enemies looking for ammunition to attack her image and credibility.

The chemise dress was a high-waisted gown of light cotton muslin fastened with simple drawstrings and decorated only with cotton ruffles and a few dainty ribbons. Those who had previously attacked the Queen for spending obscene amounts of money on fashion now scorned her for essentially wearing underwear as outerwear. The chemise dress was the antithesis of the French court's usual grand displays of wealth and status. In shedding her structure and stately luxury, the Queen lost some of the armour of her position. In addition to the taint of appearing in public in underwear, the chemise dress was associated with Creole workers of the West Indies, who were considered of unimaginably lower status than someone of French blood-royal. The Queen's supporters no doubt used the polite term for the dress, *Chemise à la Reine*. Others may have raised a satirical eyebrow at the alternative name, *Chemise à la Creole*. In short, the dress was light on fabric, but heavy with uncomfortable implications.

Undaunted, Marie-Antoinette had her portrait painted in this new style, then exhibited publicly. It created a storm of criticism. Image has always been crucial to upholding the power and status of the ruling classes, and in a more stable regime perhaps the Queen's popularity might have survived. But amid the surge of anger, idealism and destructive energy that culminated in revolution in France, a queen who had been scorned as tainted did not seem untouchable.

Following a humiliating arrest and her incarceration by the revolutionaries, Marie-Antoinette did not long survive the execution of her husband, the King. She followed him to the guillotine in October 1793. The last portrait of the many that were made of her is a simple sketch by the artist Jacques-Louis David, who watched her pass in a tumbril with her hair cropped ready for the stroke of the blade, stripped to the vulnerable indecency of her underwear – not a chemise dress, not a fashionable whim: simply her chemise.

Whatever problems it may have caused Marie-Antoinette, the chemise dress was a daring, fresh and youthful style that would soon come to embody the spirit of the late Georgian era, in the form of the 'Empire' style frequently associated with Jane Austen's novels, or with the alleged egalitarianism of France during the revolution.

A few society ladies may have shed their chemise to appear in one semi-transparent layer of cotton or silk alone, but these were the daring, affluent exception. In general, women continued to wear their cotton or linen chemises as underwear, regardless of the dress on top. However, one elegant Russian woman visiting Paris in the 1790s wrote, 'You just cannot imagine what adorable chemises they are: when you put one on and take a good look at yourself in the mirror, you will be amazed at how easy it is to see through!' It is perhaps unsurprising that the new, light dresses were sometimes referred to as 'pneumonia gowns'.

Shifts were also the perfect costume for characters in the Gothic horror tales that were popular at the time, described thus in the 1802 *Ladies Monthly Museum*: 'the close, all white shroud-looking, ghostly chemise undress of the ladies, who seem to glide like spectres, with their shrouds wrapt tight about their forms'.

SENSIBLE V. SENSUAL

From the 1820s onwards new styles superseded the Empire dress, and the chemise was once again relegated to an unseen role as faithful undergarment. Nineteenth-century industrialisation created a surge in the availability of cheap machine-made lace, which led to increasing embellishment of women's undergarments. At first this was nothing too risqué – the white-on-white embroidery with pierced holes known as *broderie anglaise* did not upset Victorian notions of propriety too greatly. Many women still preferred the sturdy protection of plain linen or cotton or, as the century progressed, the freedom and alleged-healthfulness of the wool combinations mentioned in the previous chapter, in place of the chemise. Combinations were more structured than chemises and were therefore less bulky under well-tailored suits for women or tight-waisted gowns. According to *Science of Dress* expert Ada S. Ballin, 'The chemise is a bulky article and makes them look stouter than is natural to them.'

The term *lingerie* originally referred to the collection of linen garments prepared for a woman's entry into married life, known as a 'trousseau'. In the previous chapter we saw how the London dressmaker Lucy Duff Gordon, trading as Lucile Ltd, revolutionised the perception of what underwear should be. Lucile's concoctions of flower-tinted cobweb lace took courage to buy. Some women had to return their purchases, after spousal disapproval; others returned to Maison Lucile for repeat orders – at great expense.

More conventional women slowly followed suit. Mrs Pritchard, a fashion writer in 1902, declared in a *Ladies Realm* article, 'The old-fashioned idea that underwear must be absolutely hideous in order to be virtuous is, I am thankful to say, passing away;

and now the woman of refinement, be she rich or poor, endeavours to have dainty lingerie.'

Silk underwear was considered cheapest in the long run and most charming. Somehow the chemise survived the modernisation of underwear, shrinking in size and now perhaps being woven of new 'art silk' fabrics, such as rayon. In jersey wool or cotton, it became a vest. It was long enough to cover the kidneys, and soft enough to protect the body from a corset or girdle, just as the chemise had done for several centuries. Some young women of the late twentieth century expressed puzzlement at elderly relatives who insisted on wearing their bras over a vest; this was actually the last gasp of the practice of having the chemise under the corset.

FLAPPER STYLE

The chemise once again found favour as dress more than a century after Marie-Antoinette had first flaunted it as outerwear. During the First World War the 'shift' dress was hugely practical for women doing war work. It was similar to the government-issue tunics provided for factory workers; however, it was by no means a uniform, but rather a fine example of clothes adapting to environment: simple styles were needed, society was ready for such changes, and so they became more mainstream.

The shift dress simply popped over the head with minimal fuss and fastenings. After the war, despite the machinations of fashion houses that wanted a return to more profitable structured styles, the shift dress continued to dominate completely. Hiding the body but occasionally revealing the knees, it was *the* dress of the 1920s, in transparent cotton for tennis or of beaded net for evening wear.

Now known as the *flapper dress*, it pushed the boundaries of what was considered feminine and decent. It went against more established customs of requiring complex constructions that confined the body, covered the flesh and cost both time and patience for the wearer. A shift dress was easy to make, easy to wash and easy to wear – perfect for women without servants, who wanted to make the most of their day.[2]

The inevitable backlash against the shift dress of the Twenties saw a craving for fitted clothes, worn over the latest incarnation of the chemise as an undergarment – the slight, slim, thin-strapped *slip*.

PETTICOAT GOVERNMENT

'Charlie's dead . . .'

'It's snowing down south . . .'

While the slip reigned, there were many colloquial phrases that could be murmured with a discreet nod towards the knee region, to indicate that a person's slip was showing.

Take a chemise, change the fabric from sturdy to slinky, cut off the sleeves, add ribbon straps, embroidery and lace . . . and you have a slip. Such a dramatic customisation said a great deal about the new freedoms, dress forms and fancies of the inter-war decades. These were not modest garments designed to withstand a pounding in the wash-tub. From the peach and tea-rose satin slips of the Twenties and Thirties to the turquoise and yellow nylon versions post-Second World War, the slip was a pleasure to wear – and to behold.

Worn over bra and knickers, the slip was still considered an essential component of a woman's wardrobe until as late as the 1980s. It performed the age-old function of acting as a buffer between outer garments and the skin. It was also a last bastion of decency: going without a slip was as naughty in the 1950s as going without a chemise in the Regency period. Slips of the 1960s combined bra with underskirt, while below the exaggerated masculine angles of the 1980s power-suit the contrasting allure of feminine lingerie might include the slip. A modern revival in foundation garments has seen a new generation of slips on sale, in advanced-technology textiles that can cling, cool, slim or sway.

2 The shift dress was revived once more in a shorter, bolder, more boxy style during the mid-1960s. These later shift dresses came from couturiers such as Balenciaga or were run-up at home, sometimes with more enthusiasm than skill.

A 1915 petticoat. Petticoats were a protective layer and a glorious, gorgeous indulgence.

One close cousin of the chemise that is rarely found in the modern wardrobe is a petticoat designed to give bulk. *Petticoat* was originally a term given to a skirt that was meant to be seen – another element in the game of hide-and-seek that underwear has played throughout costume history. 'Petticoat' also referred to the voluminous breeches worn by men in the seventeenth century, which were so generously cut that Samuel Pepys noted it was possible to fit both legs down one side.

However, once coats and breeches fitted closer to the male body in the eighteenth century, the term 'petticoat' became inextricably associated with all things female. Hence the term 'petticoat government' to refer to the idea of female power.

Eighteenth-century dresses, known as *robes* or *mantuas*, were purposefully wide open at the front to show the visible female petticoat (which we would now call a skirt). The *polonaise* style actually hitched up the robe around the sides and back as well, to reveal even more petticoat in a glorious display of expensive excess.

For affluent females, these visible petticoats could be made of satin embroidered with silk, have silver-gilt thread and spangles or ruffles of silk and ribbon. They matched or contrasted with the robe. They were often quilted with beautiful designs of quills, feathers and flowers, and might also be quilted for extra warmth – no small consideration in homes without central heating or double-glazing. In 1714 the editors of the *Spectator* magazine even suggested petticoat embroidery as a tactic to prevent young girls idling away their hours shopping and gossiping. The everyday petticoats of middle-class and even working women might still bear witness to quilting skills, or a penchant for bold stripes.[3]

Regardless of status or spending power, there was always a plain, practical petticoat layered beneath the outer one – an underskirt known as a *dickey*. The dickey took the name 'petticoat' for itself, once fashion moved towards closed robes in the last quarter of the eighteenth century and the visible petticoat was relegated to unseen undergarment status once more.

From the 1820s onwards petticoats held sway for a century. Their dominance was greatest during the years of Queen Victoria's reign, when the fashionable silhouette demanded spreading skirts and a bulky bell-shape around the legs.

How was this bulk to be achieved? The techniques involved were a credit to the inventiveness of the age. Starch was used as a natural aid for layers of cotton and muslin; horsehair textile gave a stiff – if prickly – shape. If time, eyesight and sore fingers were no consideration, then cording, ruffles and fabric tucks could be inserted for weight and width; plaited straw was a quicker, cheaper alternative. With the advent of mouldable rubber, some Victorian petticoats were invented with inflatable inner tubes, although it is doubtful whether many of these progressed beyond the patent-pending stage.

3 As she aged, Lancashire woman Elizabeth Shackleton appreciated the warmth of a petticoat. Writing in 1759, feeling every one of her fifty-four years, she noted, 'I left off my very old green quilted Callimanco petticoat and put on my new drab Callimanco quilted petticoat. God grant me my health to wear it and do well.'

The 1840s saw a soft alternative to the heavy horsehair petticoat – feathers. A diarist in 1842 heard gossip that Lady Aylesbury had forty-eight yards of fabric in her gown and a feather-filled petticoat, 'which swells out this enormous expanse and floats like a vast cloud when she sits down or rises up'.

To take the bulk to extremes, the hooped petticoats of the sixteenth and eighteenth centuries were once again revived for use and abuse. In one of the most ludicrous of all fashions, hooped petticoats were stiffened with canes or whalebone or were structured over metal cages. The cage style became known as the *crinoline* – we shall see more of it in action in the chapter on dresses.

With or without a crinoline, a little adroit manoeuvring of skirts could reveal a tantalising glimpse of lace edging, or even coloured petticoats. Paintings by artists such as Henri de Toulouse-Lautrec, Mary Cassatt and James Tissot show skirts covering petticoats of the late nineteenth century in all their frothy, ruffled, dirt-gathering glory.

SILK AND SUGAR

Silk petticoats were coveted as the ultimate luxury garment in the nineteenth century. The sound of silk skirts rustling was referred to as *scroop*, and it was deliberately created by fabric manufacturers who adulterated pure silk with tin salts, to give it a crisp finish and satisfying weight. The Victorian cult of petticoats was revived in the middle of the First World War, as a frivolous reaction to the pre-war hobble skirt, which was exceptionally, impractically narrow. Now fashion decreed that the sound of silk petticoats should no longer be as significant as scroop, but a more subtle *whisper*. Then in 1947, responding to the further austerity of the Second World War, Christian Dior reintroduced voluminous skirts that were stiffened with horsehair and petticoats.

The flamboyant skirt circumferences of the New Look

persisted into the 1950s and 1960s, leading to wonderfully exuberant petticoats of paper nylon or starched cotton. These petticoats did not whisper – they positively crackled. Sugar solution was a sure way to stiffen petticoats to 'full-up net', although such sugared petticoats had a tendency to droop when wet. One woman the author spoke to remembered as a girl being bored at a party and idly sucking on her sugared petticoat as a sweet way of passing the time. Drying a sugared petticoat also presented some difficulties, with girls reporting petticoats getting stuck fast to hot-water tanks, smouldering over living-room lampshades or attracting flies and wasps on the outdoor washing line.

In spite of these drawbacks, many women and girls enjoyed wearing petticoats. Vera Clarke, born in Lancashire in 1939, loved the fun fashions of the Fifties and early Sixties: 'I had a skirt printed with rock 'n' roll figures and a stiff petticoat with "See You Later Alligator" embroidered on it.' Such elaborate frou-frou was a far cry from the humble, limp linen chemise.

Where are the petticoats, slips and chemises now? Those women still wishing to follow the old-fashioned advice of 'keeping your kidneys warm' today have delicate 'thermal' vests and base layers. If a slip is worn at all, it will be of an ultra-modern textile – usually in discreet beige or black – that will claim to contour the body. Reducing bulk, not creating it, is now the main aim of foundation garments.

KEEP YOUR SHIRT ON

It was a scene that made television history – and made pulses race. Actor Colin Firth strode into immortality as Mr Darcy in the 1996 BBC production of *Pride and Prejudice*. Having partially stripped to swim on a hot day, Darcy's subsequent unexpected encounter with Miss Elizabeth Bennet while still in a state of partial undress is an exquisite portrayal of desire and embarrassment – and it's all thanks to that billowing white Regency shirt.

Jane Austen's character Mr Darcy would have worn a shirt similar to this one, a style of 1807.

'The wet shirt scene was supposed to be a total male-frontal nudity scene...' admitted scriptwriter Andrew Davies. Yes, Mr Darcy was originally intended to be nude for his meeting with Miss Bennet, on television at least; not in the original 1813 novel by Jane Austen, in which characters may display the eponymous pride and prejudice, but certainly no flesh. In the novel there was no swimming, nude or otherwise; however, the television version needed to make an impact on a late twentieth-century audience, whose concepts of impropriety were probably very different from Regency sensibilities. In fact it would have been tremendously shocking for Miss Bennet to see Mr Darcy in his shirt, let alone topless or completely undressed – a gentleman's shirt was an item of underwear, comparable to a female shift. If the coat was removed in company, it was swiftly replaced by a *banyan*, or dressing gown, so that the shirt was covered once more.

The male shirt served the same purpose as a woman's shift – it was a buffer between body and outer clothes, a washable sweat-absorber and a long-tailed substitute for drawers, if these weren't worn.

As the first layer of male attire, it was the most intimate. As the final layer of undressing, it is also the last bastion of prosperity. To 'sell the shirt off your back' signifies desperation for funds; if someone will 'give you the shirt off his back', it is the ultimate act of generosity.

As one of the most basic items of clothing, shirts are often used as a symbol of civilisation and humanity. In the *Tarzan* series by Edgar Rice Burroughs, Tarzan the ape-man contrasts the 'savage' freedom of his bare skin with the layers of civilisation added by clothes. That said, Burroughs continually plays with the idea that clothes do not necessarily make the man, as Tarzan is frequently more gentlemanly than the Westerners with whom he interacts. Tarzan himself quickly learns that the shirt, a seemingly civilised garment, is often used for hiding a gun.

CUT, COLOUR AND CLASS

Regarding the cut of a man's shirt, the essential design in Western Europe remained fairly constant across several centuries, with a wide, rectangular body, very full sleeves, and underarm gussets. The back yoke – a shaped section of fabric between the collar and shoulder blades – was a relatively late invention to improve the fit across the back. Shirt ends were originally rounded, and longer at the back than at the front, enabling them to be tucked around the buttocks. With so much fabric in a shirt, it was quite a feat to fit it snugly into narrow sleeves and snug breeches or pantaloons. Then, in 1855, the 'tunic' shirt was introduced. Instead of the usual over-the-head style with buttons to partway down the chest, this shirt had buttons all the way down the front and could therefore be put on like a jacket. It was, in essence, the origin of the modern front-opening shirt.

Far from being the voluminous tents of fabric worn previously, late Victorian and twentieth-century shirts were pared down to more body-contoured shapes. Managing to be snugly fitted without being *too* constricting became a tailoring virtue; Blyth's of Edinburgh claimed in 1898 that they could supply a soft cotton shirt for two shillings and sixpence, which 'fits perfectly and is cut right at the neck, so your collar will not torment you'. By the twentieth century shirts acquired the straight edges of equal length that are so familiar to the modern male.

Since the shirt was worn by all men, it was important to be able to show distinctions in status and class. Cut alone was not sufficient. Textiles spoke volumes: the choice of fabric was a strong denominator of rank, profession and spending power. Very fine linen characterised the shirts of wealthy men, right through from the Middle Ages to the nineteenth century, when good-quality cotton took precedence. Silk – traded from the East throughout Western history – was the most luxurious fabric, although harder to tailor or wash frequently and thus never destined to eclipse the best linens in popularity. Silk next to the skin was also a touch too decadent for some. 'These be goodly shirtes indeede,' scorned Elizabethan purist Philip Stubbes, 'and such as will neyther chafe their tender skinnes . . . nor yet make perforation into their lillie white bodyes.' Stubbes was appalled that some shirts cost as much as 'ten pounds a pece' and that such luxury was too easily available to men of lesser ranks, aspiring above their proper status.

The smock-frock shirts – or *smocks* – worn by farmers and rural labourers in southern England and northern France offer an example of apparently lower-status garments of good quality with exquisite design details. They followed the old style of over-the-head shirt, having an open neck and tunic-style cut. Novelist Thomas Hardy described Dorset farm workers in the 1870s 'in snow-white smock-frocks . . . marked on the wrists, breasts, backs and sleeves with honeycomb-work'. This labour-intensive puckered 'honeycomb' stitching became known as smocking. It was popular in children's frocks long after the smock itself fell victim to a late nineteenth-century preference for regular fitted shirts, waistcoats and jackets.

At the very bottom of the status scale come hair shirts. To don a hair shirt is traditionally a religious act of penance, the physical discomfort of a coarse cloth next to the skin showing repentance for whatever sins one may have committed. The 'hair' in question could be goat hair, horsehair or just rough burlap cloth. The Christian Old Testament refers to penitents in 'sackcloth', which is presumed to be the notorious hair shirt. Hair shirts were reputedly worn by figures including Thomas à Becket, Emperor Charlemagne and Mother Teresa. In Molière's 1664 play *Tartuffe*, the eponymous hero shows his arrant hypocrisy by wearing his hair shirt inside out, to avoid the irritation.

Along with cut and material, colour was an important indicator of a shirt's quality or purpose. Although shirts of the sixteenth and seventeenth centuries could be decorated with delicate blackwork embroidery, white was the predominant colour. The fabric was bleached with ammonia and made whiter-than-white by the addition of indigo dye or commercial 'blue' – a small block of 'blue' added to the wash gave a pleasing bright tint. The practice continued into the twentieth century, with Reckitt's being the dominant brand of 'blue' in Britain. Sun-bleaching was also an option, with lavender bushes sometimes being used as fragrant natural clothes horses.

Having said all this, clean linen was not always a priority even for men who could afford the laundry bills. Diarists and satirists commented on the dirty sleeve ruffles of aristocrats, as well as their filthy hands. It took the influence of Georgian dandy Beau Brummell to raise the standard of personal hygiene and spread the notion of frequent changes of shirt. Fastidious from his student days onwards, Brummell revelled in the exacting requirements of dressing as an officer in the 1st Royal Hussars. When he became friends with George, the Prince Regent, Brummell's popularity and sartorial influence were assured – for a while at least. Brummell preferred attention to detail over excessive embellishment. Clean shirts were an important part of this. When asked for the secret of his widely envied style, he recommended 'very fine linen, plenty of it and country washing'.

By the nineteenth century cascades of ruffles at the chest were giving way to a smoother shirt front, in keeping with a taste for classic simplicity inherited from Brummell. King Edward VII popularised a new fashion innovation towards the end of the century: the low-fronted waistcoat for evening ensembles. The shirt was slowly but surely coming into view as outerwear. But exposing a shirt front was not without its perils. The snowy-white expanse of shirt fabric might indicate enough wealth for regular clothes-washing, but it also rendered the wearer vulnerable to the danger of stains and spillages. Edward VII's grandson, the Duke of Windsor, recalled a pre-opera dinner at Buckingham Palace when the King dropped purée of spinach on his spotless white shirt. Both Queen Alexandra and Queen Mary attempted to scrape the spinach off, but the stain remained. Instead of changing his shirt, the King took great delight in dipping his napkin in the spinach and using it to draw a picture on the ruined shirt front. Rank has its privileges.

In contrast, coloured shirts were originally associated with lower-class men who could not afford high-quality bleached cloths and the money required to keep white fabrics white. Fabrics ranged from rough homespun to brushed cotton flannel. When the American Civil War put a squeeze on cotton production, linen shirts became popular for a while. Later, flannel acquired quasi-superstitious associations. One London surgeon observed that the preparation for operations included cutting clothes from the bodies of very poor patients, as they tended to 'put on a flannel shirt or vest and keep it on till it almost falls to pieces'.

A starched blue false front from the early twentieth century.

Sporting a false shirt front was also considered a feature of lower- and middle-class trade. False fronts – also known as 'cheats', 'dickeys' or 'tommys' – were starched, edged shapes of fabric fastened to the chest to cover the actual shirt between collar and waistcoat, to hide dirt, darns or creases. The author of the 1838 *Workwoman's Guide* provided a pattern for their construction: 'These are worn by men and boys, to put on over a soiled or tumbled shirt, to give a neat appearance; they are, however, seldom used, it being much better to put on a clean shirt at once.' Sold in a variety of fabrics and patterns, dickeys were also an easy way to vary the colour of the shirt front.

Working-men's shirts might have coloured stripes or, in the case of pioneers and lumber workers in the North Americas, thick plaids and checks. Meanwhile blue or red stripes, in particular, were popular for well-off chaps enjoying boating, punting and competitive rowing in the 1830s. Such gentlemen were deliberately dressing beneath their station as a sign that they were relaxing, at leisure, away from the normal rigours of clothing etiquette. Because of their association with low-status menswear, such shirts were not, at first, considered acceptable away from the river. They were, in fact, the earliest 'sports' shirts. Fifty years later came the *polo shirt* with its turned-down collar, followed by the cricket shirts of the 1890s, which were front-fastened with pearl buttons, no less.

The association of colour with working-class shirts did not wholly deter others from wearing it. Some Victorian dandies in the 1840s and 1850s chose zany fabrics; statement shirts included prints of prima ballerinas and of monkeys eating bananas. Possibly the most exotic shirt recorded was embroidered with pink boa-constrictors! Later, flashy dressers of the Edwardian age – called *knuts* – flaunted bold pink shirts, with clashing orange ties. The trend for plain one-colour shirts was established by about 1900. They gradually became acceptable for office wear in the 1980s, with blue shirts being the most popular, and pin-stripes leaving their working origins so far behind as to be considered the most professional pattern.

However, First World War austerity dampened such flamboyance in clothing, and during the turbulent decades between the two World Wars coloured shirts took on a distinctly sinister range of meanings.

The black shirts worn by Italian *Arditi* troops in the First World War were chosen as a uniform for the followers of the Fascist Benito Mussolini, accessorised with a black fez, tie, trousers and belt. By 1934 all Italian schoolteachers were required to wear these black shirts as a sign of allegiance, and it was only with Mussolini's downfall in 1943, when Fascist uniforms were banned, that such regulations were lifted.

In a show of solidarity with Mussolini, Sir Oswald Mosley also instituted black shirts for members of the British Union of Fascists. The BUF magazine stated in 1934, 'If you should join us, we will promise you this: when you have put on the Black Shirt, you will become a Knight of Fascism, of a political and spiritual Order.' Mosley made it clear that the shirt was intended to break down class barriers: 'In the Black Shirt all men are the same, whether millionaire or on the dole.' Britain would not tolerate the movement, and in 1936 a Public Order Act put an end to paramilitary uniforms.

Choosing a strong block colour for group identification is a basic tactic in creating cohesion of image. Irish Fascists in the early 1930s adopted blue shirts, and so acquired the nickname Blueshirts, although their movement fizzled out after a few short years. They shared their animosity to communism with the Falange militia in Spain, established by José Antonio Primo de Riviera in 1933. Blue Falange shirts were meant to appear serious, straightforward, sincere and proletarian, perhaps owing to cheap workaday fabrics such as blue denim and blue cotton drill. Once Francisco Franco's version of the Falange achieved dominance in 1939, after the horrors of a civil war, fresh converts to his ideologies were known as *new shirts*, to distinguish them from the *old shirts* of the early Thirties.

However, it was the brown shirts of the National Socialists in Germany that would endure the longest and inspire the greatest fear. The choice of brown was in fact a matter of convenience and utility – brown shirts happened to be readily available from military surplus stores in the early 1920s, when Adolf Hitler needed a cohesive but cheap uniform for his Sturmabteilung (SA) troops. It was men clad in brown shirts who clashed with their communist rivals, and men clad in brown shirts who descended on Berlin after Hitler's rise to power in March 1933. By then the shirts – and many other uniform items – were being produced by the menswear manufacturer Hugo Boss. The company continues to thrive today, long after the founder's death, though occasionally troubled by litigation from people demanding recompense for the enforced labour they did for the company under the Third Reich.

After the wars, aside from the African-American dandies of the 1940s, the use of colour did not revive significantly until the arrival of bold 'Hawaiian' print shirts into mainstream wardrobes of the 1950s. Psychedelic patterns and colours were the province of fashion subsets in the 1960s. They exploded into mainstream casual wear in the 1970s, when acrylics – which took and held vibrant chemical dyes easily – were a washable (if non-breathable) modern alternative to cotton.

COLLARS AND CUFFS

Aside from the emergence of the shirt front, historically only the collar and cuffs of a shirt would show in public. Never shy of displaying expensive lace, rich men from the sixteenth century onwards added extra ruffles to their sleeve ends. As well as emphasising the wearer's wealth, these protected the jacket cuff from fraying and could also hide unwashed hands. They were otherwise decidedly impractical, which in a sense was precisely the point of such conspicuous consumption: only a man of means and leisure could afford such an affectation; labouring men needed no-nonsense sleeve ends. Ruffles were also not without their perils, as one of the eighteenth-century extreme fashionistas known as *Macaronis* recorded in his memorandum

4 This entry was most probably a spoof diary rather than the real thing. It was featured in the *Lady's Magazine* of 1772.

book: 'My lace ruffles burnt in reaching the candle to examine Jem Bluster's waistcoat, which was embroidered by himself.' [4]

As Beau Brummell's influence came to dominate male costume in the late eighteenth century, cuffs lost their frills and became quite severe starched cylinders, tucked discreetly inside the jacket sleeves, only to emerge into view in the 1880s as stiff, smooth cuffs suitable for use as an impromptu notepad by men such as Sherlock Holmes. This kind of starching was a rather crippling feature. In *The Science of Dress* 1880s clothing expert Ada Ballin warned wearers: 'high collars of starched linen are in every way objectionable, preventing ventilation, hampering circulation, and being incapable of absorbing perspiration. The *Masher* collar is a thing to be avoided with horror – a very instrument of torture.' Mashers were the late Victorian incarnation of the dandy, with elaborate and particular toilettes, including a high, exaggerated collar.

Ballin's advice seems to have fallen on deaf ears. Fashion and etiquette combined to keep people encased in stiff shirts and collars. In fact, to the disgust of conservatives, the 'New Woman' of the 1890s mimicked menswear as a sign of her strength and independence. She donned starched shirts and collars that were shaped to fit the female form, but were otherwise a clear appropriation of male style.

The "MARGARET."
Three-fold Linen Collar, reduced to 3|6 half-dozen; 7d. each; Four-fold Linen, reduced to 5/9 half dozen, 11½d. each.

"PATTI" CUFF.
Three-fold Linen Cuff, reduced to 4/3 half-doz., 8½d. per pair; 5/6 half-doz., 11d. per pair; 7/6 half-doz., 15d. per pair.
Collars and Cuffs made to order. A Large Assortment of Ladies' Colored Linen Collars and Cuffs, from 1/2½ per set.

"ALEXANDRA."
Best Three-fold Linen Collar, reversible corners, round and square. Reduced price, 7d. each, or 3/6 half-doz.

The 'New Woman' of 1892 wanted her own version of the stiff male collars and cuffs; hers have female names.

Prior to this, women had worn the looser, decorated and genderised version of the shirt known as a blouse. In a multitude of colours, styles and fabrics the blouse has been a mainstay of the female wardrobe since it first became popular in the mid-nineteenth century. The 'male' shirt has also been appropriated by modern women, albeit with darts for a feminine fit and usually with an open collar.

Blouses could be soft and frilled or with a starker cut. Here, a blouse from 1920 with a very modern and very low V-necked collar.

There is clearly a tendency to show formality through stiff garments and accessories and informality through loose clothes. The starch of the shirts, collars and cuffs – whether worn by women or men – projected an impression of capability, seriousness and even professionalism. These were all laudable qualities for a society that valued hard work and respectability. As a concession to practicality, Victorian shirts did at least have detachable collars and cuffs, which could be changed daily, even if the shirt had to last a little longer without washing.

Men dressing on a budget might achieve the starched look cheaply by resorting to paper collars and cuffs. These could be bought by the dozen or half-dozen, and discarded when too soiled to wear. Neither these nor the linen varieties were kind to the wearer. Even royalty complained of the discomfort – 'Starched Eton collars invariably encircled our necks, and, when old and frayed, cut into our skin like saws,' wrote the Duke of Windsor, feelingly.

Starch at least had the advantage of resisting impregnation by dirt, and the notion that a white collar denoted higher status has persisted to the present day, with the class distinction of terms such as 'blue-collar worker' (a labourer) or 'white-collar worker' (one in a professional, clerical or managerial role). The tyranny of starch was only eroded by the new informality of the late 1920s when soft shirts were worn with softer cuffs and collars. Being over-starched led to the accusation of being too formal and serious – a *stuffed shirt*, in fact, according to Edwardian slang.

Shirt studs of the early twentieth century – shirts, collars and cuffs were originally fastened with removable studs rather than buttons.

LETTING IT ALL HANG OUT

Informality, once conceded, could not be reversed. Shopping catalogues and fashion magazines in the 1930s began to print images of middle-class men without jacket or waistcoat – an informality previously reserved only for working men and sportsmen. That such pictures were considered acceptable in conservative clothing catalogues shows a truly seismic shift in thinking about how a man could appear in normal society.

Next came the loosening of the tie and the rolling up of shirt sleeves – something that would have been unheard of for Queen Victoria's sons. Fortunately for those who prefer comfort to starch, the twentieth century saw men under-dressing for most occasions. While older generations in the 1940s and 1950s may have kept their waistcoats on and their cuffs buttoned, younger men's shirts reflected the gradual erosion of class and cultural constraints. In recent times the cult of informality means that while men dressing for a night on the town may still wear a smart shirt, it is likely to be untucked and open at the collar. In fact, dress codes have relaxed so much, it can now be acceptable for modern men to work tie-less or in short-sleeved shirts, and the polo shirt is generally acceptable day wear. In many modern companies even T-shirts can be worn and in some industries this is almost the norm, such is the revolution in notions of appropriate wear.

There is one final twist in the underwear-as-outerwear story of the shirt. It concerns the male *vest* – an article of underwear adopted relatively recently, in the nineteenth century. Originally the vest's introduction was as part of the wool-next-to-the-skin cult, although flannel versions were also popular, as well as cotton string vests. Matched with long johns, the vest ensured that the Victorian or Edwardian male could face the world with warm kidneys and an extra layer of respectability. It is perhaps because the vest took on the shirt's mantle as the most intimate garment, closest to the body, that the shirt was free to become what it is today: purely an outer garment, not underwear at all.

The vest has endured some difficult times. 1934 saw the release of the Frank Capra film *It Happened One Night*, starring Clark Gable and Claudette Colbert. The most memorable scene in this delightful comedy consists of Gable and Colbert unwillingly sharing a motel room. The camera focuses on Gable undressing for the night. Cinema audiences across two continents gasped as he unbuttoned his shirt to reveal that . . . he *wasn't wearing a vest*. According to urban legend, sales of vests plummeted. So catastrophic was the fallout, the story goes, that underwear manufacturers contacted the film studio to remonstrate and demand that the next time Clark Gable undressed on-camera, he would wear a vest under his shirt.

Shortages of commercial underwear were severe for men in the Second World War. Thrifty knitters could make this 1942 vest and shorts set, if shop shelves were bare.

However, the march of informality was relentless, with or without Clark Gable's influence. Vests, like shirts, eventually came out from under other layers, to appear as outerwear. This was in the form of sleeveless tops unfortunately known as 'wife-beaters' in the US, because of their association with the stereotyped image of a disaffected, violent man. Actually first favoured by twentieth-century firefighters as a protective layer, string vests were then co-opted by body-confident gay men in the 1980s, as well as for fetish looks for both straight and gay wearers – all very far removed from their original discreet function. Sports vests, or singlets, are now emblazoned with team names, numbers and sponsorship emblems and are usually worn to show off a well-toned physique.

With shirts and vests in full public view in many modern cultures, the dilemma of how to help a modern audience appreciate the shock Elizabeth Bennet felt on encountering an informally dressed Fitzwilliam Darcy can more readily be understood. The 1996 BBC production, for reasons of discretion, chose to keep the shirt on rather than flaunt full nudity. In doing so, it inadvertently proved that even in our modern age of informality and exposure, a male shirt on show can still have the allure of intimate underwear.

THE SOCK DRAWER

I'd rather know that the seams of my stockings are straight than wear diamonds.

JOAN CRAWFORD

THE LOST SOCK

Considering the incredible usefulness of socks, it is quite remarkable how often they are lost. The curse of the 'lost sock' is of less concern than it was in the past, as socks are now an immensely cheap item, but historically sock owners took great care to keep their socks in pairs.

In the nineteenth century, for example, each pair of socks or stockings would be neatly marked in red ink or thread with the owner's initials and an identifying number, so that they could be reunited after being laundered. The early twentieth century then saw new socks sold with the toes joined by a discreet but sturdy stitch – a forerunner of the plastic tags that are now used for the same purpose.

When conservators opened one suitcase recovered from the debris field of RMS *Titanic*, the garments neatly folded inside included a pair of unworn socks, of finely knitted black silk. Their owner had not survived the ship's sinking.

As well as being lost in the laundry, socks are also lost or overlooked in most costume histories. It is rare that they are accessioned into museum collections, unless they have special provenance or are of exceptional beauty. As ever with clothes, it is usually valuable or sentimental items that survive wardrobe culls and general de-cluttering. Fortunately, it is also owing to the propensity of the humble sock to be lost or mislaid that we have surviving examples from the past, and therefore a reasonable amount of information about early foot coverings.

Artist's impression of one of the socks found in the Egyptian King Tutankhamen's tomb, in 1922.

The socks with arguably the most ancient pedigree were, ironically, intended to be worn throughout eternity. When Howard Carter and his team opened up the tomb of Tutankhamen in 1922 they discovered treasure – a great deal of it – but they also salvaged several undyed linen socks from the tomb's antechamber, ready to sheath the young king's feet in the afterlife. These socks date back to 1323 BCE. Their Egyptian name translates as 'the pharaoh's foot-warmers', and it was no faux pas to wear them with sandals. They are now on display in Cairo Museum, though somewhat eclipsed by the more dazzling artefacts in the collection.

A lost sock from a far colder climate is the twilled-wool bootee recovered from Vindolanda – one of the Roman military outposts along Hadrian's Wall in northern England. While it is believed to be a child's sock, Roman soldiers stationed along Hadrian's Wall certainly wore socks for warmth, too. In 1973 archaeologists uncovered a collection of partly burnt wooden postcards at Vindolanda, dating from the first and second centuries AD. Amongst these was a letter written to a soldier that reads: 'I have sent you two pairs of socks from Sattua, two pairs of sandals, and two sets of underwear ...'

Moving forward a few hundred years, the Coppergate archaeological dig in York unearthed a Viking sock from the ninth century, constructed from a knotting technique known as *narl-binding*. Surviving Anglo-Saxon socks have the cheerful addition of a red stripe, courtesy of the dye known as madder. Fragments of knitted socks have also been recovered, still with two ivory needles stuck through them.

SHOW A FINE LEG

Medieval and Tudor socks were simply short stockings, called *half-hose. Long hose* were essentially full leg coverings – what we would recognise as stockings today. Those who made hose were known as *hosiers*. The term survives to modern times as the rather archaic word *hosiery*, which usually refers to tights and stockings, although it technically covers socks also.

Stockings – long hose – were by no means only female wear during the Renaissance. Before the general adoption of trousers by men a mere 200 years ago, stockings were far more visible on male legs, filling the gap between boot and tunic hem and going under the short, puffed breeches known as trunk hose. Early hose were made of close-fitting cloth or knitted to stretch around the legs. They acquired the sophistication of proper seams and fashioning from the twelfth century. Very long varieties were tied onto a waistband or belt with metal-tipped laces called points.

Hose could be associated with flamboyance and erotic display, and might come in gaudy colours with embellishments; one tenth-century poet mentions lichen-red hose, while King Sigurd Syr, a minor Norwegian king, wore blue hose with long laces in the early years of the eleventh century. However, the pinnacle of leg display was probably during the sixteenth century, when stylish Tudor men wore a variety of hose, sometimes cut on the cross of the fabric, for a better fit. Ever at the forefront when it came to flaunting status and sexuality, Henry VIII had six pairs of black silk knitted hose. Fancy designs at the ankle seams were known as clocking, as they resembled a *cloche*, or bell-shape.

1 Stubbes was appalled at the cost of silk hose, and the fact that even men of limited income indulged in them: 'And to such impudent insolency and shameful outrage it has now growne, that everyone almost, though otherwise very poor, having scarce forty shillings wages by the year, will not stick to have two or three pairs of these silk neather stocks, or else of the finest yarn that can be got.'

A French townsman of the fifteenth century shows off his long hose. In the original image the hose are a pleasant shade of purple to match his purse.

Not everyone approved of such masculine indulgence. In Shakespeare's play *Twelfth Night* censorious and self-involved Malvolio is tricked into peacocking before Lady Olivia and is made ridiculous through his choice of legwear: 'He will come to her in yellow stockings, and 'tis a colour she abhors; and cross-gartered, a fashion she detests.'

Stockings are also reserved for special mention in Philip Stubbes' vitriolic *Anatomie of Abuses,* an excoriating attack on 'ungodly' fashions and customs of the late sixteenth century: 'They are not ashamed to wear hose of all kinds of changeable colours, as green, red, white, russet, tawny, and else what, cunningly cut and curiously indented at every point with quirks, clocks, open seams . . .'[1]

2 Mr Eddy of 43 Dean Street, Soho, advertised in newspapers between 1798 and 1800 offering a range of prosthetic devices from trusses to leg irons and also 'False Calves to shape the legs'.

Nevertheless, the fashion for attention-grabbing continued unabated and by the seventeenth century male hose were edged with lace so deep it both filled the bucket-tops of wide boots and cascaded over them, in an ostentatious display of wealth. Black or white was preferred by gentlemen, but other colours such as silver, grey, green and carnation could also be seen. Further embellishments were added to the basic construction, such as embroidery along the seams.

Some men went to extraordinary lengths to achieve a fashionable calf shape: they padded their stockings. Parchment calves were one possibility, although calves of down were more effective. Padded stockings were advertised for sale in London newspapers.[2] A gentleman's tailor might also offer the service, as seen in this delightful scene from R. B. Sheridan's *A Trip to Scarborough*:

Lord Foppington: The calves of these stockings are
   thickened a little too much; they make my legs look like
   a porter's . . .
Mr Mendlegs: My lord, methinks they look mighty well.
Lord Foppington: Ay, but you are not so good a judge of
   these things as I am. I have studied them all my life.
   Pray therefore let the next be the thickness of a crown-
   piece less.
Mr Mendlegs: Indeed, my lord, they are the same kind I
   had the honour to furnish your lordship with in town.
Lord Foppington: Very possibly, Mr Mendlegs: but that was
   in the beginning of the winter; and you should always
   remember, Mr Hosier, that if you make a nobleman's
   spring legs as robust as his autumn calves, you commit
   a monstrous impropriety, and make no allowance for the
   fatigues of the winter.

The practice of padding the calves was fertile ground for all kinds of satire, both on paper and on-stage. Ben Jonson's *Cynthia Revels* includes the malicious line of gossip, 'They say he puts off the calves of his legs with stockings every night.'

Military men were at particular risk of being ridiculed as *spindle-shanks*. When the French captain Jean-Roche Coignet – a veteran of many campaigns, including Waterloo – published the memoirs of his military career he was honest enough to confess to a certain anxiety regarding the slenderness of his legs. Needing extra bulk, Coignet took to wearing three pairs of silk stockings, along with false calves bought in Paris at the Palais-Royal – 'And so I sported a good-looking pair of legs.' However, real difficulties arose when Coignet was seduced by an attractive older woman:

> I felt mighty awkward about undressing, and particularly about how I was to hide my wretched false calves and my three pairs of stockings. What a fix I was in. If only I could put out the candle, all would be well. However, somehow I managed to hide them under the pillow; but it damped my spirits considerably. And the problem of how to get them on next morning tortured me. Fortunately my beauty got up first to make things easy for me, and went into the next room with her maid to dress. I lost no time, and at once set about pulling my three pairs of stockings on under the bedclothes; the difficulty was to avoid twisting them awry, and I only succeeded with one leg, but madame never noticed.

The adoption of long trousers in the late eighteenth century would put an end to the pressure for a shapely male leg, with two exceptions: silk hose were still required for very formal evening wear early in the twentieth century, and for servants in livery. Urchins in the 1850s joked that they were going to splash the footman's stockings with mud, then 'stick pins in his calves to see if they were real or stuffed'. Ten years later a servant, John Thomas, travelling to the seaside with his employers, was described as having 'his calves revised and hair powdered after the toils of unpacking'.

As late as 1914 Punch *magazine could still publish a satirical cartoon about a footman inflating pneumatic stockings to enhance the calves.*

Even once they were hidden by trouser hems, male socks continued to attract attention in the twentieth century, but usually only when worn by dandies such as the dancer Fred Astaire. Producer Samuel Goldwyn commented that Astaire 'wore enormously loud stockings, which would draw your eyes to his feet, which were his thing . . . Remember how he walked? He always had his hand in his pocket, and the pants were a little short so you could see the stockings, so that you could see the feet.' Astaire's 'stockings' would have been long socks reaching to mid-calf.

It took the Duke of Windsor's influence to render long, 'loud' socks acceptable for upper- and middle-class males in the 1920s, particularly diamond-patterned argyle socks. The Duke explained, 'my favourite sport became golf, and here I found more scope for indulging my freedom of taste in dress'. However, gaudy socks were only for leisure wear, specifically golf, when

Argyle socks with breeches on a cyclist of the 1890s.

they were teamed with knee-length breeches. The association of sport and long socks survives not only in golf, but also on the football pitch, where players have the equivalent of historical stockings pulled up to their knees, and sometimes over, in bold club colours.

Stockings is no longer a word comfortably associated with men's leg coverings, even when it is merely referring to long socks. From once being both practical and fashionable, stockings for males are now of the sheer, mid-thigh-height variety, associated exclusively with fetish wear. They are likely to remain with these underground associations until a new shift in costume aesthetics accepts breeches or skirts as everyday menswear.

For those who wish to show a touch of individuality, socks (along with ties) offer an opportunity to deploy colour in the otherwise limited palette of business apparel. The modern male is more likely to have a five-pack of novelty socks from a supermarket than to follow the rules of style connoisseurs such as contemporary expert Nicholas Storey, who advises having socks that match trousers. Even Storey can't resist a smile at the thought of red socks, however. 'Maybe it is something to do with a glimpse of the daring and dashing lurking beneath the trousers, suggesting these qualities may lurk in the wearer too.'

A GLIMPSE OF STOCKING

Historically, women haven't let long hemlines hamper their own delight in displaying attractive stockings, which followed the usual variations, according to budget. Royal stockings in the Tudor court were typically of silk, and often embroidered.

Even when fashion dictated skirts to the floor, female stockings of the sixteenth to nineteenth centuries were still designed with dainty embroideries and subtle patterns in the weave around the foot so that, should the ankle show, it would show to advantage. These designs included flowers, leaves, lozenges and crowns.

However, by the mid-nineteenth century obtrusive embroideries and elaborate designs were cautioned against. This was not only to avoid the temptation of exposing the legs in an improper fashion, but also to hide over-wide ankles. Expert advice cautioned, 'If the foot and ankle be pretty, it is not for the wearer to call attention to it; whilst if, as is more commonly the case, the ankle be characterised rather by quantity than quality, concealment becomes an object.'

As with shirts, white was a sign of status, because it implied the money to spare for frequent laundering. Mary, Queen of Scots wore a pair of white knitted stockings for her execution in 1586. Bolder colours suggested character and confidence but wearing red stockings came at a price: compounds of tin were used to fix red dyes, and people could react badly to them. In addition, aniline dyes of the late nineteenth century used irritant chemicals, meaning that red, yellow or even black stockings were often woven with undyed fibres at the feet, to avoid staining or inflammation of the skin.

The stocking colour considered most dangerous of all was

blue, though not for any chemical reason. One member of a group of fashionable intellectuals formed by Elizabeth Montagu in the 1750s happened to wear blue stockings. That this blue-limbed person was actually *male* was irrelevant to those who wanted to mock the group for being predominantly female. The male in question, Benjamin Stillingfleet, was laughed at when he arrived at Montagu's house in Mayfair wearing woad-blue woollen stockings, showing that much of the ridicule was directed at the colour, not the context. 'Bluestocking' neverthe-less became a derogatory term for a woman who neglected traditional female accomplishments in favour of scholarly pursuits. The term became inextricably bound up with the hotly debated topic of women's right to education. Satirists and detractors were quick to slander intelligent women as failing in their primary duty to present an attractive appearance, as here in *The Enlarged Devil's Dictionary* by Ambrose Bierce:

'They call me a blue-stocking!' madam exclaimed;
'Pray why, of all ladies, should I, sir, be named
From the hue of my stockings, which man never spied?'
'Nor ever desired to,' the villain replied.

Whether cotton, wool or silk, plain or embellished, stockings were a relatively secret garment for women – until changes in society transformed them into visible accessories more vulner-able to snags, stares and stains. This exposure was, of course, linked to rising hemlines. Skirt lengths had flirted with the calves in the 1830s, and the crinoline cages of the 1850s and 1860s had often revealed legs as they swayed, but it took global conflict – the First World War – to challenge the status quo of hidden limbs. Women needed shorter A-line skirts to be able to do their war work safely and efficiently.

Cotton lisle stockings were the norm for everyday wear at this time. The fibres would be twisted slightly and singed with a gas flame to give a fine feel. They would then be mercerised – treated with caustic soda – to add a silky lustre.

Post-war hems rose and fell for a while, but soon settled at knee-grazing height. This led to an increase in sales of all types of stockings, as well as products for depilating the legs. Many women took to wearing rayon, more glamorously known as *art silk*. Rayon was far more affordable than real silk, but had a similar look, even if nothing could compare to the feel of the genuine article. The cheapest stockings were sold as 'singles' in Woolworths, so when one was damaged beyond repair, it could be replaced without having to find the money for a pair.

Cole Porter summed up very succinctly the new attitude to legs being on show: 'In olden days a glimpse of stocking was looked upon as rather shocking / Nowadays, heaven knows, anything goes.' With female legs routinely on display, eroticism now came from the amount of leg on show rather than the sense of naughtiness from gaining an accidental glimpse. Regardless of where the male gaze could wander, the revelation of legs in stockings represented important freedoms for women – the literal freedom of movement and the symbolic freedom to be relatively uncovered in public without shame.

There was even a further revolution in colour: not only were legs 'out and about', but they were being flaunted in flesh-colours, as if *bare skin* were on show. It takes an effort of imagination to appreciate just how shocking this was in the 1920s. Tales were spread of the 'first woman in the village' to wear such flesh-coloured stockings, as opposed to black, white or cream – how very daring!

EMBARRASSING TO GO WITHOUT

Stockings are extremely impractical compared to the thicker fabrics of trousers as leg coverings. Yet despite the inconvenience and expense of buying stockings – which were sure to snag and ladder and needed nightly washing – going bare-legged was not at all acceptable between the wars, except when swimming or hiking. How then to balance the shortage of stockings during the Second World War with the requirement to be ladylike? Supplies of raw silk were quickly requisitioned by the government at the start of the war, and stockings made from DuPont's wonder-fabric – nylon – were only available in the environs of American airbases later into the war. In the meantime women resorted to a variety of ingenious solutions to create the appearance of stockings, such as dyeing the legs with gravy browning, coffee grounds, used tea leaves, wet sand or, for the less thrifty, shop-bought leg make-up. 'It was embarrassing to go without,' remembers one woman from the war years.[3]

The Second World War saw the adoption of socks as acceptable everyday wear for women. One German woman in Norway used socks to send a political message. She had noted that Norwegians who were anti-Hitler all wore a red article of clothing, so 'the first thing I did was knit myself a pair of red knee socks and always wore them'.

3 Leg make-up continued to be used into the 1950s, rather like modern fake tans. The application process was made to sound pleasant; the reality was probably more blotchy: 'Legs should be as carefully made up as your face. Well made-up legs are pretty, and can save you stocking money in warmer weather . . . After a bath, place a towel round your legs, and without rubbing, dry entirely by patting. Choose a colour that is slightly darker than your skin, but not too dark, if you are fairly pale and not sunburnt.'

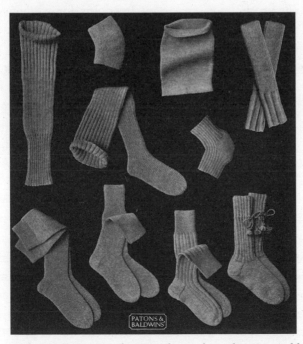

1940s socks came in many shapes and sizes; home knitters could also make knee-warmers (centre, right) and leg-warmers (top left).

Ankle socks went well with the rather dashing slacks of the Forties, and invariably it was younger women who chose short socks over stockings. Alarm at the rise of teenagers with their own morals, opinions and spending money created a backlash of disapproval against so-called bobby-soxers – 'young females who distinguished themselves for their intemperate and moronic behaviour at the public appearance of crooners and suchlike', according to one lexicographer.

ALL THE WAY TO THE TOP

Tights became fashionable as teenage hemlines reached thigh-high in the mid-1960s. They had already been around for some time; essentially they are the distant descendants of shaped medieval hose for men that rose to the waist. Flesh-coloured tights were also worn under light gauze dresses by more outré Regency women, fashioned like earlier long hose rather than with the tight, integrated pant-top of modern tights. Since Regency women wore them to suggest nudity under their transparent gowns, a taint of immorality remained attached to tights when they were adopted by circus acrobats and actresses during the nineteenth century. By 1913 a magazine editor at a fashionable South of France hotel was shocked to note women in transparent gowns 'through which the outlines of their figures could be traced almost as clearly as if the women had not been clothed at all. Some of them wore tights like a circus girl.' These visible tights were alleged to have 'a decidedly immoral effect on our children'.

However, only fifty years on from these censorious words, tights were everywhere. Innovative blends of cotton, nylon and elasticated fibres gave them unprecedented qualities. Form-fitting and self-supporting, tights provided warmth and freedom of movement. Female legs became a glorious gallery for colourful textile art, with printed, woven and appliqué patterns. Rather than seeming promiscuous, tights, with their waist-clinching coverage, had a strange asexual innocence, particularly

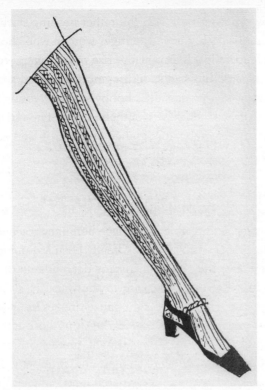

Ribbed tights from 1967 – most definitely meant to be seen.

when sprinkled with Mary Quant's signature daisy motif. They revealed the body, but didn't allow easy access to it.

The modern woman now enjoys almost universal acceptance of nude legs in most social situations, though this comes with a corresponding emphasis on leg-hair depilation. She can choose from an extensive range of practical or novelty hosiery, including tights, socks, stockings, knee-high 'pop' socks, below-ankle trainer socks and subtle low-cut shoe liners. The thickness of hosiery is now measured using the denier system, with 10 denier being light and fine and 40 denier being more of a winter weight. Tights reign supreme, in a multitude of patterns, colours and weights. And with many tights now being structured to lift buttocks and flatten bellies, they have become support garments in their own right.

And what of stockings? They have survived as a more sensual alternative to tights, from seductive lace-top hold-ups to the pleasing sleaze of black fishnets. Vestiges of historical construction survive also, with back seams and Cuban heels carrying with them an echo of past decades of sophistication.

PULL YOUR SOCKS UP

Socks and stockings did not always remain exactly where the wearer might wish, frequently yielding to gravity and requiring care and attention to keep them in place. Thus wrinkled socks and stockings can imply a slovenly attitude, hence the phrase 'to pull one's socks up', meaning to improve one's behaviour. Shakespeare uses the same motif to signify Hamlet's distraught state of mind:

> his stockings fouled,
> Ungartered, and down-goes to his ancle;
> Pale as his shirt.

Less literary but equally dishevelled are the stockings of Nora Batty, a Yorkshire housewife from the BBC television series *Last of the Summer Wine*. The character had signature thick lisle stockings rumpled around her equally thick ankles, and the name Nora Batty quickly became synonymous with such wrinkled hosiery.

Prior to the synthetic elastic fibres now incorporated into almost all hosiery, it was decidedly tricky for anyone to keep socks up and stockings smooth. *Garters,* to tie the hosiery in place just above the knee, were perhaps the most straightforward answer.

By the fourteenth century male garters were made to be seen; to see a female garter, on the other hand, implied intimacy and possibly immorality. According to popular legend, the Most Noble Order of the Garter was established in Britain in 1348, when the Countess of Salisbury's blue garter slipped to the floor at a court ball, whereupon King Edward III quashed any ridicule to which she might have been subjected by picking it up and tying it round his own knee, saying, '*Honi soit qui mal y pense*' – 'Evil be to whosoever evil thinks'. Quite how this occurrence led to the founding of a prestigious Order of Knights is not recorded. Presumably it began as a noble whim and was then established as a bona fide honour. Other stories place the origin of the Order in the reign of Richard I, linking the garter to those worn by crusading knights. The Order was – and still is – a privilege predominantly reserved for Knights rather than Ladies. Knights of the Order wore a blue velvet garter edged with gold upon their left leg. Modern Knights and Ladies eschew the garter – certainly unsuitable with trousered legs, and out of keeping with modern clothing aesthetics – to wear a Garter Star on their chest. Membership of the Order now signifies admirable public achievement, though it is represented by a rather private garment. As well as emperors, shahs and queens, modern members have included former British prime ministers Margaret Thatcher and Winston Churchill, climber Sir Edmund Hillary, and Baroness Manningham-Butler, former Director General of the British internal Security Service, MI5.

One woman's garter might have resulted in it being proudly displayed by the King, but for women in general showing a garter was indecent, plain and simple. In Elizabeth Gaskell's delightful novel *Cranford*, elderly spinster Miss Matty knits garters of such beauty that the narrator jokes, 'I should feel quite tempted to drop one of them in the street, in order to have it admired.' Miss Matty, however, found this little joke 'a distress to her sense of anxiety'.[4]

Made of wool, tape or ribbon, garters were usually tied over the stocking above the knee, or else could be buckled around the top of it. Clearly, however, they were liable to loosen and drop. Various measures were taken to prevent this eventuality. Miss Matty knitted her garters in the simple, clinging pattern known, appropriately enough, as *garter stitch*, which would

4 There is also a lovely scene where Miss Matty whiles away a May morning knitting an elaborate pair of garters. We are told that ' . . . the difficult stitch was no weight upon her mind, for she was singing in a low voice to herself as her needles went rapidly in and out'.

help them to stay in place. The first 'elastic' garters were originally bands made from linked circles of fine metal. In the early nineteenth century true elastic began to be made by webbing linen, silk or cotton with threads of rubber. It was used for the tops of gloves and for garters. However, there were health concerns about elastic garters impeding the circulation, leading to the 1870s innovation of suspenders – front supporters attached to female corsets, with clasps to hold up stockings. A multitude of variations on this concept were patented, including one by a female inventor for combinations with special slits inserted so that the suspenders could slot through discreetly. The addition of rubber-covered metal buttons on the clasps also afforded greater comfort. If the button was lost, women used a small coin as a replacement – or even a Mint Imperial sweet!

Both garters and suspenders might be fitted with a neat pocket in which a sixpence could be stored for emergencies.

This suspender belt from 1920 has all four clasps at the front of the legs, and a waist belt.

Dress experts issued guidelines for correct foundation garments. While Victorian corsets generally had one pair of suspenders at the front, increasing to a pair at front and back by the Edwardian era, there were other models with even more appendages fastening stockings to corset. These had the effect of pulling against each other to hold stockings up, while stretching the corset smoothly down. According to one 1920 Women's Institute manual, three pairs of these suspenders were considered normal, four 'for stout women'. Many younger women of the 1920s rejected this restrictive carapace and reverted to elastic garters with rosettes, bows, flowers and glittering rhinestones, all intended to be glimpsed while performing jerky contemporary dance moves.

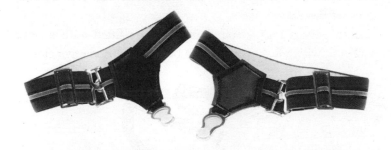

Sock suspenders, or Boston Garters, were necessary to hold men's socks up before elasticated tops.

Elasticated sock tops, hold-up stockings with semi-adhesive bands, and tights have rendered suspenders obsolete, except as part of an erotic ensemble. The garter has fallen out of favour even more, and apart from those worn by the Order of the Garter there are really only two forms in frequent use. The first is the pressure garter, which – contrary to previous concerns – is designed with the express aim of impeding the circulation. It is worn by air crews flying at high altitudes and by astronauts, to stop too much blood or water moving up to the head during intense G-forces or weightlessness. Astronaut Helen Sharman wore these pressure garters during her time on the *Mir* space station and found them very uncomfortable indeed. Such garters - also known as *braslets* - are related to the metal upper-arm garters once worn by clerks to keep their cuffs pulled away from paper.

Secondly, wedding garters are still a familiar part of bridal rituals, though now in a purely decorative, not supportive form. Originally ribbons were worn by the bride, around her leg, to give as gifts to the groom's friends, as referenced in Robert Herrick's 1648 poem 'Hesperides': '. . . let the young Men and the Bride-Maids share Your garters.' They were usually the 'something blue' of the wedding rhyme. Gradually the ribbon garter became a prize to be won in competitions by young men at the wedding. In the East Riding of Yorkshire, men used to race for the bride's garter, but only once the vicar had gone home, because they raced naked.

WOOLLY WARMTH

As we have already noted, socks and stockings are hard-working, practical garments. They act as a buffer between skin and shoes. And since they are easily removed and washed, they have long been recognised as being helpful for hygiene, not least to avoid the lamentable issue of bad-smelling feet. The 1859 *Ladies' Guide to Perfect Gentility* recommended washing feet twice a day in very hot weather - 'and the stockings should be changed twice a week in winter, and three times in summer'.

But most importantly, socks are worn for warmth. As extremities, feet are liable to get cold. In extreme conditions they are vulnerable to frostbite - loss of sensation will be followed by a loss of toes and, if the condition is not treated, the spread of gangrene can prove fatal. In that kind of situation, humble socks can quite literally save your life. Until the late twentieth century wool was the warmest kind of sock available, and was the preferred choice for mountaineers or polar explorers.

When searchers discovered the body of George Mallory on Everest in 1999, seventy-five years after his final, fatal attempt on the summit, he was found to be wearing three pairs of wool socks. Tests at the Southampton University Textile Centre and by the University of Leeds, using replica garments (including socks) created by knitting specialist Joyce Meader, revealed that Mallory's clothing was adequate for the climbing conditions – and in some cases an improvement on modern gear. Had Mallory not fallen beyond the reach of help from his climbing companion Andrew Irvine – breaking his leg in his descent – he might well have found his clothing quite adequate for surviving Everest's summit and returning to camp.

Wool wasn't without competition. From the eighteenth century onwards cotton became more affordable for everyday wear. Cotton was imported in bales, then processed for both home-spinning and the new cotton factories that were springing up around Britain like mushrooms. Machine-woven cotton stockings could be quite fine and elegant, with patterned stitching around the ankles. So popular was the fibre, and so profitable for the manufacturers, that it became known as King Cotton. However, silk was still the most coveted and luxurious of foot coverings. Jane Austen aspired to silk stockings but, at four times the price of cotton, these were often beyond her budget. Those she did own were not trusted to the laundress; she washed them herself at home. Quality was everything. In a letter to her sister Cassandra, on 26th October 1800, she declared that she greatly preferred 'having two pairs only of that quality to three of an inferior sort'. Her contemporary Lord Byron was considerably wealthier – his accounts show that even while on board ship, the only stockings he sent to the laundry were silk.

NEW USES FOR OLD SOCKS

Over the years socks and stockings have also found a number of uses not related to feet. Perhaps the most bizarre of these occurs in the Viking *Laxdaela* saga and describes an angry mistress using a stocking to beat her servant – a sign of her social superiority. More conventionally, socks are used to store

Mistrust of banks is no new concept. Parochial banks of the eighteenth and nineteenth centuries were notoriously unstable. Servants in particular were said to have a stocking 'which they keep carefully concealed, the contents of which are to help their possessors to furnish a lodging-house, or take a tavern, when the time arrives at which they think fit to assert their independence and retire from the servitude which they have all along tolerated for the purpose'.

savings (perhaps under mattresses or up chimneys) and to make puppets; stocking masks also distort the faces of bank robbers.[5]

But perhaps the most famous secondary use for socks or stockings comes on Christmas Eve, when they are hung from the mantelpiece to receive gifts from Father Christmas. In the past, such socks usually contained nuts, sweets and an orange in the toe; recently, commercially produced sock-shaped sacks testify to the exponential increase in gift expectations.

One very special Christmas sock was taken on Captain Robert Falcon Scott's 1901–4 *Discovery* expedition to the Antarctic. As a festive alternative to polar rations, Scott secretly carried a Christmas pudding with him, 'stowed away in my socks (clean ones) in my sleeping bag'. For Christmas 1902 he and his companions boiled the pudding in cocoa and decorated it with a piece of artificial holly. That sprig of holly went on to fetch more than £4,000 at a Christie's auction in April 1997. The fate of the sock is not recorded, but Scott's hut at Cape Evans, now preserved as a heritage site, was found to have 'socks hanging up to dry' long after Scott himself had frozen to death on the return leg of his journey to the South Pole.

In 1915, three years after Scott's last expedition, Allied soldiers trapped behind enemy lines in war-torn Belgium were guided to safety by a network of helpers, including nurse Edith Cavell, who was later tried and shot by a German firing squad for her involvement in this enterprise. In order to prevent trackers from being able to follow them, they pulled their socks on over their boots so that their distinctive English prints would not be recognised.

DARNING MUSHROOMS

Modern socks are as disposable as they are indispensable – they are often discarded when holes appear in them, or if a pair cannot be matched. Historically, however, great care was taken to extend the life of one's socks.

Socks were washed often and thoroughly; the 1838 *Workwoman's Guide* paid particular attention to male hosiery:

'Men's and boys' stockings should be steeped, and stewed in cold water and soap, in a slow oven, or boiled.' They were then to be hung by the toe to dry, to prevent lumpy foot ends. Holes were to be mended quickly before they spread – 'A stitch in time saves nine'. Wooden darning 'mushrooms' would be used as a support while mending socks. Surviving socks and stockings from all eras often show signs of mending, sometimes with neat, almost invisible darns; occasionally with complete re-footing.

Some skill at darning – including for chaps in the RAF in the Second World War – was indispensable for helping one's socks last longer.

In the twentieth century women's magazines published tips on how to mend stockings with a fine crochet hook, or professional stocking-menders were seen sitting cross-legged in dress-shop windows, applying perfectly matching thread to the hole. One of the punishments for female prisoners during the years of militant suffragette activity in the early twentieth century was to be given mounds of unclean socks to darn.

There was clearly a fine line between thrift and slovenliness. An Irish author, Miss Owenson, who was at the height of her fame in the Regency period, had a modish haircut and flamboyant mantle during public appearances, but it was observed that 'when the foot was stretched out at the heel it was covered with a dirty silk stocking with a long "Jacob's ladder" at the heel'.

The stigma of having visible holes in socks has remained into modern times. The author's mother was terrified that Social Services would 'have words' if they saw her children going to school with holey socks.

In short, whether you are navigating the ephemeral dangers of high society or the very real dangers of high altitude, socks and stockings are a valuable, if underrated, asset. They ought not to be overlooked, no matter that they are notorious for hiding themselves in awkward places. In this vignette from the charming 1931 novel *The Fortnight in September*, the Stevens family prepare to end their annual holiday at a seaside guest-house:

> . . . as he was taking a last look round his room, Mr Stevens saw one of his thick grey walking socks right up in a corner under his bed. It was funny how something like that happened almost every year. He felt his collar tighten and his face grow hot as he reached under to get it: it was covered in dusty fluff and he had to hit it smartly on the back of a chair before it was clean enough to stuff in his mackintosh pocket.

STAY LACES

Mrs Jervis gave me her smelling-bottle, and had cut my laces . . .

SAMUEL RICHARDSON, *PAMELA; OR,*

VIRTUE REWARDED, 1740

THE INVENTED BODY

The human body is an utterly remarkable piece of engineering. The complex articulated skeleton provides a structure that holds the internal organs and onto which muscles can attach; skin confines the contours of flesh. And yet, wonderful as it is, for more than five centuries of human existence this engineering was not considered adequate. From the sixteenth to the twentieth centuries an artificial torso structure was considered obligatory in Western culture: the corset.

The term *corset* comes from an early French word *corse*, meaning body. This is exactly the function of a corset – it is an alternative torso; a body put onto a body. For English speakers, the term *stays* was used interchangeably with corset until the late eighteenth century, when the French won out, being considered more refined.

Clothes are a fairly reasonable second skin on the human frame, providing extra warmth and protection, but what are we to make of the need to wear a structure of artificial 'bones' and fabric 'muscles'? Corsets have a perversely self-fulfilling existence: you only *need* a corset for core strength if you have always worn a corset and thus neglected core muscles. Granted, there

1 Buckram was a
coarse hemp or linen
cloth made stiff with
gum.

are many forms of corrective corset worn for medical purposes, such as rounded shoulders, back injuries and hernias. And an armoured breastplate or Kevlar body-vest may offer essential protection in combat situations. However, the majority of corsets in history have been worn simply to follow the demands of culture or fashion. Overwhelmingly they have been about creating a fashionable female shape and helping to define what it means to be female, or at least ladylike.

TIE HER STAY LACES

Laced bodices gained popularity in female gowns from the Middle Ages onwards. Gradually garments started to become shaped to fit the body, rather than merely enveloping it in belted fabric. This shaping took on new stiffness with the introduction of integrated boning. These long, thin 'bones' mimicked the bones of the skeleton, though they weren't actually made of bone, human or otherwise. Reeds and cane provided the earliest stiffening; later the keratin mouth-bristles of the baleen whale, used for filtering food, were found to be strong, yet relatively flexible.

In the late sixteenth century women's bodices took on an unprecedented rigidity and a starkly defined shape: vertical strips of boning were stitched within layers of fabric to create a conical torso, which compressed the diaphragm and waist. The next step was to create an independent structure to be worn under any bodice – the portable body shape: the *corps* ... the corset.

Buckram[1] and canvas layers were the most common fabrics for corset-making. A corset so constructed could practically stand up on its own. It was wrapped around the torso, covering the nipples, but pushing up the breasts. Before the nineteenth century, corsets often had straps coming over the shoulders from the back, to be laced into place at the front. The main fastenings were almost always at the back, and the wearer essentially had to be sewn into her corset whipstitch-style, via a long stay lace

2 After some debate
it was decided that
the below-waist
approach was the
only convenient way.

Stays of the 1780s created an inverted triangle shape, compressing the diaphragm, but leaving the hips free.

(like a modern shoelace), which threaded through rows of eyelets down each side of the back opening. This technique of using one lace to oversew the corset edges was known as strait-lacing and gave rise to the expression 'to be strait-laced', meaning morally tight – a clear indication that corsets were once integral to the notion of female sexual decency.

The only way to exit strait-laced stays in a hurry was to cut the stay lacing. Once, during a modern demonstration of how to wear eighteenth-century torso-moulding stays, a well-dressed lady approached the author for a closer look. She observed the boning of the stays, the severe narrowing of the waist and the strait-lacing at the back and then said, 'My dear, I have a question. I should like to know – how *did* they get ravished?'[2]

The form of the corset changed to suit fashion; the fabrics changed according to technological advances. Whalebones were replaced by metal 'boning' in the nineteenth century, when front-clasping corsets also made an appearance. Sprung steel had more twist and therefore allowed greater movement. Lacing techniques changed to use two threads that could be self-tightened, using long loops left at waist-level. Although in the twentieth century boning was superseded first by rubber elastic, and then by nylon power lace, the principles of the corset remained the same – to confine, control and civilise the female form.

Binding the body was no new concept – it was familiar to babies from the medieval era onwards. It began at birth, with a process of wrapping the infant's body in long strips of cloth known as swaddling bands. These bands bound an infant's limbs close to the body to keep it still and secure. This was a very different ethos from the modern emphasis on stimulation and freedom of movement, but it was a response to the real possibility of malformed bones from conditions such as rickets.

Having an immobile baby made childcare far simpler for the parents, but deeply uncomfortable for the infant, motionless in waste-soaked cloth. Advances in ideas about childcare led to the eventual unravelling of swaddling bands during the nineteenth century. Political and social reformer Elizabeth Cady Stanton described relieving the suffering of one swaddled child in the 1840s: 'When I took out the pins and unrolled it, it fairly popped like the cork out of a champagne bottle.'

Once out of swaddling bands, toddlers from the sixteenth century onwards might progress to simple stays with buttons and laces and some boning. One set of child's stays from around 1730 was worn by a young English boy called Francis Harmer, born in 1725. His stays are of bold pink wool, with a cheerful floral cotton lining, and are evidence that stays were not always limited to girls.

After a certain age – roughly four or five years old onwards – the genders divided. In general, boys were encouraged to exercise vigorously and have freedom of movement, without corsets; girls were more confined, both in activity and in clothes.

Aristocratic girls of the sixteenth and seventeenth centuries were dressed as miniature adults for formal occasions and portraits, complete with stays. Even going down the social strata, girls at every level wore some form of stays from puberty onwards.

Wearing full stays for the first time could be quite a traumatic rite of passage. At first the stays would be 'half-boned' – there would be a half-inch space between each bone. Elizabeth Ham remembered going into half-stays in 1792 as 'very nearly purgatory'. Seventy years later, Louisa May Alcott, of *Little Women* fame, used novel-writing as a platform to attack the custom of corseting growing girls. Her story *Rose in Bloom* sees the young Rose's fashionable Aunt Clara battling liberal Uncle Alec over whalebone stays. Dr Alec calls them an 'instrument of torture', scoffing, 'As if our own bones were not enough, if we'd give them a chance to do their duty.'[3]

3 Alec goes to burn the offending stays; Clara begs him not to: 'they are full of whalebones and will make a dreadful odor'.

Usually it was the older women in the family who colluded with contemporary ideas of health and fashion to force a girl into stays. When one teenage Victorian girl complained her stays were stiff and uncomfortable, and said she wished it were bedtime so she could take them off, the response from her equally stiff maiden aunt was pure shock at hearing such an indelicate idea: 'Hush, hush! You must bear it for a time,' says the aunt. 'You will soon get used to it.'

Not all girls acquiesced. In the 1880s, when Charles Darwin's granddaughter Margaret was put into stays aged thirteen, 'she ran round and round the nursery screaming with rage'. Margaret's sister Gwen simply took hers off, was re-corseted, then removed them again. The family governess despaired at this supposed wickedness. Gwen recalled, 'I had a bad figure, and to me they were real instruments of torture; they prevented me from breathing, and dug deep holes into my softer parts on every side. I am sure no hair-shirt could have been worse to me.'

After five centuries of corset dominance, sensibilities slowly shifted towards more ease of movement, leading to girlhoods dominated by the Liberty bodice. Although first produced at the beginning of the twentieth century, the Liberty bodice is perhaps best remembered by those growing up since the Second World War. It was promoted as a lighter, looser alternative to full stays. It was often fleecy inside and worn in response to warnings of the dire consequences of not keeping the kidneys warm. Despite these apparent benefits, the bodice

The famous Liberty bodice was an Edwardian invention popular until the 1960s. This advert is from 1917.

is not always remembered with affection by those who baked in it all summer, and who spent the winter fiddling with the suspender straps and rubber buttons. The buttons were for fastening the front, and for holding up drawers and petticoats, which would be too heavy to stay up on a child's slim hips. The early bodice designs were like miniature full stays, with steel boning, but these were soon replaced by simple, comfortable boneless versions. According to advertising text in the late 1930s, the supple, reinforced seams enabled the wearer to 'Stretch, bend and touch your toes. As free as air to bend as you like – so soft and well-cut that you forget you have it on.' It is doubtful whether many girls agreed with this statement.

Some girls may have rebelled against the confines of the corset when they were first laced in, but for adults corsets were an unquestioned aspect of everyday life, as reflected in an interesting collision between West and East during the early eighteenth century.

In April 1717, during an ambassadorial visit to Adrianople, Englishwoman Lady Mary Wortley Montagu went to view the scenes in a Turkish bath. She was intrigued to see the Turkish women were socialising entirely without corsets, or indeed clothes of any kind – 'in plain English, stark naked, without any beauty or defect concealed'. She then declined an invitation to undress and try the baths herself, showing her stays as a reason for not doing so. In an interesting twist on the Western notion that Turkish women had limited social freedoms, Lady Mary realised that her companions at the baths 'believed I was locked up in that machine, and that it was not in my power to open it, which contrivance they attributed to my husband'.

For years in the West it was considered essential to support, distort and confine the figure within a corset. Here, the ideal female form for 1915.

4 In January 2010 a Tesco supermarket in Cardiff banned customers from shopping in nightwear, 'To avoid causing offence or embarrassment to others'.

For Lady Mary, it was perfectly natural to be confined in a carapace of stout cloth and whalebone. For the Turkish women – believing Western men 'tied their wives up in little boxes, the shape of their bodies' – it was equally natural to have an untethered torso.

Until relatively recently in Western history, going out without a corset on would be like doing the weekly supermarket shop in pyjamas today – it might happen, but rarely, and would invite ridicule.[4] The 1890s *Pear's Cyclopaedia* stated of corsets that 'almost every woman wears them where Civilisation reaches nowadays'.

A loose figure was associated with loose morals and bad behaviour. Edwardian suffragettes were accused of both – Sylvia Pankhurst battled for the right not to wear a corset when she was incarcerated for pro-suffrage activities. The prison wardress was furious that she should suggest such a lack, and Pankhurst and other female prisoners were issued with 'a curious sort of corset reaching from neck to knees'.

The association of corsets with proper ladylike confinement only intensified through the nineteenth century, and well into the twentieth. The corset added a layer of moral protection. It was never worn directly against the skin, but instead laced around the chemise or combinations. This created unsightly red marks on the skin, from the compressed fabric. It did protect the corset from grease and perspiration, which was very necessary, since they were difficult to clean – the steels had to be removed from their casings and the fabric scrubbed with soap and a nail brush. Women born before the 1950s would find it almost impossible to conceive of wearing foundation garments – corsets or girdles – next to the skin.

One young woman in the 1940s apparently horrified her mother by going to a dance in a green organza blouse and *no corset*. She was told to go and add one, in case any young men at the dance should actually feel her body beneath her blouse and slip. She also came under pressure from her mother to wear a corset to work in an office. She used to take it off after leaving home, roll it up and only wrap it round her again when returning in the evening.

When chemises and combinations were replaced by vests in the twentieth century the corset was dutifully worn round the vest. Even when girdles – foundation garments that purely covered the abdomen and hips – replaced the full-torso corset, many conservative women continued the practice of putting girdles and bras on *over* their vests, even as late as the 1990s, to the puzzlement of younger generations who had never known the principle of hidden layers.[5]

5 This practice continued with elderly ladies into the twenty-first century. Nursing-home staff report on the difficulties of getting patients with dementia out of worn and dirty corsets, such is their importance for decency and familiarity.

IN AN INTERESTING CONDITION

Shockingly, pregnancy stays were also common for controlling the expanding abdomen of a mother-to-be. Elaborately boned examples survive from the eighteenth century, and from the Regency era: 'to compress and reduce to the shape desired the natural prominence of the female figure in a state of fruitfulness'. Later nineteenth-century maternity or 'gestation' stays had increasingly hefty amounts of boning and lacing. Strong boning supported the back, while extra gussets of lacing at the left and right of the abdomen supported the bump, rather like a modern elasticated maternity band, and at least allowed for the embryo to expand sideways. The need to hide evidence of fertility in this way was part of an inherent sense of shame about reproduction, which continued to be felt in Western culture until very recently. The absurdity of this attitude did not go completely unnoticed. Ada Ballin, Victorian author of *The Science of Dress*, deplored the fact that 'Many ladies who are hoping to become mothers, either through ignorance and vanity, or through feelings of modesty, which led them to try to conceal their condition, so press in their bodies by tight, stiff stays, that their children cannot grow properly.'

Happily, by 1913 common sense had started to prevail and the Glaxo booklet of advice to new mothers-to-be – *Before Baby Comes* – firmly advised discarding corsets during pregnancy,

6 One of the earliest
references to a
baseball game in
England is that
enjoyed by the young
heroine of Jane
Austen's novel
Northanger Abbey,
completed in 1803.
There is no mention
of the clothes worn at
the game, but we can
presume a light
cotton day dress for
the heroine.

explaining that 'Baby's growth and movement must not be interfered with by anything that restricts the mother's organs.'

SPORTS AND CORSETS

From the late nineteenth century the 'New Woman' asserted her right to expend energy and explore the world. While any woman enjoying vigorous exercise such as walking, cricket, baseball or mountaineering would wear her everyday outdoor clothes, corsets included, she at least had the option of so-called 'sports' corsets, which were somehow supposed to support the sportswoman without interfering with her movement. [6]

Cotton or satin ribbon corsets were thought to be more 'breathable' for horseriding and bicycling because of the slight gaps in the tapes and because they didn't sheath the hips as much as regular corsets.

Golfers, meanwhile, made do with full-length corsets containing extra 'spiral' steels designed to give some twist. Sports corsets may have been less formidable carapaces than the structures underlying fashionable costumes, but they were also a rather cynical sales ploy from manufacturers looking to coerce more active women into keeping their corsets on, regardless. Similarly, ladies being rowed upriver in the summer of 1913 were persuaded by advertisers that they could enjoy their boat-based picnic in *Corset Gaine*, which claimed to have the softness of a caress, but maximum support for muscles and 'reducing' powers.

Active women who quite understandably wished to do away with corsets were viciously criticised. Such criticisms usually originated from the fashion industry, which stood to lose a fortune. Conservatism permeated the popular press. In 1917 *Vogue* magazine ridiculed a woman's 'absurd willingness to support her figure without external aid'.

There were exceptions, of course. Some female munitions workers who played in the hugely popular football leagues of the First World War took the radical decision not to wear corsets under their jerseys and shorts, but such liberation was an anomaly. At the start of the Second World War corsets had mostly morphed into girdles, but Viyella could still offer sports foundations in white and peach, fastened with washable rubber buttons, supported by Lastex shoulder straps and enlivened with a lacy stitch.

FIGURE-FORMING FASHION

If corsets truly had been adopted for health reasons alone – to aid posture and offer gynaecological support – they might have been tolerably rational garments made to suit the age and condition of their wearer. And if corsets had only been worn as a sign of respectability, they might have remained at sensible proportions. But because in reality they were inextricably bound up with the demands of fashion, they were often structured beyond medical logic or reason, assuming an almost fetishised status in the historical wardrobe.

It wasn't enough merely to have a body and to be female. Fashion dictated the precise shape of the 'natural' feminine form, which had nothing truly natural about it. Artifice was everything. The body had to be reshaped so that clothes fitted well, rather than clothes merely covering the body, as they tend to do on a modern woman. The dressmaker had the exacting task of using corsets to achieve the fashionable figure. The 1805 *Book of Trades* stated: 'The ladies dressmaker must know how to hide all defects of the body and be able to mould the shape by stays while she corrects the body.' As late as 1902, after more than four centuries of the corset's dominance, *Ladies' Realm* magazine summed up the situation clearly – 'the corset is the most important item in a woman's wardrobe, for she cannot be in fashion unless her corset is'.

Each season saw adjustments to the corset shape. Each generation demanded novelty. The stays might elongate to a point over the belly, or flare to hip-tabs. They might give an hourglass figure, or a smooth, column-like effect, all as fashion demanded.

Fashion dictated the shape; the corset created it. In turn, dresses and bodices were cut to fit the newest corset styles. The body beneath was subsequently pinched in, puffed out or flattened (or sometimes all of these at once). It was widely recognised that *fashionable* was not synonymous with *natural*.

However much an age might admire healthy curves and even rotundity, fashion decided exactly where that flesh should be distributed. The suspenders that were added to the corset's hem in the late nineteenth century had the added advantage of smoothing out the 'roll' of flesh that was inevitably lurking beneath the corset's constraints. *Embonpoint* and *avoirdupois* were dignified – if rather supercilious – terms used to describe excessive flesh. Any flesh not considered a sign of fecundity or sexual attractiveness (and this always varied, depending on the aesthetics of an era) was strictly surplus to requirements. For example, in the late Georgian age a column-like silhouette was fashionable, and so long stays were considered vital to restrict 'the too abundant mass of fattening matronhood'. Similarly the large lady without a corset during Victorian fashions for narrow waists was described as a monstrosity.

Over the five centuries of the corset's supremacy, the constant for most fashionable corset styles was a narrow waist. An unwise amount of tightening at the waist gave rise to an effect likened to a pillow tied with string in the middle. Taken to extremes, the greatest distortion could be achieved by tight-lacing – specifically, lacing the corset, leaving it to 'breathe' for a period of time, then tightening the laces further until the internal organs had been jostled into conformity and the diaphragm was compressed.

Many of the modern beliefs around tight-lacing are drawn from a superficial grazing of inflammatory sources that either boast of hand-span waist measurements or else berate those women who tried to achieve them. However, although fashion frequently advocated an extremely narrow waist, this by no means went uncontested. When the 1840s saw the fashionable waist shrinking, Victorian medical 'experts' indulged in lurid

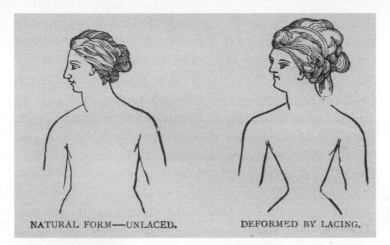

NATURAL FORM—UNLACED.   DEFORMED BY LACING.

As this 1890s illustration shows, the Victorians were well aware of the distortions caused by tight-lacing.

7 The author of *The Science of Dress* claimed to have seen corsets at a fashionable stay-makers measuring only fourteen inches: 'It is no rare thing to meet ladies so tightly laced that they positively cannot lean back in a chair or on a sofa, for if they did they would suffocate.' She asserted that the 'natural waist of a well-formed woman of average height' would be twenty-seven to twenty-nine inches.

descriptions on the anatomical dangers of tight-lacing . . . even as pseudo-science still pronounced corsets indispensable for the female form. Battle lines were drawn between those who advocated tight-lacing as aesthetically pleasing and those who abhorred the 'spider-waist'. Tight-lacing was blamed for indigestion, hysteria, spinal distortion, consumption, liver complaints, heart disease, cancer, and early death. Gwen Raverat recalled visits to her Aunt Etty in the 1880s:

> Whenever I went to stay with Aunt Etty, soon after my arrival, I would feel her fingers fumbling in my waist-belt, to make sure I was not tight-lacing; for she suspected every young person of a wish to be fashionable. She used to tell us a dreadful moral tale about a lady who laced herself so hard that she cut her liver *right in half*, and died in consequence.

Whether stories of livers being punctured by ribs due to tight-lacing were scaremongering or sad reality, such tales were enough to make many women cautious of doing damage to themselves. It is doubtful that the rumoured sixteen- or seventeen-inch waists could realistically be achieved by any except the naturally slender or perversely persistent.[7]

8 According to *The Workwoman's Guide*, 'It is impossible to give any particular patterns or sizes of stays, as they must, of course, be cut differently, according to the figure, and be variously supported with more or less bones or runners of cotton, according to the age, strength or constitution of the wearer.'

9 The Kyoto Institute in Japan has a late sixteenth-century ironwork corset, most likely worn only on formal events for impact, or else simply crafted as an example of metal-working expertise.

Studio photographs from the 1850s onwards do show a reassuringly robust number of heavyset women, with their bodices straining around the structure of hidden corsetry.

CONSTRUCTING THE CARAPACE

A corset had to be well constructed to cope with all the demands placed upon it. There was a spectrum of control, ranging from immovable carapace to tolerable encasement. For added attraction, the stiff buckram could be covered with heavy cottons, satins and silks. Before the invention of sewing machines capable of coping with corsetry in the mid-nineteenth century, professional stay-makers had the unenviable job of hand-stitching these thick layers. Home-made corsets of cotton and linen ensured that those who could not afford to buy support would not have to do without.[8]

Such home-made corsets were less likely to have the formidable sturdiness of professional stays but they were still complex garments that needed time, skill and application to construct – all qualities lacking in the young heroine of Flora Thompson's novel *Lark Rise to Candleford*:

> She was supposed to be making stays for herself from narrow strips of calico left over from cutting out larger things, which, when finished with buttons and shoulder straps, would make a lasting and comfortable garment. Laura always wore such stays; but not of her own making. If she had ever finished those she was working on, they would, by that time, have been too small to go round her.

At its most robust, a corset could seem almost like a form of body armour, and so in the sixteenth century corsets were sometimes referred to as 'hauberks' (a hauberk being a shirt of chain mail). Catherine de Medici, Queen of France between 1547 and 1559, was rumoured to have a corset of openwork steel covered in velvet.[9] Tragically for the Empress Elisabeth of Austria, her corsets could not provide the protection of proper body armour. On 10th September 1898 she was jostled by an unknown man while walking along the promenade at Lake Geneva. Shortly afterwards she collapsed. When her corsets were cut open, a stab wound was revealed and she soon bled to death. The corset hadn't deflected the blade; worse, it kept the wound hidden and prevented Elisabeth from feeling the symptoms of her injury, thereby delaying potentially life-saving treatment.

One very proactive take on the notion of corsets as armour was the innovation of cardboard corsets, to be worn during suffragette clashes with police in Edwardian London. Grace Roe, a young hockey-enthusiast, prepared to join a suffrage deputation at Westminster by fashioning a special corset of cardboard, moulded in the bathtub, then fitted to her figure with cotton-wool padding to protect her breasts.

LIGHTER, BRIGHTER, MORE HOPEFUL

At the lighter end of the scale, Regency corsetière Mrs Barclay claimed that 'ladies of the first distinction' enjoyed her *corset de Grace*, which was allegedly 'conducive to health, ease and comfort'. Presumably this meant the use of cording instead of bones, and a lighter-weight canvas, though details are not given. In the early nineteenth century, Covent Garden dressmaker Martha Gibbon advertised stays designed to avoid undue pressure, while in the mid-nineteenth century Mme Roxy Caplin offered corsets with elastic fronts (for ladies who sang) or stays with invisible spinal support.[10]

Mass-production of corsets in the late nineteenth century meant there was no excuse to be without. Each new batch of designs claimed to improve on its predecessors. By the end of the century the hourglass shape was dismissed as unhealthy and the corset dipped below the bust-line, creating the infamous S-bend, which forced the wearer into a so-called 'Grecian curve' that distorted the spine – hardly healthy, either! Corsetières confidently advertised the new long corsets of the Edwardian

10 Martha Gibbon's 1800 stays could also have padding for 'persons to whom nature has not been favourable'. Roxy Caplin's book, *Woman and Her Wants*, was a rational exploration of anatomy and how it interacts with corsetry.

era as being based 'entirely on Anatomical Principles' because they *only* compressed the abdomen.

A nineteenth-century scrimshaw busk, a rigid element of the corset about the size and shape of a school ruler, made from wood, bone, ivory or metal, and designed to keep the front straight and upright.

Edwardian corset manufacturers usually described their wares as 'dainty', 'little' and 'charmingly trimmed' - adjectives at variance with the reality of the size and construction of the actual corset. A promotion for the London Corset Company in 1902 boasted, 'Now the corset of the hour is not only a necessary garment, but an extremely beautiful one; no longer a stiff armour horribly contorting the figure, but a beautifully moulded little construction of dainty silk, batiste, or brocade, with the least possible number of bones.'

During the First World War, far from discarding corsets to carry out war-work, women relied on them for comfort and support. Canny manufacturers took advantage of the mood of war-weariness to advertise mood-enhancing corsets, such as the 'Magneto' corset of 1916:

> From the moment when you put them on a ceaseless stream of Magnetic Power permeates your whole body from head to heel. The joy of New Life, of New Health and New Vigour thrills through every nerve. You feel a different woman. Your outlook upon life is different – brighter, happier, and more hopeful.

All this for just a penny shy of six shillings.

RUBBER ROLL-ONS

Corsets per se were not intended to be instruments of torture. Professional corsetières had good knowledge of how to measure and mould the human physique. As late as the mid-twentieth century highly trained fitters, such as those from Spirella or Twilfit, attended the customer in store or visited them at home. Clients were carefully measured and then steered towards purchasing the appropriate style for their body type. Customer loyalty was strong towards brands that seemed to offer the desired effect. Then, as now, the difference between the exaggerated physiques depicted in fashion magazines and corset catalogues and the reality of their own bodies must have been disheartening to many women. The sheer persistence of the association of a sleek form and narrow waist with attractiveness is quite obvious to the costume historian. It begs the question: just how 'large' was too large?

These questions became particularly pertinent as more and more flesh was revealed during the increased 'undressing' of the 1920s and 1930s. Skin-slimming fashions would need a new kind of foundation garment – the girdle.

Originally girdle belts were worn outside the clothes by both men and women from the Middle Ages onwards and were both decorative and practical. By the twentieth century 'girdle' was instead the preferred term for an elastic corset, usually sitting below the bust. Many styles kept boning, and some even had laces. For those struggling to find stocks of girdles during wartime shortages in 1916 the *Ladies' Fancy Workbook* advertised a knitted girdle for 'women inclined to obesity', with sizes starting at just twenty-four inches.

Corsets of the mid-1920s were all about suppressing curves.

The First World War saw the introduction of simple shift dresses, which hid the curves, but this did not mean the body was left to bulge or wobble without restraint. A girdle or corset was still an invisible essential. Skin-skimming fashions of the mid-1920s onwards demanded a small waist, but also – ideally – hips and bust as close to non-existent as possible.

Corsets and girdles fortified with elastic clamped down on the figure like fancy sausage skins to help achieve this look. From the 1930s there was the revolution of the fully elasticated rubber *roll-on*. The wearer rolled it up, stepped into it, then unrolled it over her hips. This was considered very modern when it first appeared:

> My Gran was a bit trendy and was one of the first to have a latex type roll on garment which she always said made her feel like a piece of rolled bacon but the feeling of relief when she removed it was bliss.

Despite the lighter weight and better fit of elastic-based corsets, they were hardly seductive garments. The rubber webbing puckered horribly, forming ugly ridges. To stop the roll-on actually rolling over while in action, Warner introduced featherweight boning at the waist. As with other kinds of corset, they were not the easiest of garments to get into – one gent in the London Blitz of the Second World War complained how his missus was never ready to run for shelter during an air raid: 'You see, she always wears one of these 'ere abominable belts and it takes quite a time to put on,' he said. 'Abominable' was, of course, the husband's rather appropriate term for the 'abdominal belt'.[11]

Despite shortages of rubber and metal in the Second World War, women fought to have some money set aside for corsetry. The British government included corsets in their controlled scheme of garment production under the CC41 label – known as 'Utility wear'.

11 Lancashire housewife Nella Last said her corsets were 'museum pieces' by the end of the war. Writing her diary for Mass Observation in November 1949, she noted that she had last had a new corset in January 1940, and that there was a two- to three-month waiting list for delivery of a new Spirella.

12 *Fibre K* was
DuPont's working
name for Lycra nylon
elastic, first
introduced in the US
in 1958, with the
trade name Lycra
announced in 1959.

*A 1946 Gossard girdle, promoted as a glamorous form
of control for women at work.*

The CC41 scheme continued after the peace of 1945, but Utility corsets didn't pinch the waist enough to suit French designer Christian Dior. In 1947 Dior decided to re-create the Victorian hourglass figure in his first ever solo collection – the famous New Look. He called it a 'natural' feminine look compared to the austere, boxy lines of the war years. To achieve the 'natural' look, the garment bodices were cleverly engineered with sturdy internal boning and 'waspie' waist corsets. These soon gave rise to a surge of interest in corsets as *seductive* garments, particularly the black-net 'Merry Widow' designs.

From the 1940s the speed of change in textile technology was phenomenal. The artificial fibre known as rayon was well known from the First World War onwards, but it deferred to nylon and polyester for foundation garments. Lastex was a stretchy yarn made of cotton, silk or rayon wrapped around rubber threads, invented in 1925 and continuing to be popular until it was superseded by power net. Power net was an elasticated lace that could be made up into very attractive forms of control. Berlei *Controlette* promoted a 1950s corset for the fuller figure with 'perfect comfort and perfect control without a single bone'. Warner retaliated with a 1961 boneless and virtually seamless Lycra corselette called a Birthday Suit.[12]

By the 1970s the body stocking was the most advanced form

of foundation garment – as light and flexible as a second skin. This skin-clinging all-in-one garment stretched from throat to ankles and acted as tights, girdle *and* bra. It perfectly suited a growing trend for leaving the body unstructured by hefty foundations. Instead the figure would be sculptured by a craze for 'Keep Fit' workouts, such as those led by television guru Diana Moran – called the 'Green Goddess' in her skin-tight body stocking – or actress Jane Fonda.

The trend for body-contouring fitness has been with us ever since, whether via weight-training, Pilates or muscle-vibrating platforms. However, those affluent enough to afford gym membership can also afford excesses of food and drink, and the average human physique usually needs more contouring than casual exercise regimes can offer, in order to attain the sizes most frequently flaunted on modern catwalks. For those who still feel the need for artificial shaping there are modern foundation garments. Many have eschewed boning completely, aside from under-bust support; advanced textile technology offers smoothing, control and support without it. However, boning or no boning, the continuing popularity of foundation garments must make us wonder whether the cult of the smooth waist is an inevitable side-effect of cultural needs to appear toned and youthful. Are we confined and shaped – corseted – by our cultural norms, or will the wheel of fashion ever turn in favour of big bellies and 'apple' waists?

SUPPORT AND SEDUCTION

The bra is a relative newcomer on the underwear scene, though we do know of very old examples. Wool or linen bandeaux breast-bands are referenced in Ancient Greek imagery and literature, and lightweight medieval bras have recently been discovered in Austria. There are also rare examples of bust support in the early nineteenth century, such as a 'racer-back'-style bra in the Kyoto Institute costume collection. But the fact is that when bodices were specifically constructed to support the bust, and when corsets were designed to cover it, no bra was needed.

It was during a phase favouring vast pillow-like chests in the Edwardian era that corset designs began to drop below the bust, to concentrate on confining the diaphragm and hips. The 'monobosom' bust was thus left unfettered, save for the chemise or combinations. Boned *bust bodices* of net and coutil cotton were required for support instead. These wide, shaped bodices had thick shoulder straps and sometimes shaping for each breast – they were essentially hefty versions of what we would call bras.

Shown, folded, is a cotton and lace French bust bodice of 1915 – essentially a light, front-fastening bra.

The term *brassière* is itself of uncertain origin. It was probably adopted by English-speakers to replace 'bust bodice' because French was considered more refined. The French themselves refer to a *soutien-gorge*, or throat support. Brassieres were first referred to in the US as early as 1893 – specifically talking about breast-bands to be worn under high-waisted dresses – and in the UK in about 1912. They were sold alongside bust bodices during the First World War.

There were varying designs of early bras. A pre-war booklet for expectant mothers describes how to make a nine-inch-wide breast-band at home from unbleached calico, fastened at the back and provided with shoulder straps, and with darts under the bust for a neater fit. The guide recommended that 'holes should be cut for the nipples so that they are not pressed upon'. Contemporary with this band is the more advanced design of two triangles of fabric with ribbon straps, patented in the US in 1913 by American publisher Mary Phelps Jacob. As 'Caresse Crosby', the design was sold to Warner's corsetières. Jacob's patent is world-famous, but is easily pre-dated by an 1889 German design by Christine Hardt, though this does not seem to have gone into manufacture.

The supremely popular Kestos bra of the Twenties, Thirties and Forties was also designed by a woman – Mrs Rosalind Kestos – on the same principle of triangles with shoulder straps.

As with corsets, bra styles changed with fashions. When breasts became surplus to requirements in the mid-1920s there were bras to help flatten them; a thriftier method of binding bosoms was to push them into the armpits, then bind the upper torso with bandages. This latter technique was used by the author's maternal grandmother, who was never of slender build. Gradually, however, the bosom returned to fashion, and from the late 1920s it could benefit from the first proper shaped bust cups, bust uplift and spiral stitching.

The Kempat bra of the 1930s, like the Kestos brand, favoured a light structure. Small, pointed breasts were fashionable.

Early bra-makers advertised sizes by using evocative names such as 'Princess' and 'Queen', giving chest-girth inches for guidance. By the 1930s, with the focus fully on the bust once more, information became more specific. Marshall & Snelgrove might offer an uplift brassiere in strong net for the 'small to average figure', then translate this into 'sizes 32 to 38'.

Then as now, sizing was subjective. 'Small', 'average' and 'outsize' were vague terms. 'Sizes 32 to 38' was not much more helpful. It was Warner's who first acknowledged the discrepancy between the bust measurement and chest measurement; in 1935 they introduced specific cup fittings for the first time. Promotional images showed how the letters A, B, C and D corresponded to bust size. By the 1950s Warner's soothed potential customers with the reassurance:

> Darling, you'll never be 'average' to us. Warner's know that nature never meant women to be squeezed into 'standard' sizes. So Warner's 3-Way-Sizes were designed to fit you and you alone.

Double-letter cup sizes have now been added to the range, and the alphabet stretches at least to L – a reflection of the increase in female stature in the decades since then.

Sizes might be fairly standard, but the shape of the bust still followed fashion. Perky pyramids could be created by spiral-stitching. These were also known as *bullet bras* and *teenage torpedoes* because of their conical shape – and their impact. Popular between the Thirties and Fifties, they had the great disadvantage of collapsing at the tip when meeting an obstacle. Cotton-wool balls stuffed into the apex of each cup were one way of avoiding this embarrassment.

Adding inches to the bust was no new trend. Examples of eighteenth-century stays with bust pockets survive, which would take padded inserts.

Well over a century later, the Configurateur corset claimed to have the shaping required to transform 'any Thin Bust to exquisitely lovely proportions of captivating (natural) beauty'. As early as 1920 (before breasts were obliged to go into hiding) women feeling inadequately endowed were encouraged to make their husbands proud by using the Joujou bust supporter, made of pink or white rayon. It was apparently 'absolutely firm, and there is not that unpleasant feeling when taking exercise'.

1940s tips for the 'flat-chested lassie' included camouflaging the condition with ruffles of ruched baby ribbon, sewn inside a bra. Some girls simply resorted to stuffing their bras with socks, although these had an embarrassing tendency to stray from where they had been placed. A young lady from Hull named Helen recalled the excitement of her first-ever ride on cable cars in the 1960s. She had padded her bra with socks for the occasion. As the cable car rose ever higher, she looked down and saw, to her chagrin, a solitary sock sitting forlornly on the ground far below.

Inflatable bras, briefly popular in the 1950s, had their own self-evident perils.

THE BRAS THAT WERE NEVER BURNED

The 1960s was a confusing crossover era. The corset and girdle were still essential to support-structured evening wear, and still 'the done thing' for daily wear, but they were difficult to equate with the new baby-doll look that young women were adopting, or the growing sense of sexual freedom. Light net or thin cotton bras catered for the younger customer.

Young women of the 1960s rejected heavily structured foundation garments. This 1967 bra is small and light.

Then came 1968, and the myth of the bra-burning 'Women's Libbers'. To denounce the racism, consumerism and objectification of women represented by the Miss America beauty pageant in Atlantic City, feminists gathered outside the venue symbolically dumped bras and other traditionally female objects into a rubbish bin. TV cameras picked up on the Women's Liberation sign, and commentators then made the connection between draft-dodgers during the Vietnam War burning their call-up papers. At no time were bras removed or burned. The media attention ensured growing awareness of the Women's Liberation movement, but a backlash against it quite groundlessly associated feminism with bra-lessness and bra-burning.

HELLO BOYS

Traditionally bras were designed for an unseen supporting role. To avoid detection, they could be backless and, from 1938, strapless. Dresses even had small loops on the shoulders, with press-studs to keep bra straps in place. Rebellious young women might show coloured bras under pale blouses from the 1950s onwards, but the idea of visible underwear-as-outerwear was first flaunted worldwide by the pop star Madonna during her 1990 'Blonde Ambition' tour. She took to the stage in a conical bra designed by Jean Paul Gaultier, inspired by the whirlpool-effect 'bullet bras' of the Thirties. Vivienne Westwood had already parodied Establishment styles by the open wearing of corsets as a symbol of female empowerment, most notably in her 1987 Harris Tweed collection, but Madonna's Gaultier bra opened the floodgates on visible brassieres. Designers were quick to create patterns and features that would look good when worn under low-cut tops, or with the straps visible.

The most iconic modern bra is undoubtedly Gossard's Wonderbra, first developed in the 1950s but relaunched to great effect with a bold advertising campaign in 1994, featuring supermodel Eva Herzigová wearing the bra, along with the slogan 'Hello Boys'. Although the promotion heavily sexualised the bra, as did Madonna's public performances, there was at least now a sense that breasts and brassieres were something that could be talked about openly. Shops could therefore also make a more public display of the growing range of bras designed for breast-feeding, or those created for women who have undergone a mastectomy.

In the modern Western world, cultural expectations regarding breasts are as strong as control of other parts of the female anatomy – notably the waist – was in the past. Breasts have been the most eroticised area since the 1990s (longer, if the topless model shots of tabloid newspapers are taken into account). Cleavage is considered highly desirable in the non-topless woman, though female nipples are – rather prudishly – to be shielded in moulded T-shirt bras. Perhaps influenced by exaggerated digital images from computer gaming and Internet pornography, the ideal figure for the second decade of the twenty-first century seems to be for a woman without belly, hips or thigh flesh, but with a large gravity-defying bust. This can be achieved by a combination of foam-moulded bras, 'chicken-fillet' silicon inserts and significant underwiring – not to mention cosmetic surgery; the body itself is now cut and stitched into the desired foundation shape for the clothes it will wear. As an added extra, large, rounded buttocks are now also heavily eroticised, leading to distorted nude or semi-nude poses by celebrities and models wishing to emphasise breasts *and* bottom simultaneously.

BODY BELTS FOR MEN

Men have not been completely exempt from the tyranny of body shaping. Admittedly for a brief, glorious period in the sixteenth and seventeenth centuries large stomachs were considered both masculine and fashionable, so the *peascod* belly was created by stuffing doublets with bombast (sawdust or horsehair) – hence the term *bombastic* for someone who is full of their own import-ance. However, peascod bellies notwithstanding, stays of strong cotton, leather or webbing were invaluable for riding, as well as for military men and those out hunting or engaging in violent exercise.

For all that men might mock women's vanity and the artifice of female corsets, the dandies of the eighteenth and nineteenth centuries also strapped on whalebone corsets to appear younger and slimmer. These were given grand names, such as the Apollo, the Cumberland or the Brummell bodice – named after George 'Beau' Brummell – and their wearers were heavily satirised in mass-market cartoons. Although he was naturally athletic in build, Brummell himself still used expensive cashmere stays to enhance his physique, though there is no evidence that his stays were the same as the advertised Brummell bodice. The Prince Regent, another George, aspired to Brummell's elegance, but with a fifty-inch waist he needed the help of stays – in particular, a foundation belt referred to as a 'Bastille of whalebone', in honour of the feared confines of the Parisian gaol. When Prince George left off his stays there were caustic comments about his bad figure.

By the twentieth century the preferred term for male corsets was 'body belt'. Some were undoubtedly designed for medical support, but there were still boned belts that were corsets in all but name, such as those on sale during the First World War, which had fleecy lining for extra warmth. If warmth was the main requirement, then women were encouraged to knit body belts for men on active service. Such items were also commercially available; the pure wool belt was advertised as 'most useful for our soldiers in the trenches'.

Men called to action during the Second World War were also targeted by corset-makers. Advertisements for the Linia Belt used images of a handsome RAF pilot to promote a corset that claimed to brace and tone muscles and massage away fat – claims that are echoed by modern adverts for tummy-fat reducers.[13] A rival product from Woodlands Surgical Chemist went one step further and boasted that its body-conforming belt 'takes years off your age' for only twenty-one shillings, post-free.

The demands of war work in 1940 helped patriotic promotions of the Linia body belt.

BODY BEAUTIFUL

If a corset once represented civilisation, the modern attitude to foundation garments reveals much about the revolution in personal freedom. They are no longer a required item and we can, if we choose, 'let it all hang out'. At the same time the history of corset-wearing shows a steady and inexorable transition from corsets symbolising respectability to corsets flaunting sexuality. Basques and corsets are now worn as lingerie items, for fancy dress and fetish wear, or as part of fabulous fantasy ensembles in the goth and steampunk world. The human body is far less hidden under layers of clothing, and underwear enjoys the limelight more.

Alarmingly, for all the technological brilliance of modern foundation garments, which are designed to control or conceal, the unclothed body is now sculpted more than ever. However, toning and control are now supposed to be achieved primarily through exercise. Instead of the carapace of the corset, there is the drive to strengthen core muscles. When taken to extremes, the need to present a socially perfect body has become linked with eating disorders, low self-esteem and depression. The modern age might mock the whalebone corsets of the past, but both women and men now choose to undergo cosmetic surgery to enhance or suppress their figures. It is difficult to say which is the more deluded.

One Victorian dress expert summed up the contradiction of wanting natural beauty to be artificially structured: 'Had Venus been compelled by a cold climate to drape herself, we have little doubt she would have worn stays, to give her clothes the shape they lacked and without their aid could not maintain.' Perhaps the truly modern Venus would avoid figure-forming clothes by turning to surgery and so appear naked once more.

DRESS RAIL

Captain Winstanley: 'Sixty guineas for a dinner-dress!
   That's rather stiff. Do you know that a suit of dress
   clothes costs me nine pounds, and lasts almost as many
   years?'
Mrs Winstanley: 'My dear Conrad, for a man it is so
   different. No one looks at your clothes.'
   M. E. BRADDON, VIXEN, 1879

LADIES AND GENTS

At some point – or points – in human prehistory, clothes for
women and men diverged. Without pictorial or written records
it is impossible to know exactly when or why this happened,
but it did. In this chapter we consider the nearly universal association of long, skirted garments with female wear.

The concept of dresses and skirts as purely female items of
clothing is so firmly entrenched in Western culture that many
people are still hugely discomforted by practices that disturb
this norm, such as cross-dressing men.

There are, of course, many cultures worldwide where long,
skirted clothes are very comfortably worn by men as the norm.
In such cases it's a question of semantics: we might view these
men as wearing female skirts or dresses, but their cultures have
their own specifically male words for items of clothing of this
sort. The long *djellabas* worn by men of North Africa – past and
present – and the male *thwab* of the Middle East are dresses in
all but name, but they are culturally distinct. Even in English

1 What's in a word?
The smock-frock was
a basic male farmer's
garment worn from
the Iron Age to the
nineteenth century –
showing that the
word *frock* was not
always used
exclusively for a
female dress. Smock-
frocks could be
beige, blue, or
madder red; lime-
green is also
recorded. The highly
skilled traditional
English smocking
stitches were a late
addition.

such long, loose non-trousered garments are usually referred to as robes or tunics, if worn by men.[1]

As awareness increases about the wide spectrum of gender identification, we are increasingly brought up against cultural assumptions about clothes. The reasons for the gender divide in attire are complex and must be social rather than practical; even if we subscribe to the over-simple theory that females in prehistory were the 'gatherers' and not the 'hunters', tunics and leggings would surely still be the practical choice for occupational clothing. The same goes for domestic and agricultural roles: there is no overlying reason for housework to be carried out in skirts, any more than cow-milking or crop-harvesting – all jobs performed by women in the past.

And yet, despite such practical issues, the gender divergence began. It spread across many different countries and it consolidated over the last fifteen centuries to give us our modern ideas of what is male and female in clothing. The division is so iconic that it is used as a shorthand for gender all over the world: the silhouettes of figures in a skirt and in trousers on the signs for *Ladies* and *Gentlemen* toilets.

The modern lavatory sign for *Ladies* shows a figure in a roughly knee-length skirt – a relatively modern innovation. Dress and skirt styles have changed tremendously over the centuries, with an abundance of different designs. In this chapter we'll see how dress structures, shapes and hemlines have adapted to follow fashion's dictates . . . and to conform to cultural pressures.

CREATING THE FASHIONABLE SILHOUETTE

Whatever the whims of fashion or the demands of culture, women's dresses have veered between simply covering the figure and actively controlling or even distorting it. As we have already seen in previous chapters, functionality is not necessarily a priority in clothing.

Dress structure is also dependent on available time, technologies and fabrics. Thus the earliest gowns in Western history were loose and rectangular, made out of whole lengths of cloth in order to minimise waste. With the exception of elite garments, it made sense to reduce the cutting and sewing required. The cloth used was often woven on upright looms that were actually kept inside the household. All stitching was done by hand. At most, these early dresses might have gores – triangular panels of additional material – for an A-line skirt. Classical styles were simply pinned into place to reduce seams. There are also Germanic dresses from the Roman era woven on a tubular loom, which did away with the need for any side seams at all.

Once a household had enough disposable income to buy fabric, rather than producing it within the family, there was potentially time for crafting more complex styles. It was during the medieval era that gowns morphed into more sophisticated constructions, which moulded the body instead of simply flowing over it. Later, the Elizabethan era saw the separation of a dress into two parts, bodice and skirt. Then from the sixteenth century onwards it wasn't enough simply to *wear* clothes; the bodice in particular had to be *fitted*. Professional dressmakers – known as mantua-makers – now faced the dilemma of how to give a woman a flattering fashionable figure through the medium of dress.

A fifteenth-century gown with trailing sleeves and skirt – not for the working woman.

The bodice-and-skirt structure dominated dresses until the second decade of the twentieth century. In the seventeenth and eighteenth centuries bodices and skirts were usually separate, but of matching fabric, to give the impression of a complete ensemble. The late Georgian era did see a surge of popularity for complete gowns, still with a fitted bodice. To some extent, a gown could be adapted to fit different figures, as bodices were, at this time, frequently pinned into place, rather than having set fastenings. However, the bodice part of the dress still comprised a complex set of shapes, so a good fit was no mean feat. Home dressmakers took patterns from existing gowns until later in the nineteenth century, when enterprising publishers began to distribute paper patterns in ladies' magazines.

A 1740s gown worn over side hoops.

As ever, women frequently expected more from their dress than it was capable of giving. According to the Regency guide *The Mirror of the Graces*, a woman's gown was to remedy defects of the figure 'without interfering with the pleasures of the palette'. The same guide wryly commented, 'The Mantua-maker's customers are not always easily pleased.'

In general it was the bodice of the dress that fitted most precisely, over the carapace of a corset. All bodices of the nineteenth century pulled the shoulders back; most flattened the belly and compressed the lungs; many compressed the waist. Bodices between the 1840s and early 1900s routinely had whalebone strips inserted for additional structure. They also had an internal belt, which fastened tightly around the waist to prevent them swivelling out of place.[2]

Below the waist, the skirt grew in width from the 1820s onwards, peaking with extraordinary circumferences in the 1860s, then shrinking to quite restrictive dimensions from the 1870s onwards. While the long, straight gowns of the Regency era were considered scant, they were positively broad compared to the sheath dresses of the late Victorian age. One tight black satin evening dress of 1893 was referred to as a Sticking-Plaster Dress because it was such a clinging, second skin. By 1898 these body-skimming skirts were under attack by the fashion press – 'how to sit down or get up gracefully in one of these sheath-like garments has not been demonstrated satisfactorily'.

2 From the 1860s women tried the combination of blouse and skirt, rather than a matching bodice. This eventually gave us the easy informality of the modern top-and-skirt combination.

Gowns from c.1912 show a stately silhouette. Vast hats balance the very narrow skirts. The wearer walked with caution.

Then came the Edwardian fashion for a straight silhouette, named *Directoire* in reference to styles dominant under the revolutionary government in France of 1795–9, known at that time as the Directoire. The Directoire line required thigh-length stays and a decorative pole or furled umbrella for support while walking. Directoire dresses might also boast a *hobbled* skirt. The ludicrous hobble style had a short but well-satirised lifespan in around 1906–12. It saw the fabric of the skirt so tightly fitted around the legs that it was impossible to take a full stride. To emphasise the restriction further, some hobble gowns had a sash wrapped about the calves. Out of sight, hobble garters looped in a figure of eight just below the knees to further hinder movement.[3] English couturier Lady Lucy Duff Gordon (trading as Lucile Ltd) took credit for the style, declaring with perverse pride, 'I launched in Paris the silliest, most helpless, most irresponsible fashion that women have ever submitted to.'

The style was all very well – if ridiculous – on ornamental occasions, but it made even a simple everyday task such as trotting for the omnibus a considerable feat. Fashion writer Edith Russell barely managed to escape the stricken liner *Titanic* in 1912, impeded as she was by a hobble dress just half a yard in width around the ankles. Coincidentally Lucy Duff Gordon was also travelling first-class on *Titanic*, though she escaped in more manageable clothing than Edith. Ironically, the hobble style coincided with the struggle for female suffrage – as women fought for greater social and political freedoms, fashion retaliated with this perverse restriction.

1917 evening gowns.

Fickle as ever, fashion decreed wide skirts a few years later. However, this coincided with the requirement for women in Europe to shed their decorative role and take on more hefty work due to the First World War, and it was a short-lived trend. By 1918 women had become used to wearing rectangular shift dresses cut in what was known as the *barrel line*. These simply popped over the head without significant shaping or internal boning. They soon evolved into the iconic low-waisted loose shift of the 1920s, now known as *flapper* style. In turn these body-denying shift dresses were discarded in 1930, in favour of longer, leaner dresses and a whippet-woman silhouette.

Long and sleek – a crêpe afternoon gown of 1930. Elegant but unforgiving for those with a less-than-lean figure.

Not all designers liked this new narrow cut. When the couturier Mainbocher escaped from Paris in the autumn of 1939, hoping to avoid a German invasion, he remarked, 'There are too many women whose thighs cannot stand to be silhouetted and over caressed by the too straight skirt.' The 'pencil' skirts of the late 1940s and 1950s were so tight they needed a slit – like the Edwardian hobble skirt – for even the meekest of movements. This slit was sometimes given a modest insert of fabric to hide the back of the legs. It was referred to as a 'Piccadilly pleat', presumably because the sex-workers in Piccadilly did not trouble with one.

THIS HAD BETTER BE GOOD

Wartime austerity between 1941 and 1949 (when clothing rationing was in force) meant frugality of fabric by necessity rather than by choice. Dresses had few pleats, flares or embellishments. Shoulders were boxy and showed a 'can-do' attitude. Full-length evening gowns were discouraged. A brave shabbiness prevailed. In Britain restrictions were placed on commercially produced civilian clothing styles, in order to minimise wastage of fabric and factory resources.

No wonder, then, that women were stunned by the launch of an exuberant new silhouette in 1947, a mere two years after peace was declared. It was inspired by the wide gowns last seen during the First World War (and, before that, in the 1860s) and it exploded on the French fashion scene thanks to the talent of a designer who had kept a low profile during the war – one Christian Dior.

Carmel Snow, editor of the US fashion magazine *Harper's Bazaar*, was present at Dior's first solo fashion show on 12th February 1947. It was in a Paris still struggling with fuel and food shortages. The city desperately needed to reassert its dominance as the centre of the fashion world, after too long under Nazi occupation. Just before the first mannequins sauntered into sight, Snow whispered to Dior, 'This had better be good.'

It was beyond good. It was superlative. Ernestine Cartier, fashion editor of the UK edition of *Harper's Bazaar*, referred to the new sloping shoulders, cinched waists and long, vast skirts as the New Look. The name stuck. While it undeniably had impact, the New Look was another gloriously impractical style:

4 She wrote a diary entry on 8th January 1948: 'The "new line" seems to have ousted points problems, the poor quality of coal and even the weather, when women are talking.'

Post-war New Look dresses at Harrods. The new flamboyance of such dresses was a welcome antidote to wartime austerity.

Vogue editor Audrey Withers found herself needing to pick her skirt up in two hands to get onto a bus, just like women of her mother's era, two World Wars previously. Indeed, since most fabric was rationed and budgets were tight, few women could flaunt the new style to Parisian extremes. One Barrow-in-Furness housewife noticed that suddenly the only ones in fashion were 'dowdy old grannies and maiden aunts' who had never abandoned the Great War fashions for narrow waists and wide skirts.[4]

There were several ingenious options for acquiring longer, wider skirts on limited resources. Blackout fabric – opaque cloth used to make curtains to prevent lights inside a house showing and thereby providing a target during an air raid – could be dyed and jazzed up with appliqué designs, preferably with Parisian motifs; thick bands of material could be added at the skirt waistband to give extra length. If the fabric didn't match, that was no problem – it would be hidden by a jacket. Patchwork skirts and dirndls used up fabric scraps.

Further ingenuity was needed to create the ideal silhouette of the New Look, which Dior called the 'natural' feminine silhouette. In reality, bodice-boning, bust pads and hip pads were skilfully employed in his designs to present the hourglass shape of a mature woman.

Some said the New Look made women look more feminine, inspiring new-found gallantry amongst men – 'workmen on ladders nearly fell off them, glimpsing frilly petticoats; the forgotten ankle became interesting again'. Others complained that the longer skirts meant that legs were too hidden. The British government condemned the style as wasteful and promptly encouraged designers to produce it for export only, to bring much-needed revenue into the country. 'Can anyone imagine the average housewife and businesswoman dressed in bustles and long skirts . . . running for buses and crowding into tubes and trains? The idea is ludicrous,' scoffed no-nonsense Labour MP Mrs Mabel Ridealgh. And Hollywood's premier dress designer, Adrian Adolph Greenberg (known publicly simply as 'Adrian'), rejected Dior's so-called feminine styles as dowdy and dumpy. As a young girl, future world-class designer Vivienne Westwood was taken to see a local woman wearing what her mother referred to as the 'horrible' New Look, in the heart of Derbyshire's Peak District. However, Dior's glamour and exuberance actually inspired many of Westwood's later couture creations.

More symbolically, it was recognised that the New Look was a step backwards in terms of dress freedom for women: having enjoyed easy-to-manage skirts during the war, women now had to contend with legs encumbered by yards of fabric. One *Picture Post* journalist complained of the skirts, 'Our mothers freed us from these in their struggle for emancipation . . . in our own active workaday lives there can be no possible place for them.'

But despite such criticisms, the New Look was one of the most significant fashion events of the twentieth century. It remained popular until the early 1960s and has been regularly reincarnated. Dior went on to create A-line, H-line and Y-line dresses. However, it was a British designer Mary Quant who would create the next fashion innovation to shock the world. It was all about *length*. Or lack of it . . .

To set the scene for Mary Quant's contribution to the fashion revolution of the 1960s we must first look back in time once more. An overview of historical styles across the last 2,000 years at least reveals one consistent element to female dresses before the First World War: legs were most emphatically *covered*.

The requirement for covered legs for Western women was entrenched even in the Classical era, when both women and men wore loose tunics. While the outfits for women and men in Ancient Greece and Rome were often extremely similar in terms of fabric, drape and fastenings, male garments often revealed the calves, while the female equivalents were consistently long.

In the following centuries this distinction was maintained. A medieval man might have peacocked in particoloured hose, showing a shapely, gartered leg, but the medieval woman would need to hitch up her gown just to reveal an ankle. Even centuries later, when the coquettes of the nineteenth-century Moulin Rouge nightclub danced the legendary Can-Can, it was their untethered legs that were the featured attraction – all the more erotic for being forbidden in the outside world.

This charming gown from 1828 is called a Walking Dress. The skirts are still long and full – it is for strolling, rather than hiking.

Covering the legs was not sufficient for those truly dedicated to following fashion. There are many historical styles termed *walking dresses* because they were intended for wearing while shopping, promenading or paying visits. However, two dress fashions in particular conspired to reduce walking to a dainty shuffle. The first, the hobble skirt, which favoured extreme narrowness, has already been discussed. The second significant restrictive style concerned the *length* of the dress.

A French princess requires help to wear and display her trailing gown in 1470.

Wearing impractical skirts was a way for a rich woman to disassociate herself from the perceived vulgarity of needing clothes that were fit for working in. Further back in time than the Edwardian hobble skirts, there had been several eras in which this impracticality took the form of hemlines so extremely low that movement was hampered. This exaggeration is seen in some fifteenth-century gowns that had excess fabric held draped over one arm. Similarly, elite dresses in the Georgian era trailed to the feet, requiring the addition of an internal system of attached ribbons looped through metal rings in order to control them: when the ribbons were tightened, the skirt looped up in graceful swathes known as a *polonaise* style – a style mimicked a century later in the walking dresses of the 1870s. The mid-eighteenth century also saw a graceful, yet impractical style known as the *saque*-back gown, in which yards of fabric integral to the gown were pleated at the nape of the neck, to fall and spread behind the body right to the floor – where they swept up dust and snagged on floorboards!

At various times between the Middle Ages and today, excess fabric has also been structured to fall behind the wearer in a train, regardless of the inconvenience to the wearer or any other person in the vicinity. A delightful vignette from the Regency era depicts the chief peril. Picture Miss Elizabeth Ham, a young lady of fashion, excited to arrive at a ball, where she will be meeting her beloved. Her gown of delicate blue satin and sprigged Indian muslin has a long train – equipped with a loop on the hem, so that once the train has been admired on arrival, it can be raised off the floor for dancing. Elizabeth duly made her entrance, with her sister Mary just behind. Mere moments later Elizabeth had to beg a friend – one Mrs Jones – to help her re-pin the train to her waist. She recounted the episode:

'How did this happen?' said she.
'Mary trod on it,' I replied.
'Did you not turn round and give her a slap in the face?' was her reply.

Clearly ladies did not learn from such wardrobe malfunctions, and dress trains remained a trip-hazard fashion feature. Such was the aggravation caused by trains in 1860s Vienna that a secret society dedicated to suppressing them was rumoured to operate. The society's members objected to the way sweeping skirts raised clouds of dust to clog eyes and lungs, and asserted

5 Similarly, in 1896 a society called the Rainy Day Club of New York City tried to persuade women to shorten their skirts to at least four inches above the ground, 'thereby freeing the wearer from the dangers of spreading contagion by carrying into the home germs of disease'.

that trains were an obstruction to street traffic. Their tactics apparently involved treading on, and tearing, any trains spotted in public. According to society guidelines, this was to be done 'as if by accident, and a thousand apologies should be offered to the lady for the awkwardness alleged to be the cause of the accident'.[5]

DUST HO! THE LONG DRESS NUISANCE.
(WE CAN ASSURE THE DARLINGS IT BY NO MEANS IMPROVES THEIR DEAR LITTLE ANKLES.)

A Punch *cartoon of 1863: 'Dust ho! The Long Dress Nuisance!'*

As Charles Darwin's theories on human evolution from primates gained credibility in the 1870s and his ideas entered popular consciousness, one Victorian dress expert went so far as to compare the train to a 'quadrupedal tail', which was 'harrowingly suggestive of the ancestral ape'. By the end of the nineteenth century fashion editors grudgingly conceded that the train was appropriate for the drawing room, but not fit for muddy streets or the bushes and briars of the country. Yet trains and trailing hems endured long after it was socially permissible to wear shorter skirts, evidence of the fashion rule that Darwin never mentioned – 'survival of the prettiest'.

As late as 1954 the dangers of trains were still being warned against (in verse, no less) by fashion writer Betty Page:

Madam if you don't train that train
Your calculated entrance may be all in vain.
Control those yards and yards that trail,
Or find your escort treading on your tail.

Trains on formal gowns, such as for weddings or coronations, were at least carried by bridesmaids and other bearers, and were explicitly worn to display status. Such trains have survived into modern times – perhaps most famously when Lady Diana Spencer walked up the aisle of St Paul's Cathedral on 29th July 1981 for her marriage to Prince Charles and she was followed by more than eight yards of ivory silk taffeta, with seven bridal attendants to manage it.

Modern brides may well find the management of long skirts a novelty more than a frustration. It remains to be seen whether the hard-won freedoms of women in the twenty-first century can one day be countered by a resurgence of clothes that demand a hobble, a waddle or serious numbers of safety pins to remedy hem-treading.

RISING HEMLINES

When one realises the extent to which long dresses were historically the standard, it becomes easier to understand just how extraordinary short skirts and dresses were when they began to make an appearance.

It should be noted, in all fairness, that the ankle had appeared, deliberately, on several occasions in Western history. In the early eighteenth century shoe-tops and stockings were on show, while flirty gowns of the 1800s and 1830s might reveal a neat boot or sandal ribbons. However, it was the First World War that saw the first consistent calf revelation, as hems shortened to accommodate women's march into war work. As already noted, the war also saw the introduction of over-the-head shift dresses with minimal fuss and fastenings. These lengthened after the war, but easily saw off competition from wide 'picture' gowns introduced by designers anxious to keep women in elaborate ensembles. By the 1920s the shift dress was firmly established as ultra-modern. Necklines, backs and armholes were all scooped to show as much skin as possible.

Dresses – and manners – of the mid-1920s were truly revolutionary, and quite a shock for those who revered Edwardian etiquette and clothing conventions.

To match this general skimpiness, hemlines of the mid-1920s rose to graze the kneecaps, though not without attracting considerable disapproval, particularly from older generations who had grown up with the general rule 'None so bold as to display her ankles in town'. In 1916 the uniform of a wartime VAD (a nurse serving in the Voluntary Aid Detachment) was officially to be no shorter than nine inches from the ground. And yet a mere ten years after this ruling, flighty young women were actually rumoured to be *rouging* their knees a pretty pink colour to draw attention to them. A cartoon of 1926 captures something of the daring of these novel short hems: a young wife awaits guests, and her husband surveys her new gown rather critically, suggesting it is a little short and low-cut. She replies, 'Well, I don't know. They are coming to see me, aren't they – not the dress?'

Shorter hems meant increased spending on stockings and depilation creams, as well as a new drive for gymnastics and exercise to keep the body toned, now that it wasn't hidden. Such was the tyranny of fashion that women who did not wear a modish hem length might well be considered frumpy. In the 1930s Mussolini reportedly advised Hitler that fashion was one thing even a Fascist dictator could not control: 'Any power whatsoever is destined to fail before fashion. If fashion says skirts are short, you will not succeed in lengthening them, even with the guillotine.' However, according to a 1950s expert, English women were rather lax in following hem-length fashions: ' . . . when skirts shorten, no self-respecting French girl would wear her skirt at last season's length . . . alas, with English girls, these subtle changes of taste hardly register at all'.

Hemlines dropped to the calf again in the 1930s, but quickly rose once more as a new World War brought shortages and rationing in Europe and Limitation Orders in the United States. We have seen how Christian Dior then defied the trend for boxy clothes and austerity by introducing the legendary flamboyance of the New Look in 1947, but he later also initiated a drop in hemlines to cocktail length – mid-calf. The new length suggested maturity, glamour and sophistication. What could possibly break its dominance on the fashion scene? Nothing short of a revolution.

It is now time to return to Mary Quant, and the drama of the miniskirt . . .

MINI REVOLUTION

In 1958, a year after Dior's untimely death, Mary Quant's shop Bazaar, in Chelsea, began to produce girly shift dresses, a far cry from the sophisticated structure and glamour of contemporary gowns. They were also a complete contrast to the formal suits of the 1950s, which had made teenagers into clones of their mothers. The gymslip styles were often sleeveless, and sometimes the skirts were only twelve inches in length. Quant launched an ultra-modern, short 'tent' dress in 1960 – a relatively unstructured style that hung from the neckline, hiding bust, waist and hips to give a baby-doll silhouette. However, 1963 is now revered as the year to remember: it was then that Quant's *miniskirts* hit the London scene.

1960s minidresses were icons of the decade – fab, fresh and fun.

In nylons, neons, block patterns and plastic, the miniskirt perfectly captured the zeitgeist of 'new', 'modern' and 'young'. Minis were so easy to wear, particularly when patterned tights covered the legs from toe to waist. They gave young women a sense of freedom that was perfectly matched by greater availability of the contraceptive pill and the slow-but-sure collapse of conservative moral structures. They were also incredibly easy to make, compared to the complex structuring (and yards of fabric) needed for the New Look. A yard or so of fabric could be bought at the local market on Saturday morning and made up into a minidress in time for a night out.

Minis were provocative in as much as they caused many raised eyebrows, but at the same time they were often sexually rather anodyne. Promoting the miniskirt look were new mannequins – or 'models', as they were becoming known – with almost pre-pubescent bodies. 'Twiggy' (the modelling name of Lesley Hornby) was the iconic model of the mid-1960s. She was young, super-thin, rather gawky and slightly puzzled-looking. Gone were the sophisticated mature curves of Dior's New Look.

Quality, finish and longevity were not the main criteria in clothing construction in the 1960s. Clothes were promoted for *now*. Some outfits were even paper-based and disposable; others were wipe-clean PVC. Above all, they were intended to be cheap – worn for a while, then discarded in favour of a new frock. Inexpensive acrylic fabrics and plastic products were relatively new on the scene and they were not always reliable. One girl, who turned to home dressmaking to make copies of Quant designs, was mortified when her nylon dress zip literally melted and came apart at the teeth in disco heat.

French designer Pierre Cardin took the Quant-style short shift dress and matched it with Emilio Pucci's swirling psychedelic patterns. This eye-catching combination filtered back to the high street and to home dressmaking. It became almost universal for women, regardless of age or size, and remains the iconic image of Sixties clothing to this day.

However, not all top designers were impressed with the new hemlines. Distinguished British couturier Hardy Amies disliked the vulgarity of the miniskirt, feeling its skimpy proportions meant there was little to challenge a designer. As for his most illustrious client, Queen Elizabeth II, she certainly could not be coaxed into the mini. Though her skirts were shortened some-what, she insisted that her knees should be covered as much as possible when sitting down at royal functions.

In the late 1960s, once the mini had run its course, the maxi-dress was strenuously promoted instead. The maxi, as the name implies, was a floor-length look, the opposite of the mini. The switch wasn't merely for novelty – fabric manufacturers were keen to reintroduce styles that required more material. Their wishes were fulfilled when they succeeded in backing a new fashion for faux-Edwardian maxi-dresses with pie-crust collars to ruffle the chin and nylon lace to ruffle the toes.

It was Welsh businesswoman Laura Ashley who truly popularised this romantic maxi-dress. Drawing on her love of vintage fabrics, she capitalised on the inevitable reaction against Sixties trends for ultra-modernity, geometrics and 'Space Age' fashions by launching nostalgic country-style cottons, with *broderie anglaise* petticoats and pretty floral prints. She dominated the British fashion scene from the 1960s to her death in 1985, after which her company continued to sell classic nostalgic designs.

The mini was routed – but only temporarily. It reappeared as a tight thigh-topping pencil skirt in the 1980s, teamed with barely-black tights and court shoes; the 1990s went even higher, with strips of skirt charmingly nicknamed 'pussy pelmets', as well as pleated mini-kilts.

For all the jostling by designers and retailers to get women to update their wardrobes on an almost weekly basis, from the 1970s onwards women could freely choose their own hemlines for the first time in history – mini, midi or maxi – without fear of being ostracised as an oddity. Given the precedence of previous centuries, when hems were unremittingly *long*, this truly was a remarkable state of affairs, for all that it seems perfectly natural and normal to the modern woman. Essentially there might now be 'on-trend' hem lengths, but in deference to our modern desire for choice, fashion can today only suggest a hem length, not dictate it.

THE FALSE RUMP

Thus far we have dwelt on the way in which a dress constricts the torso, and how it hides or reveals the lower legs. This is only part of the story. There are other parts of the female form to be considered, each of which have been deemed erotic and therefore worthy of focus and exaggeration at some point in history.

Let us begin with the behind.

The plaintive appeal 'Does my bum look big in this?' is familiar in the modern world. But at certain times in history a large derrière has been so coveted that extensive padding was worn under the skirt to create the impression of one. A variety of techniques and textiles were used to achieve this extra volume, and the accessories crafted to give bulk were known as *bum rolls* or *bustles*. Bum rolls – also called 'false rumps' – were generally pads formed of coarse fabrics stuffed with wool or horsehair (although it seems that foxes' tails were the fourteenth-century bustle of choice). They could be relatively small and kidney-shaped, set just below the shoulder blades to help the dress flare out over the behind, or on the buttocks for added volume; or else they could be curved wide around the hips and lower back. Such rumps were pinned or tied into place at the waistline.

Easy to make at home, rumps and rolls were also produced and sold professionally, made of shaped cork. Eighteenth-century ladies would purchase theirs in a charmingly named Rump Shop. Cork rumps had the advantage of being used as a flotation device, if newspaper reports are to be believed – a story circulated in the *St James's Chronicle* of June 1778 in which a lady's life was saved by her big, buoyant cork rump when she fell into the Thames at Henley: 'She was towed to shore by a gentleman's cane, without the least injury but wet petticoats.'

Bustles, confusingly, could be similar to bum rolls in that some versions were stuffed fabric shapes, called *bustle pads*. Bustles might also be sewn from layers of starched ruffles, or crafted from curved wire netting. Servant girls on a tight budget could pin three kitchen dusters as a cheap substitute to shop-bought bustle pads. In a daring attempt to defraud British Customs of revenue from imported fabrics, in 1847 one aged lady used her bustle structure to conceal twelve yards of French velvet, more than forty-two yards of Valenciennes lace, a dozen handkerchiefs, three dozen pairs of white gloves, nine pairs of silk stockings, a pair of stays - and a wig. How much these valuable smuggled goods weighed is not recorded, but the fact that it was feasible for them to be concealed in this manner gives some idea of the extreme sizes that bustles could attain.

This was by no means the pinnacle of bustle fever. After making a discreet exit in the 1850s and 1860s, rumps returned to distend the skirts of women in the 1870s, this time being formed of steel, wood or cane cages, which, concertina-like, could collapse around the wearer when she sat. By the 1880s the bustle was so prominent it was a veritable shelf projecting out behind the wearer, prompting a frenzy of satirical cartoons in *Punch* magazine. However, after this glorious heyday, bustles dwindled slowly out of fashion.

USEFUL AND ORNAMENTAL.

Such were the extremes of the 1870s bustle that cartoonists had great fun inventing new uses for them.

It's all too easy to mock the absurd proportions of the past. And yet are bum rolls and bustles any more ridiculous than modern methods of buttock enhancement? These include fabrics designed to contour the rear, cheap foam knicker-inserts to provide a shapely behind, and even unstable silicone injections – which are liable to leave their injection site to meander elsewhere in the body, potentially causing horrific lumps and even spinal damage. Compared to such heinous possibilities, a mere bustle doesn't seem such a ludicrous alternative.

GREAT CAGES

We have seen how dress lengths, necklines, sleeves and rumps have varied. Now let us take a step back to get a full view of the widest skirts in history.

The first hooped skirts were seen in the sixteenth century. As much architecture as tailoring, they were made from a scaffolding of wood, or canes or whalebone, which tied around the waist and jutted out over the hips, being flatter at the front. Elizabethans called their hoops 'farthingales', a distortion of the Spanish word *verduga*, meaning *green wood* – the preferred material for constructing hooped skirts at the Spanish court. The skirt fabric was gathered to fit over the top of this structure, falling to a straight hem. Extremely narrow bodices with exaggerated points over the belly balanced the hoops and gave the impression of a fashionably tiny waist. They featured in the magnificent portraits of queens and noblewomen from the period, though never became a universal female style.

Hooped skirts then dwindled and disappeared until the early eighteenth century when they returned with a vengeance, reaching the most extraordinary dimensions – they might be almost as wide as their wearer was tall, requiring a graceful sideways manoeuvre in order to pass through doorways. The grandest hooped skirts were reserved for highly formal occasions, in particular court appearances. The vogue for vast hoops collapsed somewhat in the 1770s, perhaps because of the

Court dresses of the 1750s had particularly wide, narrow hip panniers to give astonishing displays of luxury fabrics.

contempt that the popular press displayed for them, but they were only replaced by smaller collapsible side hoops.

Controlling one's hoops was apparently an all-absorbing concern. 'How very few can manage them!' was the lament of the character Lady Delacour in Maria Edgeworth's 1801 novel *Belinda*. We are told that Lady Delacour's friend, Lady C–, can pass for genteel without hoops, but in them she is 'as little able to walk as a child in a go-cart'. *Belinda* was published at a time when hoops were awfully old-fashioned and generally seen only at court functions presided over by Queen Charlotte, consort of King George III – the insistence on hoops at court was all part of emphasising the prestige of the palace. In fact, hooped skirts contrasted woefully with the new fashion for slender, lightweight gowns in the first decade of the nineteenth century.

When the fashion for hoops was next revived in the 1850s, it was a craze that crossed all classes. These Victorian *crinoline cages* took their name from heavy horsehair-and-wool petticoats termed 'crinolines' – the word supposedly a distortion of two French words: *crin* is the word for horsehair, gathered from the manes and tails of horses and then woven into a dense, durable fabric; and this was sometimes combined with *laine*, or wool. Not surprisingly, lighter canvas petticoats supported by hoops slotted into the fabric became an attractive alternative to horse-hair, but the name stuck. Steel cages were still more appealing, as the light metal hoops merely needed vertical strips of linen, leather or canvas to give them shape; they collapsed down to a flat oval when untied from the waist.

Fashion plate from the Journal des Demoiselles, *1858. Crinoline cages were not yet at their widest.*

The Industrial Revolution had not only given the West mass-production (bringing down the price of certain goods), but also mass-printing, enabling the distribution of fashion images. That, in turn, created a desire to acquire. Increased earning power gave even working women an opportunity to buy non-essential items of clothing, albeit of inferior quality or second-hand. Fashions such as hoops were no longer limited to those with wealth, particularly once the steel cage came on the market mid-century. These mass-produced cages sold in their millions and made fortunes for their manufacturers. Innovations such as plate-glass display windows in shops and newly laid pavements also meant the mass uptake of shopping as a leisure activity during the nineteenth century.

of the 1864 novel
*Revelations of a Lady
Detective,* found her
crinoline a nuisance
while chasing a
criminal down into a
London sewer pipe:
'When I had divested
myself of the
obnoxious garment,
and thrown it on the
floor, I lowered myself
into the hole and
went down the
ladder.'

Before dismissing crinolines as a perverse monstrosity, it is worth remembering just how cumbersome the number of petticoats required to attain the fashionable skirt circumferences of the mid-nineteenth century would be. One ageing lady missed her steel cage, when it went out of fashion in the 1870s. She reminisced in the 1880s, 'It kept your petticoats away from your legs, and made walking so light and easy.' Victorian women also found cages rather convenient for hiding evidence of pregnancy, which was no small advantage in an age when to be 'in an interesting condition' was not to be made public, whether or not the pregnancy was in wedlock.

These considerations aside, hooped skirts – like other extreme fashions before them – were mocked for their sheer impracticality. Where doorways were not wide enough to admit hoops, women had to crush their cages and shuffle in sideways. To sit on a chair with arms would be a laughable proposition. Squeezing into a carriage or omnibus caused great inconvenience to other travellers; some vehicles carried signs asking women to take off their cages and leave them hooked on the outside of the vehicle. Many theatres and music halls were obliged to widen seats at their venues to accommodate hoops, which was of indirect advantage to any men who wished to stretch their legs out more.

Although it was not unknown for ladies to take part in physical activities while wearing crinolines (even climbing mountains, in a few cases), on the whole they were the enemy of exercise. Perversely, one gentleman looking back on the Victorian era deplored the demise of the crinoline for precisely that reason, declaring that it 'had at least prevented women from taking part in any sport more unfeminine than croquet or archery'. He was disgusted by the twentieth-century spectacle of hoopless 'young women stumbling in heavy skirts across the playing-fields of England and America, brandishing ineffectual bats and sticks'.[6]

There was another, more common complaint from men: hoops repelled boarders. At a ball, gentlemen found their access to fair damsels frustrated by the broad carapace of the hooped skirt, which was likely to bash the shins of anyone bold enough to attempt a waltz.

On the other hand, given that hoops were notoriously difficult to control, there was always the chance of sighting a lady's lower limbs: a breezy day brought bracing views, as crinolines were blown high. Diarist Sir William Hardman recalled the year 1863: 'Women getting into omnibuses, Servant girls cleaning door steps and virgins at windy seaside watering places, all show their "–" on occasion.'

More than humour, it was the horror stories that made the headlines in Victorian newspapers and magazines. Crinolines weren't just a danger to decorum – they could be lethal.

The reading public thrived on sensational stories of women dragged to their deaths when their hooped skirts caught in carriage wheels or factory machinery. Coroners' reports of such accidents make sombre reading. One such case was the agonising death of seventeen-year-old Caroline Marshall, entangled while oiling the shaft of a glazing roller at a paper mill. Another tragedy was the death of Harriet Moody, twenty-two, caught in revolving shafting at a Leeds cloth mill.[7]

Far too often the urge to follow fashion prevailed over common sense. Manufacturing employers were clear in their disapproval of crinolines, as this 1860 poster at a Courtaulds silk factory demonstrates:

The present ugly fashion of HOOPS, or CRINOLINE, as it is called, is, however, quite unfitted for the work of our factories. Among the Power Looms it is almost impossible, and highly dangerous, among the Winding and Drawing Engines it greatly impedes the free passage of Overseers, Wasters etc, and is inconvenient to all. At the Mills it is equally inconvenient, and still more mischievous, by bringing the dress against the Spindles, while also it sometimes becomes shockingly indecent when the young people are standing upon the Sliders.

7 Such gruesome stories contrast with reports of women whose lives were saved by their hoops – such as the maidservant saved from drowning in 1735, or one Mrs Williamson, who survived a fifty-foot fall from the ruins of Kenilworth Castle thanks to her crinoline getting snagged on the wall.

Hooks were provided in factory cloakrooms for hanging crinoline cages during working hours, or they were simply banned outright.

By 1870 the enormous crinolines had been subdued to more discreet proportions. Volume was pushed to the rear. Hooped petticoats were replaced by bustle cages protruding from the back of the legs like a humped armadillo back, and by the late 1880s hoops were strictly *démodé*, though not dodo-dead. During the dark years of the First World War fashionable society girls took up the crinoline again as an antidote to austerity and grief, a deliberate contrast to the eminently practical wartime suits. The Germans called this fashion the *Kriegskrinolin*, or War Crinoline.

There was another brief revival of the crinoline just before the Second World War curtailed extravagance once more. This time it was associated with nostalgia for a romanticised age of gallantry and coquetry, and was epitomised in the crinoline gowns worn by actress Vivien Leigh in the 1939 Technicolor film *Gone with the Wind*. These 'Southern Belle' costumes were inspired by original 1860s styles, with hints of 1930s flair to give modern appeal. Before the film's release, a fashion writer of 1939 gushed that the new fashion of the crinoline had 'glamour and sweetness combined in every fold' to recapture 'the charm of frills and flounces . . . and fragrant flirtation'.

Girls might dream of a dress like Scarlett O'Hara's, but, from late 1939, war was the reality and thrift the watchword. Dior's 1947 New Look revived wide skirts again, with the crinoline to support them. With the exception of Vivienne Westwood's 1985 forays into hoop-territory, the crinoline's last appearance was in the 1950s, to support the continuing New Look style. This time the hoops were made of plastic, and they were managed with far less grace than Victorian crinoline cages. Many are the tales of girls going out for an evening of fun in the Fifties, only to find their hoops up around their ears as they sat at the back of the bus. There were also lightweight plastic hoops for grander gowns: gazebo-like in structure, which could be collapsed concertina-style into a hat-box for transport.

Will the crinoline be resurrected once more as anything other than a freak of high fashion? We can only speculate that the current Western philosophy of personal freedom will eschew any return to bulky clothing encumbrances. Not to mention the litigation implications of crinoline-related accidents.

HOW LOW CAN IT GO?

As well as dictating hem lengths, dress shapes and skirt widths, etiquette has always varied on the subject of how high or low a dress neckline should be. Today, in the West, a plunging neckline excites little comment or censure. In the past, cultural conventions dictated the level of décolletage – how much flesh it was acceptable to bare. At times, such as in the early eighteenth century, it was not only permitted but expected for women to show a considerable amount of bosom. Equally, at other times (the late nineteenth century, for example) women would have been aghast at the thought of revealing their neck, let alone their throat, shoulders or bust, such was the tyranny of convention.

Of course how much flesh went on show was very much a question of context. Dress styles always depended greatly on the status of the woman in question, the time of day and the social situation. From the seventeenth century to the mid-twentieth century one general rule was that the bust and shoulders should be covered before the hour of dinner. During Queen Victoria's reign this rule led to quite startling contrasts in dress styles over the course of one day: morning and afternoon garb would leave the neck and hands bare (if indoors), while the evening saw the bust on display and bare shoulders, but arms covered by gloves reaching above the elbow.

Whether custom permitted dresses scooped as low as the nipple line or required collars grazing the chin, women always had the tricky task of balancing the need to display flesh for purposes of attraction with the requirement to hide flesh to avoid connotations of impropriety. A young unmarried woman

A fashion plate from the Ladies' Magazine *of 1813 shows a fully covered figure (left) in day wear, and the throat uncovered for evening attire (right).*

might wish to appear attractive and charming to eligible males, but also suitably virginal. It was also the case, very unfairly, that a Lady of Quality exposing flesh at a Victorian ball would have potentially different connotations from a lower-class woman with an equally low neckline walking the city streets.

The rule of keeping covered before dinner included absolutely all social engagements undertaken before that time, such as shopping, sport and even weddings. There was no question of brides entering church in the strapless corset-topped gowns that are so popular in the early twenty-first century.

There was a variety of methods for observing this rule: dresses might be designed to cover all, but one might also utilise accessories that filled offending lapses in fabric. These included scarf-like lengths of fabric called neckerchiefs or *fichus*, popular in various forms throughout the last two millennia. And for women in the post-Classical West, the neckerchief also filled in the gap between the head covering and the dress. Rectangular or triangular, plain or frilled, it remained a wardrobe staple until the early twentieth century. Some neckerchiefs were of sturdy cotton or linen, others of silk gauze or a cotton so fine they revealed almost as much as they covered.

A different way of adapting the neckline was to use sections of shaped fabric to fill in a cleavage. Known as *modesty pieces, tuckers, shades, inserts* or even *bosom friends,* these were widely used from the late eighteenth century right up to the 1930s. They could be quite complex little accessories, rather like a blouse without sleeves, which fastened with a drawstring under the bust, then rose to an attractive nestling of pleats under the chin. During the late Georgian era, when gowns were generally cut low on the bust, a tucker was essential for both warmth and modesty.

Wearing a modesty piece wasn't without its perils. Having survived the ruin of her train mentioned earlier, Regency belle Elizabeth Ham next suffered the mortification of getting her lace tucker hooked into her dance partner's regimental coat. This caused a very public intimacy, torn lace and a lot of confusion as she attempted to disengage herself.

An instinct for pretty accessories led many women to over-indulge in their coverings. Nineteenth-century necklines could have tuckers inserted *and* a fichu draped round them. By the Edwardian era a fichu of cascading ruffles was worn *over* a high-necked dress. Edwardian women perhaps had the most to endure from high necklines – the necks of their dresses were supported by coils of steel or celluloid inserts. However, in 1912 the 'Peter Pan' neckline startled the fashionable world. It was a round neckline that barely covered the collar bones, named after the youthful hero of J. M. Barrie's play *Peter Pan*. After this date only older women and those of conservative taste kept dress-necks high. The outbreak of war in 1914 was a prelude to further revelations of flesh: the V-neck became fashionable during the First World War, followed by a loose, wide boat-shaped neckline.

8 According to Victorian expert Mrs Douglas, bosom friends could also be padded to give extra curves, although women were to beware of letting such minor deceptions signify a thoroughly mendacious character. Actress and writer Mae West summed up the padding issue best with one of her acerbic quips: 'What the good Lord has forgotten, we'll put there with cotton.'

Day dresses of the post-First World War era were comparatively too scanty to cope with the exuberance of Edwardian fichus. Modesty pieces became flat rectangles of tucked crêpe fabric or dense lace in muted colours, which were pinned within the V of the neckline or held in place with press studs. For those constrained by tight budgets, a pretty modesty piece was a thrifty way to vary the look of a dress.

And who wore these neckerchiefs and inserts? The short answer is, prior to the 1930s, almost everyone. Of course there were variations depending on age and fashion. Regardless of these, modesty was a strong consideration. Warmth was another: pneumonia and tuberculosis were serious, even fatal diseases prior to the successful introduction of antibiotics in the twentieth century, and low-cut dresses might prompt concerns about health. Personal comfort was also a factor – the desire to keep cosy in houses without double-glazing or central heating meant that women of the eighteenth and nineteenth centuries made *bosom friends* of fur flannel or knitted wool. These bosom friends were to protect the chest and throat from chills, as well as unwelcome attention.[8] The 'Sanitary' ballgown of 1890 even had an underbodice of kid leather as protection against the flu. As late as 1899 there were warnings that fashionably low evening dresses led to influenza, 'of which fatal lung diseases are the common result'.

At various times there were other, more aesthetic considerations that caused women to cover up. One eighteenth-century critic declared bare throats 'not only repugnant to decency, but most exceedingly disadvantageous to the charms of nine women out of ten'. Much of this sort of disapproval was rather cruelly directed at older women; their exposed flesh was considered either too plump or too shrivelled and sinewy for public display. On the whole ladies no longer in the first (or even the second) blush of youth had a choice about whether to show flesh or cover it, regardless of prevailing fashions. There was one crucial exception: Queen Victoria insisted that all ladies presented at the royal court *must* have a low décolletage, regardless of age or aesthetics. This custom harked back to the British court of the eighteenth century and was rather at variance with the greater emphasis on demure dressing generally prevalent during Victoria's reign – it was all a question of upholding established etiquette. The practice of posting officials at the entrance to the state apartments, in order to ensure bosom covers were removed, was only discontinued in 1903.

Well into the twentieth century even the most celebrated women were not free from the complexities of neckline etiquette. Hollywood movie stars were dressed in glamorous gowns designed to display the female form to best advantage. However, in America prudishness battled with glamour in the form of the 1930 Motion Picture Production code, informally known as the Hayes code, after one of its chief supporters. The code was designed to combat Hollywood's reputation for risqué behaviour (both on- and off-screen) and established a series of rulings, including one against 'suggestive nudity'. Essentially this meant no navels, no bare buttocks and no cleavage on show – not even a *hint* of cleavage. Before the code was replaced by a ratings system in 1968, handkerchiefs, ruffles and nude-coloured net were used to camouflage bare flesh.

The actresses themselves felt an understandable ambiguity about the way in which they were packaged for public consumption. It is that same ambiguity seen throughout the history of female dress – that constant conflict between the requirement to show the body and the requirement to hide it.

Actress Joan Collins complained that, at most, she could get away with one-and-a-half inches of cleavage before a floral accessory was added: 'in went a disgusting flower'. Other actresses lamented the emphasis on a bustline: 'Must I always wear a low-cut dress to be important?' asked Jean Harlow. When filming the 1977 blockbuster *Star Wars*, Carrie Fisher had the opposite issue. She said, 'they had me tape down my breasts because there are no breasts in space'.

Clearly the twentieth century saw a remarkable relaxing of social etiquette and dress codes. By the 1970s necklines could equally well plunge to the navel or rise in a pie-crust frill under the chin. The 1980s saw an even greater disparity of styles. For day wear there were shift dresses, which dropped from high necks and wide shoulders all the way to the knee without showing anything of the body beneath ... and contrasting 'body-conscious' dresses in form-fitting Lycra that had low, scooped necks and back, no sleeves and little length. The legacy for women in the twenty-first century is perhaps a greater sense of choice. High neck or low neck, all styles are available to wear, regardless of age, status or the time of day. The individual woman must navigate herself the more subtle modern etiquette of what may be considered desirable or appropriate.

CONSPICUOUS CONSUMPTION

Hoops, trains, puffs, pads, minis ... our review of many centuries has demonstrated several factors underlying the wearing of dresses and skirts. The demands upon gender, predominantly. Taste, naturally. Fashion's perversity, too. And woven through all of these is the influence of hard economics. Dresses are an excellent way to display wealth. Costume across the centuries shows direct connections between dress materials and trade; between skirt sizes and social status. Whichever fabrics were most difficult to source or expensive to produce, those were the ones seen on display at royal courts and in wealthy families.

Silk is a case in point. It was brought to Europe via the famous Silk Road from China for many centuries, until sericulture was introduced to Sicily in the ninth century. Beautiful and relatively difficult to obtain, silk was displayed to advantage in medieval silk-velvets, Renaissance silk-damasks and the exquisite woven silks of the eighteenth and nineteenth centuries. Spreading such luxurious fabrics over panniers, hoops and bustles was a blatant display of conspicuous consumption.

During all periods prior to the twentieth century, royal courts set the fashion for elite families and set a challenge as to who could dazzle the most. The body beneath the dress was often a mere prop for the fabric structured around it. Queens and mistresses might own hundreds of gowns, sometimes only wearing them once. Not only were these made of the most sumptuous silks and satins, but they were hand-embellished with pearls, semi-precious stones, gold and silver threads, silk ribbons, spangles and coloured embroidery. Skilled fabric manipulation added extra flair, displaying serpentines, ruffles and rosettes. Heirloom lace worth a small fortune was added to the cuffs and throat. Hip panniers of the mid-eighteenth century or crinolines of the nineteenth were so wide they could provide a fabric panorama far larger than the woman wearing the dress.

Even after the French Revolution supposedly brought in a simpler, more democratic style of dress, wealth was still very much apparent in richly decorated fabrics and trimmings. When the Empress Josephine of France was divorced from Napoleon in 1809 she owned almost 900 dresses. Increasingly elaborate rules of etiquette as the nineteenth century progressed demanded a different dress for each distinct social event, including (but not limited to): breakfast, walking, visiting, riding, taking tea, carriage-driving, spectating sports, informal dinner, formal dinner, balls, card parties and theatre visits. It was an insidious method of inducing women to boost industry, and therefore the economy, by compelling them to purchase more fabrics and employ more dressmakers. Those who could not afford the very best dresses could merely aspire, mimicking elite fashions in less sumptuous fabrics.

Stepping down from the level of the ultra-rich, even wealthy families maintained their clothing carefully. Frankly, it is hard for the modern person to appreciate just how expensive fabric once was and how deliberately it was flaunted; how carefully it was maintained. It is only recently that clothes have become so disposable. Before the late twentieth century they were an investment. Nothing went to waste. They were worn well, altered to suit changing fashions, cut up for smaller garments when necessary, pieced into patchwork quilts, torn into rags or sold via the thriving second-hand trade. Ladies' maids coveted their mistresses' cast-offs. Unmarried women might bequeath their clothes in their wills, and this did not just refer to the nobility – humble spinsters also left legacies, such as one Jane Skelton of the Vale of York, whose probate will of 1800 details: 'First I give unto my Sister in Law Hannah Burnett my grey silk gown striped silk gown black silk cloak and skarlet cloak half a dozen white cloth aprons one dozen of my best Caps half a dozen pair of my best Ruffles one dozen of Napkins and two Tea Chests.'

Unfortunately, the spiralling rise of clothing consumption in the nineteenth century meant that those in dress shops, textile factories and clothing sweatshops worked harder than ever before to meet demand. The adoption of the sewing machine – a common fixture in homes and workshops from the 1870s onwards – did mean that more garments could be produced at speed. It also led to a greater workload and an increase in skirt swathes and trimming. Seamstresses dreaded the notoriously busy London 'Season' of upper-class social events, when thought-less clients ordered gowns at short notice and work was done throughout the night to ensure that dresses were completed on time. Clothing expenditure was still a large part of a household budget, but since garments were so much easier to make and buy, they were no longer usually worth bequeathing in a will.

It was the nineteenth century that consolidated the rules governing dress etiquette. Woe betide the woman who wore the wrong gown in a certain situation, or who failed to pack the requisite number of outfits for a weekend away. The advice to a Victorian lady was: 'At breakfast she should be fresh and dainty as the morn; a plentiful be-sprinkling of lace and ribbons well befits the early day.'

For those on a limited budget, this etiquette created a demand for gowns that could be enlivened for evening events, as an affordable alternative to a complete change.[9] Back in the early and mid-twentieth century even housewives preferred to have a distinction. They would do housework in a 'wash' dress and pinny, then change into something fresher for the afternoon, with particular emphasis on looking nice for when their husband came home from business.

In the twentieth century the stranglehold of etiquette was at least loosened. Artificial fabrics such as rayon and nylon were promoted as cheaper rivals to silk, so a woman on a budget could feel she was dressed to impress. Social changes, such as the relaxation of class codes and growing emancipation for women, meant that conspicuous consumption would no longer be reflected primarily in the amount of fabric on display in a dress.

Where does this leave us in the twenty-first century? When we look in the modern woman's wardrobe, any dresses and skirts usually feature relatively meagre amounts of fabric, and relatively cheap fabrics at that. Conspicuous consumption has shifted from volume of display to a focus on the cachet of the designer's brand. The minidresses of the 1960s forced fashion houses to promote logos and labels as part of the garment's intrinsic worth, above the actual physical worth of the garments' materials, and this is the ethos that remains with us today.

If we can sport a logo or brand on any garment to advertise our spending power or taste, why wear dresses? After all, trousers have been perfectly acceptable wear for Western women for several decades, and women today lead varied, active lives – far more so than in the past. However, there are still those who consider dresses 'more feminine' than trousers. Slacks may be practical, yet plenty of women still opt for a skirt or dress at work. Like many professional women, politician Margaret Thatcher had to find a balance between looking capable and not offending gender sensibilities in the 1980s:

As a working lady, I choose clothes which are plain but have a good cut. Like others in business, politics or executive position, clothes are really a background to the personality. My dark navy silk dress has brought me good luck ... I had it made in 1982. I wore it in the Falklands year, to New York to address a full assembly of the United Nations and it came through that all right.

In the 1980s dresses still dominated the work scene, along with blouses and skirts. Since then trousers and skirts have become interchangeable. But leaving the world of work, or more specialised clothes for sports and outdoor exercise, dresses arguably still take centre stage when it comes to special occasions and seduction.

1980s dresses enjoyed flirting with ruffles and asymmetry.

A DRESS TO IMPRESS

On the subject of seduction, in the 1960s British designer Hardy Amies predicted that near-nudity would be the fashion of the future:

> Ladies entertaining at home will wear loose frocks which will clearly indicate that they veil a naked body. The woman who knows her business of being a woman will understand instinctively how to manipulate such a garment to suit her ends: to seduce her man or to keep him.

Amies was rather naïve. He assumed that the function of the dress is to attract a male. He underestimated the appeal of dresses for the way they make a woman feel in herself. Dresses can provide a whole range of kinetic sensations and communicate a whole range of emotions. They can be floaty, flirty or fierce; beautiful or bold; made of dramatic satins, sleek PVC or ethereal gauze. It's not surprising that, etiquette aside, for special occasions skirts and dresses still seem to be the primary choice for many women. On the fabled 'red carpet' of A-list invitees, trouser suits are rarely seen. The appetite for consumers of celebrity magazines is for glamour and sensation – all of which, it still seems, a gown delivers best.

'Princess dress' is a modern phrase used to describe an iconic gown reminiscent of fairy-tales and Disney films. Such a dress creates a moment of wonder when it is first seen. It is transformative, an aspiration. It is the opposite of ordinary, death to mundanity.

Wearing a party dress was once a defining moment for a young girl. Patterns, fabrics and styles would be endlessly debated, until the magical moment of being seen in the whole ensemble. Fashion magazines happily played on this desire for transformation, emphasising romance and beauty. It is no coincidence that the 1950 Disney film *Cinderella* caught the public imagination, in a decade looking to put the wreckage of a World War behind it – a world that wanted the sparkle of magic.

Not every Cinderella found her prince at the local party. Actress Dame Thora Hird recalled her first ball, hosted by the local Co-op, when she was sixteen. She wore a beautiful eau-de-Nil dress with a handkerchief hem – marvellously fashionable in 1927 – only to see it ruined when a waiter spilled soup in her lap. More dramatically, a young debutante en route to a 1940s Hunt Ball came across a drunk driver injured in a car crash. Her *Gone with the Wind*-style organza ballgown got crushed, muddy and blood-stained as she put her newly acquired first-aid skills into practice. She later recalled arriving at the ball and crouching 'in a dark corner wishing for bed or oblivion'.

Of course, the ultimate occasion dress is the wedding dress. For some brides, it is synonymous with the fantasy of the princess dress and should have swathes of luxurious fabrics and a twinkling tiara. For others, it is a more subtle affair.

10 Blue has long been assumed to be associated with the Catholic Virgin Mary and thus suitable for females, but in England a 'blue gown' once referred to a harlot, as this was the colour of prison dresses worn by prostitutes in the Houses of Correction of the seventeenth century.

Wedding clothes have always been special for elite families, whose marriages marked political and financial alliance; new clothes showed the importance of the occasion. However, from about the fifteenth century onwards it was no longer adequate to hand-fast in a partnership: the wedding had to be solemnised by the Christian sacrament of marriage. This increased formalisation of the marriage ceremony at all levels of society led to a more general rise in dresses made specifically for weddings. Increasingly, non-elite brides would choose a new gown that could be worn for *Sunday best* after the wedding. Before the twentieth century this dress would always have a high neckline and covered shoulders.

In the eighteenth century aristocratic weddings made a display of silver fabrics and threads, which filtered down the classes as a *white* wedding gown. The idea of a white dress (though not as brilliant as modern optical whites) specifically for a wedding was consolidated by the Victorians, who were happy to invent traditions where none existed.

Cream, grey, ivory and straw-coloured were also perfectly acceptable choices for a wedding gown. According to one traditional rhyme, blue was a good colour for a bride: *Married in blue, love ever true*.[10] The rhyme also stated: *Married in green, ashamed to be seen*, and this superstition forced some brides away from this colour, perhaps because of the connotations of envy, or possibly because of the old expression 'to give a girl a green gown', which referred to a grass-staining sport not to be practised before marriage. Red was traditionally considered too passionate a colour for weddings: *Married in red, wish you were dead.*

Gradually the wedding dress came to be for that one day only: a symbol of something special. By the 1920s, movie actresses and royal brides were the inspirations for the gown design, which moved further and further away from an everyday 'best' dress. Despite the great expense of fabric, embellishments and accessories, the one-day-only dress would afterwards be folded away in tissue paper and put into storage: too old-fashioned to be worn by any daughters when they reached marriageable age, though in times of austerity the gown might be dyed and retrimmed as a dance dress. In a combination of thrift and sentiment, some brides cut the train or skirt from the wedding dress to make a christening gown for their new baby.

During the Second World War brides had to become very inventive if they wanted to be married in traditional white. Coupons were pooled to buy dresses on the ration, and gowns were hired or borrowed. Truly canny brides learnt how to cut the triangular seams of parachutes – legally obtained or otherwise – to make silk or nylon gowns.

A 1952 wedding dress, portraying the romantic optimism of the post-war bride.

More than any other dress, the wedding gown is steeped in superstition – at least, it was. The seamstress would tuck a strand of her hair into a seam for luck. Couture gowns might have a blue bow, a pin or a silver coin and be stained with a spot of blood from a virgin in the workshop, all lucky talismans.

Modern brides are now likely to order their outfits online from cleverly presented standardised designs. Even if they try a dress in-store, it will probably be one of many identical versions, mass-produced in an anonymous workshop overseas. The wedding and the dress have become the ultimate expression of aspirational consumption. In the twenty-first century a controversial fad called *trash the dress* even sees brides deliberately getting their gowns filthy or soaked as part of the sequence of amusing wedding photographs.

But the wedding dress, wonderful though it may be, is not the end of the story. Whether following on closely from the wedding or out of wedlock, customised dresses have always been required to accommodate the increasing swell of pregnancy. Maternity dresses have had a slow, discreet evolution. Before the twentieth century day dresses with forgiving waistlines were worn, and gowns were pinned more loosely across the torso. Nursing dresses occasionally survive in museum collections, with slit openings hidden by a ribbon or pleating. Late Victorian tea gowns were of a loose style that hung from the shoulders without the need for waist-boning, so they had the advantage of enveloping an expanding figure. During the First World War magazines began advertising clothes specifically for the 'mother-to-be'. From then, 'maternity wear' was a growth market. Early adverts portrayed remarkably svelte, bump-free bodies, reflecting the centuries-old prejudice against showing one's condition in public. Even for a significant portion of the twentieth century women in the final term of pregnancy were expected to keep their condition concealed as much as possible, with smock tops and loose coats or capes. It is only since the 1990s that designers and shoppers have embraced the idea of sleek, chic (elasticated) maternity wear that bears no resemblance to a tent.

A WORD ABOUT KILTS

From the Middle Ages on, Scottish men of the Highlands wore bright, tartan wool cloaks pleated, tucked and belted around the body. These were called *kilts*, and the name remained as the drapes evolved into the stylised pleats of a fitted skirt.

Kilts and tartan became a symbol of Scottish national identity, particularly after the 1707 Act of Union and the 1745 rebellion, when the English banned Scottish males from wearing lengths of plaid cloth, kilts or trousers. Scotsmen were to be in breeches like the English. The ban was lifted in 1782, in time for the British monarchy to indulge in a persistent love-affair with Scottish tartan, including the kilt. Queen Victoria had Balmoral Castle decked in tartan from ceiling to linoleum, while Prince Albert created a knee-length 'German kilt' and designed royal house-hold plaids to match the so-called traditional weaves being invented by the English company Wilson & Son in the early nineteenth century.

Such is the status of the kilt that there is no implication of emasculation for men who choose to wear it. The twenty-five battalions of the Black Watch regiment were amongst those men who wore military kilts during the First World War. They were such ferocious fighters that the Germans named them 'Ladies from Hell'. The Black Watch are said to have prided themselves on being 'True Scotsmen' – that is, wearing kilts without shorts or pants – but military kilt drawers were on sale at this time, also in tartan.

The modern man's kilt.

Some kilt-wearing men have confessed to enjoying the freedom of movement, the flow of fabric around the legs and the lack of fastenings when visiting the lavatory. The twentieth century has also seen new male skirt styles, such as the Utilikilt, first fashioned out of military surplus trousers in 2000.

It will clearly take time before other versions of the skirt are accepted as regular menswear, rather than as national dress or a groom's wedding outfit. Even metro-male footballer and underwear model David Beckham couldn't kick-start a new trend when he wore a sarong in public in 1998. The pressure of cultural norms is still too strongly weighted in favour of a gender division for skirts.

As for women, looking to the future, if we discount Hardy Amies' fantasy of nearly-nude women in gossamer gowns waiting at home to ensnare a mate, it seems likely that a range of dresses and skirts – whether casual or formal – will not be ejected from the wardrobe any time soon. They will, however, undoubtedly continue to jostle for space with shorts and trousers, jeans, jeggings and leggings. And with whatever unpredictable variations come next...

THE TROUSER PRESS

Heigh! Ho! In rain and snow
The bloomer now is all the go.
Twenty tailors take the stitches,
Twenty women wear the breeches.

MID-NINETEENTH-CENTURY AMERICAN DITTY

A BARBARIAN GARMENT

Trousers are a staple of modern Western attire, essential for the male wardrobe; almost always in the female wardrobe as well. They are worn for state occasions and sport, for weddings and work. In wool, denim, linen, leather, PVC or polyester, trousers are everywhere. And yet 2,000 years ago the cultured Roman elite scorned them and despised those who wore them. Trousers were a garment for *barbaroi* – barbarians – in the form of the Germanic and Celtic tribes who threatened the self-awarded civilisation of Rome. Roman soldiers may have adopted leg coverings in cold climates, but only Germanic auxiliaries succumbed to wearing actual trousers (probably copied from the Celts), and this was never done in Rome, since there were sumptuary laws (laws limiting materials or styles seen as immoral or extravagant) that forbade trousers in the heart of the Empire.

Paradoxically, during the two millennia since, trousers have come to represent respectability, professionalism and, at times, gender dominance. They are an almost universal garment in the Western world, having remained long after togas, tunics and

A romanticised nineteenth-century image of an ancient Gaul. The 'barbarian' trousers are prominent.

bare legs have been dismissed as undignified for men. And despite 2,000 years of insistence that trousers are a strictly male garment, they have now been adopted by women to such an extent that they might even be considered gender-neutral. The answer to the question 'Who's wearing the trousers?' is: almost everyone.

What do we know of the earliest Western trousers? Archaeology gives us indirect evidence, such as Viking buckles from around the ninth century CE. Where there are buckles there might once have been belts, and these might conceivably have held up trousers. This argument is strengthened when the buckles are found in the pelvic area of human remains at excavated burial sites, which is sometimes the case. That said, there is always the possibility that a buckle comes from a shirt belt, as with the leather belt found with the Iron Age bog-body in Tollund, Denmark. Textiles are far less likely to be preserved in burials than metal items, so any items that are found need careful interpretation to understand their original form and function.

Rare though they are, some trousers have survived the depredations of time. Woollen examples dated to no later than the third century CE have been found in Germany, and a particularly good pair was excavated at Thorsberg, Denmark, with a well-made waistband and six belt loops. Found with a cache of items indicating they had been worn by a warrior, these trousers have integral feet – rather like a very sturdy pair of tights. It's a style also described in later Viking sagas.

Evidence of trousers also comes from art and other historical imagery. The Romans loved to depict the warriors and captives of conquered nations, and so there are stonework representations of *barbaroi* in trousers from the Classical era. Stone monuments of the Viking age also depict them, and imagery of trousers is seen in manuscript illuminations from the fourth century CE onwards.

From all this evidence we know something of the original shape of trousers, and that they were worn under belted tunics. While the modern wardrobe is probably limited to long trousers, also known as slacks, and cropped trousers known as shorts, in history there has been quite an exuberant choice of male leg coverings. The earliest trousers seem quite narrow around the leg and baggier at the hips. The trouser legs would be bound with cloth gaiters or wound with leather straps just below the knee while riding, or to keep them clear of mud while walking or working in the fields.[1]

Another word for trousers was *breeches*, which we now associate with an obsolete kind of trousers reaching just below the knee. Having survived the contempt of the Romans, long trousers next had to defer to the supposed superiority of these short breeches. The medieval and Renaissance years saw an increasing erotic interest in the male leg, better shown off in breeches, and the lexicography of legwear also broadened to include certain types of trouser-esque garments referred to as *hose*, which, as we've seen in an earlier chapter, were usually snug-fitting stockings or socks. However, sixteenth- and seventeenth-century trouser hose were rather fabulous and fantastical in design.

1 Lower leg straps, sometimes known as 'yarks', were worn in the North of England until the nineteenth century. Agricultural workers in the England/Scotland border territories also bound their calves with straw for protection.

The extraordinary exaggeration of Renaissance trunk hose.

Knee-length, easy-fitting *canion hose* from Italy bedecked the fashionable male thigh, while *trunk hose* (sometimes gaily partnered with canions) bloomed out over the buttocks . . . indirectly giving us the term swimming trunks for male swim shorts. Trunk hose were often created from sumptuous fabrics, slashed, pinked and beribboned, and constructed with great gusto so that they puffed out from the hips and rear. This is the iconic look of famous Tudor gentlemen. Some elite men went so far as to pad their trunk hose all round, for extra flamboyance – and to give a stronger contrast to the sleek legs beneath. Padded with bran, horsehair or rags, these hose were perhaps not the most sensibly constructed garments, as evidenced by the account of a sixteenth-century gentleman who was so busy 'talking merrily' with a group of ladies that he failed to take account of the chair nail that had ripped his trunk hose, causing the bran inside to cascade out – much to the amusement of the ladies and the embarrassment of the gentleman.

The Renaissance codpiece, a bag to cover the crotch gap on male hose,
was later replaced by a buttoned opening, then by the zip fly.

Breeches were the men's leg covering of choice by the seventeenth century. The wide, loose breeches favoured by sailors
were known as *slops* – giving rise to the term 'sloppy' for slack
clothes and, by association, slack behaviour. *Petticoat breeches*
of this century were so exaggeratedly wide that they were essentially divided skirts that fell to the knee and ended in flamboyant
fringes and frills. They were a favourite with elite men. However,
the battle lines would soon be drawn between trousers and
breeches, not simply in a frivolous fashion duel, but in conflicts
between different classes and opposing nations. The wearing of
trousers or breeches became a significant political – and sometimes criminal – act.

CLASS AND NATIONAL IDENTITY

In the sixteenth century Irish clothes still retained some rural
elements dating back to Norse influences, including trousers.
Amongst the many sumptuary laws imposed by English

overlords was the insistence that only clothes 'after the English fashion' should be worn. This would mean breeches instead of trousers. A similar quashing of national identity occurred in Scotland, against the Scotsman's plaid trousers, or *trews*. Clothes were a powerful weapon in wars of cultural supremacy. In promoting breeches over trousers, the English were also attempting to define what was civilised and what was barbaric – just as the Romans had done. Those who chose to wear trousers were not only rebelling against sumptuary laws, but were asserting their own sense of nationhood in the face of domination and assimilation. Significantly, it was only a male garment that represented national identity or barbarity; the cultural meanings of female garments were almost exclusively limited to modesty, or the lack of it.

The battle for dominance between breeches and trousers continued for another 200 years. The final confrontation would be waged in the ballrooms and gentlemen's clubs of the late eighteenth century ... and under the shadow of the French Revolution, when the wrong choice of legwear could be the first step on a journey towards the 'National Razor' – the guillotine.

The beautifully fitted silk breeches worn by the aristocracy in the reign of the French king Louis XVI – the 1770s and 1780s – were known as *culottes*. They distinguished elite men from commoners. As political and social tensions mounted in the prelude to the 1789 revolution, differences in legwear came to represent much more serious distinctions between those perceived as privileged and those who believed themselves oppressed.

Sans-culottes – 'without breeches' – was the term for radical left-wing working men in long trousers (known at this time as *pantaloons*). Disturbingly assertive and often militant in their sabot clogs and red caps, *Sans-culottes* were easily recognisable icons of the new order in France. King Louis was first deposed, then decapitated. A period of violence and mass execution known as the Reign of Terror ensued – the association between trousers and uncivilised behaviour, once again.

However, revolutionary politics were complex and the *Sans-culottes* were eventually suppressed and dispersed by other groups eager for power. When Napoleon Bonaparte came to full power as Emperor in 1799 – a mere ten years after men in the trousers of the *Sans-culottes* waved the tricolour flag of revolution – he reinstituted the wearing of silk suits, as a boost to the Lyons silk industry. In an ironic turn of the Fashion Wheel of Fortune, he also asserted his own quasi-aristocratic importance by imposing the wearing of breeches at the new court.

NUDITY AT A DISTANCE

Breeches themselves were undergoing a material revolution of their own at this time. A revival of appetite for all things Classical led to a Europe-wide interest in Greek and Roman statuary throughout the eighteenth century, bolstered by the antique 'souvenirs' brought home by wealthy travellers from their Grand Tour of Classical sites. Since the statues appeared to have been made of plain, unadorned marble, it was assumed that whites and neutrals were the chosen tones of Classical garb, and so fashionable breeches were made from pale nude-coloured fabrics supposedly mimicking statuary.[2] They also accentuated the athletic male physique, reflecting the era's love of robust male sports. Buff breeches were popular for riding – buff being soft but durable buffalo leather. They were so close to the skin tone of the Caucasian men wearing them that 'buff' became a figurative term for bare skin, hence the expression 'in the buff'. The desired effect of pale breeches was 'nudity at a distance' – almost as if the wearer were trouserless. It was a natural extension of this idea to think of breeches as almost underwear themselves, and therefore sexualised and faintly shocking. They took on a range of euphemistic names, all signifying a certain prudery, despite the very public appearance of the garment: *inexpressibles*, *don't mentions* and *unwhisperables*.

Eighteenth-century breeches shrank to become close to skin-tight, although they had baggy behinds to enable the wearer to

2 Twenty-first-century research using cutting-edge scientific techniques has irrefutably established that Classical statuary was, in fact, painted with gaudy colours or given bold gilding. Reconstructions are dazzling and encourage a completely new way of approaching Classical aesthetics. Persian trousers featured on a sarcophagus from around 320 BCE and a horserider from the Athenian Acropolis (built around 490 BCE) are now seen to have been in a yellow, red, blue and green 'harlequin' pattern.

ride astride. One manservant at the time dared serve at table 'in a pair of filthy nankeen breeches made to fit so extremely tight that a less curious observer might have taken them for no breeches at all'. Being so tight-fitting at the front left little room for the contents of the trousers. The habit of pushing one's genitals down one leg or the other gave rise to the notion of a gentleman telling his tailor which side he 'dressed' on, so that an extra amount of cloth could be added on that side, particularly on riding clothes.

TROUSERS TAKE CENTRE-STAGE

Just as few in the Roman Empire could have predicted its fall to so-called barbarians, before the 1790s no one would have supposed that trousers would bring about a tremendous upheaval in Western menswear. How were trousers able to break the supremacy of breeches, to assume a position of dominance that has now gone unchallenged for more than two centuries? Essentially it all came down to the vanity of one man: George 'Beau' Brummell.

Flush with inherited wealth, as a young lieutenant in the Tenth Royal Hussars in the 1790s George Brummell enjoyed spending money on dressing well – we have already met him briefly in our exploration of shirts. Brummell thought he looked particularly fine in the long pantaloons that were part of his military uniform, so he took to wearing them as part of his normal ensemble, stretched taut along his athletic limbs by means of under-foot stirrup straps. His pantaloons were of stocking-weave black or nude fabric or soft buff. An alternative style hugged the leg to mid-calf, to be worn with long hose (stockings) and boots.

Such was Brummell's appearance, confidence and influence that elite men soon began to prefer pantaloons to breeches. Lord Byron was an early adopter of trousers, as they helped to hide his lameness. Given his extraordinary celebrity, Byron's backing of the trend can only have advanced it further. Byron preferred trousers of nankeen or white jean, which had to be washed after each and every wearing. However, his accounts show that in 1812 he bought two pairs of tartan trousers with matching gaiters. 'Tartanitis' continued to afflict Britain for several decades, with all manner of gaudy pseudo-tartans being appropriated from original Scottish plaids. Suddenly Scottish *trews* were in vogue, for those caught up in a pro-Scottish fervour, fuelled at this time by the supremely popular novels of Sir Walter Scott. Brummell was probably appalled at such a distortion of his neat, discreet style.

Sadly for Brummell, a feud with his partner-in-style Prince George – soon to be King George IV – coupled with incontinent spending compelled him to choose exile abroad over debtors' prison. By 1837 his poverty was so great it is recorded that he was obliged to stay indoors while his single remaining pair of trousers was being mended (for free) by a loyal local tailor.

From being considered lowly and barbaric, pantaloons – shortened to 'pants' in North America – became the norm for men at almost all levels of society by the start of the nineteenth century, and indeed were defined in one dictionary as 'A nether habiliment of the adult civilised male'.

Breeches were also retained throughout the nineteenth century for sports and military display. The German Kaiser's cousin, Prince Friedrich Leopold of Prussia, was sewn into his breeches to give the closest possible fit, and once fainted when they cut off his circulation. In Russia the Chevaliers Gardes on duty at gala occasions for the ill-fated Tsar Nicholas II smeared their elkskin breeches with soap to avoid creases and wore them without drawers. Paired with a tailored Norfolk jacket, breeches were sturdy enough for tough climates. When, in 1871 on the shores of Lake Tanganyika, Sir Henry Stanley uttered the famous line, 'Dr Livingstone, I presume?' Livingstone was in breeches tailored by Norton & Sons, who dressed royalty and various heads of state. Similarly, Lord Carnarvon wore bespoke breeches from the famous tailor Henry Poole when opening Tutankhamen's tomb in 1922.

An Edwardian gent's riding suit, with breeches.

Jodhpurs, wide at the hips and tight below the knee, were a good substitute for baggy-at-the-knee breeches when riding, giving flexibility or control as needed. They were named after the Indian state of Jodhpur because they were made popular by one of the Maharaja of Jodhpur's polo-playing sons in the 1890s. Riding trousers called jodhpurs are still worn by modern horseriders, male and female, albeit in skin-tight cotton Lycra. Breeches have survived in other traditional country sports: when out shooting for game, breeches are still preferred by traditionalists. They are bought from specialist suppliers, made up in variations of browns and greens, to be better camouflaged in the hunter's chosen landscape.

With the exception of such specialist occasions, breeches most certainly do not feature in the modern wardrobe. A few bold individuals attempted to revive the fashion – most notably Edwardian dandy Oscar Wilde, who liked his in rich-coloured velvets – but notwithstanding a very brief reappearance in the 1970s, as a female fashion, breeches have been ousted. Trousers rule.

DRAINPIPES AND NARROW-GO-WIDES

Over the last two centuries trousers have continued to act as a barometer for respectability and rebellion. There have been many variations on the basic design. Some of these were begun by a few innovative individuals, while others were appropriated from occupational clothing and workwear.

For the stylish Victorian gent there were peg-tops, which were wide at the hips, or narrow-go-wides, which were the original flares. If a man sported trousers of a garish, patterned fabric they were known by the wonderful name of *howling bags*.

Trousers crease easily in the seat and behind the knees, particularly if they are made of tweed wool or linen, which have a tendency to look rather baggy. The idea of deliberately adding vertical creases down the trouser leg is sometimes said to have been popularised by King Edward VIII in the early twentieth century. The style is said to have taken his fancy when, following a riding accident, a local cottager pressed his trousers with a crease at the sides. More likely the long crease was made popular by the use of a trouser press in the dressing room – a wood and metal structure for keeping trousers uncrumpled overnight. It inevitably left a crease where the trousers were folded, which was then incorporated as a fashionable detail.

The Edwardian gentleman liked his trousers narrow. Because fashion likes to react (under the guise of innovation), the next generation donned ludicrously wide trousers known as *Oxford bags* during a two-year trend in the 1920s. At the pinnacle of this fad twenty-inch-wide legs flapped around the wearer's calves – a flaunting of fabric deplored by the conservative *Tailor and Cutter* magazine, which lamented, 'From such like excesses good Lord deliver us.'

For chaps of the Twenties and Thirties, trousers were relatively uninspiring. Either narrow or wide; with turn-ups or without. Blues and browns dominated the palette. However, by the 1940s young men were once again ready for rebellion. This time it took the form of ludicrously low-crotched *Zoot* trousers worn by fashion-conscious African-American men. These, and baggy trousers worn by the hip *Zazous* of Nazi-occupied France, offered an opportunity to parade a new style and mock prevailing fashions for their austerity or conformity. The reaction against them was severe and violent, as we shall see later in the chapter on suits.

The straight trousers of the 1950s and the *drainpipes* of the 1980s were throwbacks to narrow Edwardian styles. In between were the wonderful floor-sweeping *flares* of the 1960s and 1970s, which, while reflecting the less-structured, more easy-going standards of some sections of society, also shocked older generations – just as they were meant to. One variation on 1970s trousers was for exaggerated high waists flaunting multiple buttons. An adopter of the trend recalled, 'There was talk of mythical, hopefully apocryphal, ten-button monstrosities, the waistbands climbing higher and higher, hitting our chests.' They were to be worn with several belts and in 'every lurid shade imaginable'.

It's quite remarkable how quickly a popular trouser style can look dated. The last few decades have seen high waists, but also belts barely hugging the lower pelvis. Crotches have been genital-compressing or knee-skimming. Design details include zip flies, button flies or drawstring waists. Neat tailoring gives a city-slicker look; camouflage fabric and superfluous pockets and loops show an urban warrior. High-fashion catwalk shows draw attention with exaggerations such as bondage trousers or bumsters, but these are usually too bizarre for the average man, who prefers simple variations on the same theme.

THE BREECHES PART

By far the greatest show of prejudice regarding trousers occurred not when civilised men chose them over tunics or breeches, but when women dared to wear them.

That trousers are a male garment, and that it is therefore wrong for women to wear them, was such a deep cultural assumption that it has taken centuries to overcome, and it is by no means a given that all societies will contemplate trousered women with equanimity. There are still Western men who judge skirts to be the only attractive, appropriate female attire, regardless of what a woman's own choices may be. One self-appointed expert claims that women who wear trousers are 'deliberately making themselves unattractive and like lemmings are rushing over a sartorial cliff'.

As we saw when discussing skirts, exactly why trousers became equated with men and skirts with women is a matter for speculation and debate. Evidence from the Classical era onwards demonstrates that women engaged in occupations where skirts were clearly a liability. Far from form following function, existing norms were simply adapted, as when longer-skirted riding habits were designed to enable women to ride side-saddle rather than astride. Otherwise the logic was: if women couldn't do certain activities in their clothes, then those activities were not suitable for women. For example, it is telling that when a male observer at an eruption of Vesuvius in 1788 noticed women near the volcano crater, he criticised them on the grounds that their escape from potential lava flows would be impeded by their long skirts, rather than suggesting that they might be better able to move more freely and safely in breeches. Much of the cultural prohibition has been bound up with notions of propriety, sexuality and modesty. For many centuries the female body had to be covered, with only select eroticised zones disclosed.

However, there is evidence that breeches were openly worn by European working women as part of rural costume from at least the ninth century. Female farm workers occasionally raided their husband's clothes for old trousers to labour in. Others protected their legs with trouser ends as gaiters. These are instances of practicality winning out over fashion, and perhaps such low-status discrepancies could be overlooked. Not so trousers on more elite women. A woman in breeches or trousers upset artificially created gender roles. According to one Viking law code, cross-dressing was such an anathema that a wife could signal her desire for a divorce by wearing breeches. And the notion of trousers representing masculine authority survives in the modern expression 'Who's wearing the trousers?'

It wasn't until the nineteenth century that the phenomenon of women in trousers became a matter for public debate. At that time the demands of the Industrial Revolution and the rigours of the North American pioneer expansion westwards both led to a minority of women wearing trousers. Farmsteaders in the new territories of America and Canada sometimes did fieldwork and housework in cotton blouses and canvas trousers similar to those being boldly worn by women working at the pitheads of northern England. These northern women – mainly from Lancashire – were such a novelty that photographers created printed images of these 'pit-brow lasses' that were circulated around more affluent households, where the only trouser-like garments for females were decorative undergarments such as *pantalettes* and *leglets*.

The infamous 'Bloomer' trouser suit (left) contrasts with the more traditional dress (right), here featured in an 1863 American fashion magazine.

To keep power firmly in the hands (or around the legs) of the patriarchy, obvious trouser-wearing for women had to be resisted. In most cases this took the form of immense social pressure. In some instances trouser-wearing was technically illegal for women, as in France in the nineteenth century, although the French rules were relaxed during the 1850s, when female provisioners known as *cantinières* wore skirted uniforms in the Crimean War. These bonny *cantinières* were quite an inspiration for civilian women wanting a taste of trousered freedom.

From the late 1840s onwards a movement for female trousers gathered momentum in the Western world – and ridicule. A Turkish-style of trouser was adopted for wear in the parlours of late 1840s America, but even these modest, ankle-gathered trousers worn under knee-grazing skirts and petticoats caused a huge backlash. The criticism was so severe that even stalwart feminists such as suffrage-campaigner Elizabeth Cady Stanton were forced to forgo them because of public ridicule and persistent persecution.

This style of trousers was attributed to American women's-rights activist Amelia Jenks Bloomer, and they took her name – the Bloomer Suit. However, she was only one of their most public proponents and was actually not the first. The original trouser suit was worn by Elizabeth Smith Miller, with the full approval of her father, who said that a long skirt was a symbol of woman's degradation. Cady Stanton recalled the excitement of Mrs Miller's be-trousered visit in the winter of 1852. She found it remarkable to watch Miller ably climbing a set of stairs with a lamp in one hand and a baby in the other, while she laboured in heavy skirts. Once in the 'bloomers' herself, she wrote:

What incredible freedom I enjoyed for two years. Like a captive set free from his ball and chain, I was always ready for a brisk walk through sleet and snow and rain, to climb a mountain, jump over a fence, work in the garden, and in fact, for any necessary locomotion.

For the modern woman this thrill of freedom is – thankfully – dulled by familiarity. However, it is worth looking back at this fight to change attitudes, to realise how much we take for granted and to consider how many unchallenged cultural norms there may still be.

Detractors of female trousers were not limited to the crowds of mocking youths endured by Miller and Cady Stanton. On both sides of the Atlantic nineteenth-century 'experts' and idealists entered the debate on the suitability of trousers for women. Objections were raised firstly on aesthetic grounds. The divided skirts that replaced the Bloomer suit were compared to a baggy, ill-made petticoat that did nothing to flatter a corpulent woman. Further attacks were founded on the belief that trousers were a threat to the idea of femininity. Worst of all, female trousers were seen as a threat to the status quo. Equated with the professional male who travelled from the home to enter the world of work, trousers were too closely associated with the behaviour of the provocative Victorian 'New Woman', who was becoming increasingly vocal in her demands for social and political freedom. And if she couldn't stride out in trousers, she could at least appropriate *knickerbockers* for sporting wear.

KNICKERBOCKER GLORY

The word *knickerbocker* for male breeches caught on after the publication of Washington Irving's satire, *Knickerbocker's History of New York*, in 1809, as George Cruikshank's illustrations showed the fictional Dutch hero in knee-breeches. Eight decades later it became firmly associated with a topic even more satirical than Irving's tale: women wearing them in public.

The Rational Dress Society, established in 1881 to promote 'a style of dress based upon considerations of health, comfort, and beauty', coordinated a campaign to raise awareness of alternatives to layers of heavy petticoats. In particular it promoted controversial bifurcated garments. Since any trousers openly copying menswear were too outlandish for respectable society, the options available were: knickerbockers under skirts or discreet divided skirts.

Divided skirts – also known as *skirt knickers* – were essentially a very loose pair of trousers that buttoned onto the stays or the bodice. They often had an extra layer of fabric to hide the separation of the legs. We would now call them culottes. According to one dress expert of the 1880s, the divided skirt gave a 'wonderful sense of freedom and lightness'. Even something so apparently innocuous was vilified by the *Lancet* medical journal as 'unnecessary, and in many ways detrimental to health and morals' – hardly a judgement based on scientific analysis. The less prestigious *Ladies' World* magazine, on the other hand, defended skirt knickers: 'the subject of many jokes by the other sex who have not laboured under the difficulty of long skirts flapping around their ankles'.

A cyclist from 1896 takes advantage of the new freedom of movement offered by bifurcated garments.

By the 1880s the energetic New Woman had gained a mechanical ally in her march towards more rational dress: the tricycle and, following on from it, the bicycle. Cycling was a craze like no other in the late nineteenth century, and even critics conceded that cycling might be more practical for women in breeches – as long as these were kept hidden. Sport had already led the way with the adoption of knickerbockers for fencing and riding.[3] Now the cyclist of the 1890s and 1900s could dust off the idea of a Bloomer suit for visible use, although innovations to hide the bifurcation were as awkward as they were ingenious: button-on overskirts, flapping leg-capes and modest ankle-guards.[4]

NATTY AND WORKMANLIKE

The societal attitude to women in trousers followed the usual trajectory of such things – a new idea in clothes is first attacked as obscene, ridiculed as absurd, then tolerated with suspicion, and finally accepted as if it had always been worn. In earlier centuries trousers had been considered unacceptable for certain classes of men, after all.

Consider this attack on female trousers by the author of *The Gentlewoman's Book of Dress* in 1894: 'Think of our grandmothers knitting by the fireside in a kind of adapted pyjama suit! What of a Sister of Mercy dispensing charity in a rational bifurcated costume, or of a nurse tending her patient in emulative breeches?'

A First World War worker in the newly formed Women's Land Army seems bemused by her breeches and boots. They are at least fit for purpose.

These words were meant to paint an absurd picture, one of a world gone mad, and yet they were somewhat prescient. When the First World War convulsed the world two decades later, there were indeed pyjama suits for women, recommended for wear during night-time Zeppelin raids. Frontline nurses usually wore long skirts, but the ambulance drivers and motorbike dispatch riders were certainly in bifurcated costumes, and breeches were worn as uniform by members of the newly created Women's Land Army. Female industrial workers were so proud of their patriotic war work that they posed in canvas trousers and tunics at photographic studios. It was a startling contrast to the idealised image of pre-war femininity – chiffon tea gowns and fur-swathed hobble gowns – or even those novelty Turkish trousers. Engine-cleaners walking home from the locomotive sheds were described as natty and workmanlike in their trousers. Since trouser-clad women were vital to the war effort they were not only endured, but were routinely promoted in mass-market photographic images.

Author Vita Sackville-West described the sensation of wearing trousers for farm work in 1918: 'in the unaccustomed freedom of breeches and gaiters I went into wild spirits; I ran, I shouted, I jumped, I climbed, vaulted over gates, I felt like a schoolboy let out on a holiday.'

Journalist Dorothy Lawrence wasn't so positive at first. In 1915 she appropriated the uniform of a British sapper in order to disguise herself in an attempt to make first-hand journalistic reports from the frontline:

I was left alone to struggle with unknown buttons, braces, and the division sum of how to make a big body go into a small size of trousers! Eventually I got in by a series of jumps, jerks, and general tightening up!

Conversely, Flora Sandes, originally a Red Cross nurse in Serbia, actually spent most of the war as an active combatant in the Serbian Army – in breeches. She wore them on the battlefield, and later when receiving medals from royalty. During the war her skills and bravery earnt her the rank of sergeant-major. She became a significant public figure in Britain, using her fame to inspire patriotic fundraising for the war effort. She was even presented to Queen Mary, in full military uniform, including trousers. After the war she lamented the difficulty once her life in active service was over: 'It's a hard world where half the people say you should not dress as a man and the other half want to punish you for dressing as a woman.'

WHO'S WEARING THE TROUSERS?

Old prejudices die hard. The years of relative peace after 1918 saw European countries trying to rebuild; people wanted to repair family life as best they could and 'get back to normal'. Regardless of their war service, women were pressured into resuming their decorative or domestic pre-war roles. In the 1920s the only women wearing trousers publicly were bohemians at parties and those in Oriental-style pyjama suits at foreign beach resorts; wealthy women also showed their modernity by skiing in trousers. However, there could be no magical return to a world before war. Change might have slowed, but it was now inevitable.

Hollywood actresses gave trousers a certain glamour, even if most women didn't have the nerve to copy them. Marlene Dietrich, for one, looked fabulous in well-tailored slacks. In 1933 she said, 'I am sincere in my preference for men's clothes – I do not wear them to be sensational ... I think I am more alluring in these clothes.' Katharine Hepburn enjoyed similar androgyny, commenting, 'I like to move fast, and wearing high heels was tough, and low heels with a skirt unattractive. So pants took over.'

But while the connection between trousers and authority continued to make some people uncomfortable about women wearing them, it also fuelled rebellion in others. Lancashire housewife Nella Last recorded in her wartime Mass Observation diary:

I suddenly thought tonight, 'I know why a lot of women have gone into PANTS – it's a sign that they are asserting themselves in some way.' I feel pants are more a sign of the times than I realised. A growing contempt for man in general creeps over me.

The cut of 1940s trousers was fabulously stylish.

Clothes expressed the need to move on from the war and its aftermath. This forward-looking mentality helped to make informal calf-length capri pants and shorts fashionable for leisure wear in the 1950s. It was just the beginning; society was changing and both women and men were questioning a whole range of cultural norms. It would take at least three more decades before trousers were fully acceptable in all aspects of a woman's life, but the bold clothing innovations of the Sixties broke down classic assumptions about gender and clothes. Once the trouser taboo was broken beyond repair, there were high-profile promotions of smart trouser suits by couturiers such as Yves Saint Laurent in the 1960s. Trousers on women were considered almost futuristic, and thus appropriate clothing for the space-age ethos of the new 'modern' world.

Where could trousers go next? Almost anywhere they wanted (though it took time for trousers to become as universally acceptable for women as they were for men). Bianca Jagger wore a trouser suit for her 1971 wedding to pop star Mick Jagger. It was controversial, but the style was soon copied. From then on, trouser fashions could be applied almost indiscriminately to male and female styles.

Complete normalisation of trousers for females has not *quite* been achieved. There were still tales of professional women in the 1980s being forbidden to wear trousers at work. Although the ban on trousers in the Royal Enclosure at Royal Ascot was finally lifted in the twenty-first century, the 'number-one' uniforms for military servicewomen still usually include skirts, and there are still many schools that effectively ban trousers for female pupils by only offering the option of skirts.

FRONTIER PANTS

There is one version of trousers that has achieved true universality, regardless of gender, all around the globe: jeans.

Jeans came from the sort of humble beginnings the Ancient Romans would have enjoyed deploring – as durable workwear for North American miners and loggers. In the 1870s a collaboration between two entrepreneurs, Jacob Davies and Levi Strauss, brought together denim cotton, copper riveting and patented extra-strong seams. In doing so, they created Levi Strauss & Co., and so began the phenomenon of jeans. Jacob Davies' contribution was in the strengthening of trouser seams with copper rivets previously used on horse-blanket straps. Levi Strauss himself was a dealer in fabric, clothing and boots in San Francisco and therefore an experienced distributer.

Jean is a twilled cotton cloth – that is, woven with parallel diagonal ridges – while the word *denim* refers back, obliquely, to a fabric called *serge de Nîmes*. The original serge from Nîmes was twilled wool. At some point during its use as a sturdy work fabric it was conflated with 'jean'. Hence, denim jeans. Denim quickly became irrevocably linked to the American cotton textile developed in the eighteenth century, and to men's workwear. The first style of jeans were bib-and-braces overalls, later reduced to waisted trousers only. Levi customers had started calling their denim trousers 'jeans' by the 1920s.

Jeans began life as bib-and-braces work overalls, then evolved into the trousers we know and love today.

Eventually other companies promoted their own denim trousers, and competition between brands was all-out by the twentieth century. In the 1950s the company Lee Jeans directed their promotions at the newly vocal and financially liberal teenage market, taking advantage of the generational disapproval of jeans, which were associated with informality, rebellion and slovenly behaviour. Elvis Presley wouldn't wear jeans on-stage, but Eddie Cochran set a fashion for double-denim in 501 jeans. Bikers and 'bad boy' actors such as Marlon Brando, James Dean and Paul Newman teamed their jeans with leather jackets.

The most iconic jeans are arguably Levi's 501s. These are button-fly loose-fit jeans, launched as lot-number 501 overalls in 1890, and relaunched in 1986 via a provocative television advertisement featuring a well-sculptured male model undressing in a public Laundromat. They were briefly the most popular jeans on the planet, until they became so widespread that they couldn't possibly be 'cool' any more.

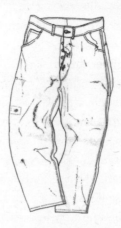

Vintage work-jeans from the 1930s – well worn,
yet now highly collectable.

Vintage jeans can be immensely collectable. The first pair of Levi Strauss jeans sold for $3 in 1870. In 1949 a pair of 1890s Levi 501 jeans was found in Calico Silver mine in California's Mojave desert. After patching and wearing them, the finder contacted Levi Strauss & Co., which bought them for $25 dollars. In 2001 the oldest known pair of jeans – dating from the 1880s – was acquired by Levi Strauss for $45,000.

Each generation – or each fashion trend – likes to adopt its own style of jeans, whether loose or tight. For 1960s British Mods, 501s with turn-ups vied for dominance with white Lee jeans. The on–off trend for skin-tight jeans between the 1960s and 1980s led to all manner of contortions, with wearers having to bathe in the jeans in very hot water to ensure the best fit. There were numerous scalding incidents, some blue-dyed flesh traumas and the need to have the restrictive jeans manually hauled from the body by a helper.

Colour is also an important fashion element with jeans.

Molecules of the indigo dye only sit on the surface of denim cotton, causing an inevitable fading of colour as the dye is rubbed off. This colour fading became part of the aesthetic attraction; so much so that modern processes include the stone-washing of denim for a distressed effect, and even pre-ripped jeans for a lived-in look, supposed to mimic the origins of jeans as workwear that took a battering. Perversely, the more damaged the jeans, often the higher the price tag.

Denim jeans might be a universal trend, implying homogeneity, but the fabric also adapts well to customisation. Hippy jeans of the Sixties and Seventies were often wildly embellished with appliqué and embroidery, while punk fashions gave their denim a sharp edge quite literally, with studs and razor slashes. Revivals of the 'individualisation' trend in the 1990s cynically involved pre-customised designs, so that every customer could look individual in the same way. In 2001 Lee Cooper revived a brief 1970s fad for male jeans with a padded crotch, called Pack-it jeans.

Jeans are egalitarian, at least up to a point. They can be budget-priced or high-end couture; body-hugging as jeggings – jean leggings – or gender-neutral when baggy. According to fashion designer Victoria Beckham, 'jeans have become not just the backbone but spinal cord, ribcage, and, for some of us, the whole skeleton of a woman's wardrobe'.

Jeans are indeed a standard of almost *any* modern wardrobe, and there are a host of other trouser styles to choose from alongside them. Far from being the scorned leg coverings of despised foreigners that they were 2,000 years ago, trousers have assumed their place as the most common, and the most practical, clothing for the legs – for men and women alike.

COAT HOOKS

It was a bitter night, so we drew on our ulsters and wrapped
cravats about our throats ...

SIR ARTHUR CONAN DOYLE, 'THE ADVENTURE OF THE
BLUE CARBUNCLE' IN *THE ADVENTURES OF SHERLOCK
HOLMES*, 1892

WRAPPING UP

Coats are not always considered the most glamorous of garments,
despite being crucial to our comfort. They are essentially a
protective outer layer. Almost unthinkingly we pull them on
for warmth, or to keep dry in wet weather. But we should appreciate them for that role – without the covering of coats or cloaks,
humans could not have thrived in wintery conditions, or indeed
under intense sun. And we would not be able today to explore
extreme environments such as the polar regions or the surface
of the moon, without insulating outer garments.

Even the most drab-looking covering may carry a world of
secrets, stories and symbolism. There is a coat in a Second World
War exhibition at a small heritage airfield in deepest Lincolnshire.
It has three big buttons, two patch pockets and one white label
at the breast with a row of numbers. Simply made, faded and
badly stained, it is unprepossessing in appearance – but this is
no ordinary coat.

It was picked up by a Belgium woman named Elise Marachal
on her arrival at Ravensbrück concentration camp in Germany
in 1944. Ravensbrück was a Nazi women-only prison. Although

Elise Marachal's life-saving coat from Ravensbrück concentration camp.

not intended as an extermination centre, it still had appalling death-rates for political prisoners, Jehovah's Witnesses, Jews and other perceived enemies of Germany's Third Reich. Elise had been arrested, along with her mother, for helping to run the hugely successful Comète escape route for Allied airmen trapped in enemy territory. She recalled the moment she first grabbed the coat: 'We passed tables loaded with clothes that had been taken from the dead. We were allowed to take a minimum of underwear, a dress, and a coat.'

Elise's coat was her protection during nights on stone floors and dawn roll calls in drenching rain. The number sewn onto the breast replaced Elise's name for camp officials, part of the dehumanisation process. A red triangle on the upper sleeve showed that she was a political prisoner, while the white cross on the back of the coat was, she noted, 'to serve as a target in case we fled'. Elise kept the coat after the camp was liberated as 'a vivid reminder of a nightmare which I am glad to be rid of. It has witnessed all the horrors of a Nazi concentration camp during the war.' An ordinary coat with an extraordinary story.

Elise Marachal's coat undoubtedly saved her life. The primary function of the first coats, wraps and cloaks was exactly the same: they protected the vulnerable human form from soaking, freezing or sunburn. In this chapter we'll see how coats and cloaks are inextricably bound up with both survival and status. Central to these twin themes is the fur coat.

FUR FOR SURVIVAL

Fur is supremely efficient. Over millennia it has evolved to provide warmth and waterproofing. Some animals have fur that alters its thickness and colouring to suit the season, as with the stoat, which has brown fur during the warmer months that changes to the highly coveted white fur, known as ermine, in winter – the better to camouflage it against the landscape.

The earliest human coverings were animal skins, either complete with fur or stripped to the plain hide. Such furs would today be known as 'wild fur', for having been hunted in the wild, as opposed to being artificially farmed. It is facile to look back on the 'wild' use of skins and fur and call it cruel. Every single part of an animal was put to some use by early human-kind, as food, clothing, thread, glue, grease, weaponry, decoration and storage. Whole treated animal skins were worn as cloaks, fastened around the neck and shoulders.

Fur and animal skin were the primary source of warmth and protection for early humans. Furs then continued to be worn throughout human history in companion with woven textiles. The first fitted fabric coats with seams and sleeves date back to the Persian Empire, approximately 3,000 years ago. Fur – while never vanishing completely from human attire – very much took a back seat to fabric, which had far greater potential for styles and production techniques. Nobles in various times might have cloaks lined or trimmed with fur to show wealth and prestige, such as Renaissance cloaks lined with miniver (literally hundreds of soft squirrel-belly furs stitched together), but on the whole it wasn't commonly worn. At least, not until a revival in the nineteenth century . . .

The popularity of fur coats at that time is bound up with

increased prosperity in the West – such garments are expensive and require considerable disposable income – and with improved technology for mass-production. Expanding trade and travel routes were also crucial: fur-trappers in Siberia, Alaska or Canada could take advantage of new train networks and speedy steam-powered ocean voyages to get furs from the wild to the furriers and so to customers.

All continents have been targeted by hunters and trappers for the international markets, and Siberia is said to have been colonised largely due to the ever-expanding quest for sable furs. Few animals were safe from the trappers. Fox, squirrel, rabbit, beaver, mink, wolf and stoat were common European furs, but Europeans could also enjoy pelts hunted further afield – sable, lynx, chinchilla, chipmunk, ocelot, monkey and bear. Considered particularly attractive was the fur of newborn Karakul lambs, cultivated in what is now the Republic of Uzbekistan. Fashioned into coats, hats or collars, it was called 'Persian lamb' and also *astrakhan*.

By the early twentieth century the appetite for fur was at its height. Even domestic cats were not safe. According to a 1917 overview, *The Fur Trade of America*, hundreds of thousands of felines were annually slaughtered for fur, and 'it is a profound mystery how so many become commercial prizes without their devoted owners obtaining an inkling of their destiny'. Novelist and Hollywood scriptwriter Elinor Glyn decided not to wear dead fur for a 1939 literary lunch date at the Dorchester Hotel. Instead she draped her (live) cat Candide around her neck as a stole. This sudden obsession with fur went far beyond any need for warmth and waterproofing. Fur was a status symbol of the elite, and an aspiration for those of far lower status.

FUR FOR FASHION

Anything that expense and rarity place beyond the grasp of the average person almost immediately acquires a glamour and mystique. It is also almost immediately adopted by the privileged and flaunted as a symbol of status. We can place fur in the same category as diamonds or caviar. Although supply chains and improved transport had suddenly made it much more available, fur was still extremely expensive. And in addition to a significant initial outlay for a coat, fur accrued further status by being expensive to care for. Over summer months it might need storing in a professional fur-safe free from moth and uninjured by contact with chemicals. Quality and rarity contributed to its exclusivity. It is easy to see, therefore, how a beautiful fur coat became the must-have item for those who were rich and wished to flaunt it.

Few animals were safe from those who coveted the glamour of fur. Here, a 1930 foalskin coat.

Sable and mink were two of the most coveted furs of all. Paris fashion directrice Ginette Spanier declared that the passion for mink was impossible to explain: 'Everywhere in the world the mink coat is the label of success. Why, for heaven's sake? There are other furs: sables, for example, which are so much more expensive . . . But I admit I have wanted a mink coat all my life.'

Further down the price range were furs dyed to look like more expensive pelts (although expensive furs were also dyed for novelty value). The cheapest fur was undoubtedly *coney* – rabbit fur – rivalled only by *musquash*, a fancy name for the fur of the muskrat rodent. These lower-end coats were the kind that would have been purchased by some young women during the First World War, with the wages earnt from their factory war work. As one middle-class lady declared in Birmingham: 'I think it's disgraceful all these munition makers and their fur coats; they're getting too much money.' A munitions worker smartly retorted that she worked a seventy-two-hour week for just a pound, and 'what sort of fur coat did she think she could buy after paying for her living out of that?' 'It's more than they ever had before,' said the lady, 'and they don't know how to spend it.' 'And do the rich always know how to spend their money?' replied the worker.

Between the late nineteenth century and the 1970s women who couldn't afford a full fur coat sported collars and cuffs of fur on wool fabric coats. These were often detachable, so that they could be used to glam up different coats. By the 1920s, when Hollywood stars were hugely influential fashion icons, large turn-up fur collars were seen on all but the most mundane coats. From the First World War onwards there was also a trend for wearing the whole animal – usually a fox pelt or two – slung around the shoulder or across the chest and fastened with a clip at the muzzle. It was common to see such stoles with the heads, tails and feet attached, complete with claws and glinting bead eyes.

In the 1940s fur capes overtook stoles in popularity, usually with wide, built-up shoulders – and dangling clawed feet. Sleeker stoles of the 1950s were often made up of many tiny squirrel pelts. By the Fifties it was not unusual for a middle-class woman to own a full fur coat for special occasions, occasionally altered to suit prevailing styles. Meanwhile elite women had to search ever further afield for eye-catching new pelts. In 1962, when meeting the US Ambassador to Rome, Jackie Kennedy began an ill-considered fashion for leopardskin coats: the subsequent boom in trade depleted leopard numbers catastrophically. Both Queen Elizabeth II and Elizabeth Taylor also wore leopardskin coats. The US only banned imports when African leopards were almost entirely wiped out, a decade later.

Fur coats of the 1970s were often combined with leather for dramatic effect. Far less stylish were the 'Afghan' coats worn by hippies, with fleecy sheepskin on the inside and cured leather on the outside, so-called because they were originally worn by Afghani tribespeople. They were imported to Britain in the mid-1960s and became popular after members of the Beatles were photographed wearing them. Cheap 'knock-off' versions of the coat were notoriously prone to giving off a strong odour when damp.

But fashion's love-affair with fur was set to change. The use of fur for fashion in modern times is tremendously controversial. For everyday life in the West we have no need of fur for warmth or waterproofing –these aspects are simply side-effects of a fashionable fur garment. Since 1980 animal-rights activists have publically rejected the use of animal pelts in fashion. Organisations such as PETA (People for the Ethical Treatment of Animals) are committed to banning fur-farming, in which animals are deliberately bred for their pelts. Extremist groups such as the ALF (Animal Liberation Front) are classed as domestic terrorists within the United States, such is the level of violence they use against facilities with captive animals, and against employees of these facilities.

Fur has now become so controversial that extraordinary fur coats are rarely even exhibited in museums. When they appear in public they cause frissons of envy from those who still venerate them, but may equally well provoke acts of violence from detractors. Fur coats were once emblematic of high status, disposable income and chic style. Now, in many Western households, they lurk in attics and at the back of wardrobes, housing moth larvae and waiting to be pulled out into the light of day and optimistically listed on online auction sites, or donated to charity shops.

However, this is not the whole story. While the general perception in the West is that fur is no longer acceptable, the first two decades of the twenty-first century have actually seen an extraordinary *increase* in the farming and wearing of fur. The lure of fur tempts many women – and it is almost exclusively women who wear luxury fur coats – to shrug off the no-fur ethics of the 1980s and 1990s to take advantage of fur's glamour. Much of the world market for fur is driven by the post-communist consumerism of Russia and China, with a super-rich elite taking up the age-old tradition of using fur to show wealth.

Fur evokes complex responses. Animal-rights campaigners object to the cruelty of farming creatures for their pelts; fans of fake fur – which was first worn in the 1940s, due to wartime shortages of real fur – overlook the environmental implications of manufacturing textiles from petrochemicals. And many fashion designers love the creative potential of fur. There are immense design possibilities in fur's shape, pile, colour and contrast with other textiles. Furs still have a sensual attraction in their texture, weight and appearance. Whether the modern consumer – or designer – resists such glamour is a matter of conscience.

CLASS AND CLOAKS

Leaving fur aside, we must return to woven textiles to chart the evolution of the modern coat – a garment that few wardrobes would now be without. It is a long story, which begins not with a garment boasting sleeves, but with the *cloak*. The cloak – an enveloping piece of fabric, either straight or shaped, wrapped around the upper body and draped from the shoulders – was a staple garment in the Classical world. The sixth-century BCE Greek fabulist Aesop famously recounted the fable of how the sun and the north wind had a competition to compel a traveller to remove his cloak. The more the wind tried to blow the cloak off, the more the traveller pulled it close, only to shed the layer quickly when the sun blazed at its hottest. Long before coats were shaped and embellished, the cloak served as an outer garment.

The earliest cloaks were animal-hide wrappers, as we have already noted. However, as time went on, cloaks could also be made of plain or felted wool. For example, one cloak found in a Danish tomb dated to the third or fourth century BCE was made of dark sheep's wool and fastened with bronze links. Advances in weaving technology brought wool, linen and silk mantles, some shaped to the body, others created by draping a straight length of cloth around the body and fastening it with pins, brooches and belts, to suit taste and fashion. A wrapper worn by women in Classical Greece, known as a *himation*, was taken up by the Romans, who were ever-eager to assimilate Greek culture. They adapted and converted it into a high-status garment for elite males – the iconic *toga*.

The basic Roman toga was a large semicircular shaped piece of lightweight woven wool, folded and then draped around the male form. The great size and impracticality of the toga made it the perfect garment to signify a distinction between labourers and landowners. It added prestige and literal physical presence to the tunic base layer of the Roman male, and required grace and dexterity to wear successfully. Small folds of cloth could be made into pouches at the belt; large folds were drawn up as hoods over the head, for shelter, discretion or mourning. While the toga might be of plain cream wool, the cloaks and the robes beneath came in all colours, although the emperors Caligula and Nero attempted – with limited success – to restrict all purple hues to the Emperor and his family.

High-status men of Germanic and Scandinavian cultures eschewed the Roman toga and kept to their cloaks, using fur linings, fine fabrics and embellishments to denote their elite status. As ever, lower-status men aspired to nobler styles, but with cheaper fabrics, or they wore hardier cloaks more suitable for their labours.

Smartly shaped cloaks characterised the silhouette of the elite Renaissance man. They were essential wear for the gentleman in Tudor and Jacobean courts, though discarded for dancing. Renaissance cloaks rose up around the neck, fitted neatly on the shoulders, then flared out around the arms to elbow-length, in a style intended to show flair and draw attention down to the legs. To prevent the cloak from interfering with the wearing of one's sword, the bulk of the fabric would favour the opposite side from the scabbard. The story of Sir Walter Raleigh spreading his cloak with a flourish over a puddle impeding the passage of Queen Elizabeth I may be a delightful fiction, but it is certainly true that the act of sacrificing an expensive and high-status garment would have represented extreme loyalty. A portrait of Raleigh from 1588 that hangs in London's National Portrait Gallery depicts him wearing a cloak hung over one shoulder. It is black, velvet-lined and turned back with sable, and has sun-rays worked in silver, each ending in three large pearls. Not something to be walked on lightly.

With their size and versatility, cloaks were a superb means of showing status. Unlike a coat, the cloak could be worn in such a way as to expose the finery beneath, rather than covering it. Cloaks that trailed along the ground, requiring assistance, emphasised status through their very impracticality. Monarchs and aristocrats paraded in cloaks of damask, velvet and satin well into the eighteenth century, adding braid, spangles, bugle beads, gems and lace as they saw fit. Cloaks were one of the defining garments of a monarch in coronation portraits and were worn by peers on state occasions.

Such display was all well and good for elite occasions, but the cloaks of working women and men were thick, warm and enveloping, without all the excess fabric and embellishment. It was in the rural population that cloaks endured the longest, in the form of Irish mantles, Scottish tartans and the scarlet cloaks made famous by the fairy-tale of Little Red Riding Hood. Peter

Kalm, a Scandinavian botanist visiting Britain in 1748, noted that 'the English countrywoman when she goes out visiting wears a scarlet cloak', resorting to a brown mantle for everyday wear. Country gentry apparently liked their scarlet cloaks for donkey-riding, gardening and informal walks, and silk-lined red wool cloaks made well-appreciated wedding presents. There is an unsubstantiated story from Wales and Jersey that when Napoleon's forces were considering an invasion of Britain at some unspecified date between 1799 and 1805, they were afraid to land, because of the sight of English soldiers in their red coats – although in reality they were women in scarlet cloaks.

Working people continued to wear cloaks well into the nineteenth century, though the garment had long had a rival in the shawl. The shawl has an ancestry as old as the cloak. It is a plain or decorated length of fabric with plain, straight ends or fringing; rectangular, square or triangular in shape. A shawl can be wrapped around the head and knotted under the chin – as industrial workers of the nineteenth century did. It is good for huddling in for warmth, but can also be arrayed around the body as a graceful decoration. Plain-weave woollen shawls were strictly functional; silk and cashmere shawls woven in elaborate designs were status garments – both sumptuous and highly costly. The eighteenth century saw an immense increase in the textile trade between Europe and India, Egypt, Persia and Turkey, and exotic imported shawls were highly coveted by Western women; the artful wearing of a decorative shawl came to denote the status of a *lady*.

SHAWLS – THE SIGN OF A LADY

It was said that the Empress Josephine of France surpassed all other ladies in the elegance of her shawl-wearing. Madame de Rémusat, a lady of the French court, recalled that Josephine had between 200 and 300 shawls and that 'Bonaparte, who thought she was too much covered with these shawls, would pull them off and throw them in the fire. Josephine then called for another.'

A lady of 1813 displays her shawl as a decorative accessory, arranged with seemingly casual grace.

The heroine of a Jane Austen romance would not have her shawl over her head and knotted under her chin to stave off cold and rain, as the mill-workers of the Industrial Revolution did. Rather, she would have draped it in the crook of her arms in imitation of Classical statuary – all the better to show off the Indian pinecone design upon the fabric. This design came to be called 'paisley', after the Scottish town where imitations of the original Indian shawls were produced en masse from the early nineteenth century onwards. Norwich shawls of cotton or silk, first made in 1784, were also highly coveted, particularly when hand-embroidered. As the demand for shawls grew, manufacturers began to market printed wool shawls for ladies of more reduced means. The import, production and retail of shawls became big business and a very prominent part of the Regency woman's shopping experience. Consider this advertisement from the *Morning Chronicle* in 1818:

> Dress shawls – the most elegant and extensive selection of dress, damask, tissue, wove and superb India and British shawls, particularly worthy of the attention of Ladies leaving Town for the Watering Places, may be inspected at Howes, Hart and Hall's India and British Shawl, Linen and Muslin Warehouse 60, Fleet-street.

It seems shawls could also be turned to more comedic uses. In 1837 the ageing Countess of Cork was a notorious kleptomaniac, with a penchant for purloining silver cutlery while dining out. She almost met her match while visiting the Archbishop of York, whose daughters decided to trick her. They wrapped the Archbishop's pet hedgehog in a shawl and left the resulting bundle in the hall. True to form, the Countess couldn't resist pilfering it, taking the whole bundle into her carriage. She was alarmed to discover the hedgehog, but quickly rallied and commanded her carriage to be stopped at the first pastry cook's shop it passed. Putting down the carriage window, she demanded, 'Bring me some of your nicest cakes.' The baker hurried to oblige. When he returned, the Countess took the proffered tray, tipped the cakes into her lap, placed the hedgehog on the tray, then returned both to the astonished baker, with the command to her coachman, 'Drive on.' She was then able to enjoy a tasty snack while admiring her new shawl.

Cloaks were still an option for ladies of the 1860s wanting warmth. They displayed to advantage over wide crinoline hoops.

The nineteenth century was the shawl's heyday. Mid-nineteenth-century hooped skirts were the perfect wide structure for displaying shawls with paisley patterns, tartan weaves or fringing to their best advantage. Ladies' coats did exist at this time, but they were, of necessity, loose and cloak-like, in order to fit over the dress styles beneath. It would take a few more decades before coats won the role of most popular protective covering and, even then, shawls would remain popular with poorer women, as they were more versatile (and generally cheaper) than a tailored coat.

One particular shawl survives as evidence of one of Victorian London's most horrific crimes – the 1888 slaughter spree of 'Jack the Ripper'. The shawl has been authenticated as belonging to the Ripper's fourth victim, Catherine Eddowes. The identification is not without controversy, as the shawl – a silk floral rectangle – was not originally listed in Eddowes' effects by the police; Metropolitan PC Amos Simpson allegedly removed it from the crime scene. It was later offered at auction in 2007 after a stint at Scotland Yard's 'Black Museum' of crime memorabilia. The current owner of the shawl, amateur detective Russell Edwards, claims to have used mitochondrial DNA recovered from the shawl to establish a connection with one of the original murder suspects, a hairdresser named Aaron Kosminski. For those who dispute Edwards' findings, the search for the Ripper's identity still continues.

More affluent women of the later nineteenth century abandoned shawls in favour of cloaks – specifically stylish short mantles with proud turned-up collars. They could be lined with lambskin, dripping with jet beads and textured with thick frills, ribbons and braid; they marked the confidence of the 'New Woman' and the consumerism of the burgeoning middle classes.

Cloaks, coats and shawls all had to be chosen carefully. Late Victorian experts such as the author of *What Dress Makes of Us* were at hand to advise. Young women were told that shawls would age them. Tall women were told to keep clear of long cloaks: 'The one who can wear the long cloak in an unchallengeable manner is the short, stout woman.' In turn, the short woman was warned away from short capes with fluffy collars to avoid looking like 'a smothered, affrighted Cochin China chicken'. One imaginative schoolgirl said her mother – dressed thus – 'looks as if her neck were encircled by bunches of asparagus'.

By the First World War cloaks were limited to formal evening wear or, in felted wool form, as part of a traditional school ensemble or nursing uniform.

The 1960s and 1970s saw a brief flirtation with a particular kind of cape borrowed from Central and South America – the *poncho*. It is traditionally a simple sheet of fabric with an opening for the head, sometimes with a hood attached. As a woven textile it has been part of Native American cultural life since even before the reign of the Incas, dating back to at least 500 BCE. By the mid-nineteenth century North American troops in the Civil War had waterproofed versions, which could also serve as groundsheets and basic tent coverings. The ponchos fashionable in the 1960s were gaudy knitted or crocheted versions in nylon wool, purely part of a fun trend – and there have been occasional half-hearted revivals since then.

CLOAK AND DAGGER

Where cloaks survive in the modern Western world, it is in their most dynamic forms – to signify power, provide a disguise and create a dramatic display. They provide swirl and panache during Hollywood sword-fight scenes, and dark glamour for Gothic characters.

Such is the historical association between full cover and disguise that many Westerners may be uneasy encountering an all-enveloped body. The expectation is that visible clothing gives strong clues about status, gender and profession – in short, an identity. When this identity is wrapped up out of sight, it can lead to social confusion. Thus, if women wear full *burqas* – a traditional Islamic choice of dress, covering head, face and body – it can trigger unintentional associations for people brought up in a society that associates disguise with a potentially fearful unknown, even though such fear is entirely unrelated to the original purpose of the *burqa*.

Cloaks and secrecy are entwined throughout history. Furtive, scheming actions are described as *cloak-and-dagger*, and with good reason. A large, dark cloak made the perfect cover for night-time crimes. In 1766 the Spanish government attempted to minimise the threat of thieves in disguise by banning men from wearing the archetypal long cloak and broad-brimmed hat.

Sensationalist literature of the nineteenth century loved tales of cloak-and-dagger drama.

Since Tudor times, melodramatic villains on stage and screen have made the most of the full-circle cape as they declaim their wickedness and incite fearful delight from the audience. The effect is highly visual and so, not surprisingly, is referenced less in the printed word; more in live action or film. Count Dracula, one of literature's most iconic dark figures, has been portrayed on stage and screen in a multitude of different black cloaks, with or without blood-red lining. In Bram Stoker's original 1897 novel the cloak is mentioned only once, but to great effect, as the horrified narrator Jonathan Harker observes Count Dracula's dark power:

> I saw the whole man begin to emerge from the window and begin to crawl down the castle wall over the dreadful abyss, face down with his cloak spreading out around him like great wings.

Elsewhere in the novel the Count's attire is barely noted, beyond references to the colour black. Even so, modern filmography usually presents a formal gentleman in immaculate evening attire, including the visually dramatic silk-lined opera cloak.

Further along the spectrum between crime and punishment is Alexandre Dumas' vengeful hero Edmond Dantès in the 1844 novel *The Count of Monte Cristo*. Having been wrongly incarcerated by his enemies, Dantès becomes an extraordinary figure of justice. He is described as wrapped in a cloak that conceals his figure, with the moon just bursting through the clouds above; but, like Count Dracula, Dantès is far more cloaked in cinematic interpretations than in ones on paper. Somehow a mere greatcoat would not have the same effect.

Not all cloaked disguise is deemed dangerous or sinister; sometimes it leads to fun and flirtation. Masquerade balls of the seventeenth and eighteenth centuries created an exciting atmosphere of mystery and speculation; with identity hidden, there was the possibility for out-of-character and risqué behaviour. At eighteenth-century masquerade balls, revellers hid beneath an all-covering cloak called a *domino* – originally a hooded clerical coat – matched with an eye mask. With most identifying features hidden, the masquerader could indulge in the frisson of anonymous flirting or even more vigorous indiscretions.

Cloaks and the disguise they afford can also be crucial for

survival. In some versions of the Cinderella tale, the heroine escapes bullying and the threat of incest by hiding in cloaks made variously of moss, leather and donkey skin. Conversely, in the Chinese Cinderella-style story, the heroine Yeh-hsien dazzles a king when she wears a magical cloak spun from kingfisher feathers. There are echoes of this enduring idea that cloaks can confer status in the expression 'to reclaim the mantle', meaning to take up power again, as if donning a high-status cloak.

Incorporating all these elements of crime, justice, power and disguise are the cloaks, referred to as *capes,* of twentieth-century superheroes. Graphic-novel artwork thrives on exaggeration and dramatic style, which are amply provided by the lines and flare of a cloak. The modern counterpart to vengeful Edmond Dantès could be Batman of DC Comics, created by Bob Kane in 1939. Batman is even known as the Caped Crusader. His cloak has evolved from bat-wing cape in the original artwork – inspired by Leonardo da Vinci's ornithopter sketch – through the camp, nylon capelet of the 1966 US television series, to a twenty-first-century vast black rubber-effect creation with fetishistic overtones. At the noble-superhero end of the spectrum, capes are more colourful and fluid – as with Superman's blue-and-red ensemble. They offset the typically skin-tight superhero body costume. Such cloaks are, in real terms, outrageously impractical – even 'suicide machines', according to one scientific forum. It would, for example, take far more than a fifteen-foot fabric span to enable Batman to glide or parachute with his cloak.

Visually, the cloaks of heroes and villains are very obviously anachronistic – signifiers of someone flamboyant who acts outside the rules of society (and basic aerodynamics). For the foreseeable future at least, cloaks remain in the realm of fiction and fantasy. For real life, we put on a coat.

FASHION'S FANCY

Coats are essentially an over-jacket with sleeves, collar and perhaps cuffs; long or short, fitted or loose, civilian or military.

Coats took over from cloaks in the late nineteenth-century wardrobe, leaving cloaks to dwindle into relative obscurity. Cloaks simply did not suit new social sensibilities at this time, which had a greater respect for neat tailoring and the practical shaping of coats. Neither women nor men wished to be hampered by a cloak's fabric folds. Coats were far better suited for the faster pace of life in the twentieth century.

A quality coat was an investment for the twentieth-century woman's wardrobe – some would say it still is. Women on limited budgets chose classic styles that would last several seasons, regardless of fashion's vagaries. For those who could follow fashion, every season brought fresh colours and novel details. The Twenties saw wrap coats, or neatly pieced tailored coats that echoed the streamlining of Art Deco architecture and new super-fast transport. The late 1930s saw a shoulder-padded silhouette, which continued through the Second World War until the launch of the sleek-shouldered lines of Dior's New Look. Of necessity, more than a few Forties coats had been born as blankets, then dyed, cut and stitched for new life as a coat. Greater confidence in Fifties' Europe brought more flamboyance.

Post-war exuberance is clearly expressed in this 1952 wool swagger-back coat.

Swag backs and broad skirts then gave way to boxy cropped coats in the Sixties, or hem-dragging long coats in the Seventies. Those of the 1980s and 1990s echoed the Forties' look, with immense shoulders once more, bulky sleeves and all-enveloping fabric. And so it goes on: a parade of changing shapes and styles for impatient consumers eager for a new look to their wardrobe.

MACS AND MANY-CAPED COATS

There is a medieval expression – '*Cucullus non facit monachum*' – meaning 'a cowl doesn't make a monk' (that is: don't judge on appearances). However, humans still instinctively do judge on appearances, and in public encounters the overcoat or cloak may give a strong first impression. For men, coat fashions are perhaps less eye-catching and colourful than womenswear, but after the suit, the coat was arguably the most significant item of menswear in the twentieth century. Out on the street, your choice of coat showed what sort of man you were, or at least what sort of man you wished to be.

As with womenswear, overcoats were the death of men's cloaks. For men, it was the eighteenth century that saw the transition from cloak to coat, with caped greatcoats as the evolutionary link. These caped coats were favoured by coachmen at first, as a practical way of keeping warm and dry on the job. Some of the looser styles of greatcoat were known by the delightful name of 'wrap rascals', as seen in a waspish article in the *London Evening Post* of 1738:

> There is at present a reigning ambition among our young gentlemen of degrading themselves in apparel to the class of the servants they keep ... some had those loose kinds of great-coats which I have heard called 'wrap-rascals' with gold-laced hats slouched in humble imitation of stage-coachmen; others aspired at being grooms.

In a striking example of the elite looking to the 'street' for clothing inspiration, greatcoats were taken up by fashionable gentlemen. As with cloaks, coats were (and arguably still are) heavy with class-meaning. The cut, fabric and styling details of coats could reveal a great deal about the wearer's wealth, status and profession. Through the nineteenth century there were many variations on the basic style of overcoat. Some involved subtle changes of cut and stitching; others had more distinctive collars, capes and pockets.

Fictional detective Sherlock Holmes favoured the heavy *ulster* style, which still retained a shoulder cape. The *Chesterfield* was of a more conservative cut, designed for the Edwardian gentleman looking to cover his modern lounge suit. Such coats might be water-resistant, but to be truly waterproofed the nineteenth-century gentleman would choose a *mackintosh* coat.

The popular Chesterfield style of coat, conferring a certain gravitas.

In 1823 Charles Mackintosh submitted a patent for a cloth waterproofed with India-rubber. He gave his own name to the coat produced using his patented process, and so the mackintosh or mac was born. The first models were a dull brown or dark green. One downside was the fact that because the cloth had been sealed with rubber there was no escape for sweat, which had odorous implications. A correspondent to the *Gentleman's Magazine* in 1839 complained, 'A Mackintosh is now become a troublesome thing in town from the difficulty of their being admitted into an omnibus on account of the offensive stench which they emit.'

Two decades later, the 1850s saw the first foldable pocket mackintosh, useful for sudden showers. Mackintosh coats have retained a space in the modern wardrobe. Mackintosh capes, on the other hand, although on sale in the 1940s, were to be eclipsed by a handy lightweight waterproof coat called the *anorak*, available from the 1940s onwards. Waterproof anoraks are a hybrid of hood, coat and cloak; the fewer seams, the better. The original anoraks of fish-oil-coated caribou or seal skin were worn by people indigenous to the Arctic regions. Western versions were of oiled cotton fabric. Owing to their popularity with stalwart train-spotters, today 'anorak' has become a semi-affectionate term for a focused enthusiast, often with a passion for statistics and a certain lack of stylishness. There is also the *kagool*, an anglicisation of *cagoule*, the French word for the Westernised version of the anorak made of waxed cotton, and then later nylon. In the 1960s kagools that could be folded and conveniently stored in little matching bags were popular. Mary Quant launched a stylish range called *pac-a-macs* in vibrant colours with transparent plastic panels. It was inevitably easier to get folding macs *out* of their carry-bags than it was to fold them precisely enough to fit them back *in*.

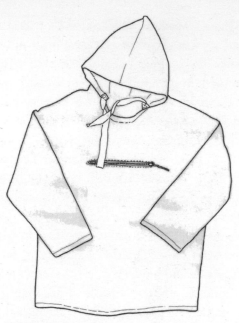

A 1940s anorak worn by the Special Boat Section – an army commando unit with the nickname 'The Cockleshell Heroes', owing to their use of limpet-mines to sink four German ships in 1942.

Returning to the mackintosh, waterproofing fabric was not a new technique when Charles Mackintosh first patented his process. Canvas sailcloth could be rendered waterproof with tar, and jackets treated in this way were worn by sailors in the eighteenth century, hence the British term 'tar' for a sailor. The word tarpaulin derives from the application of tar to a *pallium* – the Latin for cloak. From the 1930s onwards, heavy tarred canvas was superseded by lighter cottons, waterproofed with linseed oil and so known as *oilskins*. Oilskins have only recently been replaced by PVC coats for extreme wet-weather protection. However, while oilskins and macs were all well and good for heavy-duty use, a classy Victorian gentleman would abhor the stiff functionality of the former and the sweat-inducing seal of the latter. Fortunately, an excellent alternative was at hand from 1856, thanks to an innovative technique by Hampshire draper Thomas Burberry.

*Seafarers of the nineteenth and twentieth centuries found
waterproofed coats essential.*

Burberry realised that if the individual strands of wool yarn
were waterproofed, rather than the finished woven fabric, then
a garment made from the resulting fabric would be far more
breathable, because the textile would not be thickly clogged
from a uniform coating of oil. The idea was not entirely of his
own devising – he had watched local shepherds using sheep's
wool grease, lanolin, to coat their smocks, then made the conceptual leap to a more localised coating. Burberry tried his
yarn-specific treatment in making a closely woven wool called
gabardine (the close weave contributed to the waterproof properties). The process was a huge success, enabling him to establish
a company that continues to flourish to this day. It was Burberry
who supplied explorer Ernest Shackleton with waterproof gear
for his 1914 Antarctic expedition.

1914 was a significant year for Burberry in other ways. As

Shackleton sailed south, the guns of August had already begun firing the first salvos of the Great War. Burberry and other coat manufacturers would now turn their attention to kitting out the armies of the Allies. In doing so they would create an iconic wartime coat that remains a classic a full century later – the *trench coat*.

OFFICERS AND GENTLEMEN

The trench coats of the First World War were strictly for officers and not the regular Tommies. Historically officers in the military were well born, or at least wealthy enough to buy a commission and all the kit required to go with it. Their coats, therefore, were emblematic of their class. Trench coats were adapted to the particular demands of modern warfare – they needed to be camouflaged rather than flash, with strictly utilitarian details. These included buttoned pockets, waterproofing, a reinforced storm flap across the shoulders, a turn-up collar and shoulder straps for rank badges. They also included the subtle addition of underarm vents, which were very necessary to avoid sauna-like sweating. Both Burberry and Aquascutum clothing companies claimed the honour of inventing the trench coat, though it was essentially a nineteenth-century style brought up to date. It was readily taken up by patriotic civilians – male and female – and became a staple of post-war wardrobes. The trench is just one of the range of coat styles for men that arose in the twentieth century. But some of the others also had a military background.

There was the naval *duffel coat*, popular from the 1940s, and now perhaps most associated with the children's book character Paddington Bear, created in 1958. Duffel is a coarse, thick Belgian wool. It was considered perfect for those serving in the Navy, due to its warmth and ease of fastening: a duffel typically has wooden toggles and rope loops instead of buttons, so that it can be easily done up with cold fingers or gloved hands. The hood is generally wide and loose, so that it can be worn over a warm, close-fitting cap. During the Second World War General Montgomery wore a long camel-coloured version, accessorised with a beret. After the war, government surplus stocks hit the civilian market and the style remains intermittently fashionable to this day.

Another military style is the *bomber jacket*, a cropped blouson-style coat that began life as a warm, sheepskin-lined garment for the aviators of the First World War. The snug cuffs and zip fastenings ensured its continued popularity among airmen, making the look iconic of Second World War aircrews on both sides of the Atlantic. In Britain it subsequently gained a new generation of fans among the defiant scooterboys and skinheads of the 1970s, who wore an American-style nylon bomber with a distinctive orange lining. The 1986 hit film *Top Gun* then introduced yet more young people to the bomber jacket, with glamorous scenes of actors playing naval pilots. The current incarnation is as an overcoat for hip-hop artists. There's no predicting who'll wear it next.

A bomber jacket (centre) gave post-war civilians a sense of identification with aviation heroes of the Second World War. Trench coats, also shown here, were still popular long after the First World War.

Not all male coats are military in origin. Some have a definite working-class ancestry. The loose, single-breasted *donkey jacket* has been associated with working men since the mid-nineteenth century. The distinctive waterproof patches on the shoulders were supposedly an innovation of a Staffordshire tarpaulin manufacturer, to protect pottery workers from dripping water. The coat was adopted by radical subcultures such as punks and skinheads, but is also familiar in images of the 1980s British miners' strike. Satirists were quick to criticise former Labour Party leader Michael Foot for apparently wearing such a casual low-status garment during the Remembrance Day service in 1981, when other politicians had chosen longer, more formal coats. In fact it was just a good-quality short coat and not a cynical political ploy to look like a worker, but clearly coats and class are intertwined.

FIGHTING THE ELEMENTS

How do historical methods of warming and waterproofing – such as wool layers, oilskins, rubber macs and Burberry gabardine – compare with modern textiles? Since the 1950s we have enjoyed the innovation of waterproof PVC fabrics; since the 1970s we have had more breathable Gore-tex technology. Is newer definitely better when it comes to coats and protective wear? In fact, recent studies show that both ancient and modern protective clothing methods have their merits. An interesting case study is the clothing of mountaineer George Mallory.

Born in 1886, Mallory was a gifted and experienced climber. In his 1924 attempt on the as-yet-unconquered peak of Mount Everest he wore sturdy Harris tweed and Grenfell wool. A widely travelled missionary named Sir William Grenfell had developed this particular closely-woven wool only the year before, to keep him protected on his journeys in Newfoundland. Mallory failed to return from his Everest expedition, and critics have since speculated that he wasn't properly equipped for the ascent. However, following the 1999 discovery of Mallory's body on

Everest, experts have been able to disprove the popular misconception that Mallory was poorly dressed during his final, fatal ascent. His tailored wool short coat was found to be more manoeuvrable than many modern equivalents, and the combinations of layers were judged windproof, waterproof and warm. Vanessa Anderson, a specialist textile researcher, examined clothing recovered from Mallory's body and concluded, 'What impressed me is the strength and quality of the materials they used and how well they were tailored to withstand conditions on Everest.'

However, the ultimate protective cover-all will not be found in any domestic wardrobe. It is the fireproof cotton suit worn by NASA astronauts – treated with a flame-retardant chemical called proban – along with the space suit designed for extra-vehicular activity, which moon-walker Buzz Aldrin called 'a 100-percent fully contained living environment'. With a burgeoning interest in wearable technologies – including clothing that responds to environmental stimuli, clothing with inbuilt tracking chips and clothing that tracks its wearer's vital signs – it is possible that we will all be wearing coats straight out of a science-fiction film sooner than we think.

SUITS YOU

----

1 It is now theorised that Alexander wore an ancient version of Kevlar as his armour. Specialists at the University of Wisconsin-Green Bay have reconstructed Linthorax – laminated layers of linen, which Plutarch describes Alexander wearing at the battle of Gaugamela in 331 BCE, and which may be depicted in the famous 'Alexander' mosaic recovered from Pompeii.

It is recorded of Alexander the Great, that in his Indian exped-ition he buried several suits of armour, which by his directions were made much too big for any of his soldiers, in order to give posterity an extraordinary idea of him, and make them believe he had commanded an army of giants.[1]

R. BRIMLEY JOHNSON, *MANNERS MAKYTH MAN*, 1932

SUIT PSYCHOLOGY

Perhaps the ultimate elite suit – or set – of clothes is the suit of armour. Designed to accentuate the physique of the wearer to make him appear more impressive and powerful, as well as to offer protection, it retains its ability to command attention even when standing as an empty sentinel in stately homes and museum collections. While they are very different in appear-ance, the fabric suits of civilians are still a kind of carapace, designed to present the wearer and their body in a specific way.

In fashion terms, a suit is two or more garments of the same or contrasting fabric, designed to be worn together. For European men of the sixteenth and seventeenth centuries this meant a doublet and hose, or doublet and breeches, but for eight-eenth-century Scotsmen it meant a jacket and trews. For women, the suit was a bodice and skirt 'habit' for riding. The suit's evolution – with or without the addition of a waistcoat – is interwoven with the history of Westernisation. The suit still represents status; it can be a statement of individuality or, more often, of conformity. It is no exaggeration to call the suit an act of social engineering - a quasi-conscious manipulation of human behaviour through clothing - that is still very much part of the modern wardrobe.

PEACOCKING

Previous eras had seen complete outfits composed of matching or complementary components, but the suit reached a form recognisable to modern eyes in the eighteenth century. It was mostly a three-piece ensemble - jacket, waistcoat and breeches - in a range of fabrics and colours. Suits for professional wear were usually of wool or blends of wool, silk and linen. Their colours were relatively sombre, their buttons somewhat subdued. Suits for showing off at social events were inevitably of silk, glimmering with embroidery and embellishments. Some royals took such decoration to extremes - in July 1791 George, Prince Regent to King George III, was dressed to celebrate his father's birthday. The *St James's Chronicle* described his suit of rich-coloured striped silk with a waistcoat embroidered with silks, silver and semi-precious stones. The coat and waistcoat were covered in spangles and had diamond buttons to match the ones on his breeches. According to the *Chronicle*, it formed a most magnificent appearance.

Eighteenth-century elite suits boasted beautifully embroidered waistcoats in very pretty colours.

Prince George was a peacock, and a plump one at that, but he was not unique in presenting his wealth and position by means of his suit. The royal courts of Europe were all places of extraordinary display. Silk took up dye like no other material, reflecting light and acting as a glossy background for dazzling, multicoloured embellishments. Suits might shine with medallions, spangles, pearls as big as peas, jewels, silver thread, glass, gold foil and silk ribbon embroidery. Such was the cost of the haberdashery, let alone the fabric, that metal threads from suits were sometimes unpicked and recycled. This was known as *drizzling* or *parfilage*, and was considered a pretty pastime for leisured ladies. However, theatre-goers were not safe from the drizzling tools of unscrupulous gold-collectors out to add to their collection – the gold could be recovered from textiles through burning, then sold for reuse.

A suit from the 1740s with a skirted jacket, deep cuffs and breeches –
perfect for the elite Georgian gentleman.

Surviving suits from the eighteenth century are testament to a superb standard of embroidery at the time, both professional and domestic. Classical motifs and *chinoiserie* were popular, but it was flowers that bloomed on most men's suits of this era, in sprigs, bouquets, vines and cascades.[2] When taken to extremes, a man might be accused of excess or bad taste, but pastel fabrics or flowered embellishments would not invite charges of effeminacy. Suits gloried in colour and in the stylised beauty of the natural world.

Like the plumage of real peacocks, part of the lavish suit's function was to intimidate other males and attract females on the lookout for a wealthy mate. Of course there was always the danger of not looking beyond the suit to see the character of the man beneath: 'Good Heav'n! To what an ebb of taste are women fallen, that it should be in the power of a laced coat to recommend a gallant to them!' cries a young man in Richard Sheridan's 1813 play *A Trip to Scarborough*.

All this excess is undoubtedly alien to most modern suits. While there was a slight trend for embellished female suits in the 1980s, this was a *faux luxe*, often with hasty machine embroidery and plastic sequins. True suit exuberance, eighteenth-century-style, survives now only in the theatrical splendour of the Spanish bull-fighters *traje de luces* – suit of light – or perhaps in the encrusted suits of London's famous Pearly Kings and Queens.

Such splendour came at a price. During the French Revolution of the 1790s some aristocrats paid for their extravagant ways with their life. Court clothes, which had kept thousands of French silk merchants, weavers and embroiderers in trade, became symbolic of privileged decadence and disloyalty to the new regime. In these turbulent years of political upheaval some canny men kept a set of court suits *and* a set of more sober revolutionary costumes so that they could dress to tally with the prevalent political mood. The revolution was a sobering influence on suits and was partly responsible for the muted styles and colours worn by the modern male.

2 *Chinoiserie* is the fashionable use of Chinese and pseudo-Oriental motifs in objets d'art, fabric, furniture and even architecture.

Contemporary with unrest in France was a shift in the way gentlemen showed superiority of birth and breeding. Ironically the icon of this shift was not an aristocrat, but the uncommon commoner George 'Beau' Brummell, whose name should by now be familiar. When he inherited his fortune in 1799, he set about spending it not on spangles or silks, but on plain-seeming suits of superfine wool. Superfine suits have a longer, smoother nap than broadcloth, which is a plain-weave wool with a light nap. With his athletic figure, exquisite taste and strong character, Brummell become synonymous with the new vogue for subdued suits.

George 'Beau' Brummell in the suit style that he made famous.

For a while the Prince Regent – admiring Brummell – aspired to dress with as much quality and restraint. Dark coats of green or blue were eased onto his considerable frame over comparatively plain, short waistcoats and set off by buff-coloured pantaloons. Ostentation and extremes of fashion were now considered vulgar. Brummell was reported to say, 'If John Bull turns around to look after you, you are not well dressed; but either too stiff, too tight, or too fashionable.' John Bull here signifies the stereotypical bluff Englishman. The fashion for apparent simplicity carried its own superciliousness, of course, and Brummell sneered at those he considered badly dressed. One gentleman found himself under scrutiny and demanded to know, 'Is there anything the matter with my coat?' 'For heaven's sake my dear fellow,' sneered Brummell, 'don't misapply names so abominably! It is no more like a coat than it is to a cauliflower – if it is, I'll be damned!'

At this time the coat in question was a *tail coat*, a form of jacket with long tails. These tails were vestiges of the excessively wide, stiff coat skirts of the seventeenth- and earlier eighteenth-century male coats. Coat tails, if worn correctly, were not divided when sitting down, but flipped up behind. A style known as the *spencer jacket* was also popular with both men and women in the late eighteenth and early nineteenth centuries. It reached just below the shoulder blades in length and was neatly tailored, fitted and fastened. It was said to have originated with the 2nd Earl Spencer, who burnt his coat tails while warming himself by the fire. According to the story – quite possibly apocryphal – he pragmatically ordered his valet to neaten the ends, and so the fashion was born.

MADE TO MEASURE

Ideally a suit would be built around a straight, strong figure. A good fit could show off a physique honed by riding, boxing or perhaps fencing. However, not all gentlemen were so energetic. For less magnificent figures the tailor had techniques of cut to hide any defects, and to show the figure to best advantage. If a less-than-athletic gentleman seemed to cut a fine figure in his suit, it was really the underpaid (if *ever* paid) tailors who deserved the credit.

Tailoring was a respected but often poorly paid profession, mostly associated with men. By the eighteenth century London's West End tailors had gained a reputation for world-class quality, a reputation that is still alive today. Tailors gained customers by word-of-mouth recommendation. Occasionally their names can be found on paper or parchment labels hidden in a yoke-lining or back pleat of the suit jacket. Suit labelling today still tends to be discreet – in contrast to the modern fad of blazoning a designer name prominently on leisure wear.

The best tailors were famed for their sense of self-worth. In a *Punch* magazine cartoon of 1863 a rotund bewhiskered gent in a loose, wrinkled suit is being measured at a West End tailor's. This new customer begins to say, 'I've had my clothes from –' The tailor interrupts him, 'Clothes! Jus' so, Sir! He! He! We may concede you to be Clothed, Sir! But we re'lly can't call you Dressed; we can't, indeed!'

A first-class tailor mastered all the skills of cut, fit and finish. There were many different systems of cutting, and the best of these were shared in tailoring journals. Victorian gentlemen were measured for their suits with a humble yet crucial innovation – the standard inch tape. The measuring tape was said to have been invented by a tailor named George Atkinson, inspired by seeing a scale of inches used in foot measurements. In the right hands, the tape ensured that a suit would be a perfect fit.

English lawyer and world traveller William Hickey described a 1799 outfitting:

> I went to a tailor named Knill, to whom I had been recommended as a fit person to equip me *comme il faut*. He advised my having a dark green with gold binding, dark brown with the same, a plain blue and, for half dress, a Bon de Paris with gold frogs,[3] all of which he spoke as being much worn and of the highest *ton*. I bespoke the four suits accordingly.

A fictional fop of 1772, featured in an article in the *Ladies' Magazine*, was far less impressed with his tailor. His diary entry reads:

> Mr Casaque came to try on my pea green suit. Memo: sleeves too wide, pockets too high, skirts too long, and most frightfully made altogether: shall not pay his bill these two years by way of punishing him.

As fashions changed or as the wearer changed shape, a suit could be altered. Eighteenth-century tailors could 'take out a fish' in order to improve fit. This meant adding darts, a technique of cutting out a narrow triangle of fabric, then stitching the edges together. Wrinkles were always a concern. One gentleman confessed, 'I have imbibed strong prejudices against wrinkles even in my coat for fear they may next invade my face.' The early nineteenth century saw the introduction of a waist seam onto the skirted coat – called the *frock coat* – which avoided many fabric wrinkles at least.

A frock coat dating from 1915.

In addition to their skills in cutting and fitting, tailors could correct anatomical asymmetry and create a fashionable figure by means of padding. In the words of the tailor Schneider in Edward Bulwer Lytton's 1828 novel *Pelham*:

> We want a little assistance though; we must be padded well here, we must have our chest thrown out, and have an additional inch across the shoulder ... all the Gentlemen in the Life Guards are padded there, sir, we must live for effect in this world, sir. A *leetle* tighter round the waist, eh?

Satirists were contemptuous of any form of female artifice, but their pens were not nearly so strident on the subject of male suit-padding – unless it was taken to foppish extremes, such as Regency fops described as 'mere walking pincushions pinched in and laced up until he resembles an earwig'.

The fashionable shape was sculpted with layers of linen, cotton, buckram and wool, all oversewn with neat rows of stitching. The padding was generally more discreet than the fashionably vast bellies that had been created by bombast in the sixteenth century. This use of bombast – or stuffing – gave rise to the subsequent use of the word to mean inflated language. The particular use of padding varied in accordance with the currently fashionable silhouette. This could mean an inflated pouter-pigeon chest in the 1820s and 1830s, for example, or the broad shoulders – known as American Shoulders – that have rarely been out of fashion since they became prominent in 1875. In the words of a modern suit aficionado, 'any good suit has a chassis and much can be achieved to amplify the good and to hide the defective, by padding, pinching, darting and stuffing – especially around the shoulders and waist'.

It is not only men who have made the most of a suit's potential for showing oneself to best advantage. Much as we may think of the three-piece suit as a male ensemble, women have long been appropriating it, or elements of it, in their own wardrobes.

WELL-TAILORED WOMEN

Elite ladies and well-to-do women of the seventeenth century took advantage of tailoring skills for their riding suits, known as *habits*, which had a neat fit on the jacket to contrast with the long, wide skirts that were designed to cover both legs while riding side-saddle. Some people worried that this fashion blurred distinctions of gender. Samuel Pepys was not pleased to see women in riding jackets like his own: 'nobody would take them for women in any point whatever, which was an odd sight'.

One anonymous essayist warned Victorian women not to be too 'mannish' by wearing double-breasted jackets with 'the suggestiveness of a wide chest and the need of unchecked breathing'.

But some women clearly appreciated being able to adopt a more masculine style. Sarah Ponsonby and Eleanor Butler were cohabiting Welsh spinsters of the late-Georgian era, who came to be known as the Ladies of Llangollen. They were said to look 'just like two old men. They always dressed in dark cloth habits with short skirts, high shirt collars, with cravats and men's hats, with their hair cut short.' [4]

Author Radclyffe Hall controversially took suit-wearing to an extreme. Ten years before her 1928 novel *The Well of Loneliness* gave voice to the prejudice and unhappiness endured in the secret world of homosexuality, Hall was painted wearing a brown skirt and a masculine frock coat. As her confidence grew, she eschewed skirts altogether to wear only tailored trouser suits.

Tailor-made suits for women – or 'costumes' as they were also known – usually comprised a fitted jacket, a waistcoat and a long skirt. Eminent tailors such as Redfern made stylish walking suits for the bold New Woman of the 1890s onwards. Tweed was one of the favoured fabrics, and the tweed skirt suit with blouse and pearls became a standard uniform for well-bred country-women until the late twentieth century, paired with thick stockings and sturdy shoes.

4 Society eventually came to accept their upper-class eccentricity, but tailored suits only became widespread in Europe from the 1870s.

A double-breasted jacket and loosely pleated skirt suit from 1929.

Fashions in female suits changed far more dramatically than the male suit, which tended to have minor shifts in cut, colour and detailing. Suits accorded with the currently fashionable silhouette in much the same way as dresses. They were often of fluid, knitted fabrics in the 1920s and 1930s, particularly the easy-fitting knitted wool or rayon jersey made popular by Gabriel 'Coco' Chanel from the First World War onwards. Forties' suits suffered from wartime clothing constraints (more on that shortly), while suits of the Fifties seemed to upholster women rather than allowing them freedom of movement – something that came in the Sixties.

Tailoresses – the now-outmoded term for female tailors – are often overlooked in histories of costume, but they were quietly present throughout the nineteenth and twentieth centuries. Their skills were unquestionable, even if unlauded. In the tailoring trade they were noted for their abilities in handling expensive fabrics, in moulding the canvas structures of complex suits and in exquisite hand-finishing. While there were few famous tailoresses, men in the tailoring business knew a good thing when they saw one – in the 1950s royal couturier Hardy Amies approached a tailoress working at a rival fashion house. 'Did you make what you're wearing?' he asked. When she replied that she had, he offered to hire her on the spot. For the record, Amies' offer was declined, and the tailoress eventually became a hand-finisher with a Savile Row tailor.

Bold design details and a loose fit – an almost unisex look from 1971.

As we've already seen in an earlier chapter, there was great ambivalence over women wearing trousers before the later twentieth century. Therefore trouser suits were rarely seen before the 1960s. Gabrielle Chanel offered a black sequinned trouser suit for her 1937 collection, but it wasn't until Yves Saint Laurent famously designed a female tuxedo suit in 1966 that the world of couture began to take trouser suits seriously. Barbara Hulanicki, under her *Biba* label, specialised in trouser suits cut from comfortable synthetic jersey; Ossie Clark subverted the strict lines of tailoring with flower-power flowing lines and Celia Birtwell prints. It took the cracking of the 'glass ceiling' in the world of work during the 1970s and 1980s, and the notion of *power-dressing*, to give the female suit full focus as a corporate 'look'. The 1980s work suit was often in bold colours with strong shoulders, the overall cut boxy.

As for men, we now turn back in time once more to see how their suits underwent a quiet but definite revolution during Queen Victoria's reign, resulting in the generic off-the-peg two-piece *lounge suit* of the modern man.

PROPERLY SMART

The story of the lounge suit is inextricably bound up with the gradual easing of class hierarchies. By the nineteenth century the suit had become a signifier of aspiration, as well as a sign of established status. Wearing a suit was essential if one wanted to be considered respectable, and respectability was now an aspiration of working-class people too. However worn and grubby a labouring man's working suit of wool or corduroy might be, he would always have a better-quality Sunday Best suit, even if it meant swapping it for a ticket at the pawnbroker's during the working week. With the advent of affordable photography, even poorer men began to pay for studio portraits of themselves with all the accoutrements of a gentleman on display.

There was a tremendous social anxiety among working- and middle-class people about not being 'properly' dressed. The tailoring trade also put pressure on professional men to keep distinguished from those in 'trade'. Even in a limited palette of colours and styles, the suit could still speak volumes about the class and bank balance of the wearer. As the Industrial Revolution mechanised trade, so tailoring was often fragmented into unskilled sweatshop piece-work. This mass-production of suits satisfied a growing demand from the middle- and working classes, keen to dress above their allotted station.

Profiting from the proven commercial success of nineteenth-century mass-production methods, new department stores of the twentieth century offered 'off-the-peg' suits, and chain stores such as Marks & Spencer were able to lower prices while claiming to maintain quality. Hire shops quickly provided the requisites for one-off occasions – as they still do. It was all encouraging to the aspirational male, if depressing to the skilled tailor. Local tailors, tailoresses and dressmakers were once the staple of every small or middling town – but industrialisation and globalisation have almost wiped out such businesses, leaving only a few modern alterations shops in their passing.

However, even as lower classes dressed 'upwards', there was a new taste for informality trickling down ...

If one suit jacket represents elite men of Queen Victoria's reign, it is the frock coat. In dark hues with long skirts and silk-faced revers (lapels), the frock coat exuded dignity, confidence and Establishment. It also had strong links with professional men, as we'll see presently. The frock coat had battled for dominance with the tail coat at the start of the nineteenth century, winning the fight from the 1830s, after which it reigned supreme for elite men for at least another sixty years.

A typical morning coat.

However, there were rivals. Put simply – and the correct etiquette for suit-wearing in the Victorian age was anything but simple – there were three main suit styles to choose from, depending on class, time of day and occasion. On the formal front, an 1860s frock-coat style with cutaway skirts called a *morning coat* became increasingly common for business wear, leaving the full frock coat for conservative older gentlemen and state occasions. For more informal occasions, young men and working men, there was the *sack coat*. This was a shorter, looser jacket that hung from padded shoulders, rather than fitting close to the chest and waist, and was popular from the 1850s – for leisure wear, at least. Who could have predicted that the sack coat would outlast all other styles of suit? From the mid-nineteenth century it began to be known as a *lounge coat*.

The lounge coat, and indeed suit, provoked quite a controversy in the tailoring world. In 1879 the trade magazine *Tailor and Cutter* called men's suiting 'slipshod' and made despondent predictions about a future where frock coats and even morning coats would only be seen in museums, 'where they will serve to amuse a wondering and awe-stricken group of sight-seers'. Young men of the early twentieth century affecting the lounge suit might be sneered at as 'lounge lizards', with implied connotations of louche or lazy behaviour. Suits, it seems, could no longer be relied upon to act as a sound index of a man's social position. In 1925 *Tailor and Cutter* was still lamenting this apparent wave of shabbiness; perhaps the tailoring trade was worried about a decline in business as much as a decline in standards.

Welcome or not, however, the change seemed unstoppable. One of Edward VIII's first acts during his brief reign as King in 1936 was to abolish the frock coat as a court requirement. To older generations it must have seemed like the end of a more dignified age.

From a modern viewpoint, the concerns about slovenly dressing or informality are hard to appreciate, particularly when contrasted with the jeans-and-shirt culture of the present day.

Looking back, contemporary footage and photographs of the first half of the twentieth century show almost universal suit-wearing, albeit of the lounge style. Gone was the flamboyant peacocking epitomised by a spangled Prince Regent. Instead a new 'royalty', that of Hollywood, set the standard for smart dressing, from Cary Grant's superb suits in the film *North by Northwest* to Greta Garbo's minimalist outfits, Katharine Hepburn's trouser ensembles and the incomparable fit and flexibility of Fred Astaire's suits, both on and off the dance floor. Grant and Astaire were among the many famous clients of the London tailors Kilgour, French and Stanbury. Cary Grant provided his own suit for *North by Northwest* in 1959 – eight copies in fact, along with a spare bolt of matching fabric in case repairs were needed during filming. Astaire achieved an International Best Dressed List citation in 1979 as 'The best-dressed man of our time'.

This smart male suit from the 1960s has all the classic modern features: subdued hue, loose tailoring, long trousers and padded shoulders.

Perhaps the most iconic cinema suit-wearer is super-spy James Bond, who is often seen calmly straightening his cuffs a second after some daredevil high-speed escapade. Lounge

5 Amies echoed the canny approach of eighteenth-century tailors, boasting, 'I knew that a suit could be designed so as to show off an athletic body and, where there wasn't one, to suggest one.'

suits are seen on a large number of urban warriors in the film world. Commenting on the wardrobe of male characters in his hit 1992 film *Reservoir Dogs*, director Quentin Tarantino said, 'You can't put a guy in a black suit without him looking a little cooler than he already looks.' Seeing suits worn in such physical roles highlights an important aspect of modern tailoring – they are made for movement. Lounge jackets tend not to cling to the body; the sleeves are set with freedom of movement in mind.

Agent 007's rise in popularity came at a time when menswear design was beginning to be seen as part of the public fashion world, rather than a discreet masculine shopping experience. It was couturier Hardy Amies who broke with tradition by arranging the first-ever male catwalk of suits to buyers in Leeds in 1959 – the heart of suit textile manufacturing. There were fears that the sight of male models parading up and down would be considered ridiculous, and Amies reported that there was stunned silence at the end of the event. It was broken, however, by a Yorkshire shop manager exclaiming, 'By gum, we could sell these!' A second show at the Savoy hotel attracted 300 guests and was a huge success.[5]

A '~~Black~~ tie' dress suit.
WHITE

James Bond is also well known for his exquisitely tailored evening dress. The black and white evening suit – sometimes referred to as a 'penguin suit' – evolved from the eighteenth-century tail coat. It sobered throughout the nineteenth century to become a precise combination of jacket, waistcoat and leg coverings. Once a privilege of the upper classes, it was appropriated as common property by generations of non-aristocratic men after the First World War. 'White tie' called for a tail coat, starched white shirt, white waistcoat and black trousers. 'Black tie' now means a soft-fronted shirt with a fold-down collar and a lounge jacket. This ensemble came into existence in 1886, allegedly at the Tuxedo Park country club of tobacco millionaire Pierre Lorillard IV. Lorillard wore a 'bum-freezer' lounge suit with a black bow tie. It became known as the *tuxedo*, or dinner jacket – now casually shortened to DJ.

The black evening tail coat was eventually relegated to servants and waiters, which caused no small embarrassment to the Duke of Windsor when attending a formal reception in Melbourne. In his memoirs he recorded that his host, the Australian Prime Minister, 'waved a hand towards the end of the room and said to me: "That is my son." Seeing two men standing there, I signalled out the one in evening dress, and shook hands with him. He turned out to be the waiter.'

PROFESSION AND PRIDE

Now that we have established the most dominant styles of suit, it is possible to track back and see how the male suit in particular came to be so thoroughly associated with being properly turned out for work. Once it had shed the eighteenth-century associations with opulence and decadence, the muted three-piece suit was a sound choice to represent authority and professionalism. Novelist Virginia Woolf had no patience for the vanity of male ecclesiastical and military wear, but in her 1938 novel-essay *Three Guineas* she conceded that menswear could serve an important function as advertising the social, professional or intellectual standing of the wearer. The suit was very much the crux of professional costume. Before the twentieth century the professions were, with few exceptions, for men. They included medicine, politics, finance and office work.

In the world of medical practitioners there were no specialist antiseptic garments comparable to modern hospital 'scrubs' or the iconic white laboratory coat. This was because there was no germ-theory until 1861 and therefore no notion of the need for antisepsis. Doctors and surgeons simply wore their day wear – the suit. When Georgian obstetrician Dr William Smellie made home-visits with his forceps, he simply popped each arm in a separate coat pocket to avoid them clanking together! For the nineteenth-century male surgeon a dark frock coat was the norm, sometimes with needles and surgical thread thrust into the lapels ready for the operation. Oversleeves were added to the coat, along with an apron, but this was usually the only concession to hygiene, prior to the goal of total asepsis – a germ-free environment – becoming the norm in hospitals.

In law enforcement, the 'Bow Street Runners' of eighteenth-century London, and the 'Bobbies' established by Robert Peel in 1829, all wore uniform suits to distinguish them from ordinary civilians. These morphed into the iconic indigo-blue suits of Victorian and twentieth-century policemen – and, from the First World War onwards, the skirted suits of the first official policewomen.

In the realm of politics, statesmen of the nineteenth century wore black frock coats to convey a sense of gravitas and authority. This persisted among the older generations, until the infamous photograph of British Prime Minister Neville Chamberlain in his frock coat, holding aloft the 1938 Munich Agreement with Adolf Hitler, declaring 'Peace for our time'. The unfortunate associations with this image certainly did nothing to slow the frock coat's decline in popularity. When he became the first-ever Labour Prime Minister in 1924, Ramsay MacDonald was less than impressed with the official pageantry of Parliament, despite the King's advice on how new Labour

MPs could buy cheaper second-hand versions of the range of formal suits required. Even in the twenty-first century few men involved at the higher levels of modern politics would be seen out of a suit on formal occasions, although the suit in question will be a lounge suit.

Finance workers in London advertised their own version of the Establishment in black coats with pin-striped trousers. Even now, many companies emphasise corporate identity through suit-wearing. Corporate clothing expert John Molloy advised aspiring businessmen of the 1970s and 1980s on how to use a suit to succeed. He based his theories on in-depth statistical analysis of clothes and business interactions, and concluded that the suit was the garment most symbolic of the wearer's status, character and abilities: 'We are much more likely to believe, respect and obey the man who wears a suit than the man who does not.'

This association of the suit with power and professionalism has often posed problems for women entering the public sphere. Where the default costume has traditionally been male, women could be seen as outsiders or, worse, deterred altogether from taking on judicial or professional roles because they seem so much associated with a 'male' world.

The adoption of the suit was crucial for twentieth-century Western women in their fight to enter a wider range of employment. During the First World War, when women were required to replace men who had left jobs to join the services, the fashionable female suit of the era was converted for professional use. A loose-fitting jacket and A-line skirt in dark serge wool became staple uniform items for female clerical staff and transport workers. Suits were also worn by officers of the newly formed female military auxiliary services. It was still a shock for some sections of society to see the rail and road networks being staffed by suited women – 'Porters in Skirts!' shouted the headline of one *Daily Mirror* edition in 1915.

At this time there was tremendous confusion as to how women could dress professionally for their new office jobs without the loss of their perceived 'femininity'. There simply wasn't the easy option of a generic suit, as worn by their male colleagues. This would have been seen as mimicking men or, worse, denying their womanhood. This confusion still exists, to a lesser extent, in the modern world of work. There is no objective benchmark. Dress too sensibly and you may be dismissed as frumpy, unfashionable and unfeminine. Dress too attractively and you may be labelled sexually provocative and overly image-conscious. Would the modern woman eschew her trend-dependent suits for the limited styles and colours of a male suit? The blues, greys, blacks and browns each have their own distinctions, but overall male suits suggest a fear of standing out. Would Beau Brummell, such an antithesis to gaudiness, have approved? Perhaps even he would prefer to be distinguished by his quality and elegance, if not by loud colours and cuts.

The *uniformity* of the male lounge suit, once noticed, is striking. What purposes can this kind of standardisation of clothes serve? And what can it tell us indirectly about the standardisation of behaviour?

UNIFORMITY

In mass-produced, controlled form, a suit can leave the wearer looking anonymous and therefore make it easier for him or her to identify as part of a group. New styles of suit were used by the emerging twentieth-century communist movement to reject old styles representing rank and privilege, which were seen as unfair. In 1911, for example, Chinese revolutionary Dr Sun Yat-sen and his followers all dressed in a tunic/trouser suit with exactly four buttons and four pockets. It represented a direct contrast to the wealth and status portrayed by the traditional imperial family, who would be robed in many layers of impressive embroidered silk. Similar clothing upheaval was seen in the tumult of Russia's October Revolution in 1917.

The concept of uniformity was ideal for Chairman Mao

Zedong in the communist Republic of China during the 1966–7 Cultural Revolution. Regardless of rank or gender, Chinese people presented a united front in the same style of trouser-and-tunic suit. Colour-coding showed whether the wearer was a city worker, in administration or in the military. It became known as the 'Mao suit', and Mao himself is seen wearing it in his most iconic portraits. While this is a fairly extreme example, suits are clearly a strong weapon in the arsenal of political ideology. The propaganda power of uniform is often used in Western dystopian film and fiction.

Taken to extremes, a suit can strip the wearer not only of individuality, but also of dignity. Prison clothes are deliberately chosen to make the prisoner distinct from a free civilian. Historical prison suits had broad arrows and identifying numbers; modern uniforms are often highly visible orange jumpsuits, or anonymous grey suits.

During the Holocaust the suit became an enabler of genocide. In the concentration camps, clothes were used by the Nazi authorities as a deliberate method of dehumanisation. Most camp prisoners were issued with generic blue- or black-striped pyjama-style suits. Once the head was shaved, the ensemble negated all indications of profession, gender or class. Without individuality, there could be little empathy between guards and prisoners. Far from creating a group-bonding homogeneity, the uniform made it easy for guards to treat prisoners as subhuman, and therefore of little or no value.

Survivors of the camps were eager to return to civilian clothes and civilian life. One former prisoner was ashamed of a thought-less present bought by someone who hadn't endured the camp system for a relative in Israel after the Second World War. It was a pair of white-and-black-striped pyjamas. The relative gently declined the gift; the sight of the iconic suit was too emotive.

The institutional garb with perhaps the most shocking appearance is less murderous but still dramatically sinister, even if humane in intention. The straitjacket is part of a suit designed to control violent inmates, particularly in mental hospitals. A journalist at the turn of the last century described one designed for British female prisoners. It was made of coarse sacking, stamped with the broad prison arrow 'and having two deep pockets inside to receive the arms of the wearer, so that when the jacket is strapped together at the back, fitting round the neck and extending as far as the hip, the prisoner is powerless to harm anyone. If she tries to struggle there is nothing to injure her as would be the case with handcuffs.'

So suits can be used to send a number of different messages. They may be a simple statement of respectability and conformity, as in the case of the professional suit, but they can also be more extreme: communist suits promote an appearance of homogeneity; prison suits emphasise lack of status. And we have yet to consider the use of suits in the military, where they are used to denote both function and rank, to create an appearance of uniformity and to allow one to discriminate between friend and foe.

SUITS ON PARADE

Europe's professional armies evolved from mercenaries and feudal militias, whose fighting gear essentially followed the same lines as civilian clothes, with the addition of some items of body protection and identifying markers to avoid complete confusion on the battlefield - colours and ribbons were an easy way to distinguish between opposing groups.

As armies evolved into national forces under the closer control of a monarch, so more specific uniforms were designated. A particular suit showed allegiance externally and served to remind the soldiers themselves of where their loyalty lay. The general design was often dictated by the whims of the presiding royal family. Equally important was the use of a uniform to enforce discipline in the increasingly formalised drill exercises of European armies. The 1757 *New Regulations for the Prussian Infantry* stated, 'Recruits are not only taught to walk, stand, and exercise, but also to dress.'

By the eighteenth century European armies fought in versions of the frock-coat suit, often with the skirts of the coat hooked out of the way when on the march. For British troops the dominant colour was red – a bold, confident hue thought to give a psychological advantage on the battlefield. Sailors were in blue and were known as 'blue jackets', until they began wearing jumpers in 1890.

Just like civilian gentlemen, soldiers were often peacocks. Care spent on personal appearance represented an investment in the profession as well as pride in the regiment – often reinforced by a sense of heightened sexual desirability. 'I remember the time when I liked a red-coat myself very well and indeed so I still do at my heart,' declares the giddy Mrs Bennet of *Pride and Prejudice,* 'and if a smart young colonel with five or six thousand a year should want one of my girls, I shall not say nay to him.'

Edward, Prince of Wales, in his uniform as a colonel in the 10th Hussars.

As wars were fought in new territories, so military fashion acquired exotic paraphernalia, particularly in the nineteenth century. The fabric of the suit could barely be seen beneath epaulettes, medal ribbons, sashes, rank bands and other insignia. In turn, civilians took up military styles such as Hussar frogging, neat Zouave jackets or Garibaldi blouses as fashion fads. There were tensions, however, between the soldiers' urge to parade in theatrical uniforms and the need for practical kit for combat. 'Is there anyone outside a lunatic asylum who would go on a walking tour, or shoot in the backwoods or the prairies, trussed and dressed as the British soldier is?' fumed Field Marshal Wolseley in 1889. He likened the clothing of British generals to that of a dressed-up monkey on a barrel-organ.

It was nineteenth-century skirmishes by the British in India that threatened the long dominance of theatrical uniforms in combat. The Queen's Own Corps of Guides, eschewing the bright-red uniforms of regular soldiers, were issued with far more discreet Punjab-style suits, comprising smock, sheepskin jacket and pyjama trousers, all in a drab grey. Leather accessories were in a yellow shade of drab called *khaki*, from the Hindu for 'dust-coloured'. The Guides went into action in khaki in 1849 and were called the *Khaki Risala*, or Khaki Squadron – with the nickname 'the Mudlarks'.

The military grew increasingly interested in the potential of camouflage. Previously, in the eighteenth century, dark green had been used by the British in forest-fighting, but the muted shades of khaki suited a new ethos of practical soldiering in the late nineteenth century, particularly in the landscapes of Afghanistan or South Africa. Further informality came from the adoption of the Victorian gentleman's typical sportswear – a woollen *Norfolk jacket* and breeches, or trousers with puttees. The Norfolk had extra room across the shoulders, plenty of pockets and was belted for additional control.

When colours started to become muted for combat, male vanity could still be appeased by the exaggerated colours and embellishments of 'dress' uniforms for formal occasions. These expensive suits are still looped with gold, dazzling with polished metal and accessorised with feathers, leather and fur. A war-weary Virginia Woolf saw no hope for peace as long as the finest male suits of all were those of professional soldiers. She understood the crucial role that uniforms played in giving majesty to military endeavour, and, through vanity, in inducing young men to become soldiers. Out of sync with public military patriotism of the time, in 1938 she called the sight of a man in full dress uniform 'a ridiculous, a barbarous, a displeasing spectacle'.

Such is the power of uniform that, once demobilised, many servicewomen and men have found quite difficult the adjustment from a life in a uniform suit to the suits of Civvy Street. Gertrude George described the experience of being demobbed from the Women's Royal Air Force in 1919:

> And now the days of uniform were over. As a civilian outfit, with badges and buttons removed, it might still be worn, but most of its significance was gone. There was a real, if not always understood feeling of pride of uniform among the girls. More than anything else, this outward and visible sign caused realisation of forming part of a great community, banded together in a common cause.[6]

Men in particular grumbled about their 'demob' suits in the 1940s. Comedian Spike Milligan said his demob suit was the worst he'd ever had, while fellow comic Harry Secombe struggled to walk naturally in his, having to quash an urge to swing his arm as if marching. J. B. Priestley's 1945 novel *Three Men in New Suits* begins with the arrival of three demobbed servicemen in a country pub: 'The suits were blue, grey and brown; but were alike in being severely, even skimpily cut, and in being very new.' (In fact, the novel was written before the end of the war, and Priestley assumed that demobbed men would be issued with meagre Utility suits. After publication he inspected actual demob suits and declared them of excellent quality.) Government ministers feared mass discontent from the troops if they were

6 In 1918 and 1945, following the wars, quality clothing was hard to come by. This 'Wanted' ad from *Exchange and Mart* in March 1919 is by no means unusual: 'Two brothers, discharged soldiers, require suits, also coats and vests, 1 for work, one for evenings, chest 36 to 40.'

given inferior suits, but they did have to be mass-produced and finished at speed, so while they were not of the worst quality, nor were they of the best.

If uniforms can give such a great sense of community and belonging, why haven't standard suits been adopted in all areas of social life? Most Western countries have resisted the implementation of a standardised civilian suit to match the controlled ethos of military uniforms, probably due to a distrust of extreme left- or right-wing politics and the loss of individuality and individual freedom that people associate with them.

That said, the lines between military and civilian clothes have always been somewhat blurred, both for high fashion and informal occasions. Two areas in particular flag up this cross-fertilisation: suits for sportswear and school uniform.

SPORTING TYPES AND SCHOOL DAYS

The most obvious sporting suit is the riding suit, both the female and male versions. Riding is very much associated with hunting pinks – the scarlet jacket so characteristic of British rural history. Pinks were a feature of formal hunts in the nineteenth century, continuing up to the present day. There are now strict regulations concerning who is permitted to wear pinks, and also how many buttons they can sport on the riding-suit jacket. However, with riding being such an integral part of everyday life for those of the middle classes and above, riding garb was more often in everyday colours such as greens and browns.

For other sports, just as gentleman's dress codes dictated which styles and fabric were suitable for Town or Country wear, so there were rules governing which sports required which suit. From the late nineteenth century flannel suits with a *blazer* jacket became the sportswear for university athletes in particular. The blazer was a relatively informal jacket, in a short, double-breasted *reefer* style. It was said to have been the innovation of HMS *Blazer*'s Captain Wilmott, to make the ratings – non-officer-class crew – appear smarter during an inspection

1940s wartime boarding-school pupils show the lounge-suit uniform, cricket clothes... and how to wear a gas mask.

by the newly crowned Queen Victoria. It survives in the wardrobe of the conservative smart-dresser, in navy-blue serge with gilt buttons. It is also widespread in British school uniforms.

There has long been a debate over the pros and cons of school uniform. It can serve the same purpose as a military suit, providing group identity and a controllable homogeneity. Supporters assert its benefit in levelling different income brackets, although there are many stories of girls in particular being discouraged from grammar-school education in the twentieth century because of the cost of the uniform.

But despite grumblings about the obligation to wear a uniform – and the inevitable unpopularity of the colour, whatever it might be – the blazer in particular can still represent a sense of belonging, as well as a sense of achievement for those pupils of the twentieth century who were perhaps the first in the family to get a secondary education. MP Cyril Smith recalled, 'I remember my first Grammar School blazer. It came from a jumble sale – all my Mum could afford, but I was mighty proud to wear it.'

In some cultures uniform actually provides a link between education and the military. All Japanese high-school pupils are required to wear the same school uniform – a skirted sailor suit for the girls and Prussian military-style jacket and trousers for the boys. How appropriate or moral it is to prime children in this way must be left to the reader to decide.

SUBVERSIVE SUITS

Suits have often been taken to extremes in history, such as in the flamboyance of eighteenth-century dazzlers known as *Macaronis* or the plaid-legged *Mashers* of the mid-nineteenth century. Macaronis and Mashers were both types of male dandies, peacocking exaggerated suit styles in defiance of contemporary opinion. They took a norm and elaborated on it to such an extent that it seemed to mock more conservative clothing. Sometimes such exaggerations are simply ridiculed by others. But sometimes they are seen as a usurpation of the status quo and even as a wilful rejection of mainstream society.

By 1943 one particular style of nonconformist suit was considered so inflammatory that it led to racial persecution and city riots in the United States. This was the splendidly arrogant 'zoot' suit of African-American and Mexican-American young men. They chose to emphasise a non-subservient difference from the Caucasian 'norm' through a suit that defied the US government's wartime Limitation Orders of clothing, which favoured clothes made from reduced amounts of fabric. The defiant zoot suit had bold shoulder pads, almost knee-length jackets and voluminous trouser legs and was both emboldening and provocative to wear.

Ralph Ellison described three young men in zoot suits ' . . . walking slowly, their shoulders swaying, their legs swinging from their hips in trousers that ballooned upward from cuffs fitting snug about their ankles; their coats long and hip-tight with shoulders far too broad to be those of natural western men'. Radical black activist Malcolm X had strong memories of buying his first zoot suit in 1940, aged fifteen:

I was measured, and the young salesman picked off a rack a zoot suit that was just wild, sky-blue pants thirty inches in the knee and angle narrowed down to twelve inches at the bottom, and a long coat that pinched my waist and flared out below my knees.

Some white American servicemen considered the suits an insult to patriotism. Fuelled by racism, conflicts broke out in Los Angeles and soon spread along the Pacific coast, then to other US cities. They were known as the Zoot Suit Riots. Despite pleas for tolerance, men wearing the suits were stripped in public and even arrested. To add to their humiliation, their suits might then be urinated on or burnt.

On a less aggressive note, the zoot suit made it into mainstream musical history when it was worn by legendary jazz singer Cab Calloway in the 1943 musical film *Stormy Weather*.

The magnificent zoot suit worn by singer Cab Calloway.

The zoot suit crossed the Atlantic in the 1940s, and photographs show black men and women from the time looking stylish and confident. Zoot suits were also an inspiration for young people in Occupied France known as *Zazous*, who flaunted long, checked lumber jackets, despite rationing and restrictions. The disapproval generated by Zazous was relatively mild compared to the clampdown on similar young hipsters in Hitler's Germany. Here, *Swingkinder* – Swing Kids – were not only attacked for their Anglophile suits and their love of non-Aryan jazz music, but were actively persecuted in concentration camps, on the orders of Heinrich Himmler, who wanted this supposed degeneracy wiped out.

Post-war Britain saw a revival of Edwardian-style suits as an expression of young men rebelling against class constraints and mainstream culture. In contrast to the wide padded shoulders of the late Forties – dubbed 'American' shoulders, and associated with 'Spiv' black-market dealers – working-class lads saved up to buy slim-cut suits with sleeves down to the knuckles, brash waistcoats and tapered trousers. In 1953 a *Daily Express* headline shortened Edwardian to Teddy, and the term Teddy Boy was born. Dressed with great attention to detail, the Teddy Boys defied the norm and peacocked in unlikely urban environments. Their suits were one of several trends to make headlines in the Fifties and Sixties as their generation, who had grown up during the war, clashed with the generations who had fought through it. A strong economy with plenty of jobs meant that young people had spending power to help fuel their rejection of what had gone before.

As seen with the Teddy Boys, fashion innovated by using the past, as well as by scorning it. When the Beatles first made their mark on the music scene their image was created around suits with a distinctive gloss and modern Nehru collar. However, the iconic 1967 album cover for *Sgt Pepper's Lonely Hearts Club Band* depicted the Beatles as pseudo-Edwardians, in military-band-style suits. Surplus uniforms saturated the second-hand clothing market at this time and were eagerly taken up and customised by young people flocking to London stores such as I Was Lord Kitchener's Valet.

DRAMA AND DETAILS

Having seen how suits can be both conformist and rebellious, it's interesting to note how a broad relaxation of social conventions in the later twentieth century was reflected in street styles of the male suit. From the late Sixties onwards, fashionable suits from a mad dressing-up box of styles competed with conservative corporate suits. Non-mainstream suits were full of drama. Tartan fever followed the fame of Scottish band the Bay City Rollers. Glam-rock brought glitz and dazzle. Disco gave the sharp suit of *Saturday Night Fever*. Hippy-style suits revelled in an orgy of global cultural appropriation: Oriental, Native American, Indian, Inuit, Afghani . . .

And yet, through all the flamboyance, classic style survived as a norm. The size and shape of shoulders, lapels or pockets might change; the quality might veer from cheap and shiny to ultra-expensive; but the modern wardrobe still usually relies on sensible suits as a basis for presenting a professional image, or for group identification.

Several details of the modern suit owe their ancestry to points of pattern-cutting or etiquette in the past. Suit-jacket sleeves have been cut straight, on the curve; with cuffs or without; set with a shoulder seam or Raglan-style. Men's suit sleeves have never been short, regardless of season or temperature.[7] In the eighteenth century they were folded back into vast wings of fabric at the wrist; in the 1980s 'cool' men wore their sleeves pushed up, in a style immortalised by the costumes of the US TV series *Miami Vice*, as well as by New Romantic musicians such as British group Duran Duran. If the 1980s jacket didn't already have sleeves stitched back – revealing a neat colour-coordinated lining – the wearer might struggle to keep them shoved up the arm in this style. Scriptwriter and presenter Denis Norden resorted to using dabs of Superglue under each elbow

7 The habit of tucking a handkerchief in the jacket sleeve supposedly dates back to the Boer War. In *The Adventure of the Crooked Man*, Sherlock Holmes criticises his companion Dr Watson for this military habit: 'You'll never pass as a pure-bred civilian as long as you keep that habit of carrying your handkerchief in your sleeve.'

to hold the sleeves up. 'There are still little bald patches among the fine hairs on my forearms,' he confessed – caused by him absent-mindedly pulling off his glued-on jacket!

Aside from these variations, modern sleeves are dull tubes enlivened only by discreet rows of buttons at the cuff. These generally match the colour of the suit and are purely a decorative detail, despite the popular story that they were meant to deter naval midshipmen – in slang terms, *Snotties* – from wiping their noses on their sleeves. It's surprising how many ornamental buttons there can be on suit jackets.[8] The pair of buttons on the back of a morning coat, where the side seams meet the waist seams, are a vestige of seventeenth-century ornamental coat-skirt buttons. As for the *buttonhole*, this refers to the practice of wearing a fresh posy or sprig in the suit, for decoration and perfume. Originally the flower was tucked into the top button-hole of the jacket. From the 1840s on, a special flower-hole was cut into the top of the left lapel.

Rarely, suit jackets have buttoned pockets. During the Second World War, when there were government restrictions on the numbers of suit pockets and buttons, often there were pocket flaps with no pockets beneath, to save on fabric. These sham pockets have a long tradition, dating back to the mid-eighteenth-century, when less was not always more, and so numerous pockets added to the flamboyance of the outfit. Unlike the female tailored suit, which usually only permits false flaps to break the line, men have always benefited from a multitude of genuine pockets. These include slit pockets, scallops and flaps; also internal breast-pockets and 'poacher's pockets' in coat tails. The advent of railway travel gave rise to a ticket-pocket on the right-hand side of the coat.

One button that custom now dictates should remain undone is found on the third piece of the traditional suit – the waistcoat. The tradition of undoing the end button on single-breasted day waistcoats did not begin with King Edward VIII, but he certainly popularised it. Nineteenth-century studio portraits show waist-coat buttons straining and gaping across many well-filled torsos.

8 Buttons on military uniforms can denote details such as regiment and rank. Military cuff buttons have been used to identify human remains uncovered at battlefield sites from the First World War. Most uniform buttons were of brass or other copper alloys. Once they begin corroding, the verdigris (a green patina caused by oxidisation) is toxic to bacteria, which means that fragments of fabric surrounding the button may be partially protected from decay, even after a century in the mud of the Somme.

Edwardian collarless cotton shirts.

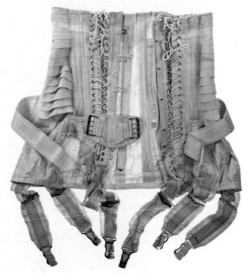

Boning, lacing, buckles and
suspenders – an early 1920s corset.

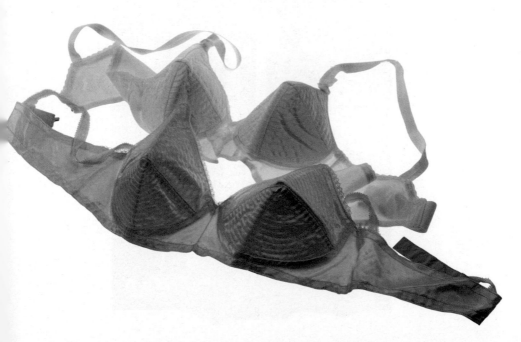

1940s 'bullet' bras with whirlpool stitching.

'Walking' dresses from 1849.

Nylon glamour from 1953.

1960s evening wear – shirt, collar, tie and jacket for him, structured dress and gloves for her.

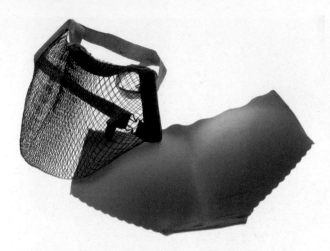

An 1880s wire bustle cage... and a 2015 pair of buttock-enhancing knickers.

A dramatic modern revival of cloaks – the 1980s.

The seventeenth-century male suit – breeches, stockings and skirted coats.

The modern suit in the making – an 1830s gentleman.

A mid-nineteenth century young boy's wool dress – very different from the clothes of modern male toddlers.

Slacks and a skirt from 1947, when trousers were still a rarity for women.

Exquisite early Victorian silk evening slippers.

A modern four-inch heel stiletto shoe... and a
twentieth-century four-inch-long 'lotus' shoe.

The famous Fair Isle knitting design.

A nineteenth-century hanging pocket
and red miser's purse, and 1940s
silver reticule.

A unisex knitted swimsuit
from the 1930s, with skirted
modesty panel.

Bonnet extravagance,
from 1828.

Gloves for townwear, warmth, evening and
motoring, plus some bone glove-stretchers.

Ready for bed in the 1950s – a man's flannel night-
dress, pyjama case and folding leather slippers.

The waistcoat was first known as a vest, and it retains this name in North America. Originally it was worn for warmth as a male undergarment and it could be quite plain. Doubling up on waistcoats wasn't uncommon. Flannel waistcoats were favoured for keeping cosy, but deplored by some as a sign of decrepitude. In Jane Austen's 1811 novel *Sense and Sensibility* young Marianne declares 'with me a flannel waistcoat is invariably connected with the aches, cramps and rheumatisms, and every species of ailment that can afflict the old and the feeble'. In this instance, sixteen-year-old Marianne is referring to Colonel Brandon, who is a mere thirty-five years old – ancient in her eyes.

A smart wool waistcoat from the 1920s. Still a classic today.

One of the earliest surviving waistcoats is a light-blue knitted vest with thirteen small buttons believed to have been worn by King Charles I when he was executed in January 1649, and to have been preserved by his physician Dr Hobbs. The King was said to have needed the extra layer of warmth in case shivering was misconstrued as fear.

Subtle styles were rejected once fashion replaced the doublet with the coat; the coat edges were drawn back to reveal a matching waistcoat in the same silk or wool as the rest of the suit. Such was the expense of fine fabric at this time that the unseen back section of the waistcoat was commonly of a plain cotton or linen, and so was known as a 'chate' or cheat. The front, however, had prime peacocking potential. Embroidered waistcoat fronts marked an aristocratic garment, or a wedding waistcoat. In general men were less likely to attach sentimental value to their clothes, or to hold onto them beyond usefulness, but wedding waistcoats are an exception, and they would have been saved because of their special value and fine quality.

Sometimes the waistcoat fabric matched the suit; at other times it was a gaudy contrast of pattern and colour. The cut and length followed fashion, sweeping low over the thighs in the eighteenth century, rising high on the chest in the era of Beau Brummell (to draw attention to the groin and legs) or settling neatly at waist level in the twentieth century. Upright collars, revers, shawl collars or collarless designs were also a matter for taste or trends.[9]

In the nineteenth century the waistcoat expanse was perfect for displaying a watch chain and fob, with the watch tucked into a handy watch pocket. It had the added advantages of hiding the braces – not something to be seen in polite society – as well as covering a possibly shabby shirt front. The waistcoat itself was tensioned to fit at the back with lacings or a strap and buckle; the latter style survives in modern garments. Being so close to the skin-covering shirt, waistcoats did suffer from sweat damage, one of the excretions known euphemistically at this time as 'body oils'. To avoid staining and damage in 1817, George, the Prince Regent, had underarm protectors sewn into a white waistcoat.

Leather waistcoats served a more protective purpose for factory or agricultural labourers. Railway porters and ostlers liked long-sleeved vests. The most extreme protection of all comes from a bullet-proof vest. One might have saved the life of Archduke Franz Ferdinand in Sarajevo in 1914. The waistcoat he was wearing was not made of Kevlar – invented in 1964 by DuPont researcher Stephanie Kwolek – but of layered silk, and was intended for the Archduke to wear on public occasions, due to the high risk of attack. Recent research at the Royal Armouries National Firearms Centre suggests that the sixteen layers of fine silk and cotton would have stopped penetration by bullets fired from a 1910 Browning semi-automatic pistol – the weapon used by assassin Gavrilo Princip on that fateful day. One might speculate that the waistcoat could have averted the First World War (or at least postponed it until another flashpoint) but, sadly, the Archduke was not wearing it when Princip fired. The Archduchess Sophie did not have the option, and her death is often treated as mere collateral damage in the history books.

For extra warmth and comfort, waistcoats could be knitted. Gradually knitwear came to replace waistcoats for casual and semi-casual wear. The adoption of this more informal style was prominent in the 1930s, when suits were matched with tank tops, sweaters and cardigans. A ban on 'Utility' suits having a waistcoat during the Second World War hastened the demise of the three-piece suit for all but latterday dandies and evening wear. The waistcoat is occasionally seen without a suit, as with street styles of the Eighties, which saw both men and women wearing waistcoats with a T-shirt and jeans. More recently, the waistcoat and T-shirt combination has been taken up by hipsters looking to add a touch of tailoring to their mostly casual style.

FUTURE SUITS

What of the future of the suit? Certainly its dominance has been challenged by leisure wear and sportswear in recent decades – called 'Freedom Clothes' by Hardy Amies. The latest incarnation of a suit for leisure is the *shell suit* of the 1980s and 1990s – a close relative of the tracksuit – rather unkindly described by one well-dressed man as 'a uniform for the kind of people whose main sporting interest is shouting obscenities at police vans outside courtrooms'. The venom and snobbery behind this comment say much about the perceived low status of the shell suit specifically. This is not a universal opinion: expensive tracksuits are now frequently worn by high-profile music artistes, and they clearly have credibility among athletes worldwide.

A light-hearted prediction from 1893 of how men's suits would look in 1978.

Predictions of future fashion are heavily biased towards prevalent taste and culture. An 1893 satirical article in the *Strand Magazine* forecast doublets, flares and flamboyant suits for the twentieth century, some of which are uncannily echoed in glam-rock stage outfits; and the last century saw future suits as being space-orientated. At the 1939 New York World's Fair the predictions for menswear in the year 2000 focused on an air-conditioned one-piece 'Solosuit' with antennae in the hat. Conversely women were predicted to wear diaphanous aluminium suits with an electrical headdress to illuminate the face. The 1960s latched onto the post-Sputnik zeitgeist with couture spacewear by Pierre

Cardin that featured space-helmet hats and white suits cut in a science-fiction style. Lurex and Lycra fabrics gave these 'Space Age' suits a truly futuristic look. They were promptly followed by the deliberate contrast of hippy suits featuring natural fibres, clashing colours, fur, fringing and beads.

Some of the most visible dapper-dressers of today are male footballers, who spend their professional time in sportswear, but show team identification off-pitch in very up-to-date suits. This is a trend pioneered by footballer David Beckham, no stranger to the world of fashion. It coincided with a drive to make football a more prestigious sport, moving away from associations with hooliganism and unruly stadiums.

The modern suit is cut for comfort, not to correct the figure. For formal occasions the suit still dominates: at weddings, many grooms and attendants hire morning-coat suits or else wear three-piece suits. Suits in sombre colours haven't yet been ousted as the standard clothing for funerals and memorial services, in spite of contemporary trends towards colours and informality. And in many workplaces the suit is still the standard way to show seriousness and professionalism. Until a more convincing status-garment evolves, the suit – with all its implications – remains an important option in the modern wardrobe.

TIE RACK

Show me a man's ties and I'll tell you who he is or who he is trying to be...

JOHN T. MOLLOY, *THE NEW DRESS FOR SUCCESS*, 1988

CHIN UP

1980s clothing guru John T. Molloy rated the tie as *the* most important status symbol. It's a small accessory that has survived many incarnations. It has been rejected by many, yet is worn by others as an unquestionable necessity. It has a range of symbolic gestures associated with it: the straightening of a child's tie on their first day of big school, the loosening of a collar after a hard day at work, the fingering of a tie end when nervous.

The history of the neckcloth charts the rise of collars – and the rising aspirations of lower classes. Ties can emphasise stability or signify subversion. Expressive or repressive, they are Old School or New Man and, indeed, New Woman.

Dressed for leisure in 1934 – but still in collar and tie.

The straightforward flat tie worn by modern men in a standardised knot around the neck has remarkable ancestors. It's quite an eye-opener to compare the tie *now* with the various ruffs, scarves and ribbons that preceded it. The tie's earliest origin dates back to the Renaissance, when it wasn't enough to have the throat and neck merely covered by costume, for neck fabric had to be flaunted.

As a young princess in the 1820s, Queen Victoria was reputed to have had a piece of holly pinned under her chin by her governess, Baroness Lehzen, to deter her from drooping her chin. Advocates of extreme neckwear in the sixteenth century needed no such contrivance. Their chins were up, whether they liked it or not; men and women attained a fashionably haughty demeanour by surrounding their neck with prodigious ruffles, which protruded out in a many-layered textile cascade, known, for the sake of brevity, as a ruff.

The Elizabethan ruff was an exquisite masterpiece of pleating and starching.

Woe betide anyone whose ruff was limp. In the 1580s acerbic observer Philip Stubbes said such absurd ruffs would 'goe flip flap in the winde like ragges' or lie on the shoulders like 'the dishcloute of a slut'. To avoid such a slovenly effect, a ruff could be displayed on a padded foundation or wired scaffolding called a *supportasse*. For extra magnificence, the edges of the ruffs might have pointed lace known as *piccadilla*, after the Latin *pica* for spike or spear. Piccadilla Hall was a popular London depot for this style of lace and supposedly gave its name to the street of Piccadilly.

Starch – called the *Devil's Liquor* by its critics – was the best method for achieving a crisp look on the ruff. In 1582 it was reported that one Belgian woman grew so incensed that her laundress hadn't starched her ruffs properly that she trampled on them and wished 'that the deuill might take her when shee wore any of those neckchers agayne'. According to the report, which is clearly a moralistic urban legend, the devil obligingly appeared disguised as a young lover and strangled her to death, leaving an ugly bruised corpse, which some no doubt saw as a fitting punishment for her pride and vanity. In addition to being starched, ruff pleats had to be reset with heated poking sticks, or pressed with small gophering irons, making them expensive to maintain as well as awkward. Neither aspect deterred the wearers, presumably because they delegated the job to menials and enjoyed the implicit superiority of such conspicuous consumption.

When the flamboyance of the ruff was discarded in the eighteenth century, it was set to be replaced by neckwear that was comparatively discreet but far more uncomfortable – the *stock*. Although some elite women wore stocks when out riding, such neckwear was overwhelmingly a male fashion. Stocks were stiff, high collars, originally worn by German and French infantry. They were simple and formal, perfectly suited to express the hauteur and detail fetishism of both professional soldiers and well-dressed civilian gentlemen. Great creativity was shown in stiffening stock fabric to achieve the right effect. Horsehair and pig bristle competed with stocks that were simply made of card or wood covered in cloth. The collar *à la guillotine* was stiffened with whalebone to achieve terrifying heights of discomfort. Slips of wood could also be inserted as extra stiffening, which was said to have caused 'the eyes almost to start from their spheres, and gave the wearer a supernatural appearance'.

Stocks were fastened by clips or buckles at the back of the

neck. When these were tightened it produced a ruddy complexion, supposedly the look of a healthy, virile man. Throats were rasped by pasteboard stocks, and heads were held so erect that the whole body had to be turned if the wearer wished to look anywhere but straight ahead. It was suggested by the anonymous author of the mildly satirical 1818 work *Neckclothitania* that men would need revolving seats like music stools to gaze around them. The author philosophised, '... what an apparent superiority does not a Starcher give to a man? It gives him a look of hauteur and greatness.'

Following the stock came the craze for *cravats* so elaborate they required the services of a patient valet and a hard-working laundress. Cravats can come in many forms, but started life as fluid scarf-shaped accessories. The first cravats are widely supposed to have been introduced to France and England by dashing Croatian mercenaries in the early seventeenth century, but there are other less romantic etymologies that suggest mangled forms of Turkish and Hungarian words – *kyrabacs* and *korbacs* – both of which mean a long, slender object. The French *cravache*, or horsewhip, is another source given for the English term 'cravat'.

Beau Brummell was famously exacting about his cravats. His valet had previously worked for one Colonel Kelly, a man so vain he had burnt to death trying to rescue his favourite boots from a fire. Visitors waiting for Brummell to appear one morning spotted the valet carrying mounds of white linen. The valet responded to their queries, 'Oh, these, sir? These are our failures.'

While dressing for battle at Waterloo in June 1815, Napoleon reportedly discarded his customary black stock to emulate the Duke of Wellington's white cravat. It was not a lucky choice. After Napoleon's defeat, a languorous cravat named the 'Napoleon' was recommended in a violet colour. This was owing to the nineteenth-century *language of flowers* – an informal dictionary in which flora were categorised as representing a specific attribute or emotion. Napoleon's flower was the violet because it grew from obscurity and its scent lingered after dark.

The fashionable Georgian gentleman had an array of cravat styles to choose from, assessed with gentle irony by a spate of specialists during the height of the cravat cult. *Neckclothitania* listed a variety of tie-tying styles, including the *Irish*, the *Nabob* and the *Horse Collar Tie*, which, the author complained, 'has become, from some unaccountable reason, very universal. I can only attribute it to the inability of its wearers to make any other.'

Cravat display became an art. One of the more exacting styles was the *Oriental*. This was so rigid that, according to *Neckclothitania*, one very tall gentleman was reportedly unable to bend his neck enough to avoid the tripping hazard of an elderly aunt, with the result that he was precipitated headlong into the lap of an old dowager, who then spilt a jug of water onto a nearby baron who was, at that instant, assiduously occupied in picking up her pocket handkerchief. It was at least advised that, in the case of apoplexy or illness, 'it is requisite to loosen or even remove the Cravat immediately'.

The *Mathematical*, having only three creases, was considered less severe and, according to expert opinion, 'This tie does not occasion many accidents.' The *Waterfall* needed a very large neckcloth and was worn 'by all stage-coachmen, guards, the *swells of the fancy* and Ruffians' as well as by the well-dressed heroes of Georgette Heyer's well-loved historical romance novels, written between the 1920s and 1970s and still in print today.[1]

High collars and tight neckcloths were by no means discarded with Brummell's decline and demise in 1840. In 1885 a clothing expert warned that tight collars and cravats could cause headaches, apoplexy and death. And as late as 1917 excessive neck constriction was linked to deafness, tetanus and sudden death.

Contemporary with the rise of the fashionable collar was a far more degrading custom – the revolting practice of enslaved black people in Britain having a close-fitting metal collar of brass, copper or silver riveted around their neck. This would be engraved with the so-called owner's details – name, address, coat of arms – in case of abscondment. King William III saw no shame in displaying a marble bust of his favourite slave at Hampton Court, complete with a very lifelike padlocked marble collar.

LOVE OF LUXURY

Neckcloths were yet another way of displaying wealth through costume, both in the textiles used and in the messages they conveyed. For example, even the apparent simplicity of a snowy-white cotton muslin around the neck could only be achieved thanks to expenditure on frequent laundering. Thus a fresh neckcloth meant healthy finances or, in the case of aristocrats with mortgaged estates and overspent incomes, the ability to defer bill-payment.

Laundry was done in batches, and multiple cravats would represent a significant expenditure in this regard. The laundry list of a German prince visiting Georgian London included no fewer than thirty neck kerchiefs, while one portable cravat wardrobe for the travelling gentleman at this time contained at least a dozen each of plain white, striped/spotted and coloured cravats; also three dozen shirt collars, two whalebone stiffeners, two black silk cravats and a small iron.

Add to this the disposable income required to purchase the textiles involved, and neckwear really does get expensive. The ruffs of wealthy Elizabethan women were made of fine cottons, but then embroidered with gold and silver designs or embellished with extraordinarily expensive lace. Such ruffs were, as the *Anatomie of Abuses* put it in 1583, 'speckeled and sparkeled here and there with the sunne, the mone, the stares and many other antiques strange to beholde'.

As men's hair lengthened in the seventeenth century, so their ruffs collapsed into wings or cascades of lace over their shoulders and down their chests. The most fashionable French and Venetian laces were outrageously pricey and were worn at court by the monarch and the richest aristocrats. Charles II spent more than twenty pounds on one lace cravat; James II spent more than thirty-six pounds on a Venetian lace cravat. In modern terms this equates to more than £1,500 for the first cravat and more than £3,100 for the second. The effigy of Charles II in Westminster Abbey sported a lace cravat fully thirty-four inches wide. Specialist laces such as Mechlin and Valenciennes were lush with designs of roses, lilies, carnations and fruit blossoms. On his imperial coronation, Napoleon went so far as to sport a rather anachronistic lace *jabot*, for maximum peacocking.[2]

After lace came the tyranny of pure-white neckcloths, but colours were not completely forgotten. In the early nineteenth century the splendidly attired Count d'Orsay wore cravats in sky-blue, sea-green and primrose-yellow. By the 1880s gentlemen could flaunt their wealth and their eye for colour with the wide-ended Ascot cravat, which has survived to this day, generally in acrylic-mix fabric, worn with morning suits as part of a hired wedding ensemble. As the wheel of fashion turned, instead of lace or white cottons and linens, silk came to dominate good-quality neckwear, particularly in the form of the now-ubiquitous *tie*.

Modern ties are a foil for sombre suits and a discreet way to advertise wealth, status and taste without appearing too foppish. They are a direct descendant of the slender ties with a neat knot at the throat, worn by Victorian gentlemen. The nineteenth century slowly saw a shift from cravats to the sort of ties a modern man might recognise: the *Royal Albert* tie of the mid-century, for example, was long and slim. It was a slow change, linked with shifting portrayals of masculinity through clothes. As Queen Victoria's reign reached its zenith there were those who shied away from tartan trousers, florid cravats and floral waistcoats, and these men found gravitas in darker colours, tighter collars and plainer neckwear.

Construction of the tie as we know it only came about in the 1920s, when tie-specialist Jesse Langsdorf patented a tie cut in three pieces on the bias, to maximise elasticity and longevity and to minimise creasing. The narrow width of fabric might not have displayed as much wealth as the giant ruffs or lace cravats, but luxury could still be indulged in, particularly with silk ties.

Twentieth-century shoppers took up artificial fabrics such as rayon, then nylon; silk manufacturers retaliated by promoting silk neckwear in Jacquard-woven designs or rich foulards. English silks – from Macclesfield and Spitalfields – had a superb international reputation, both hand-woven and, increasingly, machine-woven. Designer Hardy Amies ordered men's silk ties with silk linings to sell in his new boutique in 1953, calling them 'the most luxurious form of neckwear existing in my lifetime'. He loved the contrast of light-reflecting silk against a suit's muted colours. Before Amies, key names in art and fashion, such as Pablo Picasso, Jean Patou, Jacques Fath and the immortal Elsa Schiaparelli, had created luxury silk ties for high-end buyers, recognising that people will pay for the name on an item, as well as for its actual quality. Paul Smith, Pierre Cardin, Hermès and Yves Saint Laurent were not slow to follow. The silk tie remains one of the signifiers of a well-dressed, wealthy man.

SNOBS AND SWEATSHOPS

As we've seen again and again, one of the purposes of conspicuous consumption in fashion is to create distinctions between different strata of society. Neckcloths and ties have their own part in this categorisation. As middle- and working-class men began to adopt neckwear of one form or another, there was a very real risk of mistaking a *man* for a *gentleman* because of his clothes – and because of his neckwear. The 1818 essay *Neckclothitania* poked fun at the anxiety provoked by the 'monstrous and unnatural' supposition that all men are equal. This may have been a gentle satire, but it touched a nerve with some, when it described 'the aping attempts of the lower orders and shabby genteels to appear accoutred as their superiors'. In this case *equal* signified aspiring to greater status. Ten years on, *The Art of Tying a Cravat* highlighted the crucial role that a cravat played in signifying status on a man of rank making his *entrée* into society: 'Should this, unfortunately, not be correctly or elegantly put on – no further notice will be taken of him.'

3 Popular from the
nineteenth century
onwards, the *bow tie*
is a relative newcomer
on the neckwear
scene. It is a slender,
shaped tie, requiring
nifty fingers to
fasten . . . or the
'cheat' of a pre-tied
bow.

Ties and collars, associated as they initially were with the higher echelons of society, conferred dignity even to those whose lives were anything but luxurious. Charles Dickens' 1843 novel *A Christmas Carol* features a vignette of life in the impoverished Cratchit household at Christmas. It's a small detail, but very charming, that when Bob loans his young son Peter a proper shirt collar in honour of the day, Peter 'rejoiced to find himself so gallantly attired, and yearned to show his linen in the fashionable Parks'. Instead Peter remained with the family for Christmas dinner and promptly got the corners of the shirt collar stuck in his mouth as he plunged a fork into a saucepan of potatoes.

As the nineteenth century progressed, tie etiquette actually consolidated to create socially intricate requirements for any fellow wishing to dress as a gentleman. Manufacturing advances due to the Industrial Revolution, and changes in high-street shopping, meant that those wishing to emulate their betters had access to inferior versions of fashionable styles. 1864 saw a patent for a mass-market pre-tied tie, to avoid the sartorial embarrassment of being badly turned out. Snobs despised it; sweatshop workers wrecked their health producing it. And superior gentlemen's outfitters shuddered when middle-class men took to wearing evening suits with – oh, horror! – *ready-made* bow ties.[3]

The bow tie in 1920.

There were pitfalls to this sort of economical social posturing. The character Mr Pooter in the classic novel *Diary of a Nobody* suffers cringing social embarrassment when his patent pre-tied black bow falls from a theatre box into the pit, where it is trampled and lost. 'To hide the absence of the tie,' confessed Mr Pooter, 'I had to keep my chin down for the rest of the evening, which caused a pain at the back of my neck.'

The names of popular Edwardian tie shapes – the *Marquis*, the *Baron* and the *Crown* – certainly reflected a bourgeois desire for prestige and privilege. Middle-class men could even aspire to collars entitled *Emperor* or *Imperial*. One style, the *Premier*, reached a towering two and five-eighths inches at the back of the neck. The impulse to show dignity was, fortunately, balanced by a continued need for practicality; ties on sale in mail-order catalogues at this time were advertised as 'easily tied', 'easily fixed and always retains its shapes' or 'ready tied with band to slip round the neck'.

For those ruled by economy, good-quality silks were mimicked by silks 'weighted' with tin salts and starches to appear of far better quality than they actually were. Paper or celluloid collars were substitutes for fine linen. Wearing detachable collars meant a reduced laundry bill, because this meant the thrifty man need only pay for his collars to be washed, and not the whole shirt.[4] To save money men were advised to prolong the life of a tie by lying it flat when not in use, or by hanging it over a string fixed on the inside of a wardrobe. Worn ties were cut down to make shorter, smaller ones for sons. Thrift even extended as far as cutting ties into patches for quilted bedspreads.

Few styles of tie now survive from the innumerable historical variations in cut, cloth, colour and knot. They have been reduced to four or five, at best. The most common modern tie is generally knotted using the four-in-hand method, named after a Georgian gentlemen's carriage club. The knot is also known as the Derby or the Oxford. It has a dimple below the knot where a tie-pin may nestle. Some prefer the fatter Windsor knot,

4 The savvy shopper in 1915 could take advantage of waterproof celluloid collars, prestigiously named *Military* or *Sterling*, on sale in the Civil Service Association Catalogue and at the Army & Navy Stores for only 5½ d each. They could be cleaned with a damp sponge.

although this was once said to be the mark of a bounder. It pre-dates the Duke of Windsor – who didn't care for it – and also the claim of Jermyn Street outfitters Hawes & Curtis that they invented it in 1913.

Regardless of where it was bought and what it was made of, in the early years of the twentieth century the tight tie and the formal collar reigned supreme. Today, expectations have relaxed to the point where it is exceptional for someone to choose to wear a tie as part of their everyday outfit outside formal or professional contexts, although elderly men may still feel undressed with an open, tie-less collar.

Ties for *women* have even more complex associations.

APING THE MEN

Social rules were tested not only when men of the lower classes began donning smart neckwear, but, more egregiously, when women wanted a shirt and tie also.

Since the seventeenth century women had worn stiff collars and cravats for riding, as befitted the more formal, tailored nature of their riding habits. For less-specialist use in daily fashions, women's neckwear was softer, prettier, more 'feminine' in style. In the nineteenth century women made or bought detachable, decorative collars – *collarettes* – in fashionable fabrics, shapes and sizes, which could be worn with a variety of different bodices. As well as being attractive, these collars gave welcome variety to a limited wardrobe and were also practical, in that they sat between neck and bodice, thereby protecting the latter from sweat and dirt. Collarettes were 'of the utmost value in freshening up a somewhat démodée gown and in setting off a pretty face,' declared *Cartwright's Lady's Companion* in 1897. Home-made collarettes of gauze, lace, muslin, chiffon or velvet could be copied from fashion plates or shop displays and created at home, to save dipping into the dress allowance. Bows of ribbon, silk or cotton thread could be added to the collar for an additional dainty touch.

This female cyclist from the 1890s looks smart – if stiff – in a starched collar and tie and a tailored cycling suit.

Propriety dictated how much neck-flesh was to be covered each season; fashionable whims dictated how stiff or soft the collars. Certainly the throat or bosom was not to be uncovered before the hour of dinner. As women fought for greater social freedoms and access to education in the late nineteenth century, a trend for tailored suits and 'masculine' style reflected the need to be taken seriously and to dress decisively. By 1900 the 'Gibson Girl' look dominated the popular media. With her crisp white shirt, stiff collar and dark tie, the Gibson Girl – named after the artwork of Charles Dana Gibson – was often portrayed as bigger and bolder than the surrounding males. Ladies' linen collars as high as two and a half inches had noble female names such as *Princess*, *Gertrude*, *Edith* and *Florence*.

Florence Nightingale and other medical pioneers recognised the links between formal collars and an image of professionalism – hence the long decades of female nurses in starched detachable collars. When British nurse Edith Cavell was executed as a spy in Belgium in the First World War, the photograph most widely

5 The Edwardian
Vorwerk collar-
stiffener advertised its
attractions: 'A woven
collar band by the
yard for dresses,
jackets etc. Much
superior to ordinary
buckram. Perfectly
shaped. Ready for
use. Fast edges. In
black, white, drab,
slate 1½ to 4ins wide.'

circulated showed her in a striped cotton blouse, stiff collar and fabulous broad-ended cravat. Queen Alexandra was another significant influence in the Edwardian era. She favoured high collars because of scarring on her neck, which she considered disfiguring. Such collars were supported by spirals of steel and bands of buckram stiffener.[5]

Contrasting with this stiff masculine style, women also decorated their necks in long wisps of cambric, chiffon and lace – in homage to Classical drapery. Regency ladies had used these to complement the long lines of their high-waisted gowns; Edwardian women rediscovered them, to much the same effect. The stylish neck scarf was also ideal to showcase the streamlined designs of the Art Deco era. In direct opposition to formal male ties, these decorative neck scarves were flimsy and flamboyant. They were also potentially fatal. Outré dancer Isadora Duncan had worn long scarves all her life and in 1927, aged fifty, had lost none of her flair for the dramatic. Setting off for a test drive along the Promenade des Anglais in Nice, she flung a two-yard-long red silk scarf around her neck and across her shoulder, waving and calling, '*Adieu, mes amis! Je vais à la gloire!*' The long tassels of the scarf caught in the rear-wheel spokes as the car sped away, snapping her neck, severing her jugular vein and killing her instantly.

The tie was softened into a floppy bow for women in the 1980s.

Less floaty than a scarf, more 'feminine' than a tie, *pussycat bows* were a way of disarming the impact of a severely tailored suit, and of expressing a little femininity in a male-dominated world of work. Made in art silk and crêpe, they were added to the throat of the Thirties' long, lean silhouette. In the wartime Forties they were a contrast to the boxy, austerity look. Collars of the Fifties and Sixties were neat and sleek around the throat, but the 1970s saw a return to floppy bows for women. These were taken up by British Prime Minister Margaret Thatcher as part of her well-thought-out political wardrobe; Thatcher's clothes – with their combination of plain tailoring and soft touches – cleverly balanced implications of strength with concessions to womanliness. She did not wish to appear *mannish*, nor did she want to seem frivolous.

Her neckwear did, of course, flag up how gendered neckwear is. The male, stiff collar is associated with power and impact, whereas the female bow is seen as pretty and decorative. When Lady Diana Spencer – a poster-girl for the affluent London *Sloane Ranger* clique – posed for an engagement portrait with Prince Charles in 1981, she (the virginal newcomer) wore a pussycat bow, while he (heir to the British throne) had a traditional tie.

LOOSENING THE TIE

This overview of high collars and tight knots is surely enough to give anyone an empathetic stiff neck. Fortunately there have always been gentler alternatives to such formality. Softer styles of neckwear have a long pedigree. The 7,500 terracotta warriors of Shih Huang-ti's army of 221 BCE all have a loose neckcloth, as do the Roman legionaries featured on Trajan's column, dating from 113 CE. Much later was the seventeenth-century style known as the *Steinkirk* – a loosely wrapped scarf tucked or pinned at the chest. According to popular legend, it was adopted after French troops dressed hastily for the 1692 battle of Steinkirk and didn't have time to fasten their cravats properly.

As already mentioned, from the 1770s newly independent North American men had looser stocks than their European counterparts. They sometimes chose plain bandana neckcloths or thick, floppy ribbons called *plantation ties* because of their association with the loose styles favoured in the southern states. Cotton bandanas might be brightly coloured and boldy decorated. Being washable and multi-purpose, they were readily taken up by working men on both sides of the Atlantic as the perfect informal neckwear. English prize-fighter Jim Belcher fought his way to fame in the late Georgian era and gave his name to a dark-blue spotted neckcloth, which became acceptable wear for gents at sporting events.

And what of men who wore no neck tie at all? This was a lapse in sartorial standards permitted only to artistic types. Certain romantic portraits of George, Lord Byron in the early nineteenth century, for example, show him with a loose open collar. It is the paintings of Byron by Thomas Phillips and Richard Westall that are most commonly reproduced, with the tie-lessness accentuated by dark clothes and bold white open collars. This image suited Byron's reputation as a poet, adventurer and sexual libertine. In reality, his laundry accounts show that he owned many neckcloths, which he used on a daily basis, even while travelling in exotic territories. In 1811 a besotted lover sent him a parcel of embroidered neckcloths that had her own hair woven into the stitches.

As late as the twentieth century bare necks, bows and loose ties were associated with artists, poets and other people on the periphery of decent society. Oscar Wilde had been a classic 'offender'. Such men were also the first to wear soft turtleneck sweaters without ties as the century progressed – a very visual rejection of petty formalities.

How would the tie contend against artistic looseness, shrinking collar heights and soft cotton 'lounge' collars after the First World War? Surprisingly, there was no competition. The incentive to appear respectable was too strong, and too necessary in the job-scarce periods of the inter-war years.

However, with prosperity in Britain increasing from the 1950s onwards, ties no longer needed to be constricting or conservative. From the mid-1960s the kipper tie – a wide-ended tie reminiscent of the gutted fish, and credited both to weatherman Michael Fish and to designer Pierre Cardin – was a broad canvas for amazing prints. Ties dazzled with modern designs, taking advantage of advances in weaving technology. Nude women, psychedelic patterns, exotic motifs and cartoon characters made the shirt front a focal point in the Sixties and Seventies – unless you preferred the white tie with a dark shirt, in homage to gangster culture.

There were predictions in the heady hippy days of the late 1960s that by 1980 the tie would be dead, and it's true that the modern male clearly feels more comfortable with informality and ease than his ancestors. Sports clothes and T-shirts now dominate leisure wear.[6]

Sadly for the leisure-loving male, although the tie's tyranny has slackened, it is still going strong in certain strata of business, in school uniforms and on formal occasions. It has even made it off the planet; in 1981, when Britain's first astronaut Helen Sharman joined Russian counterparts for dinner on the *Mir* space station, one of the dinner 'guests' sported a tie, 'which duly floated horizontally the whole evening!'

Caution is still necessary to navigate the subtle social rules dictating what is admirable, acceptable or unforgivable in a tie. Male politicians err on the side of sensible. Too gaudy might seem brash; too dull and you're out of touch. Male TV presenters seem to have far more latitude in tie-expression, with fashionable, eye-catching colours being worn in contrast to more subdued suits. Male corporate workers hover somewhere in the middle of the tie-choosing spectrum: a colourful or patterned tie might be one of the few ways in which the modern suited man can express personality at work.

While on the whole few people enjoy wearing ties nowadays, ties aren't leaving us any time soon. The tie is dead; long live the tie.

6 Those who still feel constricted by a collar and tie worn at work will doubtless sympathise with John Byng, 5th Earl of Torrington, who says in one of his diary entries from 1789, 'at last home I come, clap on my bedgown, my slippers, take off my gaiters, ease my neckcloth . . .'

SHOE BOXES

Momma always says there's an awful lot you could tell about a person by their shoes. Where they're going. Where they've been.

FORREST GUMP, PARAMOUNT PICTURES, 1994

ECHOES OF THE OWNERS

A shoe is never just a shoe. It carries the resonance of whoever made it, and the imprint of whoever wore it.

Shoes carry their owners along pavements, down catwalks, across continents and along sprint tracks. They can be designed for speed, or to impede. Shoes show status – or lack of it. They enable survival and exploration. They can be objects of desire and instruments of self-induced torture. Almost all humans now wear shoes, and yet shoes are also poignantly individual.

It is the imprint of the individual within a shoe that makes each one so personal. An experienced podiatrist could examine a used pair of shoes and deduce a great deal about a person's gait and foot-health from the way the heel is worn and the way the soles and sides have been pressured. We talk of 'putting yourself in someone else's shoes' to signify empathy with another – an understanding of their perspective. This is particularly relevant when taking a historical view of shoes. If we looked back over the last few millennia, we would be dazzled by the huge variety of shoe styles and decorations, described as early as 1585 as numbering 'the sands of the sea, the stares in the skie, or the grasse upon the earth, so infinite and innumerable'. It would be impossible to catalogue them all. Instead we shall pluck a few examples out of the past to illustrate how even a solitary shoe can represent a whole human being – or even a large-scale event in human history.

For example, we could focus on a shoe that is steeped in status and occasion, such as the single one surviving from a pair believed to have been worn by Queen Victoria at her coronation in 1838. The ivory silk satin and appliquéd ribbon stripes imply wealth and personal daintiness. The interior paper label is marked with the royal coat of arms and 'GAUNDRY & SON Boot & Shoemakers TO THE QUEEN'.

A little later in history we could see the contrast of a far more practical black leather shoe, with modest black satin rosette and beading. It is still fairly small but, unlike Victoria's barely scuffed soles, this shoe has been pavement-pounding. It was lost by the militant suffragette Emmeline Pankhurst during one of the Women's Social Political Union scuffles with protesters. Definitely a shoe with a story.

One of the most significant pairs of shoes in history comes without a name. That is part of its tragedy, and the reason it was added as emotive evidence in the trial of Adolf Eichmann in 1961. A Nazi bureaucrat of Germany's Third Reich, responsible for the trains that transported many tens of thousands of innocent people to concentration camps and extermination centres, Eichmann sought to distance himself during the trial from actual physical murder, believing that his position behind a desk would absolve him of any crime. A pair of shoes was chosen from a pile of thousands remaining at Treblinka death-camp and was held up in the courtroom by Attorney-General Gideon Hausner. The pair had belonged to a child. The sight of those shoes transformed the cerebral concept of genocide into a visible, appalling reality for the people in that courtroom. An eyewitness remembered, 'We were gripped by the spell cast by this symbol of all that was left of a million children.' Eichmann was convicted of war crimes and of crimes against humanity, and was sentenced to death by hanging in 1962.

1 Drivers may spot
the occasional
abandoned item of
footwear at the
roadside, each with a
story. One lorry driver
in post-war Britain
stopped at the sight
of one such solitary
shoe, at Wrotham Hill
in Kent, thinking there
might be a pair he
could salvage for his
wife, such was the
scarcity of shoes in
the 1940s. Tragically,
not far from the shoe
was the body of a
murdered woman.
She was identified as
Dagmar Petryzywalski;
the discovery of her
single shoe eventually
led to the police's
identification of her
murderer.

Of all the artefacts exhibited at Holocaust museums and memorial sites, it is probably the piles of anonymous shoes – reeking of old leather and grime – that have the greatest impact on viewers. The imagination can conjure up a human being to suit the shoe: whether a working person in heavy boots, a dandy in dapper dress shoes, a young girl in her first heels or a child skipping in strap-and-button patent leather. When Majdanek death-camp was liberated by Soviet soldiers in August 1944, a *Time* magazine reporter described the sea of shoes spilling out of one of the camp's warehouses:

High heels, low heels, shoes with open toes. Evening slippers, beach sandals, wooden Dutch shoes, pumps, Oxfords, high-laced old ladies' shoes. In one corner there was a stock of artificial limbs. I kicked over a pair of tiny white shoes which might have been my youngest daughter's. The sea of shoes was engulfing. In one place the sheer weight had broken the wall.

Sometimes, then, a shoe has been the only remaining evidence of a person's existence. This is in part because leather is sturdy and can survive for centuries in certain conditions, as they have on the feet of bodies buried in bogs, or when lost in the mud of a Viking town. Jorvik Viking Centre in York exhibits Viking Age shoes; bog bodies of various countries and eras have intact footwear. When the wreck of RMS *Titanic* was discovered in 1985, the world was stunned to see underwater images of the prow, the deck and the huge hull; but what really brought home the human element of the tragedy were the shoes scattered in the debris field around the wreck. Many items of footwear have been recovered in pairs from the ocean floor – the bodies of their owners having long since decomposed.[1]

In this chapter we'll explore the making and wearing of shoes across time, with forays into some of the many different aspects of shoe culture. We begin with the problems arising when trying to get footwear to fit.

There is an expression to describe accepting that something is appropriate – something we are worthy of, or even an insult we deserve. We say, 'If the shoe fits, wear it'. When dealing with literal, not metaphorical shoes, getting them to fit can be rather tricky; in fact, of all clothing items, shoes are perhaps the most demanding to get right. Human feet are load-bearing, so shoes must be hard-wearing. Feet are well jointed, and so shoes must also accommodate a wide range of movements. Achieving all this *and* taking fashion into account requires considerable skill. Later in this chapter we'll see just how varied shoe styles became from the Middle Ages onwards. For now, it's worth giving credit to the craftspeople who wrestled with the problem of how to create successful footwear.

Shoes begin life as pieces of fabric or leather in the hands of a cobbler. The earliest shoes – worn at least from the Roman era onwards – were simple *turn-shoe* designs that essentially wrapped a shaped piece of leather around the foot and fastened it with bindings or toggle at the ankle or over the foot arch. There were many variations in colour, cut and fastenings, but the basic, relatively unformed shoe could mould around the shape of the foot and be padded out with sheepskin inners, if required. From the Renaissance onwards, shoes began to evolve into more complex constructions. They might have separate soles, heels, uppers and tongues, all to be stitched or glued into place. These more sophisticated styles were crafted around a wooden mould called a *last*.

Before the nineteenth century, when cobblers adopted separate wooden lasts shaped for right and left feet, shoes were made with no such distinction. They were known as *straights*. Having undifferentiated footwear resulted in a certain clumsiness of gait until the shoes naturally moulded to each foot, at which point they could be marked with L and R, for left and right; or, to be continental, D and G for *Droit* and *Gauche*.

Cobbling was hard work, requiring a good knowledge of

2 Bespoke shoes
were also crafted for
those with disabilities,
such as the steel boot
worn by Florence
Nightingale in her
youth to correct a
weakness; Lord
Byron's long gaiters
and heavy boots to
hide his club foot and
correct his gait; or the
orthopaedic shoes
made for Hitler's
Minister for
Propaganda, Josef
Goebbels, to
minimise a politically
unattractive limp.

hides and, before the full mechanisation of shoe-making in the late nineteenth century, hands that could take the punishment of stitching leather. Those learning the trade professionally (invariably females were excluded from this privilege) had to produce an 'apprentice-piece' to show their craft. Apprentice-pieces were made in miniature, to hone techniques and display exquisite skills. One of the greatest master cobblers was John Lobb. A poor Cornish labourer, he became a shoe-maker in order to craft footwear that would fit him, after an accident left one foot injured and deformed. By the 1860s he was producing footwear for the Prince of Wales. An apprentice-piece supposedly created by Lobb is in Fowey Museum, Cornwall, near his native village of Tywardreath. The company John Lobb Ltd, Bootmakers, is still trading.

Bespoke footwear – made to fit one person and no one else – was the best and most expensive means of being shod. This might entail having a unique design made up especially for one person alone, or it might mean having a standard style adapted to the individual's foot length and width.[2] Measuring of the feet was originally done by the shoe-maker directly, but as shoe shops became more prevalent in the eighteenth and nineteenth centuries, the shoe-seller would perform the task.

The idea of having a *shoe size* is very modern, but its adoption can be traced back to the mass-production of shoes in the nine-teenth century, without which there would be no standardisation of measurements.

In 1812 boots for the British Army had soles fixed to uppers by machine, which was a great boon during the Napoleonic Wars. However, full industrial-scale shoe production wasn't viable by machine until the middle of the century. Shoes were not given sizes at this time. We begin to see numbers stamped on the leather of the soles, or on the insoles, from the twentieth century onwards. The standardised sizes originally took length and width of the foot into account. They were generated by calculations that varied from country to country and originally included half-sizes for extra-accuracy – a degree of fit that is no longer universal in modern shoes. The size was represented by a number, while the width was denoted by a letter of the alphabet.

It was possible to get a relatively good fit with the twentieth-century system. However, increased standardisation now means far fewer variations in shoe sizes. It is cheaper to produce a few generic sizes than to attempt to cater for a greater variety of foot shapes. Those who fall outside the average will struggle to find footwear to fit. Even those within popular ranges of size will know that considering oneself a size 6 does not necessarily mean that all shoes stamped with a 6 will fit. Half-sizes are rare and the modern shopper often tolerates badly fitting shoes if they are fashionable or feel good for the first few minutes of wear in the shoe shop.

Nowadays few buyers trouble to have their feet measured professionally, and many people buy untried shoes straight from the Internet, on the basis of standard-size numbers only. There has been a corresponding rise in the promotion of insoles, gel soles and blister-plaster products to counteract the effects of ill-fitting footwear.[3]

3 A good fit requires good fastenings. Elastic-sided boots, with a gusset of India-rubber fabric over the ankles, were a boon from 1837 onwards, when they were patented by James Dowie. For women, the innovation of narrow straps across the foot really took off from 1927 onwards, with the adoption of children's strap shoes that became known as Mary Janes.

COBBLED TOGETHER

Looking back in time again, it's clear that cobbling was hardly a lucrative profession, despite the success of John Lobb and a few other elite shoe-makers. The romantic image of the 'poor cobbler' is familiar in folk stories and fairy-tales such as *The Elves and the Shoemaker*. The reality would have been periods of intense work with little remuneration, and times without any work at all. Trade was traditionally boosted by demands for repairs and re-soling. Prior to the twenty-first century dominance of 'fast fashion', the preference for cheap materials and a general indifference to poor quality, shoes were an expensive commodity, not to be discarded prematurely – hence the demand for repairs. Too many repairs left a shoe looking rather bungled, though, giving us the term to be *cobbled together*.

In 1852 workmen effecting repairs in what was then known as the 'Shoemaker's Room' at Corpus Christi College in Cambridge discovered a hoard of Elizabethan leather goods, including several shoes. One pair of the recovered shoes has slashes cut into the leather to make a fashionable pattern (and to allow flashes of colour from the hose within). Historians now speculate that the shoes had long ago been dropped off for repairs, as they were worn at the sole and toe, but were obviously never collected – perhaps never paid for. If they were in for repairs, this would be clear evidence that even those who could afford to buy fancy shoes still considered it an investment to maintain them.

For all the low wages of cobblers, shoes were a costly outlay. We speak of someone being *well-heeled* if they are affluent, and *down-at-heel* if scruffy and poverty-stricken (the implication is that if your heels are worn down, you're stuck for the cash to pay cobblers' bills). In the budgets of poorer households, boot-buying involved a great deal of economy. Going barefoot during summer and perhaps even winter was a necessity for children in poor families as recently as the mid-twentieth century, or else shoes might only be worn on Sundays. One visitor to Scotland in 1810 reported, 'We often see on the road men and women barefoot carrying their shoes in their hands to save the leather.' From the nineteenth century onwards careful housewives could pay a few pence into a weekly 'boot club' run by shopkeepers in the neighbourhood – essentially a savings account that encouraged loyalty to local shoe-sellers. Cheap shoes simply weren't a good economy.

With shoes such an investment, it made sense to protect them. Shoe bags were stitched to hold them while travelling, with coarse brown canvas recommended for walking shoes, and old silk for storing satin slippers. From the nineteenth century, shoe suitcases were crafted with ruched satin pockets for each shoe. *Shoe trees* are devices moulded to keep the shape of the shoe when unworn. Wooden shoe trees have recently been replaced by plastic ones, though few people use them now, being more likely to invest in plastic shoe boxes or shoe racks.

Preserving the footwear investment also required careful maintenance with polishes, waxes and whiteners. As he strutted in Hyde Park, Beau Brummell was famously asked where he got his exquisitely polished boots blacked. He replied, 'My blacking positively ruins me; it is made with the finest champagne!' This was almost certainly a case of facetiousness on Brummell's part, and not factual truth. Glossy patent leathers could be restored to brilliance with spirits of turpentine. For regular leather, from the nineteenth century, shoe polish was readily obtainable through brands such as 'Kiwi' and 'Cherry Blossom', in *black, neutral, dark tan and light tan*. Sports shoes, canvas shoes and ladies' white summer shoes would be whitened with 'Blanco', which was a dreary grey when wet, but whitened as it dried. One girl of the 1920s remembers her governess dabbing Blanco on the toes of her white boots before they entered any house when they were out visiting.

Military boot-cleaning, 1943 – all part of life in the services.

From the nineteenth century onwards, one additional way to protect footwear was to don shoe *spats*. The name is a contraction of *spatterdashers*, which were protective gaiters in use from

4 Spats may have helped prevent the outside of a shoe or boot becoming unpleasant, but what of the inside? The issue of odorous shoes has long perplexed people, leading to the advertisement of ingenious solutions such as the 'Ventilating ladies' boots and shoes' recommended by the medical journal, the *Lancet*, in February 1852, which claimed to be 'really valuable' from a sanitary point of view.

the seventeenth century; spats were a reduced form of such gaiters, designed to cover the top part of the shoe or ankle boot, and elegant enough to be worn as a fashion accessory in their own right, not just in inclement weather.[4] Usually white or dove-grey, spats had become associated by the late 1920s with American gangsters and caddish behaviour, since, according to the saying, 'a white spat may often hide a cloven hoof'.

Early twentieth-century felt gaiters.

Designing footwear that will go on, stay on and come off only when required is an art. Historically, shoes have been held in place with ribbons, strings, latchets, buttons and buckles. And what begins as a practical requirement is soon distorted into exaggerated embellishment: 'Formerly indeed, the buckle was a sort of machine intended to keep on the shoe; but the case is now quite reversed, and the shoe is of no earthly use but to keep the buckle,' laments a character in R. B. Sheridan's 1777 play, *A Trip to Scarborough*. Shoestrings were forerunners of eighteenth-century braided shoelaces, and, according to Regency courtesan Harriet Wilson, the truly pretentious man would have his shoestrings ironed. Since shoestrings were relatively flimsy they gave rise to the expression 'to live on a shoestring' – that is, on a very reduced budget.

FAMOUS NAMES

As with the makers of other items of attire, cobblers might gain a reputation and a more buoyant income by producing shoes and boots for the Royal Court (*if* their illustrious clients ever troubled to pay their bills). Those who crafted shoes worn during presentations at court could advertise themselves as 'Court shoe-makers'. By the nineteenth century paper labels inside shoes, with elaborate fonts and scrolls, promoted the name of the more prestigious shoe-makers.[5] Modern shoes still have the brand printed inside or, increasingly, a metal tag or woven logo on the outside to flaunt it.

Gradually the name of the shoe-maker became enough to sell the shoe. By the twentieth century shoe *designers* (rather than makers) were rivalling costume couturiers in fame and the desirability of their brand. Like their equivalents in the clothing industry, the most prominent designers of female footwear have, historically, been men.

Designers married engineering skills with an eye for colour and form to produce a range of styles. Such designers' work became coveted by those who could afford it. Salvatore Ferragamo, one of the biggest names in twentieth-century foot-wear, credited with inventing the 'wedge' shoe of the 1930s, also created the shoes worn by Marilyn Monroe over a breezy subway grating for the iconic *Seven Year Itch* photoshoot in 1955. More notoriously, Eva Braun chose black suede Ferragamo shoes for her April 1945 marriage to Adolf Hitler. Since their suicide pact followed shortly afterwards, it can be presumed she was buried in them, too. Famous names of modern shoe design include Manolo Blahnik, Christian Louboutin and Jimmy Choo.

Royalty have relatively little influence on mass-fashion in modern times, except in the sense that they may be photo-graphed in designer shoes and so further popularise a trend that already exists. Modern shoe designers increasingly look to have their footwear worn by celebrities, to create new cults of covetousness.

5 In the History Wardrobe collection there is a wonderful pair of yellow silk embroidered court shoes with gilt heels, worn by a 1920s English debutante. Sadly they have been partially devoured by discerning mice.

6 Finnesko is a soft fur often lined with Arctic sennegrass to absorb moisture.

Of course the primary function of shoes, however they are made, sized or labelled, is to protect the feet. Early hominids walked barefoot. Civilisation brought about the softening of the human sole and therefore a need for artificial covering. Shoes became so crucial for comfort that we found we couldn't easily function without them.

How the footwear is crafted depends a great deal on the environment that is encountered. Extreme climates lead to innovations in footwear design. For example, those walking long-distance across the sandy deserts in Africa emulate the splayed camel foot, with wide, woven sand-shoes. For hot climates, sandals are naturally the footwear of choice for the sake of keeping the feet cool. They can be made of woven reeds or cut leather pieces. One centuries-old sandal style is that of a sole with a simple toe-post. Sandals have also come to represent a certain humility, as with the simple footwear chosen by Mahatma Gandhi during his long, dignified protest against foreign rule in India in the twentieth century. From the late 1950s mass-produced rubber versions of this toe-post sandal went on sale, with the onomatopoeic name of *flip-flops*.

At the other weather extreme, warm waterproof footwear is crucial to avoid the potentially fatal effects of frostbite during exposure to extremely low temperatures. Over the centuries many cultures have adapted to winter conditions, with, for example, Native American snow-shoes, Viking ice-skates and Scandinavian skis all using cane, bone, wood . . . and eventually modern moulded polymers. Humans living in or travelling to conditions of extreme cold have long taken advantage of animal pelts – including relatively modern polar travellers, such as Sir Ranulph Fiennes, whose expeditions in the 1970s and 1980s adopted *finnesko* boots of tanned reindeer skin.[6]

Sir Ernest Shackleton's account of his heroic failed expedition across Antarctica in 1914–17 mentions the desperate need for decent footwear when he and his men had to trek across floes

A sturdy nineteenth-century hobnailed boot – the descendant of Roman hobnailed footwear.

on foot, once their ship was ice-locked and crushed – either they were ill-prepared with boot stock or they had simply worn through the pairs available. He was disgusted to find that suitcases salvaged to use as material for making boots were not 'solid leather' as marked, but mainly cardboard: 'The manufacturer would have had difficulty in convincing us at that time that the deception was anything short of criminal.' Having generously given away his Burberry boots to a crew member, Shackleton soon discovered that boots with grip could also mean the difference between life and death; he and two other men had just survived an extraordinary ocean voyage in a small wooden lifeboat, in an attempt to get help for the rest of the crew who were stranded on a remote island. The trio needed to cross the inhospitable mountains of South Georgia. Shackleton knew his light boots would be near-useless, so screws from the lifeboat were pushed through the soles to form makeshift cleats, much as the Romans added hobnails to their leather boots, to enable long-distance marching. The rescue mission was a miraculous success, thanks in part to the boots.

Boots as a general style of footwear are essentially shoes that extend up above the ankle and sometimes to the knee or beyond. Fur and hide boots have been worn for several millennia, although their style has been greatly finessed, as we'll see shortly. Boots are clearly essential for survival in certain environments. They also have a prominent position in costume history as footwear for more civilised settings, such as shopping arcades and parade grounds. Between the Renaissance and the twentieth century shoes and boots jostled for dominance. Initially it was shoes, perhaps decorated with big metal buckles or lavish ribbons, that best showed off the male leg, or peeped out from under a female petticoat. Working men and women would wear stouter shoes. The idea of wearing boots socially took a while to catch on; it wasn't until the late eighteenth century that they became the norm for both women and men as outdoor wear, with shoes relegated to elegant occasions such as balls and court functions. It's interesting to see how boots achieved this coup.

DIED WITH HIS BOOTS ON

Cloth or supple leather boots were common enough before the seventeenth century, sometimes with slender leather soles, or with wooden soles for extra sturdiness. The vast *bucket-tops* of sixteenth- and seventeenth-century men were, as their name suggests, so wide they had a tendency to collect rainwater in wet weather. In addition to filling with water, they were usually frothing with lace-topped boot-hose decorated in needlework and, according to one detractor, 'clogged with silke of all colours, with byrdes, foules, beastes and antiques purtraied all over in sumptuous sorte'. However, boots truly came into their own after the first American colonies were founded and the Georgian era in England began. Courtly cavaliers flaunted boots with bucket tops and gilded spurs, and for the less ostentatious there was a tough, cowhide boot called a great boot or *jackboot*, large enough to fit a light slipper or shoe inside – all ready to wear indoors when discarding the dirty boots. Riding boots required sleeker shapes and more elegance of form, and it was these criteria that came to be adopted by civilian boots, as opposed to the clunky weight of jackboots, which had been worn by military men and coachmen. Jackboots aside, it was a passion for emulating the military that effected the rise of the boot's popularity with gentlemen and ladies of the late eighteenth century, a popularity that endured right up to the early 1900s.

A selection of nineteenth-century men's boots, one with a riding spur.

As armed forces in the West were increasingly formalised and kitted out with standard uniforms, so boots came to be seen as smart wear for men. Military styles were frequently co-opted into civilian trends, and not just for disagreeable jobs where extra foot and leg protection was needed. Civilian men wearing military-inspired boots could feel a certain might and panache.[7]

Hessian boots, so beloved of the late Georgian and Victorian gentleman, were originally made in Hesse, Germany, and worn by German troops. They were cut lower at the back so that the leg could bend, but may nevertheless have been quite a liability in battle: wooden-heeled hessians could weigh more than two pounds each. The Duke of Wellington gave his name to a style

7 One of the most extraordinary costume innovations in history began commercial life in the 1920s as 'Mystik Boots' in the US. These boots used the newly invented zipper or zip, or *Lightening Fastener*. Goodrich launched the 'Zipper boot' in 1923 with the promotional tag line, 'Stir some woman's heart – give her footwear loveliness for the wet and slushy day.'

8 Christopher 'Clutty' Clayton-Hutton, who was technical advisor to MI19 military-intelligence service, was the pioneer designer of escape boots for the British War Office. He was also responsible for compasses concealed in buttons and the silk maps printed by Waddingtons, of 'Monopoly' board-game fame.

of campaign boots in the early nineteenth century, cut to mid-calf without a turnover at the top. The Duke's boots were crafted by George Hoby 'the Great', of St James's Street and Bond Street, and were actually best suited for horseback, rather than on foot. When one of Hoby's customers once dared to complain that his boots had split, Hoby reportedly exclaimed, 'Good God! You've been walking in them!' The leather of the Iron Duke's boots was exchanged for rubber in the mid-nineteenth century, evolving into the ubiquitous modern *wellingtons* or wellies. The North British Rubber Company, trading as Hunter boots, provided wellingtons during both World Wars – it remains an upmarket and well-known brand to this day, although wellingtons are now more associated with farming or festival-going than warfare.

As modern armies developed a finer distinction between the ostentatious uniforms worn for formal parades and the fit-for-purpose clothes of combat, boots became more subdued, such as the tight-fitting leather lace-up *field boots* with a protective flap around the front, which were created for officers in the mud of the First World War trenches.

Early aviators needed fur-lined boots to keep them warm in open and unheated cockpits. These were bulky and could in no way be mistaken for civilian wear, which, by the early twentieth century, had once more eschewed boots and half-boots for shoes in everyday outfits. During the Second World War airmen who crashed behind enemy lines couldn't run the risk of their boots being spotted and giving them away, so special aviation boots were issued. These could be converted to inconspicuous 'town' shoes by the removal of the furry, wrap-around ankle section, which could then be used to make a warm fur-lined waistcoat. Some of the boots had a hinged flap in the straight edge of the heel, with a cavity for a compass, a small file and silk maps showing escape routes. A small knife could be concealed in a cloth loop inside the boot, along with documents sandwiched between layers of rubber and fur.[8]

Regardless of Napoleon's dictum that an army marches on

its stomach, it does, in reality, march on its feet, so well-fitting, long-lasting boots were essential, though not always obtainable. In the 1940s the German Wehrmacht suffered the dubious advantage of being issued footwear that had undergone rigorous testing at Sachsenhausen concentration camp, just north of Berlin. Prisoners in a penal work detail were forced to run up to twenty-five miles a day around a 700-yard track made up of different textures – rocky, sandy, gravelly and muddy – to challenge the shoes in different ways. Guards beat anyone who couldn't keep up the pace. The ordeal proved fatal after days for some prisoners; few of them lasted weeks. The remains of the shoe-testing track are still visible today.

Despite the utterly uniform design of the modern military boot, it is such an important and personal part of a soldier's kit that somehow it can still represent an individual. This is proven most movingly by the *Eyes Wide Open* memorials created by the American Friends Service Committee after the 2003 US invasion of Iraq. A travelling national exhibition sets out memorial fields with pairs of black boots – one pair to represent every servicewoman or man killed in the conflict. Having begun at 504 pairs, the 'parade square' arrangement now tallies more than 3,000 pairs . . . and counting.

S**T-KICKERS

For daily wear, Regency gentlemen loved their hessians, and Victorian chaps doted on ankle-boots. Middle-class men of the early twentieth century, however, relegated boots to warfare, sportswear and hikes. Instead they stepped out in shoes. Not high-heeled shoes with ribbons and bows, as they had worn three centuries before; male footwear became as subdued as the suits with which it was worn. Leather lace-up shoes became the norm, with minimal decoration (perhaps holes punched in a pattern), minimal height (a slight stacked heel) and minimal attention-seeking. Boots were the province of the working man who needed something tough on his feet. Since clothing trends

9 Fashion loves to appropriate practical items and turn them into a frivolous phenomenon, as with the 1930s soft sheepskin boots worn by Australian sheep-shearers. They were adopted in the Sixties and Seventies for après-ski and après-surf, and then in the 1990s their appearance in the US television show *Baywatch* ensured their mass-adoption, mainly under the brand name of Ugg boots.

perpetually cross-fertilise, it wasn't long before the influence of workwear created a counter-culture fashion that is still prevalent today: the *Doc Martens* boot.

The blurring of distinctions between military footwear and civilian gear has no better example than the legendary Dr Martens boots. Docs or DMs, as they are popularly known, began life as a shoe with an air-filled sole, designed to ease the pain of one Dr Klaus Märtens, a young soldier who broke his foot skiing in the Bavarian Alps in 1943. Märtens' friend, Dr Herbert Funck, made the actual shoe sole from rubber bought in bulk from abandoned Luftwaffe airfields. Märtens and Funck both agreed that the shoes were so comfortable there would be a commercial market for them, but the name 'Martens' was chosen over 'Funck' to avoid linguistic crudity. Post-war Europe was only too happy to have a comfortable alternative to the basic army boot, and the first official DMs appeared on 1st April 1960 – the classic eight lace-hole cherry-reds with reinforced steel toe-caps.

No doubt because of their association with 'rough' workers and aggressive football fans, DMs came to be classed as 'offensive weapons' by the police. Graduating from association with skinheads, goths, punks and the National Front, Docs are now accepted high-street wear in a wide range of colours, being used to add a certain edge to a floral dress in some cases. In pure black, Dr Martens have been adopted by the British SAS, seeing action from the Falklands conflict onwards.[9]

LIGHT ON YOUR FEET

Ladies traditionally wore their most elegant shoes to balls and dances. Although leather boots and shoes worn during the day would do for a village dance with working people, more elite occasions called for light and delicate shoes, to match the beauty of the ballgowns being worn. Often of silk, embellished with ribbons, beads and sequins, they were known as *slippers* – not to be confused with cosy bedtime shoes. Silk slippers were hardly fit for purpose. There is a charming fairy-tale collected by the Grimm brothers in 1823, entitled *The Twelve Dancing Princesses*, in which nightly magical balls leave delicate dancing slippers worn to threads: 'every morning their shoes were found to be quite worn through, as if they had been danced in all night; and yet nobody could find out how it happened'. Real-life slippers suffered similar fates. So light were silk dance shoes that ladies sometimes took a spare pair to the balls – and there were confessions of bleeding feet.[10]

As social dancing evolved over time, so shoes altered to suit dancers who wanted the best footwear on the dance floor. When a craze for the Argentinian tango hit Europe in the early 1900s, special tango shoes were worn, with neat straps and a curved heel – perfect for the leg flicks required. Ballroom dancing was hugely popular from the 1930s onwards, and supple silver leather dance shoes were seen as just the thing for doing the foxtrot and the cha-cha-cha. Flat ballet pumps suited the heady swings of lindy hop and rock-'n'-roll in the 1940s and 1950s. After that, it was back to twisting, strutting or step-kicking around a handbag in whichever high heels were in fashion, unless you were a fan of the 1980s craze for gymnastic-style *Flashdance* – after the 1983 dance film – in which case bare feet and leg-warmers were all the rage. With Eighties street-dance styles morphing into breakdance, stomping and other energetic genres, those who truly want to show some moves are nowadays likely to wear sports shoes.

This isn't to say it's all about shoes that are fit for purpose. One Victorian dress guru wryly noted, 'It is only at their first balls that Cinderellas are indiscreet enough to wear glass slippers.' The principle of putting comfort before effect is patently untrue when it comes to choosing shoes for a night out, and impracticality has never deterred determined dancers. Modern Cinderellas are not averse to dancing in extremely high heels – as we shall soon discover.

As for sports shoes themselves, their rise from humble beginnings to a global footwear market worth billions is truly

10 The slippers of the twelve dancing princesses would have been tied *en sandale* – with silk ribbons criss-crossed around the ankle in the style of Ancient Greek footwear. As ballerinas adopted the *en pointe* style of dancing on-stage in the nineteenth century, the shoes required block toes, and it was a daily task for the dancer to darn and redarn the points to strengthen them.

astonishing. Footwear specifically designed for sports is a relatively recent phenomenon, with the exception of the Viking shoes with bone-skates attached and, later, of riding boots with champagne-coloured or mahogany tops, possibly with spurs attached. For centuries anyone who wanted to *show a clean pair of heels* – that is, to run – would do so in their regular shoes or, in the case of seventeenth- and eighteenth-century footmen hired to run alongside carriages, in thin-soled shoes called *pumps*. These were eventually adopted by gentlemen for evening wear, styled in black patent leather with flat grosgrain ribbon bows. The first spiked shoes for track athletes were worn in the 1850s, followed not long afterwards by spikes for gentleman cricketers. Modern running shoes have interchangeable spikes that can simply be screwed in, unlike the earliest designs, in which the spikes were incorporated with the soles.

Athletes of the twentieth century have been able to take advantage of ever more sophisticated sports shoes. Much of their usefulness is thanks to the nineteenth-century adoption of rubber for footwear. Shoes with vulcanised rubber soles were first produced in 1866, by Charles Goodyear (of Goodyear Tyres fame). They had cotton laces to tie the eyelets together and were intended for the leisured classes to wear for croquet and light ball games. By 1868 the design included a horizontal line around the sole, reminiscent of the lines newly marked on British ships, thanks to the 1876 Merchant Shipping Act (these were to show the limit of displacement, following scandals of overloading). The Act had been introduced by Samuel Plimsoll, who therefore indirectly gave his name to the shoes, now affectionately known as *plimsolls* or *plimmies*, regardless of whether or not they have the line.

By 1897 Sears, Roebuck in the US were selling running shoes in their stores and catalogues, although UK catalogues of this era limited their sports section to sand shoes, tennis and cricket shoes. The popular US brand Keds began manufacturing their shoes, with a rubber sole and canvas top, in 1916. These soft-soled shoes had a quiet tread and so they became known as *sneakers*; British English, meanwhile, adopted the term *trainers* for sports shoes. By the late 1970s a craze for sports shoes as fashionwear was married with a new mania for keeping fit. Since then shoe technology has become increasingly specialised, with variations of weight, sole and cushioning for different sports. Multimillion-dollar endorsement deals with sports superstars such as, most famously, Michael Jordan in the 1980s – whose name was behind the Nike *Air Jordan* shoes of 1985 – kept the trade increasing to such an extent that reports began to spread of people being mugged or even killed for their expensive sports shoes, which flaunted brand logos and distinctive technologies of lift and arch support. Sports shoes that never see exercise more strenuous than car-driving now command prestige prices. Some are so collectable they will stay virgin in the box, their tags intact.

School hockey boots from the early twentieth century, complete with rubber studs and reinforced toe-caps.

Streamlining, super-light fabric and canny construction mean that modern sports shoes can genuinely enhance an athlete's performance, and runners can now have their gait analysed to determine the best fit of shoe. Many sports have recognised that there are significant gender differences in the way movement impacts on the feet and have adjusted their shoe designs accordingly. It's all a far cry from the earliest days of football boots, for example; King Henry VIII may have enjoyed a kick-around, but he did not have studs or streamlined boots. As for women of the 1580s, it appears they simply got on with the game in their everyday garb: Philip Sidney's poem 'A Dialogue Between Two Shepherds' describes a mother who 'with skirts tuckt very hy, with girles at football playes'.

Even when football became a regular fixture at schools and sports clubs, footy players wore their everyday boots until about the 1860s, when some adopted navvy boots with heavy metal toe-caps (which must have been a deterrent to close tackles). It wasn't until after the Second World War that tough leather boots were replaced by modern lightweight boots, being adopted by the British in the early 1950s. Modern football boots have their own trends in fashionable colours and faddish design extras but, ultimately, these are just details – the need for speed is the key.

REACHING NEW HEIGHTS

At the other end of the spectrum are shoes most certainly *not* intended for speed or ease of movement.

Contrary though this concept may seem, both status and sexual desirability are linked to awkward and even foot-deforming shoes, both historically and in modern cultures. One reason for this is that exaggerated footwear styles show that the wearer has the luxury of idleness and impracticality. Pointed *poulaine* shoes of the Middle Ages were so long in the toes that men bound up the ends with ribbons tied just under the stockinged knee. Exaggerated toes were still popular in the later Renaissance. 'And handsome how should they be?' mocked Philip Stubbes in 1588, 'as with their flipping and flapping up and down in the dirte, they exaggerate a mountayne of mire?' Men also wore cork platform shoes to gain a few inches in height.

Gaining height through shoes is an age-old trick. Fashionable ladies in Renaissance Venice elevated themselves with stacked overshoes called *chopines*. Centuries before that fad, Ancient Greek actors wore booster boots known as *cothornos* on-stage, sometimes up to six inches high. In a soft leather form, these became known as *buskins* by Shakespeare's age and were synonymous with acting. In the eighteenth and nineteenth centuries wooden overshoes raised high on a metal support – known as *pattens* – were popular with countrywomen, to raise them above muddy roads or cold stone floors.

Wedge-soled shoes from 1947, promoted as 'airborne' to emphasise their comfort.

Adding height using wedge soles is a natural follow-on from using chopines and pattens. However, arched heels were by far the heel of choice until the 1930s and the introduction of Salvatore Ferragamo's wedge-heel shoes. These were followed by, but not limited to, the raised 'brothel-creeper' crêpe-soled shoes and transparent Lucite soles of the 1950s. Stacked shoes reached a peak with the 1970s craze for *platform shoes* so high that walking became a danger to limbs – and even life. Platforms were popular with both men and women, but when the style was revived in the early 1990s it was for females alone. Supermodel Naomi Campbell famously teetered over in super-exaggerated catwalk shoes with nine-inch heels and four-inch platforms designed by Vivienne Westwood for her 1993 *Anglomania* collection in Paris. Westwood was sanguine about

11 In 1999 a twenty-
five-year-old nursery
teacher fell over in
her five-inch stacked
shoes. She cracked
her head on the
pavement and died.

the tumble: 'Fashion to me is like walking a tightrope, where you risk falling off into the ridiculous, but if you can stay on that tightrope you can achieve a triumph.' The blue shoes are now one of the most popular exhibits in the V&A costume gallery in London.

White platform shoes worn by a bride at her 1971 wedding.

Away from the spotlight, uncounted numbers of platform-wearers suffered broken bones and contusions after falling in *taxi shoes* – so called because walking even short distances in them is such a difficult task.[11] One Japanese shoe company produced the warning label:

Because the heels of the shoes are high, please be careful when you go up and down the stairs. Be especially careful when you drink because you can be wobbly. We, the produ-cers, will be very happy if you keep these points in mind when you enjoy the trendy fashion.

ACHING FOR BEAUTY

Screen icon Marilyn Monroe said (breathlessly), 'I don't know who invented high heels but all women owe him a lot.' High-heeled shoes seem to be one of the most perverse accessories ever to hobble their wearer, both now and in the past. Heels are by no means a modern creation. In the Greek dialogues of

Xenophon, Ischomachus reproaches his wife for her high heels. The fashion for heels dwindled quite noticeably in the following fifteen centuries, with heels rarely seen before the 1600s. Once they reappeared, however, they were worn with a vengeance. Elite shoes of the seventeenth and eighteenth centuries could be up to four inches high. They had the wearer teetering, and the foot arched at a seemingly unwalkable angle. Peter the Great's modernising reforms of 1690s Russia included decrees that court women must wear wigs, cosmetics and high-heeled shoes. The craze for elevation was swiftly followed by the adoption of low, curving *kitten heels* and then absolute flats. After this fashion for dead-flat shoes, dancers of the mid-nineteenth century considered even one or two inches to be 'high', risking a twisted ankle while waltzing – as was the fate of Meg in Louisa May Alcott's well-loved Victorian novel *Little Women*.[12] Women from the 1860s to the 1920s favoured the neat, curved *Louis heel* on both boots and shoes.

12 In 1902 fashion guru Mrs Pritchard declared, 'the wearing of high-heeled shoes is an abomination and a dangerous institution', but conceded that it was an excellent way to conceal foot defects, allowing that 'the more sensible among us reserve the wearing of these pretty, high-heeled shoes for carriage and indoor wear'.

A 1959 stiletto shoe – sharp at toe and heel.

Possibly the most lethal heel in history – certainly where wooden flooring or walking on metal grilles is concerned – is the *stiletto* heel, named after the deadly, narrow blade of the stiletto knife, and also called the *needle heel* or *talon aiguille*. The first stiletto is credited to shoe-maker Roger Vivier in about 1954. The House of Dior was granted a licence by Vivier to produce these steel-reinforced-heel shoes, while Vivier went on to design a pair of high-heeled ruby-encrusted gold kidskin sandals as Queen Elizabeth II's coronation shoes . . . but there is no evidence they were ever worn, and there are no shoes in the royal collection authenticated as being worn by the Queen during her coronation. We must presume that she wore something fairly low-heeled and comfortable.

Why would anyone run the risk of injury or death merely to be fashionable? Why do we choose clothes that are contrary to common sense? 'You have to suffer to be beautiful,' writes modern designer Lulu Guinness inside some of her highest heels. There is certainly a price to pay to achieve a high standard of beauty in many cultures. It seems there have always been women who will pay it gladly, rather like the fairy-tale of the Little Mermaid, who swaps her ocean fins for human legs, despite the fact she is warned, 'Each step you take will be like treading on a knife sharp enough to cause your blood to flow.' Fashion designer Victoria Beckham – who has worn shoes so cleverly constructed that they need no heel, despite their arching height – confided, 'Maybe it's a Cinderella complex, but there is just such pleasure to be had in looking down at your feet and seeing something fabulous.'

Some devotees of extreme shoe styles may actually enjoy the sensation of arching the feet when wearing them. And there are certainly those – both wearers and observers – who enjoy observing the aesthetics of the feet and legs in such shoes. High heels elongate the foot, bunch the muscles of the calf and fold the toes, supposedly in imitation of an orgasmic spasm. They give a potentially attractive sway to the gait, but at the same time often denote feminine assertiveness – many business-women wear heels to work, but switch to soft trainers for the commute. It is an assertiveness bound up with vulnerability, however: a woman in high heels is unlikely to be fleet of foot if outrunning a mugger, for example. That said, sharp heels deftly applied could prove quite a deterrent.

Flat shoes can also, surprisingly, have sexual connotations. The two-tone co-respondent shoes of the 1920s and 1930s were so named because they were associated with the sort of person who would be named as a co-respondent in a divorce petition. Divorcee Wallis Simpson, future bride of Edward VIII, wore them – and that was enough to give a taint of scandal to the style.

It's as well to bear all these torturous foot distortions in mind when considering the most extreme form of footwear the world has ever known: the *lotus shoe* of late imperial China, which is believed to have started being worn around the eleventh century. To fit a lotus shoe, the foot had to be broken, curled and bound until it was no more than four inches in length, in the practice known as *foot-binding*. Much like Cinderella needing to have the daintiest feet to gain her prince, pre-communist Chinese girls were forced to aspire to tiny feet as a symbol of beauty, status and eroticism. Big feet were associated with peasantry, and were therefore a stigma.

The infamous Chinese 'lotus shoe' – beautiful silk uppers, but just a four-inch-long sole.

According to an old Chinese saying, 'If you love your son, don't go easy on his studies. If you love your daughter, you don't go easy on the foot-binding.' Foot-binding meant breaking the toe bones and deliberately allowing the flesh to rot so that the feet could be curled over into the smallest shape possible. Bindings kept the decayed flesh and the broken bones in place. The foot was then eased into the lotus shoe – the *Golden Lotus* was an ideal of four inches. The suffering involved was intense, both during the process and into adulthood. The girls were literally hobbled. Their 'reward' was a fetishistic respect for their feet and improved prospects of a good marriage. From 1949 bound feet became a symbol of national shame under communist modernisation, but for generations of women the damage was already done. Travelling in north-eastern rural China in 2013, the author spotted an ancient lady resting by the roadside, her diminutive lotus feet barely visible under black cotton trousers. For her there was no chance of bodily modernisation.

BOOT-LICKERS

From this brief overview of historical styles it is clear that shoes and boots have far more significance than as mere protection or even as attractive decoration. Through height, colour or size, footwear - like so much fashion - is very much a signifier of status. Hercule Poirot, Agatha Christie's fictional detective, uncovers an imposter merely based on the fact that she is wearing expensive clothes but cheap shoes - a crime of which no true gentlewoman would be guilty. Similarly, in George Bernard Shaw's 1912 play *Pygmalion* a Covent Garden porter notes the status of Professor Higgins through his footwear: ''E ain't no blooming 'tec - ee's a gentleman - look at his boots!'

Over several millennia of human history, those wearing shoes have come to be considered superior to those without. Slaves in many cultures were, and still are, forced to remain barefoot. One barefoot ninth-century Viking slave complained of this specific humiliation: 'I had to bedeck her and tie the shoes of a warlord's woman every morning.' If a person is judged *not fit to tie my shoelaces*, then they are below the status even of such a slave. Lower still, a boot-licker is someone who has not only debased themselves to grovel at foot-level, but who also licks the dirt from someone's footwear. And the lowest of all? Someone not even fit to lick boots, as so eloquently evoked by a character in a Conan Doyle mystery: 'This drunken hound, that he should dare to raise his hand to her, whose boots he was not worthy to lick!' On this same theme is the devastating Spanish insult, '*No llegues ni hasta el suelo de mis zapatos*' – 'You don't even reach the soles of my shoes!'

Conversely, removing shoes can be a sign of respect, such as when entering certain religious buildings, or simply at the entrance to a house.[13] In the Christian Old Testament (Exodus 3:5) God orders Moses to take off his sandals so as not to contaminate sacred ground, a practice also observed by Muslims.

A combination of height and colour of footwear have been used to denote a status beyond mere personal taste. The French king Louis XIV took to wearing heeled shoes to appear more imposing. His 1701 portrait by Hyacinthe Rigaud clearly focuses on his bold red-heeled shoes, one of the King's innovations. They had a very steep arch that thrust the wearer forward, and were restricted to nobles who were presented at court, making them highly coveted. Upstart, insolent courtiers became known as *talons rouges* – 'red heels'.

By the 1760s red heels were out of favour, replaced by white shoes, which Louis XIV now favoured to match his white stockings. However, the association of red with power and luxury remained. Ginette Spanier, one of French designer Pierre Balmain's most sophisticated employees, recalled being inspired to acquire red heels after seeing a performance of the eighteenth-century romp *Monsieur Beaucaire* as a young girl in the 1910s:

I peeled the leather off the heels of my shoes and painted them red like those of all the white-wigged gentlemen on the stage, and that is how I peacocked about school. No wonder I was unprefected or deprefected or whatever it was called.

Heeled shoes with shiny red undersoled heels were revived in the 1990s as the trademark of shoe designer Christian Louboutin, a onetime apprentice of Roger Vivier. They were promptly copied by innumerable cheaper suppliers. For a

13 In Japanese homes it is customary to remove outdoor shoes at the threshold before stepping on the fragrant and fragile tatami mats of the private interior.

quicker, home-made imitation, there is always the option of painting shoe soles with red nail varnish ...

MAGICAL SHOES

Whatever the height and colour, whatever their status, shape or size, more than any other item in the wardrobe, shoes have a kind of magic to them. This notion is taken quite literally in fairy-tales around the world, and these stories have a strong link to our real-life relationship with shoes.

Shoes are a specific mark of distinction from animals, as seen literally in the story of *Puss-in-Boots*, where the cat in question gains the ability to walk upright, to talk and outwit all other characters in the tale, once he has donned a pair of boots. In some tales the right footwear confers power of movement – quite dramatically in the case of the *Seven League Boots*, which are said to travel a literal seven leagues with each stride.

Shoes can represent extreme vanity and, as such, they can be both a pleasure and a punishment to the wearer, as in the suffering of the little heroine of Hans Christian Andersen's story *The Red Shoes*. A wealthy benefactor rescues her from the extreme poverty of going barefoot in summer and wearing heavy wooden clogs in winter. But, having committed the sin of pride in coveting a beautiful pair of red shoes *and* wearing them to church, the girl is forced to dance in the red shoes beyond exhaustion. Her only relief comes when the town executioner agrees to chop her feet off, after which the shoes – still with the amputated feet inside – set off dancing across the fields into the forest. Snow White's wicked stepmother enjoys no such respite in pre-Grimm Brothers versions of the story. In retaliation for her attempts to kill Snow White, the queen is compelled to wear red-hot iron shoes at the heroine's wedding and dance in them until she drops dead.

The most famous fairy-tale shoe is undoubtedly the glass slipper worn by Cinderella, lost at a royal ball, then used to identify her, thereby elevating her to a royal marriage. It has

The iconic shoe-fitting scene in Cinderella, here from 1938. The heroine's fortune rests entirely on the size of her feet.

come to represent a transformative moment, when lowly status can be shed for supreme fulfilment.

There are more than 700 versions of the Cinderella story from cultures around the globe, from Ancient Egyptian storytelling to Disney's trilogy of animated films. In many tales the prized shoe is so dainty that only the heroine can fit her foot inside, reinforcing age-old associations of small feet with delicacy and femininity. In a modern twist to suit the more feminist zeitgeist, the Prince in Disney's 2007 film *Cinderella 3 – A Twist in Time* asserts, 'It's not about the slipper, it's the girl who's in it.' That said, the heroine still only has size 4½ feet. Jealous contenders for the rewards that wearing the shoe will bring – that is, marriage and elevation to life in a royal palace – resort to appalling self-mutilation. 'Cut the toes off!' Cinderella's stepmother orders one of her natural-born daughters in the unexpurgated Grimm version of the story. 'Once you're queen you won't need to go on foot any more.' The Prince is only alerted to this savage deception as blood spurts from the prospective bride's foot!

In versions of the Cinderella story worldwide we encounter

the iconic shoe in many different forms – straw, embroidered velvet, cracked leather and sky-blue silk. The most famous of all the varieties is the shoe made of glass. The idea of a *glass* slipper is ascribed to French courtier Charles Perrault, who published his version of the Cinderella tale in 1697. It is assumed that while writing down an oral telling of the tale he (deliberately?) mis-transcribed the French word *vair* (presumed to be variegated fur) as *verre*, or glass. He called the shoe *la petite pantoufle de verre* – the little glass slipper. An Edwardian version of Perrault's text wryly notes that Cinderella is dutiful but not enthusiastic about wearing glass slippers to the ball, 'for glass is not as a rule an accommodating material for slippers. You have to be measured very carefully for it.'

The Brothers Grimm 1812 version of Cinderella is less picturesque – the shoe is merely 'covered with gold'. Instead of passively waiting for his mysterious amour to lose a shoe as she rushes from the ball, Grimms' prince cleverly spreads pitch on the palace steps so that her left shoe becomes stuck.

Such has been the influence of the glass slipper that it is now reproduced in modern footwear, albeit in modified form. A Frankfurt fashion house of the 1940s designed a 'Cinderella' shoe with a heel made from the remnants of Plexiglas aeroplane windshields – a reminder of how wartime Europe had to be inventive to counter scarcities of shoe leather. Sparkling plastic versions are now sold by Disney for children as part of their extensive 'Princess' merchandise range. Plenty of other modern shoes have Cinderella-like elements, for adults who want their shoes to capture some of the glamour (and success) of the original – though hopefully most women today have more options open to them than Cinderella, who can only escape drudgery and achieve economic freedom by marrying a rich man.

Another set of shoes that made an extraordinary transition from fiction to worldwide fame in real life are the ruby slippers worn by actress Judy Garland playing the character of Dorothy Gale in the 1939 Technicolor film *The Wizard of Oz*. Frank

L. Baum's book of 1900 actually describes the magical shoes as silver. The transformation from silver to ruby can be traced back to a film script dated 14th May 1938, in which the stage direction changed from *C.U. [Close up] Silver Shoes* to *C.U. Ruby Shoes*. The change was apparently made because ruby made a better contrast with the yellow brick road. Several pairs of shoes were made for the film by Hollywood costumier Adrian, each one covered in approximately 2,300 red fish-scale sequins. They cost $15 a pair to make in 1939; at an MGM sale in 1970 the first authenticated pair, recovered from a graveyard of abandoned costumes, sold for $15,000. Another pair sold later for $165,000.[14] Another pair of ruby slippers is on display at the Smithsonian Institute, as an artefact of outstanding cultural significance.

14 The ruby slippers became an icon for many people in the gay community. To be a 'friend of Dorothy' was to be homosexual.

SHOE SUPERSTITIONS

Beyond fiction, but sometimes equally fantastical, shoes hold their magic in the superstitions of daily life. In Western weddings shoes are tied to the back of cars and carriages for luck. This is rather better than the old custom at Anglo-Saxon weddings, where the bride was hit on the head with a shoe to symbolise her transfer as property from father to husband.

It is considered unlucky to put shoes on a table, as this echoes a corpse being laid out before burial; some also say that if you sneeze before you have shoes on your feet, you will be taken ill.

A persistent example of shoe magic is the hiding of shoes in the foundations and wall cavities of houses, to ward off evil influences. At Gunsgreen, an eighteenth-century smuggler's house on the Scottish Borders, renovations to the old tea-chute during the twentieth century revealed the deliberate burial of two Maltese slippers, in their own hand-made blue paper coffin. They were buried with a note *To The Finder* signed by Ann Mary Home of Paxton House in 1852:

. . . After little more than six years wear & tear in this cold heartless world where they lived only to be trampled on, nothing but the wreck of former beauty remained, and with deep regret are they now consigned by an early tomb.

ONE GIANT LEAP

This all-too-brief overview of shoes in history has hopefully given some sense of the giddy array of styles available, and the rich variety of meanings that can be attached to them. It must also leave us wondering what the future of footwear may be. What can possibly be added to the modern shoe rack, with its trainers, loafers, wedges, peep-toes, flip-flops, wellies, moccasins, Oxfords, ballet flats, Crocs, plimsolls, Chelsea boots, football boots, hiking boots, beach sandals, DMs and designer heels?

In the search for new and exciting creations, designers mine the past for inspiration. But they are also embracing ultra-modern technologies to produce shoes that can calculate the number of steps walked in a day, stay up without a supporting heel or regulate foot temperature. The 'future' influences shoe fashion, so that as NASA develops boots for humans literally setting foot on another world, terrestrial feet can feel the spring of lunar-boot styles – as with the shiny nylon Moon Boot fad of the 1970s and 1980s.

When Neil Armstrong and Buzz Aldrin stepped onto the surface of the moon in 1969, they drew the largest television viewing audience in history, estimated at 20 per cent of the world's population. The modern astronaut's boots are a complex assemblage of layers of 'Space Age' textiles. A metal woven fabric called 'Chromel-R' forms the outer shell of the boots, resisting the high lunar surface temperature and surface abrasion, with a silicone rubber sole. Alongside the iconic image of Aldrin in full spacesuit beside the American flag, the shot of his moon-boot footprint is one of the most famous photographs in history. Aldrin spoke across the vacuum of space to NASA: 'I can see the footprints of my boots and the treads in the fine, sandy particles.' Aldrin's boot-print became both a symbol of the human drive to explore and a record of a profound, unique moment – in terms of human achievement, quite magic.

JUMPER COLLECTION

... the eternal rapid click of the knitting-needles broke the silence of the room, with a sound as monotonous and incessant as the noise of a hand-loom.

ELIZABETH GASKELL, *RUTH*, 1853

FOLLOW THE CLUE

1 A ball of yarn used to be called a *clew* – through the word's association with Theseus' escape, it is the etymological ancestor of our modern word, 'clue'.

Aside from rare prestige garments worn by aristocrats or for ecclesiastical purposes, jumpers and *knitteds* (as they are sometimes known) rarely figure in books on fashion history, which favour examples of extreme styles, luxe garments and images of high-status clothes. It is also an unfortunate fact that few jumpers have survived from history, having been worn to pieces, eaten by moths or unravelled to make new garments. However, knitwear has a history as fascinating as the craft of knitting itself.

Given that examples of early knitteds are rather elusive, it seems fitting that one of the first myths associated with yarn is all about being lost. In Greek mythology, when Ariadne cleverly suggests to Theseus that he uses a ball of yarn to guide himself back out of the Minotaur's labyrinth, no mention is made of what the wool would otherwise have become.[1] Would it have been woven or knitted? Would it have made a blanket, a cloak or a more complex garment? The history of knitwear is itself a maze that we must try our best to negotiate, by following myths, memories and a few precious scraps of the yarn itself.

Knitting is a fascinating craft, exasperating to learn and supremely satisfying to master. The craft dates from about the second century CE, but we will probably never know who first thought of using flat sticks for *netting*; then one needle for the Viking knot-work known as *nahlbinding*; then two bone or wooden pins for knitting. Just two basic stitches – the knit and the purl – have created a world of complex creativity, with ribs, cables, moss stitch, drops and lace patterns becoming scarves, socks, caps, cardigans and jumpers.

The first knitting was done by hand and was time-consuming and of variable quality. At one end of the scale were the strictly male medieval and Renaissance craft workers, who had to undergo a lengthy apprenticeship before producing stunning pieces to qualify for guild entry. Many of their creations were decorative only, or for ecclesiastical wear. Jumpers per se were not yet worn, but our modern sweaters are directly descended from the immensely technical and beautiful knitted jackets of the sixteenth and seventeenth centuries, such as the finely knitted jumper-style vest in the Museum of London collection, reputed to have been worn by Charles I to his execution in 1649. It features skilful damask patterning in bands of plain and purl stich.

Less lauded were the overworked domestic knitters, who took up their needles to provide for the family or to earn a small amount of extra money. Women felt the urge to fill every spare moment with industry, and knitting is known to have been carried out at informal meetings in neighbours' houses called *assemblies*, with women gathering for company and conversation, much as modern crafters enjoy socialising at 'Knit and Natter' groups in local community centres.

The most famous gathering of knitters in fiction is that of Madame Defarge and her monstrous cronies, congregating at the foot of the guillotine during the French Revolution. Charles Dickens introduced the reading public to these *tricoteuses* – as they were called in French – in his 1859 novel *A Tale of Two Cities*, describing how they 'sit knitting, knitting, counting dropping heads'. Dickens also had his ghastly knitters encrypting the names of the executed into their stitches. Writer Baroness

Orczy picked up on the grisly image, and the fictional hero of her 1908 novel *The Scarlet Pimpernel* disguises himself as a cart-driving *tricoteuse* in order to rescue a family of aristocrats from the Terror. He is seen as one of the women 'who sat beneath the guillotine platform to knit whilst head after head fell beneath the knife, and they themselves got quite bespattered with the blood of those cursed aristos'.

In fact this gruesome portrait of *tricoteuses* is, in all likelihood, one of many knitwear myths, believed to have been lifted by Dickens from a set of unreliable memoirs written in the 1830s, long after the tumbrils of the Terror had ceased to roll knife-wards. Any original *tricoteuses* at the guillotine would have been more likely to knit the red Phrygian caps that were symbolic of the new order; they would have been some of the working women of Paris who had banded together for a protest march on Versailles in 1789 as the revolution began. They formed the Revolutionary Women's Club and were conceded seats in the spectator galleries of the new National Assemblies once the monarchy had been toppled. However, from 1793 even this token gesture of egalitarianism was denied them, and so they congregated in public. At the guillotine. The term *tricoteuses* may well have been a generic dismissive term for groups of such women.

The casually misogynistic characterisation of knitting as simply menial women's work can be seen throughout the history of the craft. While this is completely unfair (both because knitting requires great skill and because there have been plenty of amateur and professional male knitters), it certainly did have a central place in the lives of a lot of women for many centuries. Knitting wasn't only a way of avoiding idleness; women with leisure time also wanted scope for creative flair – something that wasn't available to them through the arts or academia in the way it was for men.

From the eighteenth century on, knitting was formalised as part of a female education, particularly in foundling hospitals and workhouses. It was included on the curricula of many schools – for girls, not boys. This created a skilled force of knitters who could be responsible for household knitting, but who were also drafted into outworking as professionals, for a derisory income. Stockings were one of the main items produced at first, but jumpers were set to take their place in drawers and wardrobes from the nineteenth century onwards.

STITCHES FOR SEAFARERS

In the eighteenth century – and probably earlier – patterns for hand-knitting were passed on by word-of-mouth, by chanting the complex stitch formulas for each row. This was not simply a question of stocking stitch or garter stitch, the two most basic knitting patterns; some of the creations were so complex that they required extraordinary feats of memory, as well as the ability to calculate tension and mathematically evaluate sizing adjustments in order to use them. Patterns could be specific to a particular geographical area, such as the islands off England, Ireland and Scotland: three of the most famous are Guernsey, Aran and Fair Isle.

A traditional gansey sweater.

Guernsey sweaters – also known as ganseys – have long been associated with fishermen and seamen. Fanciful writers say the cable stitch on the gansey was invented to mimic the ropes that played such an important part in the lives of seafaring men. As families and communities evolved the basic pattern into new adaptations, a myth arose that a fisherman pulled from the sea could be identified by his individual sweater. This story was enhanced by the 1904 stage play by J. M. Synge, *Riders to the Sea*, in which the jumper in question is actually in simple stocking stitch. There are no recorded instances of any such identification being made in real life. Ganseys are traditionally dark blue and they have no designated front, so if any darning needed to be done, the repaired patch could be worn at the back where it would be less noticeable.

Aran sweaters are often an unbleached natural wool colour, patterned with honeycombs, cables and diamonds. Original Aran knits kept the water-resistant natural lanolin, rather than washing it out, making them more practical as outdoor wear. Far from being an age-old pattern contemporary with the twining artwork of the Book of Kells, as one myth suggests, it is likely that Aran sweaters really began life as a twentieth-century initiative to boost dwindling household budgets.

Fair Isle sweaters are an attractive combination of many colours with a distinctive O-X-O motif – very economical if using up odd ends of wool. There are tall tales that Fair Isle patterns were originally spread by sailors shipwrecked from the sixteenth-century Spanish Armada; prosaically, these have no basis in any factual evidence.

JERSEY AND JUMPERS

The chunky-knit sweaters made on Guernsey, Aran and Fair Isle are only part of the jumper story. Machines also play a prominent role in knitwear history. The sixteenth century saw the invention of revolutionary stocking-knitting machines, meaning that knitted fabric started to be produced on an ever-increasing industrial scale. The stretchable stocking knit could be created as a flat or tubular fabric, called *stockinette*. Fine and pliable, machine-made stockinette was perfect for underwear, and well-dressed gents of the late eighteenth century might have stockinette drawers. They might also wear an early form of jumper, in the form of long-sleeved stockinette vests; a similar undergarment for women was called a *spencer*. These early jumpers came into public view thanks to a surge of interest in sports during the nineteenth century, as they were worn publicly, without any other covering, for athletics and team games. By the First World War the practice of using sports jumpers with stripes and colours to differentiate between the teams was firmly established. Our modern sports gear may have synthetic fibres, but it is otherwise not far removed from these original stockinette stops.

Because stockinette production was associated with the island of Jersey, it was a natural progression to call the snug, stretchable tops *jerseys* – still a prevalent term for sportswear in the US. A more glamorous theory about the origins of the name is that jerseys were named after actress Lillie Langtry, who was born on Jersey and was notorious for her 1870s affair with the Prince of Wales. Although Lillie did favour simple black dresses for public appearances, they were not necessarily of stockinette, and so references to her as 'Jersey Lily' are more likely to be an association with the emblematic flower of the island. There is no evidence of her exerting her charms in a knitted jersey.

Continuing with the sportswear theme, many outfits described as *sportswear* in shopping catalogues of the nineteenth and twentieth centuries are not suitable for anything more lively than enthusiastic spectating. They were called sportswear because of their relative informality and the ease with which they could be worn – qualities associated with sporty stockinette jumpers.[2] Eventually stockinette would revolutionise clothing – leisurewear in general, as well as women's clothing in particular – becoming the cotton-jersey fabric so popular in T-shirts and other tops. But this is looking ahead to the twentieth century. First we need to linger in the nineteenth, to celebrate a relative of the jumper – the *cardigan*.

2 A *Daily Advert* for a spring jumper in 1912 describes it as 'light yet warm; perfect fitting yet giving absolute freedom of motion. Slips on in a moment . . .' This jumper was promoted for golfers, and golf has retained an association with confident knitwear to this day.

The man credited with providing the cardigan with its name might well have lamented the fact that it has stubbornly resisted most attempts to elevate it from rather frumpy informal wear.

The seventh Earl of Cardigan was known for being a fastidious dresser. While in command of the 1854 Light Brigade during the Crimean War, he chose to live on his luxury yacht while his men suffered a harsh winter, low on supplies. During the winter months officers began wearing a front-fastening woollen knitted waistcoat, which then acquired sleeves as a knitted jacket and somehow acquired an association with the Earl – we must assume he wore one – becoming known as a cardigan. The Earl may have returned to Britain a war hero, after reports of the sacrificial Charge of the Light Brigade during the battle of Balaclava, but subsequent reports showed him to be an arrogant and self-deluded hero. His eponymous knitted garment has an equally ambiguous reputation, as we shall see as we move further into the twentieth century.

Cardigans for women could be smart as well as warm, but before the First World War they were likely to be associated with badly dressed bluestockings, or mannish suffragette types. This one dates from 1912.

Although the knitted coat, or cardigan, increased in popularity through the Victorian era, it was during the First World War that it became a huge success. Fuel shortages meant that being cosy and comfortable was as elusive as it was desirable. Low-paid professional knitters turned out cardigans in khaki, pansy, emerald, cornflower, cinnamon, navy and black. They were advertised as *a boon* for despatch riders, munitions workers, lady chauffeurs and soldiers. Jumpers also enjoyed a surge in popularity, with many magazines printing knitting patterns for jumpers, as well as patterns for simpler chest-warmers or woollen waistcoats.

A 1914 jumper made from a magazine knitting pattern.

During wartime in particular there has tended to be an uneasy shift from the usual complacency about women's crafting abilities to appreciation of their importance, because of an urgent need to keep troops kitted out with warm clothes. Even ladies of the royal family did not disdain knitting 'comforts', as the items were called. Queen Victoria and her daughters set the example during the Crimean War in 1854, making generous contributions of woolly armlets and mufflers to combatants and invalids. The Queen was apparently furious that they were only handed out to officers and not to the regular soldiers. On the receiving end of a huge number of such donations during this conflict was none other than Florence Nightingale, along with her stalwart team of nurses in Scutari. Initially banned by army medical staff from attending patients at the Barracks Hospital, these women instead set to sorting through donations. These included a soldier's widow's sole remaining petticoat, sent to be made into bandages, and a pair of gloves knitted by a 'servant of all work' with old fourpenny pieces stitched inside one of the fingers, 'to be given to one of the gallant defenders of her country'. Later in the century, recording her memories of the 1899 Boer War, socialite Lady Diana Cooper wrote, 'It had meant nothing to me except learning to knit and crochet Balaclava helmets and comforters.'

Knitting needles were the only weapons that women were allowed to wield at the outbreak of the First World War: 'When our troops marched away into the unknown, with banners waving and flags flying, they were furnished by the girls they left behind them with an abundant supply of woollen garments of all descriptions,' wrote a correspondent for *Ladies' World* magazine of October 1914. Men in the trenches were desperate for all warm gear, including sleeveless pullovers, jumpers and body-warmers. Convalescents might have the sobering addition of pneumonia jackets and hand-knitted stump-covers for amputated limbs.

The benefits of knitting seemingly went beyond warmth and comfort; one woman remembers, 'It was soothing to our nerves to knit, and comforting to think that the results of our labours might save some man something of hardship and misery, for always the knowledge of what our men suffered haunted us.' For the men's part, the woollies symbolised a welcome touch of home.

Just as working people had done centuries before, wartime crafters knitted as they walked, using ingenious needle- and wool-holders to assist them. They also knitted on steam trains and omnibuses during trips and commutes. There were complaints during certain committee meetings that the speaker could not be heard over the clicking of the knitting, and the New York Philharmonic Orchestra had to publish a notice requesting patriotic wartime knitters not to wield noisy needles during concerts.

On a more sinister note, knitting was also linked (improbably) with espionage. During the war rumours spread that knitting was being used by spies to send covert messages. One of the most outlandish claims was the story reported by the patriotic UK *Pearson's Magazine* in October 1918. German agents based in Britain, the article asserted, were knitting jumpers as a means of smuggling out information about Allied naval preparedness. When the German authorities carefully unravelled such a sweater, the story went, they found the wool thread dotted with many knots. By marking a vertical door frame with the letters of the alphabet, spaced an inch apart, the knots could be deciphered as words by measuring the yarn along this alphabet and marking which letters the knots touched. It was described as 'an ingenious cipher, and not apt to be detected'. Once again, it is highly unlikely this story was more than a paranoid fantasy.

Such myths aside, satirists were quick to mock the nation of knitters during the First World War. As women were drafted into sterner, industrial jobs, they found they received far more public praise for riveting tanks, sewing the linen onto aeroplane frames and welding battleships than for any domestic crafts. However, in private, knitters treasured pencilled notes received from those on service, thanking them for the gifts of warm woollies. Ironically, all the volunteer knitting had the unfortunate side-effect of putting professional knitters out of work. At least their ubiquity meant that jumpers and cardigans were assured of a role in the post-war wardrobe.

Women in particular were already benefiting from the use of stockinette for suits as well as jumpers. One of the chief proponents of jersey fabric for womenswear set up her first clothing boutique during the First World War, advertising sportswear jersey suits in the newly created *Vogue* magazine.

She was none other than Gabrielle 'Coco' Chanel, and she would begin a revolution in women's fashion that still resonates today.

WOOL ART

The early designs of Gabrielle Chanel may have been advertised as sportswear, but they bear no relation to football kits or tracksuits other than the fact that their designer saw the advantages of adopting jersey fabrics for her ultra-modern, ultra-comfortable skirt, jumper and jacket ensembles. Chanel rode the wave of fashion evolution brought about by wartime changes in attitudes to gender roles and class. She wasn't interested in corseting women like upholstery; she liked understated elegance and freedom of movement. Jersey fabric and knitteds perfectly suited this ideal. Chanel's iconic designs took knitwear to a whole new level of chic and ushered in an age of 'Jazz' sweaters with dazzling Art Deco geometry. Knitteds of the 1920s ignored the contours of the female body, to act as a textile canvas for exotic, modern designs. The public were hooked. Women's knitwear had truly entered fashion consciousness, not so much as comfy sweaters or cardigans, but as elegant, light-weight dresses, suits and tops with amazing geometric details.

The most famous jumper in history was knitted in the 1920s, at the height of knitwear's new public popularity. It is associated with the flamboyant surrealist designer Elsa Schiaparelli, although she did not actually craft it. That task was left to a now-anonymous Armenian refugee, who received a drawing from Schiaparelli of a sweater with a white *trompe-l'oeil* butterfly bow design at the neck. The nameless knitter took three attempts to perfect the design. When Schiaparelli wore it to a grand luncheon, she created quite a sensation. A prominent New York store immediately placed an order for forty such sweaters with matching skirts. Schiaparelli went on to design beautiful and daring knitwear that could be worn on quite formal occasions, including a black fitted sweater with a cascade of monkey fur down the front.

'Sweater Girl' competitions offered prizes for girls sending in photographs of themselves in their favourite jumper, such as the September 1949 Home Chat *magazine award of £100 for a British girl to rival American film-star Sweater Girls.*

By the mid-1930s curves were coming back into fashion after being sheathed out of sight for many years. Women wanting to show off the newly erogenous bust area found jumpers the perfect clinging garment. Hollywood stars teamed their knitteds with advanced brassiere construction – cantilevering and whirl-pool stitching for the bullet-bra 'teenage torpedo' look, and so the Sweater Girl was born. She was typified by actresses such as Jayne Mansfield and Lana Turner. The girl-next-door might not pick quite such a startling cone-shaped bra under her jumper, but the Sweater Girl was still a popular cover-girl image for mainstream women's magazines.

Menswear struggled to look as good.

Men were undoubtedly wearing knitteds during the inter-war years, but jumpers – and cardigans in particular – had to work hard to shake off their fuddy-duddy image, having become too closely associated with middle-aged conservatism. As the author of a popular 1940s knitting manual so tartly put it – 'When you think of knitted garments for men, you don't, if you're wise, think in terms of *what the well-dressed man will wear* – but of what the comfort-loving man will wear.' Somehow, a woman taking the common-sense approach of wearing a ribbed cardigan over a blouse or dress was seen as more stylish than a man who wanted a classic cardigan for walking the dog. The 1940s zip-front lumberjack cardigan was, says the same knitwear expert, 'definitely built for the man who likes to be carefree about his clothes – that's the nice way of putting, "for the lazy man"'.

The jumper managed to overhaul its image more successfully, but the transformation required the social status and panache of a royal. Prince Edward (later Edward VIII) had inherited his grandfather's love of smart tailoring, teaming it with eye-catching patterns and an informality that was quite scandalous at the time. Where King Edward VII had introduced a new form of knitted, sleeveless sweater for hunting, his grandson loved the far more flamboyant 'jigsaw of patterns' of the Fair Isle sweater. The young Prince Edward first wore one in 1922 while playing golf as Captain of the Royal and Ancient Golf Club of St Andrews. Six years later he was painted by Sir William Orpen in full golfing knitwear, including a sweater and argyle socks. The trend caught on with those who wanted the cachet of dressing like a prince, and soon filtered into mainstream clothing.

However, even the prince's knitteds weren't quite enough to shake off all suspicions that men in jumpers were a little soft, unless the jumpers in question were chunky knits associated with rugged work and the Navy. However, the Second World War helped make woollens more universal wear for men.

A Second World War leaflet with knitting patterns for servicemen.

When war broke out in Europe once more, women took up their needles as a matter of course to produce the usual comforts for servicemen and women. As well as supporting the troops, when government supply lines couldn't handle the volume of warm clothing required, astute knitting could also help stretch limited Home Front resources. It became a kind of domestic national service and a soothing hobby during blackout hours.

The Second World War is particularly famous for its 'Make-Do-and-Mend' campaigns intended to instruct knitters how to make woollies last. New bands of knitting were added to old sweaters to make them stronger or longer. Small holes were darned or hidden with adroitly placed embroidered motifs. 'All of you, probably, are faced with the problem of keeping warm in the wool shortage,' announced the author of *Knitting for All* – the same knitting expert who was so scathing about men's cardigans. 'You'll find that extraordinarily few of the pathetic collection buried in every knitter's rag bag drawer need finally be given up for lost.' Old jumpers eventually became kettle-holders or dishcloths or were reknitted into squares that could be made up into blankets. Not everyone lived in a household of adept darners. In her 1946 novel *Party Frock,* Noel Streatfeild created the character of Colonel Day, a man of ancient English stock, who wore three jerseys while walking his dogs during wartime: 'The bottom one was green, the next was grey, and the top one was brown. They had holes in different places, so you could see all three jerseys at the same time.'

A typical sweater from 1945 – combining warmth and daintiness... and thrift.

Even legendarily chic Parisian women sacrificed style for warmth during the austere and bitter winters of the 1940s. One lady ventured onto the streets in 'Double, triple woollies, an appropriate shawl hidden under my caped gunner's coat, my head muffled in a woollen hood, heavy knitted stockings, so thick they stand up on their own like the waders of a sewer worker . . .'

Alas for the knitter whose plans were interrupted by war, as in the case of a Hull woman who went to Hammonds department store in the city centre to buy pink wool for her cardy. She began knitting the same evening, but soon realised she wouldn't have enough wool to finish. Returning to Hammonds the following day, she found that Hitler had scuppered her plans. The store had been bombed during the night. The cardigan became a short-sleeved top instead.

The Second World War once again saw the association of knitting with espionage. This time women living near railway yards in Europe were rumoured to have coded details of train movements and rolling stock into their knitting, to be forwarded to the relevant authorities. Romantic stories or evidence of crypto-knitting? Perhaps we will never know.

Particularly during times of austerity, woollens are vulnerable to the possibility of being reworked into new garments. A jumper can be unravelled, the wool soaked, dried and reknitted. Post-war shortages meant that thrift was continued long after the peace of 1945. As late as the 1950s rag-collectors were still advertising for cast-off knitwear, paying a shilling per pound weight in woollens. In addition, non-synthetic knitteds are irresistible fodder for moth larvae, which love silk and wool fibres. Cedarwood chests, lavender bags, vilely scented camphor balls and chemical-impregnated sticky papers have all been used in the centuries-old fight against what was known as the 'Moth Menace'. Both of these reasons partially account for the fact that jumpers are so under-represented in costume collections and museum displays.

The big impetus for devising synthetic yarns wasn't to defeat the moth menace, but to produce textiles during 'total war' when materials were at a premium; such wool as there was in Europe was reserved for the military. Germany in particular focused on research into synthetic fibres in order to keep civilians clothed, and as a possible alternative to wool uniforms. Cellulose from pine, fir or poplar trees could be converted to viscose and added into rayon threads, which were then woven, wadded or knitted. Post-war, nylon and acrylic yarns came to dominate. Modern jumpers now benefit from the warmth and softness of wool mixed with more resilient yarns.

In addition to the depredations caused by moths and by yarn recycling, knitwear often hasn't been kept or conserved simply because it has not carried the cachet of other, more glamorous garments, despite the elite outfits created by Chanel and others. However, the second half of the twentieth century saw a concerted effort to promote jumpers as both fashionable and practical.

TWINSETS AND TURTLENECKS

Somehow the sweater had to shrug off its cosy connotations if it was to become more chic, and more acceptable in semi-formal social situations. For women, unfettered by the conservative conventions of menswear, this was relatively easy. Matching a neat sweater with a cardigan created the 'twinset' craze from the 1930s onwards. The style was promoted by Hollywood stars, and any knitter could aspire to it; they just needed a pattern, two needles and wool. Twinsets then capitalised on the availability of affordable soft cashmeres and angoras in the 1950s. Bras with extreme spiral stitching thrust the bust out dramatically, but the colours of the knitwear itself were muted to delicate pastels, matched with a demure string of pearls. Worn with white gloves (and a softer bustline), this was also a style suited to royalty and the relative aristocracy of the American presidential family. With opulent hand-beading and exotic glass trims, the twinset even became glamorous evening wear in the 1960s. Worn with brogues and a tweed skirt, it epitomised the conservative 'country' look. It took teenagers to subvert the fashion into something more edgy – they put their cardigans on back-to-front, for no other reason than the time-honoured urge to innovate.

Sweater fashions for 1966.

Chaps in the second half of the twentieth century faced difficult choices: to look casual but rugged and 'manly' in a thick-knit
sweater; to seem fusty and old-fashioned in a cardigan; or to
run the risk of appearing rather effeminate in more elegant
lightweight garments. To be smart, men did at least wear their
knitteds over a proper shirt and tie, and often under a suit jacket.
Knitting magazines tried to promote the sartorial potential of
men's knitwear by using photographs of well-liked actors and
TV personalities to associate jumpers with attractiveness. So in
1954, for example, readers of *Home Companion* magazine were
urged to 'Make Jon Pertwee's distinctive pull-over for Your Man'.
Knitting patterns from the 1930s to the 1970s emphasised
masculinity through the accessories of the male models seen
wearing them, who posed with pipes, gardening implements,
binoculars and a variety of DIY tools.

One style of sweater came to be associated not only with
left-wing politics, but also with possible homosexuality – two
elements that caused anxiety amongst conservative sections of

society. This was the neat, black polo-neck sweater, worn from the 1930s onwards. Its easy informality was adopted by writers, actors and teenagers – all sections of society that might represent change and challenge. In the arts world, people were potentially able to be more open about their sexuality – hence the association with homosexuals. *Beatniks* of the 1950s thrived on this rejection of Establishment. For these anti-Establishment pseudo-intellectuals, polo-neck sweaters were hip. Eventually the *youthquake* of the 1960s, and a general sense of increasing informality in daywear, made a jumper-without-shirt ensemble acceptable as smart wear.

For those with more money than youth, there were classy alternatives to both frumpy knitwear and the semi-tainted black polo neck. Scottish knitwear company Pringle had made its mark in the nineteenth century with knitted underwear. It then made the natural transition to jumpers and became one of the most elegant knitwear brands of the next century. Pringle knitwear was characterised by luxury cashmere yarns and smart argyle patterns. For men there were extremely fine, quality sweaters which, when not being worn, could be knotted casually around the shoulders, Italian-style. Pringle wasn't afraid to introduce men to pastel colours and sensual yarns. Elite labels such as Pringle, and Italian knitwear in general, helped establish jumpers as an acceptable fashionable garment. From the 1970s onwards, sweaters with trousers were a mainstream fashion for men and women, superseded only by the advent of the unisex fleece jacket – the most modern form of knitted fabric.

HAND-MADES AND SHOP-BOUGHTS

The biggest shift in twentieth-century knitwear wasn't so much a question of colour, style or label. It was the gradual ascendance of machine-knitted jumpers. It was inevitable that techniques originally successful in stocking and stockinette production could eventually be used to produce complex patterns and shaped pieces for making up into knitwear.

There was an uneasy relationship between hand-crafted and machine-made textiles. Each new industrial innovation had knock-on effects, both good and bad. Machines meant mass-produced goods at affordable prices, but they also made much cottage industry redundant, although they couldn't entirely do away with the need for hand-finishing.

The unease as machines started to take over occasionally erupted into violence; during the Luddite uprising of 1811–12 knitting frames were smashed by angry workers in Nottinghamshire. This drew attention to the plight of cottage crafters, but did not stop the march of progress, or the anguish of those caught in the toils of sweated hand-finishing. Progress was not always on a vast scale: the development of affordable home knitting machines, available from the late nineteenth century, meant that if you had the patience to set it up, you could knit a sweater in an evening. This was an extraordinary development, given how long it would normally take to hand-knit the same garment. As with the home sewing machine, it opened up possibilities of clothing the family more quickly and effectively.

For the majority of homes that didn't want (or couldn't afford) a knitting machine, there was the perk of printed knitting patterns. They had been available from the early nineteenth century onwards – though rare – but were first published by women's magazines in the early twentieth century. From then on, knitters didn't have to rely on memory. Wool producers created their own patterns too, which inevitably boosted sales of their yarns. The wool companies Patons, Wendy and Sirdar became household names, both for their yarns and for their knitting patterns.

Where knitting had once been rooted in a need to earn money, or to clothe the family on a budget, the twentieth century saw the evolution of women from producers to consumers. The swing from thrifty home-production to pride in having the means to buy ready-made clothes created a wider market for knitwear producers. Demand fostered a wider range of styles as investment in the new technologies that were needed to form complex, imaginative designs became financially justified.

From the 1940s, fresh new designers such as Maria Luck-Szanto added to the evolution of knitteds by experimenting with new, sometimes seamless ways of shaping and structuring. Luck-Szanto is known as the 'mother' of the tailor-knitting machine concept. She created models for the top couturiers of her era, including Dior, Amies, Molyneux and Hartnell. Couture houses also continued to use hand-knitters, sending supplies and precise instructions to the very best outworkers.

After the austerity of the Forties and early Fifties, increasing affluence gave preference to 'shop-bought' sweaters, and home-knitteds were unfortunately associated with thrift or poverty. Woe betide the child starting school in a home-made sweater when everyone else had commercial uniform items. However, for those living on a budget, home-knitting remained an excellent way of bulking out the wardrobe for a relatively small outlay for wool, right into the 1980s.

A burst of enthusiasm for home crafts in the 1970s did attract a zestier style of domestic knitting using bright, synthetic yarns, novelty wools and thick needles to produce a garment more quickly. Punks of the 1970s seized on knitwear as part of their anti-fashion, anti-homogeneity ethos. Perfectly respectable jumpers were deliberately sabotaged to have holes, rips and trailing threads. Designer Vivienne Westwood wove commercialism and anarchy together by selling pre-unravelled jumpers with pre-dropped stitches and deliberately droopy shaping.

By the 1980s, even though a new generation of females was being educated without a strong emphasis on home economics as a gender requirement, fashion knitwear enjoyed a surge in popularity. Jumpers, in particular, were often featured on the cover of glossy magazines, which would also have knitting patterns inside. Primary colours, outrageous shoulder padding, appliqué, embellishments – nothing was too extreme. Jumpers with novelty pictures sold well, and festive jumpers became an established Christmas-gift purchase. The brief dominance of knitwear saw one high-street chain selling jumpers boldly embroidered with the store name – *Sweatershop* – right across the chest in cheerful bright colours.

Like all fashion fads, the oversized jumper fetish eventually dwindled. In the 1990s knitting was no longer being taught in schools. Advances in machine-knit technology, allied with foreign sweated labour at appallingly low rates of pay for hand-finishing, meant that even embellished jumpers were significantly cheaper to buy ready-made. Few modern wardrobes are now without their collection of jumpers and cardigans, mostly shop-bought, with a minority nobly hand-knitted.

Knitwear is at once common and yet celebrated. Knitwear designers include the legendary Sonia Rykiel – 'Queen of Knits' – Issey Miyake, Missoni and Kaffe Fassett. Nowadays couture lines commonly include knitwear, and many designers specialise in radical reworkings of traditional structures and motifs. The digitalisation of industrial knitting machines means that almost all images, techniques, yarns and shapings can be crafted in bulk for a greedy ready-to-wear market. We have come a long way from two pins and knit-one, purl-one.

So who knits now? Surprisingly there has been a recent surge of interest in hand-crafting, including knitting, sewing and crocheting. Economic downturns might account in part for this, but considering the expensive wools and fancy designs on sale, much of the knitwear seems to be being produced for the sheer pleasure of creation.

At variance with the ethos of knitting as a traditional female activity are the many examples of men knitting. Historically, merchant seamen, fishermen and men in the Navy were adept at creating their own sweaters. Prisoners-of-war kept themselves sane and occupied by knitting sweaters with complex patterns – there are impressive examples of these in London's Imperial War Museum. But modern 'metro' man may also be seen knitting in public, and there is a small but growing sense that knitting can be recognised as a skilled craft rather than a silly pastime for dotty grannies and ageing spinsters. One man who was a pre-teen in the 1980s told the author how he took up knitting at this time – with great success – because his mother was a genius with the needles. Secondary education bullied the urge out of him until later life, when he rediscovered it. He is currently working on a knitted Dalek.

The warmth that a woolly jumper brings is emotional as well as literal. There is more to a jumper than just front, back and sleeves. The act of knitting itself is now firmly recognised as good for mental health, particularly when carried out in sociable groups – just like the assemblies of earlier centuries.

It is perhaps this combination of warmth and individuality that gives jumpers an emotive element like no other garment, particularly when they have been hand-knitted. In a recent oral-history survey on clothing, many respondents listed a sweater as their favourite garment. Liz, born in 1969, wrote: 'Favourite garment ever – a HUGE black jumper. I've had a succession of them over the years. Eventually they become so shrunk or worn people demand I stop wearing them.' Jodie, born in 1954, recalled, 'My favourite sweater was a long black tunic with cowl neck and batwing sleeves bought in C&A in 1975. I've worn it for over 30 years but it's beginning to get so thin in places I think it will disintegrate soon.' More poignantly, Madeleine, born in 1959, recalled: 'My grandma did used to knit me lovely jumpers and cardigans. My favourite was a pale lemon mohair jumper. I used to rub my lips against the sleeves. I think it was a kind of security blanket.'

Jumpers may not survive in great numbers, but those that do are tremendously personal, evoking powerful memories of loved ones. In December 1943 Barrow-in-Furness housewife Nella Last wrote a journal entry about the arrival of a parcel containing an old jersey belonging to her absent and dearly missed son. He had embroidered it with travel memorabilia in his spare time. Nella wrote: 'I gathered it up in my arms and felt it so much a part of Cliff, the thoughts and dreams, regrets and heartaches in every stitch. It felt a living thing.'

POCKET FLAPS

Can you remember how six of your friends carry their hand-bags? (By the way, how do you carry your own?) Do they clutch them for fear of a sneak-thief – squash under the arm to the detriment of both bag and coat – sling from the shoulder to bang into the faces of other luckier travellers who have got seats in a crowded bus – dangle from two fingers? Handbag-carrying is an art because a bag should be a final touch to an outfit.

BETTY PAGE, *ON FAIR VANITY*, 1954

DAINTY SADDLEBAGS

Strictly speaking, handbags are an accessory rather than an item of dress. However, they began life many centuries ago as an integral part of clothing – as the pouches formed by the belted folds of a Roman toga, or the tucks in a countrywoman's apron. Handy items such as prayer books, scissors, grooming gear and knives might also dangle from belts on decorated chains called *chatelaines*. Pouches and purses were hung externally from a belt, but might be complemented by flat, fabric bags tied around the waist with thin strings and concealed *within* garments – these were pockets. Pouches, purses and pockets are the ancestors of the modern handbag. We'll begin with the story of the pocket . . .

The word *pocket* comes from the Middle English *poket* – a pouch or small bag. Pockets are described in 1688 as 'little Bags set on the inside, with a hole or slit on the outside; by which

1 According to *The Workwoman's Guide* of 1838, 'Pockets are either worn tied round the waist, fastened to the petticoat, or buttoned upon the stays. When fastened to the petticoat, they are made of the same material, otherwise of dimity, calico, jean, twilled muslin, and sometimes of nankeen or brown jean.'

2 The design source is 'Pattern for a Lady's Pocket'. Published by Alexr Hegg at the Kings Arms, No. 16 Paternoster Row Nov. 1 1786. It was made by Mary Hebbert in 1787.

any small thing may be carried about'. Perhaps because they are so easy to store, or perhaps in tribute to their beautiful embellishments, elite pocket-bags from the Renaissance have survived to the present day; others are visible in artwork from the era. Some have elaborate fringing, some are beaded, some are even crusted with jewels – they were definitely examples of conspicuous consumption.

It is more unusual to see surviving examples of non-elite pockets, but these were universal across the last two millennia. Hidden, waist-tied hanging pockets, which resembled dainty saddlebags, were worn by women from the seventeenth to the nineteenth centuries, when skirts were wide enough to envelop them without visible lumps. A hemmed slit in every layer of skirt and petticoats allowed access to the pocket, which was often of plain linen or cotton.[1] However, pockets could also be decorated with silk embroidery and crewel-work – surface stitching with fine, wool-worsted threads – of extraordinary beauty, sometimes in fanciful floral designs and at other times with charming images of contemporary events. One surviving pair of pockets, for example, feature a chain-stitch wool design showing Vincenzo Lunardi's famous balloon ascent at London's Artillery Ground in September 1784 – his dog and cat also feature.[2] The embroidered cat shows no signs of the airsickness that apparently plagued it during the actual flight.

A flat, fabric pocket to be worn beneath the clothes, with the slit for access visible.

'What', in the words of J. R. R. Tolkien's riddling creature Gollum, 'has it got in its pocketses?' Generally the contents of a pocket were to remain private. Some pockets even contained a further inner pocket, for extra security. However, historical and literary references to pockets can give us a tantalising insight into the personal paraphernalia carried around during everyday life in the past.

When Samuel Richardson's eighteenth-century fictional heroine Pamela escapes from imprisonment by an over-amorous admirer, she packs her belongings in her pockets, which must have been truly capacious: 'I took with me but one shift, besides what I had on, and two handkerchiefs, and two caps, which my pocket held (for it was not for me to encumber myself), and all my stock of money . . . and got out of the window, not without some difficulty.'

The diary of a Regency lady, Elizabeth Ham, gives other clues. While staying with friends, young Elizabeth hid her pocket behind her pillow, but was horrified to return to her room to fetch it, only to see it 'lying on the top of the bed, with every object it had contained spread about and the letters all lying open! Those letters that Misses in their teens write to each other!'

Aside from handkerchiefs and intimate letters, pockets were the home to keys, household tools and sewing paraphernalia – the same sort of things that might also be hung from the belt on a chatelaine. Later in the nineteenth century, pockets were more frequently sewn into clothes, rather than hung from a belt. They might contain a glorious miscellany of childhood treasures, such as the 'lovely hoards' collected by Gwen Raverat – a Victorian artist – in her youth: 'pencils and India-rubbers and a small sketch-book and a very large pocket-knife; besides, string, nails, horse-chestnuts, lumps of sugar, bits of bread-and-butter, a pair of scissors and very many other useful objects. Sometimes even a handkerchief.'

Naturally, real treasures were also secreted in pockets. The money and valuable watches frequently hidden within them were too great a temptation for criminals to resist – hence the term *pick pocket* for a thief who targeted pockets in clothes (as opposed to a *cut-purse*, who simply slashed the cords attaching a purse to a belt).

Wandering hands came close to intimate parts of the body, so the notion of picking pockets also had lascivious connotations. Sixteenth-century fashion critic Philip Stubbes called handbaskets 'clokes to sinne'. He claimed loose women used baskets as a decoy, 'under whiche pretence pretie conceites are practiced . . .' When the Lucy Locket of nursery-rhyme fame loses her pocket, the sexual entendre is there for anyone who wishes to see it. According to the rhyme, Lucy's pocket was found (empty) by one Kitty Fisher – this is supposedly a reference to the celebrated eighteenth-century courtesan Kitty Fisher, although the possible identity of Lucy herself is unknown.

This decorated mid-eighteenth-century woven silk pocket-flap kept pocket contents tucked inside – although it would be no deterrent to a skilled pickpocket.

Integral pockets for seventeenth- and eighteenth-century men were hidden within the generous folds of their coat skirts. These back-pleats were originally intended to accommodate a sword jutting backwards from where it hung on the sword belt. Such pockets were sometimes fastened with buttons to discourage pickpockets, and these buttons have survived in vestigial form at the top of jacket back-vents on formal tail coats of the twentieth century.

For security purposes, corsets could be supplied with pockets sewn into their lining, as with one eighteenth-century Russian corset, where valuables could be hidden at the front neckline. Even more ingeniously, Victorian inventor Bertha Ortell patented a design for a Combined Pocket and Garment Supporter, which hid valuables in two flap-fastening pockets *and* held up the stockings via strap suspenders. Canny female survivors of the 1912 *Titanic* tragedy carried their money into the lifeboats safely in home-made corset security pockets.

Hanging pockets, tied around the body, continued to be used, including when travelling; after the spread of the rail network they became known as 'railway pockets'. They survive in mutated form as both the slim security wallet that ties around the waist or neck and as the bulging 'bum bag' so beloved of the 1980s tourist.

POSTURING POCKETS

Not all pockets were hidden. From the nineteenth century onwards, men's tailoring in particular incorporated visible specialist pockets. The point was not to see precisely what was inside the pocket; the mere fact of the pocket's existence advertised the valuable contents. So, for example, smart gentlemen such as Beau Brummell kept their snuff-box of choice in a slim pocket on the inside of the waistcoat.[3] A 'pocket watch' was, of course, named after its usual resting place. If the pocket itself was too discreet, a watch fob dangled from the pocket, or a watch chain was boldly hung across the torso to advertise the hidden wealth.[4]

Victorian ladies shaped their watch pockets with whalebone or ribbon wire to make them a snug fit for timepieces (though

3 Sometimes pocket flaps were added to garments simply to suggest a multitude of (possibly valuable) possessions – they might never actually have anything in them.

4 Large watch pockets made of a fabric matching the four-poster bed curtains were hung beside Georgian and Victorian beds to provide a safe resting place for the timepiece overnight.

they might also store smelling bottles and handkerchiefs). Late nineteenth-century medical staff later adopted a small pocket on the chest for smaller watches, which were eventually pinned to the chest instead, for ease of consultation. Five-pocket denim Levi jeans still have a watch pocket at the front hip, a vestige of a historical need. Other accessories might also merit special pockets – in the 1870s there was even a brief fad for flamboyant fan pockets of crinkled fabric on the outside of the skirt. The folded fan was slipped inside, with its decorative tasselled handle on show. Tickets for bus, rail or steamer travel were kept in ticket pockets high on the front of the jacket, not to be confused with the handkerchief pocket, which a modern dandy may still use for a notional triangle of folded hanky.

The twentieth century brought further changes. Civilians in both World Wars added large patch pockets to coats and air-raid suits to ensure they always had essential items handy during emergencies. As men's professional dress codes relaxed and jackets could be removed at work, pockets also appeared on the shirt breast. These were soon appropriated for pens – which invariably leaked onto the fabric – for sunglasses and, more recently, for the ubiquitous mobile phone. Pockets on trousers were another twentieth-century innovation, as with the multi-pouched cargo-pants pockets or the special thigh-top plastic-coated map pockets for aviators.

Pockets also play an essential role in human space travel. The Velcro-flapped pockets of spacesuits are invaluable for accessibly storing tools during extra-vehicular activity, as well as for keeping more sentimental items close. Buzz Aldrin recalled an important moment prior to leaving the surface of the moon after the historic 1969 landing: 'Instinctively my hand moved to a pocket on my spacesuit that contained a special pouch in which I carried an original mission patch honouring the men who died aboard *Apollo 1* as well as various medals honouring Soviet cosmonauts.' Aldrin's pocket also held a silicon disc inscribed with good wishes from the leaders of seventy-three nations of the world, and a gold pin in the shape of an olive branch of peace.

Pockets such as these were added to the outside of shirts and blouses in the 1920s as a neat design feature.

Menswear was able to incorporate pockets as part-garments with little difficulty. For women, the battle has long been between the desire for practicality and the urge to follow fashions which often dictated costumes that fitted very closely to the body. Many Victorian gowns were cluttered with ruffles, swags and bows over bodices of complex construction. Finding a convenient place for a pocket was not easy. One dress expert in 1894 wrote about the pocket, 'Dressmakers take a weird delight in concealing it, and you have to search for it as long and fruitlessly as for hidden treasure.' This she ascribed to a desire for revenge, pure and simple: 'It is through the pocket that the dressmaker repays (and with interest) all the annoyance her customer causes her.'

In the twentieth century designer Elsa Schiaparelli played with the issues of real and fake pockets in women's clothing as part of her passion for surrealism. Her 1940s 'Tailored Desk' suit had multiple pockets on the front of the jacket, each with large drawer-knobs instead of buttons. To add to the subversion, some of the pockets were real and some were fake. None were seriously supposed to be used to put things in, however – that would have spoiled the tailored line of the jacket.

Feeling just as playful, but with rather more political bite in her message, American suffragist Alice Duer Miller wrote a fabulous satire subverting the more ridiculous arguments put forward as to why women shouldn't have the vote. In 'Why We Oppose Pockets for Women' imagined bigots declare that pockets are 'not a natural right'; that they will 'destroy man's chivalry toward woman, if he did not have to carry all her things in his pockets' and that 'it would make dissension between husband and wife as to whose pockets were to be filled'.

The solution to pocket issues for women? Portable pockets, which we call *purses* and *handbags*.

PORTABLE POCKETS

Pockets are integral to clothing, or tied within layers of clothes. Purses – in the sense of little bags containing valuables – have the same function as pockets, but are not attached. Whether plain or embellished, leather or fabric, stitched or knotted or knitted, purses have always coexisted comfortably with pockets. The basic purse style has endured from antiquity till today – a circle of fabric or leather, gathered by a drawstring into a pouch form. The addition of ribbons or strings meant the purse could be dangled freely from the hand or wrist, rather than fastened to a belt. Such purses were commonplace, in various forms, at all levels of society. They became known as *indispensables* in the eighteenth century and, more enduringly, as *reticules*. 'Reticule' is supposedly a contraction of *ridiculous*, which was the alleged male response to this frivolous accessory. It could indeed be decorated to the point of silliness, with fringing, beadwork and tassels. The colours were far from discreet: a reticule pattern from the 1830s suggests a bag of violet and green, lined with gold silk. This little hand-carried bag was essential for women adopting the revolutionary fashions of the late eighteenth century, when hoops and bulky petticoats were discarded in favour of the flimsy 'Empire'-style gowns that left no room for the body beneath, let alone an internal pocket. Queen Victoria was not immune to the lure of the hand-carried bag. During her State Visit to Paris in 1855 she carried an enormous white reticule embroidered with a fat poodle in gold. Sadly, it seems no photographs or sketches survive.

From this basic style, which we now call the *Dorothy bag*, a dazzling regiment of hand-held bags – or *handbags* – has marched through history to the present day. It is now very difficult to say the word 'handbag' without conjuring up Lady Bracknell, the supercilious character from Oscar Wilde's 1895 play *The Importance of Being Earnest*. During the course of the play Lady Bracknell is horrified to discover that an apparently respectable suitor for her daughter was, as a baby, abandoned at a railway station in a handbag. '*A handbag?*' she repeats in stentorian tones, to the great delight of every theatre or film audience since the play's premiere.

The handbag per se is generally far more complex than a mere purse – often a well-structured leather or plastic form, with zips, clasps or buckles. The early decades of the twentieth century saw bags dangling on long chains, or slotted over the wrist. Animal hides vied with fabric bags for popularity. Leather certainly suited the woman who wished her bag to appear professional, and it soon became the norm for the daytime handbag at least. A variety of exotic skins were soon on sale, including alligator and snakeskin. For evening wear there were beaded bags that glittered in modern electric lights, and satin bags that shimmered next to satin gowns. Those looking to get a new bag on a budget could take advantage of department-store sales, or make their own. Leather crafting kits were not too daunting, or else knitted bags were a breeze.

This 1930s knitted bag, in blue wool, features a fancy innovation – a 'zip' fastener. How modern!

Bags now carried all the 'essentials' of the modern woman: her money purse, handkerchief, notebook, calling cards, gloves and, last but not least, her make-up. Applying cosmetics in public was daring for the Edwardian lady; for a woman in the 1920s it was no longer vulgar, but chic. Handbags were adapted to carry mirrors and powderpuff pockets. Dainty box-bags called *minaudières* were actually crafted as complete miniature make-up sets. From the 1950s novelty bags in transparent Lucite were all the rage, and they are still highly collectable. In fact over the last century handbags have become something of a cult.

Handbags from 1938. Leather was the most popular choice for bags, being durable and waterproof.

Today these portable pockets are vastly enlarged. They are slung over shoulders, across backs, under arms or clutched in manicured hands. Far from hiding away in the folds of clothing, we carry our pockets for all to see. In the 1960s dresses were so simple that the handbag – perhaps slung from a gold chain over the shoulder – became a status symbol in its own right. Jackie Kennedy exemplified this development. Certain styles soon became highly covetable and collectable. A modern 'It' bag might cost a cool £10,000 – and be considered an investment.

Handbags such as these 1960s styles are relatively new on the fashion scene, but most women could hardly imagine life without them.

'Designer' bags now boast coveted logos – the 'CC' of quilted Chanel bags with their distinctive linked-chain straps, or the brown-and-gold Louis Vuitton bags that have launched countless imitations, or whichever other 'on-trend' brand happens to be being sported by celebrities and aspiring fashionistas. Bags contain our portable necessities – sometimes far more paraphernalia than is strictly necessary for daily use. They also act as a barrier in public, both metaphorically (in the sense that they can be clutched for confidence or held across the body) and literally, as when Princess Grace of Monaco – the actress Grace Kelly – used her Hermès bag to disguise signs of pregnancy during a 1956 photoshoot for the cover of *Life* magazine. It was named the 'Kelly' bag in her honour.

Handbags can now command huge prices if they have a coveted label or vintage pedigree. For some women, buying and collecting bags is an addiction – and an expensive one at that. For some men, bags are an uncomfortable necessity for times when pockets simply aren't big enough. The 'man-bag' of modern times is often ridiculed, despite the fact that it is only a slight variation of sartorially acceptable bags such as the open-jawed Gladstone bag, named after the statesman William Gladstone, or the haversack, which was originally a soldier's bag to carry haver-cakes – oat rations.

However, many modern women – no matter how large their handbag collections – are still frustrated to find that the pockets of their tailored suits and skirts are fakes, or stitched shut to preserve the line of the garment. Dresses in particular have a frustrating lack of pockets, except patch-pockets added for decoration.

'Why mayn't we have Pockets?' mourned Gwen Raverat in the 1950s. 'Who forbids it? We have got Women's Suffrage, but why must we still always be inferior to Men?' It is a lament that still strikes a chord today.

IN THE SWIM

Bathing is a sport
Enjoyed by great and small
In suits of any sort
But better none at all
ANON.

DIPPING IN DRAWERS

The idea of wearing specialist clothes for swimming is relatively recent in human history. In Ancient Greece and Rome citizens escaped the summer heat of the cities to relax at coastal towns. If they bathed, it was in bathhouses or rivers and they were naked. In post-Classical Europe nudity remained the norm for river-swimming, although there are images of medieval men bathing in their drawers. Ironically, such was the change in Western European attitudes towards public displays of nudity by the gentility, when seventeenth-century spas were opened in imitation of the Roman baths, that clothing for bathing was required. So it was that Celia Fiennes, a gentlewoman touring Britain in 1687, wrote of indoor bathers in Bath, 'The ladyes goes into the bath with garments made of fine yellow canvas, with great sleeves like a parson's gown, the water fills it up so that it is borne off that your shape is not seen, it does not cling close.' Gentlemen apparently took to the waters in 'drawers and waste-coates of the same sort of canvas'.

The women observed by Fiennes were wearing loose shifts, which understandably ballooned up in the water. A century later these shifts were made of flannel rather than canvas, but were just as modest. In a lively poem of 1813 – 'Poetical Sketches of Scarborough' – it is recorded that, while dipping in the North Sea, 'the ladies, dress'd in flannel-cases, Show nothing but their handsome faces'. These fashionable bathers were quite literally *dipped*: sturdy professional Dippers were employed to seize those who were too timid to descend from the steps of their bathing machines and to push them under the waves in a process known as 'shuddering' or 'sobbing'. More independent women enjoyed a gentle immersion without such help, although swimming as exercise was not widely practised.

The fashion for swimming in a shift continued well into the nineteenth century, with bathers at Ramsgate wallowing in the shallows and letting each surge of the waves 'carry their dresses up to their neck, so that, as far as decency is concerned, they might as well be without any dresses at all . . .' A pamphlet from the 1860s described the British bathing costume as 'a chemise or shirt of blue flannel, open at the chest and tied round the neck. It reaches a little below the knee, and is just long enough to make swimming impossible, but by no means adapted either in size or shape, to effectually answer the requirements of decency.' Being able to swim in it was clearly not a requirement for the costume – yet. In fact many British people never learnt to swim, even if they lived on the coast.

It seems that not all ladies felt the need to cover up when swimming in public; in 1857 the Marquis of Westmeath attempted to introduce a bill in Parliament to enforce swimwear on those women who 'go down to the sea-bathing places and dance in the water without any covering whatever, to the great disgust of the respectable inhabitants and visitors'. The bill did not provoke any interest in the House of Lords and was withdrawn.

Since many mid-Victorian men still preferred bathing in the nude, there were many light-hearted caricatures of ladies equipped with spy-glasses who had 'accidentally' stumbled across some coastal cove reserved for gentlemen. However, sensibilities became more delicate as the nineteenth century progressed, and men were forced to adopt what one disgruntled vicar, Francis Kilvert, termed 'the detestable custom of bathing in drawers'. Reverend Kilvert's diaries recount his chagrin at having to wear drawers in Shanklin on the Isle of Wight in 1874:

> The rough waves stripped them off and tore them down round my ankles. While thus fettered I was seized and flung down by a heavy sea, which retreating, suddenly left me lying naked on the sharp shingle from which I rose streaming with blood. After this I took the wretched and dangerous rag off and of course there were some ladies looking on as I came up out of the water.

Reverend Kilvert added, 'If ladies don't like to see a man naked why don't they keep away from the sight?'

However, by the 1880s some town councils had made it illegal to bathe nude, as with this by-law of the Borough of Colchester from 1882:

> No person shall bathe from any Highway, Street, or public place without wearing drawers or such other dress covering as is necessary to prevent indecent exposure.

Nevertheless, skinny-dippers continued to plague public parks and rivers. Victorian ladies had to take pains to avoid the sight of male nudity. In the 1890s a boating expedition in Cambridge passed perilously close to a naked bather, so 'each Lady unfurled a parasol, and, like an ostrich, buried her head in it, and gazed earnestly into its silky depths, until the crisis was past, and the river was decent again'. The problem persisted into the early twentieth century, when not all children could have afforded a bathing costume, even if they had wanted to wear one – in Hyde Park in 1925 an irate female police officer, hampered by a heavy wool uniform, was photographed chasing cheeky naked boys away from the water.

As the notion of actually *swimming*, rather than *dipping*, gained popularity, so women in particular had to fight against new trends towards elaborate costumes more suited for a fashion magazine than for full immersion. Victorian bathing costumes are a treat to behold, but must have been a nightmare to swim in.

Women's complex costumes of the late 1890s were quite an impediment to actual swimming.

Nineteenth-century chaps, if not swimming in the nude, could wear home-made cotton drawers, or a one-piece costume. This was usually of a natty striped jersey fabric, and rather like a vest and drawers combined, with or without sleeves. Baggy when dry and clingy when wet, these stripy suits have remained in our cultural memory as an iconic image of the Victorian seaside swimmer.

Women's bathing suits were usually of wool or cotton jersey in blues and reds, with jaunty sailor collars, maritime piping and the occasional anchor motif. The basic design consisted of all-in-one combinations with buttons, which held an attached wrap-around knee-length skirt in place. Accessorised with silk or rubber swim caps and knitted stockings, such outfits were supremely unsuitable for energetic swimming. That said, they were praised by a fashion editor in 1896 for at least being an improvement on the idea 'that a sack arrangement tied in the middle is all that is required of us, when braving the perils of three or four inches of water'. That editor went on to recommend silky-looking stockinette for the bathing gown, matched with cork-soled sandals and a red silk turban. Appliqué anchors on the costume paid suitable homage to the nautical nature of the ensemble. The bodice and knickers were to be made separately, 'doing away with any fear of a hiatus appearing when the skirt floats on the water'.

Cap, boots, sash, skirt and drawers... this Parisian swimsuit of 1915 makes quite a style statement.

Swimming for sport was already increasing in popularity when fourteen-year-old Agnes Beckwith stunned the world, both with her record-smashing long-distance swims in the River Thames in 1875 and with her shortened, practical swimwear. As well as clocking up many long-distance records, Beckwith coached other swimmers and performed in aquatic entertainment shows at the Royal Aquarium, Westminster. Billed as *The Greatest Lady Swimmer in the World*, she wore a performance costume that showed touches of Classical themes, with draped fabric and ruching, so that the public would think of her as a water nymph rather than a hussy. Her everyday swimwear was an unadorned, dark jersey one-piece – as close to streamlining as any Victorian could get. Such was her popularity that the press forgave her relatively skimpy swimsuit, voicing the opinion that 'Young ladies ought to be able to enjoy bathing at the seaside far more than they do in the ugly gowns custom makes them wear.'

Despite this public approbation, the layers and wool for women's swimwear prevailed into the twentieth century, even if the skirt part of the costume rose to mid-thigh and the sleeves became little caps. The suit itself wasn't the only impediment to movement. Novelist and socialite Barbara Cartland recalled the aggravation of swimming in stockings just before the First World War: 'Three or four vigorous kicks when swimming, and my stockings were dangling a long way beyond my toes; they were either sucked off altogether or wrapped round my ankles like fetters by the time I emerged.' Nurse Edith Appleton also struggled to swim during her rare hours away from service during the First World War, though her difficulties were caused by a second-hand costume that was at least two sizes too big. She wrote, 'I had to swim two strokes then pull up my breeches – two strokes – and so forth, but they just about stayed on.'

SLEEK AND STREAMLINED

Post-First World War costumes were to reflect new social liberties for both sexes, leading to an increasing marriage of form and function in swimwear.

Streamlining – soon to become prevalent in architecture and transport – was already a feature of swimming costumes for those wealthy enough to afford daring designs. By the 1920s tight body-hugging jersey fabrics complemented the cult of physical beauty through sport, which dominated the Twenties and Thirties. Black costumes with low-cut fronts, backs, deep armholes, no sleeves and very short trunks rendered the wearer sleek and unisex, through the use of flesh-flattening panelling around the groin for men and across the bust for women. The addition of moulded unisex rubber bathing caps added to the smooth silhouette.

In 1926 swimmer Gertrude Ederle – the Olympic Gold Medal-winner known as 'Queen of the Waves' – wore a streamlined costume and covered her entire body in grease for insulation when she became the first woman to swim the English Channel. Clocking in at fourteen hours and thirty-four minutes, Ederle broke all previous records (held by male swimmers) of sixteen hours thirty-three minutes. Her reception as a heroic athlete was rather different from that of Australian swimmer Annette Kellerman, known as the 'Million Dollar Mermaid' because of her mass popularity at home and in the United States. At the height of her fame, at Revere beach in Massachusetts in 1907, Kellerman was arrested because she was wearing a bare-armed unitard costume that fitted every contour of her physique. It was considered too indecent for public display.

All-in-one suits for seaside swimmers of the very early 1920s – more streamlined than before, but not too revealing.

However, such were the changes in society during the First World War and afterwards that it was impossible to contain the movement towards body-skimming costumes. Women's fashions of the Twenties revealed more of their body than ever before; so did their swimwear. In the 1920s skimpier costumes, coupled with complete dissolution of gender segregation at holiday camps and public swimming baths, led to the coining of the phrase 'Lido Libido' to describe the phenomenon of amorous liaisons at the poolside.

In contrast, some respectable middle-class and working-class trippers in the Twenties, Thirties and Forties resolutely wore complete 'Sunday Best' outfits to the beach: shoes, shirt, tie, hat and wool suit for the men; blouse, skirt, corset, petticoats, stockings, shoes, hat and fur-collared coats for the women. Young girls were at least allowed the relief of tucking their layers into their knickers for a paddle.

The new androgyny of nubile swimmers was a shock to older generations who had been used to stricter delineation between the genders, the unremitting formality of menswear in public, and the allure of the well-clothed female form. 'It is deplorable,' comments the fictional detective Hercule Poirot of sunbathers on the beach. 'To-day everything is standardised.' He also complains that the sunbathers remind him of the morgue in Paris: 'Bodies – arranged on slabs – like butcher's meat!'

Advances in fabric technology were the crux of twentieth-century form-fitting swimming costumes. In 1913 the company Jantzen launched its quality rib-stitch garments. The sleek Jantzen 'Diving Girl' logo would become possibly the most recognised swimwear brand of the century, changing only to reflect updated aesthetics – she had a flat chest and straps on her costume in the 1920s; a prominent bosom and no straps at all from the 1950s. From 1925, Lastex helped suits keep their shape, thanks to the innovative combination of cotton or silk fibres wound around a rubber core, then woven into a stretchy fabric. As well as Jantzen, the other company set to make its mark on swimwear was the McCrae Knitting Mills, established in Australia in 1914. It specialised initially in knitted underwear, but launched its first streamlined swimwear in 1927, rebranding as Speedo Knitting Mills in 1928. At first the brand achieved notoriety for producing women's silk costumes with narrow straps and hardly any back covering – a *racerback* – which was considered far too revealing, even for the Twenties. Further controversy followed in 1936 when male swimmers at the Berlin Olympics competed in Speedo trunks, not a one-piece. The trunks were cut more like briefs than shorts, and by the 1960s they were very small and snug indeed. The Speedo company is still very much at the forefront of swimwear textile innovation, but the name *speedo* is often used as a generic term for tiny swimming briefs.

However, not everyone could afford Jantzen or Speedo swimsuits, and it is the hand-knitted costume that holds such an affectionate place in many people's memories of mid-century swimwear.

KNITTED COSSIES

Home-knitted costumes were the thrifty swimmer's answer to the possibly prohibitive prices of 'shop-bought' swimwear. Patterns were advertised in women's magazines – and very fetching the costumes looked in the accompanying illustrations. They were often not so appealing in reality. Sand-traps when dry, they quickly became frontless and backless when wet, sagging down to the knees and beyond. One elderly gent from Whitley Bay couldn't help but laugh as he recounted to the author his embarrassment when, as a little lad, he wore rather loose home-made knitted trunks on the beach: 'Me mother worra slack knitter!' he chortled.

Similarly, a Yorkshire woman recalled bunking off school to go to the local pool:

We hired our swimming costumes, which were very blue, very woolly and very prickly! I dived in, pulled myself out, and lo . . . there was my not ample bosom on display for the world to see! Gave a whole new meaning to the breast stroke!!

Home-made knitted costumes from the 1940s – saggy sand-trappers, but fun for paddling.

An unlucky RAF officer experienced another issue with knitted swimwear whilst enjoying water sports in the 1940s. Unbeknown to him, while poised at the top of a slide at the lido, his RAF-issue blue knitted trunks became snagged on a nail. He descended at speed. By the time he reached the end of the slide his trunks had almost completely unravelled.

Wool also attracted insect life, despite the labels on commercial swimsuits that boldly declared 'guaranteed moth-proof'. One army engineer had strong swimming skills, which enabled him to reach the safety of a fishing vessel during the evacuation of the British Expeditionary Force from northern France in 1940. However, he suffered quite an embarrassment during a post-war seaside holiday. Having ignored his wife's assertion that his woollen costume wasn't fit to wear, after six years of wartime storage, he entered the sea enthusiastically . . . and emerged to give a very public demonstration of the appetite of moth larvae.

Fortunately moths didn't care for man-made fibres, such as the nylon mixes of the 1950s. By then, Hollywood had become the primary inspiration for swimwear styles – both the trunks of big-chested actors and the suits sheathing the hourglass forms of actresses. Female costumes were heavily structured with pads, zips, boning and elasticated panels to achieve such an ideal. Bright prints reflected post-war optimism. Ethnic patterns reflected new opportunities for passenger air travel and cheap package holidays.

Once again modern fabric technologies provided new opportunities for styles and fit. Nylon created a swimwear revolution – suits that actually retained their shape and dried easily; Elastene was introduced to costumes in the early 1970s, which meant that women's suits could eventually do without internal shaping, much to the dismay of exercise-averse wearers. Neoprene was developed in 1953 during experiments by the company O'Neill, which went on to popularise long 'surf' shorts for men. The material was an important factor in the development of specialist suits for snorkelling and scuba-diving.

Neoprene was sleek and useful for covering the body in cold conditions, but the next departure for swimwear was a costume that would be the smallest ever created: the *bikini*.

BIKINI, MONOKINI, MANKINI

There were *two-piece* swimming costumes before the Second World War, but these covered a relatively large amount of flesh; they were usually made of a crinkly elastic-smocked fabric, genteelly hiding the navel. However, such demure costumes hardly prepared the world for the arrival of the bikini. The skimpy ensemble hit the headlines in 1946 when French engineer Louis Réard circulated images of it being worn by a dancer. He named the design the *bikini*, after the French atomic-bomb tests on Bikini Atoll, because this was a huge news story at the time and was symbolic of the new, modern post-war world. Réard claimed the only 'true' bikini was one that was small enough to be pulled through a wedding ring.

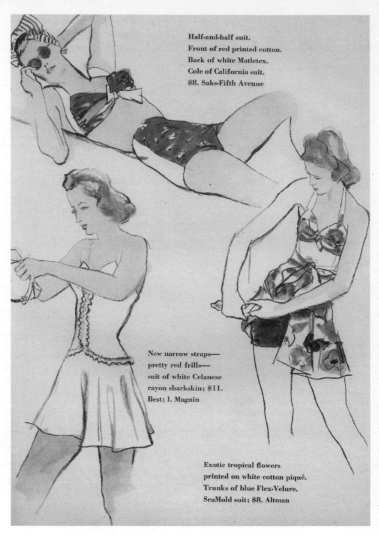

Half-and-half suit.
Front of red printed cotton.
Back of white Matletex.
Cole of California suit.
$8. Saks-Fifth Avenue

New narrow straps—
pretty red frills—
suit of white Celanese
rayon sharkskin; $11.
Best; I. Magnin

Exotic tropical flowers
printed on white cotton piqué.
Trunks of blue Flex-Velure.
SeaMold suit; $8. Altman

Two-piece suits advertised in US Vogue *in 1943.*

Despite disapproval from the Vatican and other concerned organisations, the bikini gradually became acceptable for public wear. Actress Brigitte Bardot wore one, to great effect, in the 1957 film *And God Created Woman*; another notable example was sported by Ursula Andress in the 1962 James Bond film *Dr No* – complete with knife scabbard. Two years later Rudi Gernreich's *monokini* – briefs supported by two shoulder-straps

– provided the next swimwear sensation. It was followed by the fad for crocheted bikinis in the 1970s, which were intended to reveal as much sun-bronzed body as possible.

A 1970 crocheted bikini – not for vigorous water sports, but ideal for sunbathing.

At this time men's trunks became so brief they were known as 'budgie-smugglers'. This fashion was followed in the 1980s by baggy surf shorts with mesh pouches inside. In subsequent decades, men have been able to choose between small trunks and loose shorts for everyday swimming. The one-piece, once a staple of men's swimwear, is now only seen in *wetsuit* form for those enjoying vigorous water sports, or in the second-skin racer suits of Olympic athletes. The most humorous male answer to the bikini was comedian Sacha Baron Cohen's flaunting of a neon-green *mankini* in his 2006 mockumentary, *Borat*. These *sling* swimsuits, with a groin pouch and two long shoulder straps, had been quietly on sale in France and the US since the 1990s, before the outrageous *Borat* version hit the big screen.

Gradually the season for selling swimwear in department stores changed from summer months only to all year round.

Couture houses created 'luxe' designs purely for resort wear, embellished with metal and plastic and twinned with sarongs and kaftans appropriated from other cultures. Contemporary swimwear can be found to suit every figure and every pursuit. For sport, modern swimmers take advantage of the latest textile technologies in suits inspired by sharkskin, for the ultimate streamlining. There are wetsuits and dry suits for every kind of water sport. For leisure swimming and beach promenading, elasticated nylons still dominate. Few mourn the loss of the knitted swimming costume.

THE HAT BOX

No-one knew better than Granny Weatherwax that hats were important. They weren't just clothing. Hats defined the head. They defined who you were. No-one had ever heard of a wizard without a pointy hat – at least, no wizard worth speaking of. And you certainly never heard of a witch without one.

TERRY PRATCHETT, *WITCHES ABROAD*, 1992

A HATLESS SOCIETY

Where are all the hats?

The modern house no longer has hats resting on poles, hooked above hall mirrors or on the prongs of coat stands. We own no hat brushes. We do not buy hat dye. With few exceptions, we are a hatless society.

In fact being bare-headed in public is a remarkably new phenomenon in civilised human history. Hats have, for millennia, offered protection and shown status. They have – depending on style and circumstance – indicated taste (or lack of it), modesty, frivolity or seriousness. They have hidden identity or flaunted fashion. They have been worn to blend in . . . and to stand out.

Given the universality of hats and headwear prior to the mid-twentieth century, as well as the near infinite variety of styles worn, we may well offer to *eat our hats* in surprise that an accessory which was a highly significant indicator of rank, gender, occupation and style is now really only worn for winter-warmth, as a religious or cultural requirement or on very formal occasions, such as weddings or Royal Ascot.

Hats are no longer removed as a sign of respect, or thrown down to signal the start of a fight. The elaborate staging of American graduations is possibly the sole surviving scenario where hats – in this case mortar boards – are flung into the air as a sign of celebration. Bonnets with bees in, dunce-hats and thinking caps now exist only as metaphors and in museums.

In consigning hats to history, we have lost a great deal. Like shoes, hats are immensely personal. They mould to the contours of the head. They collect trace-evidence of our uniqueness – skin cells and stray strands of hair. To an astute observer, the way a hat is donned, doffed, trimmed and tilted can reveal many clues about the wearer.

Hats can answer a wide range of needs and be used to convey all kinds of messages. Those that survive into modern times have very interesting ancestors. The sheer number and variety of hat styles means that to attempt, even concisely, to set out an evolutionary tree for headwear would be all but impossible. Instead we shall limit ourselves to looking at some of the most significant implications that hats have acquired over the years and shall examine a few highlights within each category.

HEAD PROTECTION

As with so many garments, the primary use of a hat is for protection.

In cold climates one of the best ways to retain body heat is by covering the head, usually with fur or wool. Early examples of warm hats include a bearskin cap worn by a *c.*5,000-year-old man found mummified in a glacier on the Austrian-Italian Alps, and the sheepskin hat worn by a man from the fourth century BCE, preserved in a peat bog at Tollund, in Denmark. In the following centuries there were many variations on cold-weather headgear. *Hoods* of wool were particularly popular in the Classical era, during the Middle Ages and the Renaissance;

they enveloped the head and kept the throat warm too. Fur hats had the advantage of showing prestige as well as keeping the wearer warm. The traditional Russian *ushanka* fur hat, with its fold-down ear flaps, is still worn today.

In Britain, however, wool was the preferred choice, not only because it retained heat well, but also because, historically, much of the country's economic prosperity was founded on the wool trade. People not only wore wool from inclination, but by law – as with a 1571 statute designed to support the British wool trade, which ordered the wearing of a 'cap of wool knit' on Sundays and holidays for all persons above six years old, with certain exceptions for rank and gender.[1] Despite a fine of three shillings and fourpence for each day's transgression, the Act was largely ignored and limped through its short legal life to a final repeal in 1597. Descendants of these knitted caps are still seen every winter in colder climates, albeit made of acrylic wool, and sometimes embellished with bobble tops.

1 Elizabethan knitted wool caps were found on building sites during the redevelopment of the city of London in the early twentieth century. In felted wool – perhaps in bright reds and blues – these Tudor caps would have been both warm and waterproof, and sported ear flaps for extra protection from the elements.

During the Second World War the woolly balaclava of servicemen was symbolically likened to a Crusader's chainmail hood.

For truly extreme levels of cold there was an innovation from the Crimean War. This knitted full-head covering was devised by frost-bitten soldiers and associated with the 1854 battle of Balaclava, hence its now well-known name *balaclava*. Some variations of the balaclava helmet leave the face exposed, while others cover all but the eyes. They were knitted by the ton for servicemen in the First World War, and worn in both World Wars by aviators in unheated aeroplanes. Modern polar explorer Sir Ranulph Fiennes has described his perpetual battle to keep the head warm in temperatures well below zero: 'Our ears were muffled by at least two balaclavas plus our jacket hood, and every movement of frosted clothing or of skis on crusty snow made hearing difficult.' On a more sinister note, the black balaclava is now synonymous with paramilitary groups and terrorists, both to hide identity and to intimidate.

At the other end of the weather spectrum, hats are essential to protect the head from overheating and sunburn. Woven fibre hats provided the earliest forms of protection. Conical reed hats are seen in Ancient Egyptian art from Thebes, dating to around 3,200 BCE; conical bamboo and straw hats feature strongly in Asian costume across the millennia, where they were particularly useful for field-workers labouring in strong sun. In Europe the conical straw hat worn by some outdoor workers was replaced in the eighteenth century by a straw hat with a crown and a brim; and by the more sophisticated fabric structure of the *sola topee* or *pith helmet* that is so often associated with Victorian explorers. Female agricultural or coastal workers of the seventeenth century onwards wore wide straw hats and, in the eighteenth century, devised their own cotton or linen sun bonnets, with a ribbed arch around the face, gatherings at the back of the head and a curtain of fabric to protect the neck. Nineteenth-century British soldiers adapted this protective detail during the Indian Uprising of 1857, securing a white cloth covering onto their caps, with a flap hanging down at the back. It was named a *havelock* after General Sir Henry Havelock, who went to the relief of British troops and civilians at Lucknow. An 1859 portrait of Havelock by Thomas Jones Barker exhibited at the National Portrait Gallery in London shows him wearing this distinctive neck-curtain.

The Victorian sun bonnet was further developed by the

addition of covered cane hoops at the front brim for extra protection. This practical, yet unprepossessing accessory was named an 'ugly', and rightly so. Thankfully by the 1920s a clever design for flamboyant cotton-print sun hats that twisted and folded flat for travel was available instead.[2]

Astonishingly, hats were also created with the express purpose of protecting... well, hats. The eighteenth-century *calash* or *caleche* hood was a vast contraption of silk and hoops that could safely cover caps, ribbons and wigs without crushing them. They were considered excellent for ladies walking short distances to evening parties. The earliest example of a weather-proofed garment in the London Museum costume collection is an oiled silk calash hood from the late eighteenth century. It is a far cry from the classic yellow oiled silk sou'wester that came to be worn by New England fishermen in the nineteenth century.

The idea of a waterproof hat was taken to extremes in 1920, when plans were submitted to the British patent office for an umbrella hat, intended as a 'simpler and more convenient substitute' for the umbrella. This hat was no more ridiculous than another invention – a top hat with a coiled spring inside, which would rebuff heavy objects falling onto the hat.

A theoretical Edwardian top hat to protect the wearer from falling objects.

For those who need genuine, practical head protection, hard hats are worn. They have a long ancestry. For example, Chinese

2 Somewhat bizarrely, a 1943 handbook on nursing in Blitz conditions suggested making a hat of folded newspaper for use against heatstroke, with a fresh cabbage leaf placed on the head for additional cooling properties.

3 Before the 1890s professional male cooks worked in a variety of headgear including, but not limited to, night-caps, skull caps, tam-o'-shanters, and pork-pie hats with tassels. By the early twentieth century the tam-o'-shanter had risen in height to become the iconic white, cylindrical hat. Habit and affectation established it as the norm, although most modern chefs resort to smaller, neater caps.

people drafted in to help construct sections of the famous Great Wall between the seventh and fourth centuries had woven plant-fibre hats, with light webbing underneath to act as a buffer between hat and scalp. Since then, various professions have devised their own hard hats, including the tall helmet worn by London Metropolitan Police from the 1860s onwards, the crested brass helmets of the Metropolitan Fire Engine Establishment from the same decade, and the tin helmets of twentieth-century soldiers. From the late 1930s aluminium hats were used for protection, but they were superseded by new thermoplastics from the 1950s onwards. Now modern hard hats, such as the yellow hats worn by construction workers, benefit from such extra-strong thermoplastic moulding with internal suspension straps.

GET-AHEAD HATS

In addition to the basic need for protection, at every level of society throughout history there have been hats to show occupation. In some cases a certain type of hat starts to be so strongly identified with one profession that it becomes synonymous with it. Examples of this might be the fisherman's sou'wester, the chef's white, puffed toque or the jockey's multicoloured brimmed riding cap.[3]

Occupational hats advertise expertise. If they are limited only to those who have acquired certain qualifications, then they come to embody this training or learning. Thus we have square, tasselled academic *mortar boards*, which, although rarely worn now, were once a very visible sign that a student had graduated from university. They were obligatory wear for university lecturers and secondary-school teachers until the mid-twentieth century, and are still worn at many graduation ceremonies (including North American high-school graduations). Mortar boards evolved from certain flat-topped caps worn by Christian clergy in the Renaissance, showing just how closely entwined Church and education were at this time. They got their name from their resemblance to mortar-mixing boards used by construction workers.

4 Firefighters now have highly visible yellow, thermoplastic helmets. Until 1866, when the Metropolitan Fire Brigade introduced brass helmets, leather helmets were worn. In 1937 London Fire Brigade adopted cork helmets covered with flameproof cotton and finished with acid-resistant and heat-resistant enamel.

Intended to confer dignity, the British teacher's mortar board is now irretrievably associated with an archaic educational ethos that is out of touch with a modern age.

Closely linked with the notion of advertising expertise is the use of hats to command respect. This was, of course, one side-effect of the mortar board. It is also still a crucial quality of the hats worn by professionals such as police officers and firefighters – people who need to impose order and authority quickly in complex situations. As firefighting and policing organisations formalised in the nineteenth century they often adopted high, crested helmets, which offered some degree of protection from head injuries, but also made them distinctive in a crowd.[4] The low-peaked caps of most twenty-first-century police forces perhaps suggest a contrasting desire not to appear too aloof – or perhaps their body armour, high-vis vests and multiple enforcement accessories already inspire enough respect.

Hats designed to encourage respect are, out of context, likely to inspire ridicule. Many occupation-specific hats were – and still are – more symbolic than sensible; some were even distinctly and deliberately impractical. The Christian bishop's *mitre* or the

British Grenadier Guard's *bearskin*, for example, are – when viewed out of context – improbable and rather ridiculous hats, but they carry a multitude of meanings. First, hats such as the mitre and the bearskin add height to the wearer. This gives stature, and therefore added status: the wearer can then tower over those of lesser rank. In a strongly hierarchical religious or military organisation this is crucial for emphasising relative levels of power. Second, they flaunt particular decorative and yet symbolic design details. The glossy cream-and-gold silk mitre may be said to augment the worship of God through its quality; the bearskin, by association with the bear itself, may confer connotations of powerful aggression. Military hats in particular also serve the purpose of displaying insignia, such as badges of rank and regiment.

Historically many of these occupational hats have been exclusively male, reflecting the exclusion of women from certain professions or their quasi-invisible status in the workforce: on the whole women wore their usual everyday hoods, bonnets and hats at work. Even when women joined the military, from the early twentieth century onwards, they were issued with smaller, more discreet styles of headwear, without the height – and therefore status – of their male colleagues. However, there was one area of work that came to be considered a female profession in the later nineteenth century and therefore had its own specialised headwear, distinct from any male trends: nursing.

Professional Victorian nurses wished to distinguish themselves from unqualified amateurs, servants or well-meaning relatives who tended patients at home or in hospital. Headgear was important in the battle to emphasise this distinction. Nurses' caps evolved from the fine white cotton or linen structures worn by nursing sisters of Christian religious orders from the Middle Ages onwards – although they were somewhat more subdued than the elaborate, highly wired contraptions worn by some religious women, which were intended to shield the face and signal the devout status of the wearer, but which were hardly practical for physical care-giving. As well as this spiritual association, the precise folding and pinning of starched white nurse caps denoted professionalism and hygiene, in contrast to the popular mid-Victorian image of nurses as dirty slatterns. Often unflattering and difficult to construct, the folded fabric headdresses of nurses in the early twentieth century had, by the 1970s, been replaced by easy-to-wear pre-formed caps – or hatlessness.[5]

Caring for children was also traditionally considered a female profession, and so nineteenth-century nannies had their own neat white caps, which – though similarly unprepossessing to those worn by nurses – could nevertheless imbue the wearer with status and authority in the eyes of a child. Here is the opinion of one young Victorian child from the pen of novelist Frances E. Crompton:

> We consider nurse a very cross person ... Her aprons are as stiff as the nursery tea-tray, besides being the same plain shape, and she will wear the tightest and sternest caps that ever were seen. Her caps were all strictish, but her Sunday cap was savage.

TOP HAT AND TAILS

The crowns of monarchs are the ultimate status headwear, but next in importance is the headwear worn by aristocracy and other elite groups. These might be the gold coronets of dukes and earls, the jewelled headdresses of ladies in Renaissance courts or the large plumed hats worn by Royalists of the seventeenth century. Jewels, feathers and fine fabrics for headwear were a highly visible way to distinguish nobility from commoner, rich from poor. Even the comparatively sober black-beaver bicornes and tricornes of the eighteenth century might be enlivened with a sprightly cockade or gold braid. For men, displays of status eventually settled to quite a wide class divide between those who wore *top hats* and those in *flat caps*.

5 Florence Nightingale, for all her impressive hospital management reforms, had complaints about the unflattering caps that her nurses were compelled to wear while working in military hospitals during the Crimean War of 1853–6.

The iconic Edwardian silk top hat.

Legend has it that the silk top hat was invented by a London haberdasher named John Hetherington. Cylindrical in shape and with a glossy satin surface over a felting of rabbit fur, it provoked a riot, according to contemporary reports, as the sight of him wearing it for the first time was so startling. Hetherington was charged 'with a breach of the peace for having appeared on the Public Highway wearing upon his head a tall structure having a shining lustre and calculated to frighten timid people'. However, by the late Regency period such hats were all the rage for gentlemen. It was a trend that would continue for more than a century.

By far the most typical image of the top hat in action is when it is matched with a sober frock coat. As such it represented conservatism, affluence and possibly political power. However, one of the most iconic images of the top hat is a photographic portrait from 1857 of the Victorian engineer Isambard Kingdom Brunel, standing before the giant launching chains of his iron ship, the SS *Great Eastern*. The photograph was taken by Robert Howlett, the year before the magnificent vessel sailed. In the photograph Brunel's hat is a very tall, very striking glossy beaver-fur hat, yet his clothes are clearly work-battered; the ensemble shows the fusion of his non-gentlemanly engineering background and his confident aspirations. In both clothes and deeds, Brunel bridged the divide between gentleman and worker.

Before the advent of specially constructed safety hats, women appropriated the top hat for riding, often teamed with a scarf wrapped around it. By the First World War they were riding in bowler hats, which were considered safer and more convenient.

As the frock coat was passed over in favour of the more informal lounge suit, so the fashion for the top hat dwindled too. They were, after all, expensive to buy and maintain. Gradually the silk top hat was commonly replaced by one of felted wool. Shifting etiquette in the twentieth century meant that the top hat became relegated to formal occasions – and to the silver screen. In the 1930s Fred Astaire wore 'top hat and tails' with great panache, in films designed to act as escapist fantasies for cinema-goers who were mired in the reality of post-Depression economies.

For many modern men, their first encounter with a formal hat will be with a hired grey felt topper for a smart wedding; this is also still required wear in the enclosure at Royal Ascot. For the most part, however, a welcome erosion of class structures has seen top hats relegated first to the top shelves of cupboards and wardrobes, and then donated to become a staple of Amateur Dramatic Club costume collections.

ROUND, FLAT AND FLAPPED

Further down the social scale from the top hat is the rounded black crown of the *bowler hat*, which took over from the top hat as the riding hat of choice in the late nineteenth century, until health-and-safety concerns pushed for proper hard hats in the mid-twentieth century.

The bowler is said to have been invented in 1849 by hatters William and Thomas Bowler for the famous firm of Lock & Co. in London. The 2nd Earl of Leicester's younger brother, Edward Coke, wanted a hat more practical than a tall topper for his gamekeepers to wear. However, in the muddle of history, William Coke – the earl himself – is the name traditionally associated with the hat's commission, thus giving rise to the hat's nickname: the *Billy Coke* or *Billy Cock*.

A gentleman's accessories in 1937 – bowler hat, handkerchief and cigarette.

Working men adopted the bowler on both sides of the Atlantic, and even in the American West. But traditional gentlemen's outfitters deplored it as 'an abomination in head covering', declaring, 'Men of individuality eschew it and never give it peg-room in their hat-stand.' Winston Churchill adopted a square-crowned *coke hat* as an alternative to the conventional bowler, and it became central to his identity during the 1930s and 1940s. It was also a marked contrast to the more old-fashioned silk top hat sported by Neville Chamberlain during his appeasement visit to Adolf Hitler in 1938 – an occasion when nothing but a top hat would do.

For general use, the bowler didn't long outlive Churchill's impressive state funeral in 1965. Bowler Hat Week had been launched by the hat trade in October 1950 to celebrate the centenary of the hat's creation and to boost flagging sales, but the bowler's survival was mostly limited to men working in the City of London who wished to present a 'correct' professional image, teaming it with a tightly furled umbrella. By the 1960s the bowler had become the perfect prop for parodies of the British, rather as the sombrero was supposed to signify 'Spanish' and the beret 'French'.[6] The parody did not include women, who had long been excluded from City professions except in a secretarial capacity. And because the iconic image of the City worker was always a man in a bowler hat and suit, it was difficult for women to be taken seriously as potential employees in the same roles.

An early twentieth-century wool flat cap.

Removing a cap was a sign of humility, and it was a requirement to do so before any social superior, and not just the monarch. The expression 'I take my hat off to you' is so firmly embedded in the English language that it speaks volumes about the significance of headwear in relation to social status, or lack of it. Hats themselves gave plenty of clues about the status of the wearer, so it was relatively easy to tell who should doff the hat and who should receive this honour. A silk top hat easily trumped a woollen cap, for example.

However, while a mere cloth cap may appear inferior to a more structured hat of higher-quality fabric, some caps – such as the wool-tweed flat cap preferred by men in the North of England from the nineteenth century onwards – now embody a certain pride in the class and background from which they come. This flat cap (so-called because it has no high peak or crown), with all its associations of a country living or labouring background, has evolved to be a strong anti-privilege statement. It is a close relative in shape, if not significance, to the plain-wool caps made of stitched triangular pieces worn by gentleman cricketers and schoolboys. The former advertised the team or school badge, the latter were revived in the anti-glam fashions of the 1960s and 1970s, becoming known as *Baker Boy* hats.

The basic design of a skull-fitting crown with a stiff brim endures well beyond these historical roots, in the form of the now-ubiquitous *baseball cap*. Which came first, the cap or the

7 The honour of earning a 'cap' when playing for one's country refers back to this early practice of wearing caps during football matches.

game? It was the cap – essentially the pieced-cap style worn by sportsmen and schoolboys, but with an elongated visor to shade the eyes during a game. While the cap had been worn by footballers too, to distinguish one team from another, for them it was too easily dislodged during the match.[7] Baseball fans began to wear caps in team colours to show allegiance, and now they are sold in a multitude of forms and fabrics, invariably machine-embroidered with affiliation logos or designer motifs extending far beyond baseball, to encompass almost any brand you can think of. There is no 'doffing' of these caps to show deference; in fact they are frequently used to broadcast an anti-Establishment attitude, worn with the brim backwards or sideways, as fashion or anti-fashion decrees. Strangely, modern male politicians are more likely to be seen wearing a baseball cap than a formal hat, perhaps as a ploy to appear youthful and in touch with their voters. The mind boggles at how Chamberlain would have looked sporting one.

STALKING THE TRUTH

There are too many variations of male hats to take stock of them all, but some are definitely more distinctive in history than others. Take the *deerstalker*, for example, a cloth hat introduced in the 1860s, which has become synonymous with one particular fictional wearer. Sherlock Holmes is now indelibly associated with the cloth cap with ear flaps (along with his meerschaum pipe). The hat is made in four sections on the crown, and the ear flaps have ties so that they can be folded up and secured at the top of the head. The question is: *did the Baker Street detective ever wear one*? In truth, the deerstalker per se is never mentioned in the novels. It was Sidney Paget's illustrations of the Sherlock Holmes stories for the *Strand Magazine* between 1891 and 1908 that immortalised the image of the detective in a deerstalker. Holmes does, however, wear a 'close-fitting cloth cap' with a long grey travelling cloak while waiting at Paddington station in 'The Boscombe Valley Mystery'. He is also described as having 'his sharp, eager face framed in his ear-flapped travelling-cap' in 'Silver Blaze'. The only reference to a *Scotch bonnet* – another name for deerstalker – comes when a victim of hat theft is reduced to wearing one, until his stolen hat can be found. This gentleman complains that it is 'fitted neither to my years nor to my gravity'. It is true that in 'Town' – that is, London – a gentleman who wished to follow etiquette would wear a dark hat, but never tweed or a cap.

THE WIDOW'S CAP

In contrast to the male use of hats to advertise a profession, a woman's headdress once denoted marital status.

The tradition of covering the female head has long been prevalent in the West, for all that we may now associate it with an Islamic cultural preference. The concept of head-covering is very much bound up with notions of modesty and propriety for females. Various religions may require hair to be hidden in public, or around males who aren't close relatives. Christian women were, until relatively late in the twentieth century, expected to keep their heads covered in church, unlike men, who doffed all hats when indoors.

From the fifteenth to the nineteenth centuries the tradition was for young girls to wear their hair loose until they reached marriageable age, at which point it would be pinned up and often hidden under an indoor *cap* – usually a plain linen shaped cap (with or without frills) or a frothy concoction of light cotton muslin, complete with ribbons and ruffles. Until as late as the 1910s, caps were still worn by matrons and confirmed spinsters. Jane Austen, born in 1775, was rebuked for wearing a matron-style cap when only twenty-six, which wasn't *quite* old enough to place her on the shelf. Scottish girls would wear a ribbon or *snood* net in their hair, which would be exchanged for a *coif* – a type of round-eared indoor cap – when they married. To *lose the silken snood* meant to lose one's virginity before marriage.[8]

8 Until the social upheavals of the First World War, older women acted as chaperones to unmarried gentlewomen. *Chaperone* comes from the Spanish word for *hood*, which was worn by these duennas.

9 Jane Austen, letter to Cassandra Austen, 1st–2nd December 1798: ' . . . my long hair is always plaited up out of sight, and my short hair curls well enough to want no papering'.

A highly decorated outdoor cap from 1819.

Women themselves had various opinions on the merits of wearing caps and hats. In the 1820s and 1830s, caps were used to keep the chin - or chins - in place via ruffles of tulle or lace called *metonnières* or chin stays, which were sewn onto the strings to form a chin-tucking frill. Another benefit of wearing a cap was pointed out by Jane Austen, who remarked that it 'saves me a world of torment as to hairdressing'.[9] A century later, Clara Moore, a professional hair-curler, took things a step further with an innovation for female cyclists who found their hair disagreeably dishevelled - she invented an artificial fringe of curls to be stitched or glued to a band, which could then be gripped onto one's own neatly tucked-under-a-hat hair with hair pins. The idea was imitated by at least one fashionable lady in the First World War: concerned about the impossibility of styling her hair while under threat of imminent Zeppelin raids over London, this particular (anonymous) fashion journalist attached a line of false curls to the front of her boudoir cap so that she wouldn't look a fright rushing out into the street at night. *Boudoir caps* were worn while at one's toilette, to keep waves and curls in place. They were the last of a long line of indoor caps and met their demise in the 1930s, when they were superseded by cotton or nylon hair nets.

As a lady aged, so her caps adapted. In the 1890s elderly women still wore caps in public long after the fashion for them had faded and hats were more the thing. One dignified Highland lady is recorded as having worn a black silk cap, followed by a frilled white lawn cap with long lawn strings, covered – if going out – by a black hood. Family photographs from the late nineteenth and early twentieth centuries attest to the endurance of *widow's caps* in particular. Worn by bereaved women, as the name suggests, these were fairly elaborate constructions of wire or buckram covered in crinkled mourning crêpe, perched unbecomingly on the top of the head, tied with black ribbons and encrusted with bugle beads, black lace frills and the occasional lugubrious bird.[10]

10 Death and black caps were closely associated, prior to the abolition of the death penalty for murder in Britain. The legal black cap was a small square of black cloth placed over the judge's wig when intoning the mesmerising words of the death sentence: 'To be taken from this place and hanged until dead.'

A ribbon-trimmed straw bonnet of 1819 – protecting the face and the modesty with a deep brim.

For outdoor wear, the cap would be covered by a *bonnet* – a straw or fabric concoction that was moulded to frame the face. Structured bonnets were first seen in the eighteenth century and continued to be popular until the 1870s, when they shrank into little confections perched high on wads of false hair. From the 1870s onwards, *hats* were in vogue, in a crazy cavalcade of absurd or demure styles.

THE PICTURE HAT

In addition to complying with cultural demands for modesty, headwear was one more weapon in a woman's arsenal of self-promotion. Therefore an admirer's eye might be caught by long, fluttering bonnet ribbons called *follow-me-lads*; his passions might be stirred by dainty bonnets of the late 1860s called *kiss-me-quicks* – and later by the jaunty cheap hats sold at seaside resorts with the same invitation written around the crown.

The true coquette knew that attracting admiration did not necessarily mean revealing all one's best features at once. Historical hat designs include many face-shielding fashions, such as the nineteenth-century poke bonnet, sometimes known as a *coal-scuttle*, which one writer quipped 'required a telescope to see to the far end of it'. Such long-brimmed bonnets forced the wearer to turn their head in order to see anything to the side of them, rather like a blinkered horse.

While dainty hats might be flirtatious, large hats meant serious posturing. In the late eighteenth century there was a fad for prodigiously padded hair, matched by vast hats. In 1784 Italian aeronaut Vincenzo Lunardi created such a great stir with his ascent in a balloon that it inspired an outsize hat known as the 'Lunardi'. Other hats of the time had large brims that could be tilted to reveal or shield the face.

It seems some gentlemen found these large hats frustrating. At the pleasure gardens of Ranelagh in 1772, the fictional Sir Clement Willoughby said: 'I must own myself no advocate for hats; I am sorry the ladies ever invented or adopted so tantalizing a fashion; for, where there is beauty, they only serve to shade it, and where there is none, to excite a most unavailing curiosity.' Willoughby's ungallant companion suggested that tantalising hats 'were invented by some wrinkled old hag, who'd a mind to keep the young fellows in chase'.

Female headwear could be decorated with extraordinary arrays of novelty trimmings, including fruit and flowers (both real and fake), ribbons, ruffles, feather sprays and satin pleats. 'A bonnet decorated with loops of ribbon and sprays of grass, or flowers that fall aslant, may give a laughably tipsy air to the face of a saintly matron of pious and conservative habits,' declared one dress guru in 1897. There were some trimmings that would be frankly offensive to modern tastes. The Regency era, for example, saw 'pussy-cat' bonnets made of cat skin. After several centuries of regular surges in popularity for plumage on hats - including complete birds: beak, wings and all - it took protracted campaigns from concerned societies to put an end to the mass killings of exotic birds for their feathers, beginning in the nineteenth century and succeeding in the twentieth. Sadly, this success only came after some birds were hunted to extinction, purely for vanity and display.

Not all women were advocates for large headwear. One Victorian lady recalled of her big bonnet: 'Like the hood of a carriage, the wind found its way under it, and could not come out again. It was the home of draughts, the nursing mother of face-ache and answered no purpose that would not have been more consistently performed by an umbrella.'

Leaving aside such practical sensibilities, the most famous grand hat in history was arguably that worn by Georgiana, the fabulous, tragic Duchess of Devonshire. Ever at the forefront of new trends, Georgiana chose a large *picture hat* - an oversized large-brimmed affair - for a portrait by Thomas Gainsborough in 1787. Black, bold and dramatic, it in no way overstated Georgiana's position in the fashionable world. It had a glossy ribbon trim and thick plumes. It was far larger than her head and hair combined, even though her hair was dressed in the fashionable bouffant *hérisson* - or hedgehog - style. Gainsborough's eye-catching painting of the Duchess was bought by London art dealer William Agnew and put on public display in 1876. Wealthy American banker Junius Spencer Morgan put in the highest bid for its purchase. To the horror of Agnew and Morgan alike, it was promptly stolen by a notorious fraudster called Adam Worth. When Pinkerton's Detective Agency eventually tracked down Worth and the painting in 1901, its next public display created a sensation, particularly in the world of fashion, and huge 'Duchess of Devonshire' hats became all the rage. The large hat received an additional boost when Edwardian couturier Lucile Ltd created a wonderfully oversized hat for the actress Lily Elsie in the stage play *The Merry Widow* in 1907.

Punch *magazine enjoyed mocking extreme hat fashions, such as the Edwardian cartwheel.*

The Gainsborough and Merry Widow hats eventually morphed into the monstrous cartwheel hats, which peaked in circumference about 1910. These huge creations – also known as *mushroom hats* – were worn by all ages and all levels of society, from aristocrats to maids-of-all work. They were large on the outside, and smaller within the crown. They were supported on pads of hair known as *rats* or *postiches* and secured by immensely long hat pins, which were lethal to wearers and bystanders if the point was not protected. 'Don't spoil your hat by sticking a big pin through the crown!' admonished an 1896 advertisement for the *Majestic* hat fastener – a fancy variant on the hat pin. Other patent devices included the *Phix-it Hat Pin*. Such enormous hats were a great cause of frustration to theatre audiences and crowds at sporting events.

Whatever the size, hats could be uncomfortable to wear. Two young English sisters, Gwen and Margaret Raverat, took their revenge on the tyranny of hats in the late nineteenth century. They were forced to go to chapel in Paris hats designed to look like daisies, with yellow straw crowns and frilly white papers. Sulking at the imposition, one of the girls took off her hat '... and STOOD on it, and squashed it as flat as ever St George squashed the Dragon; and no one could ever wear it again. Glory, glory hallelujah!'

For modern women there is far less fuss, now that huge mushroom hats are rarely seen. Wedding hats are the only true survivors of the golden age of head-top flamboyance. But more of the last century anon . . .

MAD AS A HATTER

Who was responsible for the fabulous and fabled hats of history? Apart from home-made creations, they were the craft of the *hatter* or *milliner*. There was scope for design flair in hat-making, but much of the labour was hard graft for low wages in sweatshop conditions. True, some hat-makers made their name and fortune: Frenchwoman Rose Bertin became the premiere milliner in late eighteenth-century Europe when she created headwear for Queen Marie-Antoinette. She had begun her career with her own shop on the rue Saint-Honoré in Paris. Once introduced to the Queen, she began creating gowns as well as hats and is credited with being the first haute-couture French designer. On the Queen's arrest and incarceration in 1792, Bertin took small gifts to her in prison, such was her loyalty.[11]

Hat-making was once a surprisingly dangerous trade. We use

11 Royalty are still among the best customers for modern hatters, owing to the fact that hats are still required for elite social events and certain state occasions. Notes of novelty do creep in, as with the whimsical hats spotted at royal weddings.

the phrase 'as mad as a hatter' with little thought for its origins in the aberrations that chemicals used in the hatting industry could cause those who worked with them. Mercurous nitrate, for example – used in making felt hats – can produce St Vitus's dance and other tremors, as well as impaired vision. The original mad hatter may have been Robert Crab, a seventeenth-century eccentric hatter who gave all his goods to the poor and lived on dock leaves and grass. The mad hatter was, of course, immortalised by Lewis Carroll in his 1865 story *Alice's Adventures in Wonderland* and its 1871 sequel, *Alice Through the Looking-Glass*.

When everyone in society was wearing hats, there was great demand for their production and decoration. But as a new informality crept into everyday life after the social upheaval of the First World War, the hat industry struggled. Towns that specialised in the trade suffered, with the decline in the popularity of headwear. For example, Luton – home of straw-hat-making – experienced a huge drop in prosperity when traditional straw boaters went out of vogue, despite a brief revival under the promotion of the dapper Duke of Windsor in 1920. The younger generation increasingly eschewed the formality of their elders and spent more money on hairstyling, and travelled more frequently under cover of motor cars – all of which made hats a less attractive proposition.

The take-it-or-leave-it attitude to hats was seen in male headgear first. Despite the emergence of fashionable new styles such as the *trilby*, not every chap felt duty-bound to cover his head when out and about.[12] There were numerous attempts to promote male hat-wearing by blatantly linking it to the suave masculinity of Hollywood stars. Frank Sinatra advised tilting the hat to look smart – 'Angles are attitude,' he said. One 'manly' hat that has survived and even thrived into the twenty-first century is the *Stetson*, a large-brimmed hat originally worn by US cattlemen, now worn by men and women across the United States and named after its best-known manufacturer, John B. Stetson.

The Homburg entered fashion thanks to the patronage of King Edward VII, who adopted the style after a visit to Bad Homburg in Germany. It remained popular well into the 1960s.

Hat manufacturers also attempted to create conceptual links between hats and professional success. However, a mild resurgence in hat-wearing in the 1920s failed to pull things back to a state of affairs where headwear was all but compulsory. In an informal poll in late 1930s London it was noted that only 23 per cent of men were wearing hats, even during a snowstorm. This relative hatlessness doesn't quite tally with our impression of mid-twentieth-century men who, we may assume, all kept a hat handy. To arrest the decline in their trade, hatters in the 1950s staged a promotional campaign with the slogan 'Get a Hat to Get Ahead', aimed at men under thirty-five years old. Unfortunately it was entirely ignored by young men of this decade, who preferred to keep their heads hat-free, all the better to display their thick 'Teddy Boy' quiffs.

HATS OFF

The hatless phenomenon also created a new dilemma for good manners. Historically, raising the hat – or at least touching the brim – was a show of deference and a sign of respect when meeting a lady. An elaborate system of etiquette was created around this simple action, known as *hat honour*, and negotiating it could cause some social anxiety. For example, was it proper to tip one's hat to an unknown lady? And should the hat be fully or partially lifted? The best way to perform the required lift included turning the interior away from the lady with a deft gesture, thereby avoiding the possibility of their glimpsing any unsightly sweat marks or dandruff within.

One confused gentleman wrote to the *Spectator* magazine in 1711 complaining that his salutations were treated as impertinence. The correspondent required the niceties to be made clear – 'if it be only to save the unnecessary Expense of wearing out my Hat so fast as I do at present'. More heinous than offending passing ladies was the horror evinced by the magazine's editors at the sight of a *woman* on horseback appropriating the act of hat honour, as if she were a dashing young gent. The editor declared, 'This is to give Notice that if any Persona can discover the Name, and Place of Abode of the said Offender, so as she can be brought to Justice, the Informant shall have all fitting encouragement.'

Far too late for the 1711 correspondent, an Edwardian etiquette manual for men clarified the basics of hat honour:

> While there is no need for a sweeping movement like that of the cavalier of other days, do not go to the other extreme and simply touch the brim with your forefinger, as many men have a habit of doing in these days. Raise the hat just clear of the head for a moment, that is the correct procedure.

HAT V. HAIR

In contrast to male hatlessness, in the first half of the twentieth century there was still no question of *women* removing their hats. A woman going out bare-headed was described by *Harper's Bazaar* as a half-decapitated creature who looked as if she was running out on a family row. Women of the last century had anxieties of a different kind. Which style was in vogue? Which the most flattering? How ought the hair to be worn with each new shape? As the Edwardian cartwheels shrank, so the hair became more subdued, until the bell-shaped *cloche* hats, first seen during the First World War, came to dominate the 1920s. Hair then had to be coiled flat on the back of the neck or cut short. Most women chose a crop, which meant that brims could be very far forward, very low and very beguiling.

A close-fitting cloche hat of 1926.

Fashion flirted with both wide brims and neat head-hugging hats throughout the Twenties and Thirties, but the real conversation pieces came in during the Second World War. In Britain, hats were not rationed during the war years, though materials could be hard to come by and money for hats could be scarce. In addition to colourful turbans for home, factory and field work, there was a fashion fad for dinky toy hats, as a nod to

Field and factory workers of the Second World War favoured headscarves and home-made turbans.

thrift. These small doll-like versions of normal hats were a playful contrast to the sombre reality of hard work, anxiety and austerity. Parisian women defied German appropriation of fabrics and fashion houses during the Occupation by wearing over-elaborate hat structures, sometimes decorated with a provocative French tricolour.[13]

The post-war 'New Look' continued couture's love-affair with headwear, including eccentric *flying saucer hats* and lampshade-esque styles; some of the pretty lace and feather concoctions looked positively edible. However, younger generations were generally happy to go hatless.

It was hair that defeated the hat. Flirty baby-doll flicks and high backcombed beehives triumphed in the 1960s. Outside hippy circles, hair was being washed more often and so could become an accessory in its own right, rather than being hidden away. The hat was on its way to being relegated to weddings, where it exploded into vibrant floral designs or footstool-shaped furriness. Brims went out of fashion, and so the brimless *toque* found favour.

Toques had a particularly long lease of life in the wardrobe of American style icon Jackie Kennedy Onassis. In contrast to the growing informality of the Sixties youthquake, Jackie Kennedy came to emphasise ladylike poise. She always wore gloves, and her solid coiffure was usually topped with a toque, known as a *pillbox* because of the shape. Her adoption of this style of hat was first noted at her 1961 inauguration as First Lady. Kennedy had sent her own sketches and notes to milliner Bergdorf Goodman, along with the note, 'I'm afraid these hats will pauperize me.' The pillbox established her as a respectable but fresh style icon. More significantly, it helped reinforce the concept of a presidential 'royal' dynasty by giving Americans a photogenic alternative to the British royal family. In an interesting twist, Jackie's husband, J. F. Kennedy, became known as 'hatless Jack' because, despite wearing a top hat at the inauguration, in general he favoured a boyish swept-hair look. This emphasised his youth and vitality, in contrast to the old order of conservative forces.

To suit the let-it-all-hang-out styles of the late Sixties and Seventies there were some very floppy hats. A craze for berets came about quite by accident: in 1967 actress Faye Dunaway wore one on-screen in the film *Bonnie and Clyde*. She received a box full of berets in her hotel room the night after the Paris premiere – a gift from some grateful makers of traditional French headwear, who, since the first US showing of the film, had seen production leap from 5,000 to 12,000 berets a week.

A true overview of hats in history could be encyclopaedic. This chapter has touched on some of the most significant trends, and has hopefully highlighted the truth that sometimes a costume custom that seems to be an inescapable fact of life is, in fact, no more enduring than any other constructed cultural constraint.

'The distinctive sign of a gentleman,' wrote an Englishman in 1854, 'is never to abandon his hat under any but the most pressing circumstances.' Alas for the hat, this pronouncement no longer holds true. Since its swansong in the Sixties and Seventies, the hat has been relegated to the role of protection against sun and cold weather, or for special-occasion wear. In most instances it is now a choice, not an obligation. Even for weddings a concoction of feather and ribbon known as a *fascinator* will suffice for women.[14] Aside from certain cultural and religious requirements for head coverings, such as the Islamic hijab or Sikh turban, the notion of headgear as an intrinsic part of the everyday wardrobe has become . . . *old hat*.

14 *Fascinators* are smaller side-pinned versions of a headdress style introduced in France in about 1680 – the *fontange*. It was named after a mistress of Louis XIV, the Duchesse de Fontanges, and consisted of ribbons and lace built over a wire structure called a *commode*.

ATTENTION TO DETAIL

Gloves, shoes, stockings, fan, jewels and handkerchief should all be in perfect harmony with her gown and with each other.
MRS DOUGLAS, *THE GENTLEWOMAN'S BOOK OF DRESS*, 1894

We've seen how key garments in the modern wardrobe can be traced back in time. Now we can concentrate on the ephemera: the accessories that seem so simple, but which all have a tale to tell. Some accessories, such as gloves and umbrellas, are in common use today – albeit having lost their historical connotations. Others, such as handkerchiefs, fans, muffs and braces, are rarely seen. And some, including the veil, have taken on quite new connotations in the West.

A lady's accessories from 1954.

The veil is a uniquely female requirement, reflecting its uses as both enhancer of beauty and a protector of modesty. For the modern Western woman there are really only two types of veil potentially in her wardrobe: the *wedding veil* and the *niqab*.

The wedding veil has provided plenty of memorable drama in literature. Picture the scene: a nineteenth-century bride-to-be wakes in the night after disturbing dreams, to see a ghastly female figure in her bedchamber, trying on her wedding veil. Next, recounts the horrified watcher, 'it removed my veil from its gaunt head, rent it in two parts, and flinging both on the floor, trampled on them'. The narrator is Charlotte Brontë's Jane Eyre.

Jane's veil – an expensive gift from her wealthy fiancé, Mr Rochester – is also rich in symbolism for her. Delicate and embroidered, it seems like a mask to her, to hide her low-born status; it is described as 'vapoury', 'strange and wraith-like'. She prefers the simple authenticity of a veil she has chosen: a square of plain, blond lace. Trying the veil on in the mirror, Jane describes herself as 'a robed and veiled figure, so unlike my usual self that it seemed almost the image of a stranger'. Instinctively she knows there is no integrity in the forthcoming union. When the madwoman – who is the wife that Mr Rochester has concealed in the attic – tears and tramples on this fine veil, she is symbolically destroying the marriage Jane hopes for.

The modern wedding veil can rarely be said to carry much symbolism; it is simply dramatic and decorative. It does, however, have a rich ancestry, having supposedly been derived from the gorgeous saffron-coloured *flaminea* of pagan Roman brides, who would be covered to conceal them from evil spirits; later, Christian Roman brides had purple and white veils. Also in bridal mythology is the idea that wealthy Renaissance brides and 'bride maids' – as they were known – would all wear identical veils, to foil any potential risk of kidnapping by entrepreneurial rivals, who could potentially force a marriage on the heiress and so inherit all her worldly goods. Some of the Roman idea of the wedding as a celebration of future fertility survives in the decoration of later veils, which may be embroidered with symbolic sheaves of wheat. However, by the twentieth century true lover's knots were a more popular embellishment, as marriages came to be seen as being more about romance than reproduction. Fashion also influenced veils, in size, shape and decoration; a phalanx of attendants was required to carry the 'cathedral-length' veil of ostentatious Victorian brides.

A First World War wedding veil, emphasising the romance of a wedding, even in dark times.

The bride's face was usually veiled before the ceremony, and then the veil was folded back to reveal the face, once the vows were taken. When Queen Victoria married Prince Albert in 1841, she did not cover her face as her contemporaries would have done, because she was a reigning monarch and easily outranked her husband-to-be. Victoria's wedding bonnet survives in the collection of the Museum of London, complete with a delicate veil. The practice of having a two-tier veil is a relatively modern introduction from the mid-twentieth century, reaching its apex in the bouffant two-tier nylon veils of the 1960s, which seemed skewered to the head with a 'miner's lamp' fabric rosette on the front. Tradition has it that a modern bride must never seen in her full ensemble before the ceremony, so many brides leave off wearing the veil until the proper moment.

The bridal veil was often a very expensive piece of luxury lace, using quality styles such as Honiton or Valenciennes. It would be treasured in silver paper and perhaps worn as the 'something old' of a bride in the next generation. Brides of the First World War might enjoy a 'something new' veil if their menfolk were serving in Belgium and were therefore able to send home packages of genuine Brussels lace, while wartime brides in the Forties might have 'something contrived' veils – lace was not rationed during the Second World War, but it could be hard to come by, and so net-curtain veils were not unknown.

Leaving weddings aside, veils were common in daily life from the Classical era until the later nineteenth century. They served to conceal the wearer's features in public places, and to protect them from dirt when travelling.[1] As the fashion for bonnets or hats dominated between the eighteenth and twentieth centuries, veils attached to these could be alluring and decorative. Spotted, sprigged or plain, they were a particularly feminine way of attracting attention while eluding obvious scrutiny.[2] Gradually these styles of veil shrank to a few inches of coarse nylon net on the pillbox hats of the 1980s, then vanished along with the fashion for everyday hats.

1 In April 1912 the *Daily Mirror* advertised the new 'Storm Queen' waterproof motor veil, with self-gripping adjuster, for 1s. 11¾d. – 'Better than ever! No knots! No Bows! No Worry! No Woes'.

2 Some saw potential in veils beyond the aesthetic: Edwardian ju-jitsu expert Edith Garrud promoted the use of female accessories in a self-defence situation, citing the veil as a useful tool for tying up a foiled mugger!

A neat face-veil from 1889.

When taken to extremes, the veil's allure – the way it conceals, but suggests the tantalising possibility of revelation – was closely linked to erotic dancing, most notably the infamous *Dance of the Seven Veils*. Parodied many times in many ways, the Dance of the Seven Veils was essentially the invention of writer Oscar Wilde, for his 1891 play *Salomé*. Salomé, Herod's stepdaughter, is given the head of John the Baptist as a reward for her dancing. Wilde's stage direction for this scene was simply: 'Salomé dances the Dance of the Seven Veils'. It was the interpretation of this name by the talented dancer Maud Allan that took Europe by storm. Allan's choreography in her production, *Vision of Salomé*, opened in Vienna in 1906. She began the dance with a breastplate of pearls and jewels above a transparent embroidered shirt and ended it in little more than a string of pearls and two oyster shells. Audiences loved the exoticism; critics disliked the papier-mâché severed head stage-prop. Ultimately Allan's downfall came about because of a smear campaign in 1918 by a homophobic right-wing British MP, who accused her of being part of the 'Cult of the Clitoris' – that is, a lesbian – which was socially unacceptable at this time. Allan was forced to hide her relationships with women and to defend her reputation in public by repudiating the claim. However, she lost a subsequent libel case and her career was irreparably damaged.

Maud Allan's dancing was shocking in that it was a deliberate casting aside of the concealment – and therefore modesty – offered by veils. We speak of *drawing a veil* over something that ought not to be seen. Veils and draperies disguised sexuality and suppressed vanity. Hanging down from a bonnet brim, or swathed around the face from a hat, certain veils offered almost complete anonymity. This anonymity sometimes signified an effacement of individuality, as when giving up a secular life and identity to *take the veil* as a Christian nun. A close association with this type of seclusion is seen in the long history of the widow's veil; like nuns, widows in the Christian West dressed in browns, whites and blacks. Although not all women wore veils for mourning – working-class women had neither the time nor the money for such indulgence – plenty of images survive of female mourners in veils of various styles. A particularly striking scene is depicted in the engraving of a 1661 royal funeral in Germany, in which the women are hooded to the eyebrow line, with a panel across the face just under the eyes and a transparent floor-length black veil over the whole face.

Regency widows are usually depicted with the veil pinned in a graceful Classical style, away from the face, while Victorian veils could hide the mourner in public and hang from the back of the head symbolically at other times. The most iconic widow of the nineteenth century was, of course, Queen Victoria herself, mourning the premature death of her husband, Prince Albert, in 1861. Victoria remained in mourning until her own death in 1901, generally adopting a white widow's cap and veil. From 1866, when she attended the State Opening of Parliament, she always had a white lace veil or a net veil over her crown.

Proponents of rational dress objected to the cost (and vanity) of full mourning from the 1870s onwards, but it was the First World War that truly ushered out widow's weeds. Seclusion behind a veil was neither practical for women doing war work, nor encouraging for servicemen and women on leave. Black armbands were preferred over head-to-toe black. Sometimes officers' wives would wear a fine silk veil while collecting posthumous awards for their husbands.

In 1952 the Lord Chamberlain ordered court mourning of only ten weeks for the death of King George VI; it had been one year for the death of King Edward VII in 1910. A famous photograph, since dubbed *The Three Queens,* shows Queen Mary, the Queen Mother and the new Queen Elizabeth all in elbow-length veils. One of the last high-profile widow's veils to be seen was that of Jacqueline Kennedy at her husband's funeral in 1963. It was a shoulder-length transparent black veil simply sewn onto a black hat.

The concealment provided by a veil might also be used for privacy or disguise. Until veils went out of daily use, a lady might wish to veil herself out of discretion, perhaps when

3 In 'The Veiled Lady'
by Agatha Christie, in
Poirot's Early Cases
(1974), a figure with
her face veiled
heightens the mystery
as well as the allure.

4 The *niqab* is a cloth
covering for the face.
It can be part of the
all-enveloping *burqa*
robe.

conducting private business – such as consulting money-lenders or a private detective – or when visiting a less-than-respectable place of entertainment.[3] There is also a long tradition of hiding the face at masquerade balls. Concealed identity in that context was associated with the potential for pleasure without repercussions. This was a particularly meaningful escapism for a woman, whose reputation was both crucial to her social standing and essential currency in the historical marriage market. Nowadays the visard or veil is more likely to be an empowering accessory for those indulging in dramatic dressing-up, or darker shades of sexual activity.

Concealment of identity is most definitely not the rationale behind the modern Islamic face-veil in all its forms, seen mostly in the West in the form of a *niqab*.[4] For a small piece of cloth, the Islamic veil has been a big source of controversy. Its adoption by women in predominantly non-Muslim countries has caused a degree of cultural collision between people who are used to communicating naked face to naked face and those whose religious convictions demand a covered face.

As with other veils, the *niqab* is a gendered requirement and there is a very active ongoing debate among different communities as to whether the face-veil is religious or cultural, preferred or obligatory. Some Islamic teachings require the face to be covered by a veil when out in public, or in front of males who are not relatives. In some people's view, the veil is a form of oppression, while others assert that it protects the female from unwanted male attention. While it may, in theory, minimise sexual harassment, it also makes the wearer highly visible, particularly in Western countries that are struggling to adapt to the sometimes uneasy relationship between secular and religious convictions.

GLOVE-STRETCHERS

A lost glove is a forlorn object. We sometimes spot one looking soggy on a pavement, or lying limp on a wall, where it has been placed by a helpful passer-by. Anyone growing up in the twentieth century may remember gloves and mittens dangling long and low from elastic that ran around the back and down the coat sleeves, to avoid such a loss. Gloves may now be worn almost exclusively for purposes of warmth (or for certain sports), but they were once a much more significant item of clothing. We still speak of *an iron fist in a velvet glove* to represent disguised power; we refer to *the gloves coming off* to mean no further genteel behaviour – as with bare-fisted pugilists fighting without restraint; and to be *hand in glove* with someone is to be a close friend, ally or conspirator.

5 This is a different etymology from *running the gauntlet*, which derives from *running the gantlope,* or a passage between two lines of soldiers. The runner would be beaten as he passed, as a form of military punishment.

Gauntlets were extra-long over the wrist. In medieval Europe throwing down a glove – or gauntlet – meant to announce a challenge publicly. Taking up the gauntlet signified accepting the challenge. These are twentieth-century woollen gauntlets.5

Back in the Renaissance, high-status gloves were a far cry from the leather or wool mittens of common people and were not to be discarded lightly. Made of silk and soft leathers, spangled and beribboned, they made costly gifts, to confer favour, or to curry it. For a truly special gift, gloves were perfumed with cinnamon, cloves, orange, musk and lily. Tourneying knights might wear a lady's glove as a love-token, as chronicled at a tournament in Hull in 1500:

> One wore on his headpiece his lady's sleeve,
> Another the glove of his dearlyng.

Exquisitely embroidered glove belonging to Queen Elizabeth I.

Queen Elizabeth I regularly gave and received gifts of clothing, and gloves are noted in her New Year's Gift Rolls. In 1598 she received ten pairs of perfumed gloves, rising to twenty-one pairs in 1603. There is a pair of leather and silk gloves in the Ashmolean Museum, Oxford, decorated with gold thread and believed to have been given to the Queen when she visited Oxford University in 1566. Why were they left behind? The speculation is that Elizabeth prided herself on her slender, shapely hands, and that these gloves were rather large and bulky. Glove-stretchers of pivoted bone, ivory, ebony and silver were later designed, for widening the finger fabric so that the hand could gradually be eased within. Such a tight fit was desirable to make the hands seem smaller and therefore more elegant.

Jasmine-scented gloves were given to the bride and groom as wedding presents in the seventeenth century, and white gloves were distributed among other guests. Gloves made gifts even in sombre circumstances. As Lady Jane Grey – Queen for just nine days – paused before kneeling at the executioner's block in 1554, she gave her maid, Mistress Tilney, her gloves and handkerchief. Similarly, at his execution, Charles I is said to have gifted his gloves to William Juxon, Bishop of London, and they were subsequently preserved by his family. For many centuries black gloves were also given as gifts at funerals, carefully graded in quality according to the status of the mourner. At one burial in 1680 eight chamois-leather gloves were given to close relatives, ninety-six cordovan leather and kid gloves to friends and other relatives, and 118 pairs of coarser sheep's leather gloves to servants and tradesmen.

Throughout history, gloves have had varying uses across different social classes. For labourers there were woollen mittens for warmth, and thicker leather gloves and gauntlets to protect the hands at work. In leisured circles, gloves were used to protect the skin and prevent it from becoming coarse, as a labourer's hands inevitably would, even with protection. The finest, most supple gloves were those called *chicken-skin*. Delicate enough to be contained within a walnut shell, they were in fact made from the skin of unborn calves, treated with almonds and spermaceti, and were particularly recommended to fashionable ladies:

> Some of chicken-skin at night
> To keep her Hands plump, soft, and white.

Gradually the etiquette of glove-wearing was consolidated for gentlemen and ladies alike. By the late eighteenth century fashion dictated the length, embellishment and fastening for each season. Although the details changed from one generation to another, the essentials remained the same. Gloves were necessary to appear well bred and became an integral part of any outfit. Etiquette manuals laid out the rules for the insecure middle-classes who were anxious not to make a faux pas. *Etiquette for Ladies* in 1837 admonished: 'To appear in public without them – to sit in church or in a place of public amusement destitute of these appendages, is decidedly vulgar. Some gentlemen insist on stripping off their gloves before shaking hands; a piece of barbarity, of which no lady will be guilty.' Gloves also conferred an advantage when dancing, protecting each partner's hands from the sweat of the others.

The best, most expensive gloves were also the most easily crumpled and soiled. From the eighteenth century onwards, magazines and household manuals printed advice on how to make bags for keeping gloves clean, and how to fold and store them after use. The 1838 *Workwoman's Guide* gave advice on making a glove bag, while *Pears Cyclopaedia* of 1919 went much further:

> Each glove should be wrapped in tissue paper after the fingers have been stretched, the thumb turned in place and the inside of the glove aired after wearing. It is a pernicious habit to roll the gloves one inside the other immediately after removing from the hands.

In a perverse rule that was typical of fashion's conspicuous consumption, the fashionable colours for elite gloves were white, lavender, pale grey or fawn – expensive to buy and difficult to keep pristine. White kid gloves were almost universal for women in the early twentieth century.[6] They attracted dirt quickly and resisted most contemporary advice on cleaning (which included rubbing with stale breadcrumbs). This no doubt accounted for the etiquette ruling that a gentleman in dark-coloured gloves should not presume to shake hands with a lady wearing light-coloured ones. For many women, white gloves were a luxury kept for best. Some, however, could afford as many pairs as they wished: a salesgirl at Fortnum & Mason's gift department in the 1930s recalled Mrs Wallis Simpson – future wife of Edward VIII – in 'the cleanest white gloves I have ever seen'.

Nylon took over from cotton and kid for many formal occasions in the 1950s, and benefited from the hand-moulding tight-fit of Lycra in the 1960s. Then informality took over from etiquette and bare hands were socially acceptable for all but formal occasions involving royalty, or for the groom and groomsmen at weddings.

When it came to non-elite gloves, different professions required variations on the basic design. Thus there was the 'thatcher's palm' to protect a thatcher's hand when pushing in straw spars, and gloves with spikes for nineteenth-century women employed to pick caterpillars off fruit bushes. As Louis Pasteur's revolutionary 1861 germ-theory took hold in the medical world, it was increasingly understood that antisepsis, and even asepsis (the exclusion of bacteria and viruses), was important. The use of carbolic acid (phenol) as an antiseptic was pioneered by the surgeon Joseph Lister and was pumped over the operating table in spray form. As a result, surgeons needed to protect their hands from irritation due to repeated exposure. From 1878 they could do so by wearing rubber gloves made using a newly invented dipping process. They had to wait until 1947 for the first plastic gloves, which still retain the name *rubber gloves* thanks to their ancestry.

Warm, waterproof gloves were essential for early motor driving and motorcycle riding, while fur mitts saved early aviators from frostbite in open cockpits. In 1902 Mrs Pritchard of *Ladies' Realm* magazine informed her readers that white doeskin military gloves were just the thing for driving and country purposes. However, as motor cars became enclosed, so driving gloves assumed a less bulky, only semi-functional form, until eventually interior heating and stippled steering-wheel covers made warm, gripped driving gloves obsolete.

Human hands are particularly vulnerable to frostbite in extreme conditions. Untreated, frostbite can be fatal. Layers of gloves – silk first then wool, quilt gauntlets then leather outer mitts – can help prevent this. However, glove-layering impedes movement, presenting an extra challenge for astronauts on extra-vehicular activity (EVA) in space. Fabric technology and design are constantly evolving to combine dexterity with warmth and protection against abrasion. Current EVA gloves fit over an intra-vehicular glove and have an outer shell of metal-woven fabric, and silicone rubber caps on the fingertips. The gloves have to be attached to the arms of the space suit with a wrist joint for flexion. There are hot pads and fingertip-heaters.

The *muff* – a fabric or fur tube – is a close cousin of fur gloves. In the seventeenth century both men and women carried large muffs as fashionable accessories, but modern hands are more likely to hold bags and mobile phones, making the muff a redundant encumbrance. *Muffetees* were a diminutive form worn around the wrist. Gradually men conceded the muff to women as a female accessory, which was carried loose or hanging by a chain or ribbon from the neck. Large versions flaunted the latest expensive pelts, sometimes with legs, tails, claws and eyes. The 1930s and 1940s saw neat little fox-fur muffs with satin linings and purse pockets. These pockets had been introduced in the 1880s to transform the muff into an alternative to a handbag. They also had other, more criminal uses . . .

During the militant suffragette campaigns of Edwardian Britain, women became adept at street-fighting and guerrilla tactics. Some of those closest to the Women's Social Political Union leader, Emmeline Pankhurst, were trained in ju-jitsu by martial-arts expert Edith Garrud – already mentioned in connection with her use of a veil to restrain muggers. During one window-smashing protest on London's Oxford Street, at Garrud's signal a team of suffragettes pulled out stones and hammers from their muffs. Damage done, they escaped to Garrud's dojo nearby and quickly changed into ju-jitsu training gear to look suitably innocent when a group of policemen arrived. Garrud was known to keep Indian Clubs in her muff. These were a form of gym equipment to build strength and agility, but made excellent weapons against anti-suffrage roughs, or police officers. Garrud was once stopped by a policeman on Regent Street who inspected her muff, looking with particular suspicion at the pocket inside. Garrud told him sweetly, 'I wouldn't have a muffler without a pocket, constable. I must have somewhere to put my handkerchief and my gloves and keys.'

THE UMBRELLA STAND

Umbrellas were mocked when they first appeared on rainy streets in the eighteenth century. But despite this initial scorn, they have endured to become a universally popular accessory, both as large 'golf'-size umbrellas and in diminutive telescopic form – in nylon and PVC, they come in all imaginable colours and novelty designs.

Umbrellas originally began life as sunshades, or *parasols*. They conferred status as well as shade on those who sheltered under them. ('Umbrella' comes from the Latin for *little shade*, while parasol means *for the sun*.) Made of paper, reeds, leaves or silk, parasols represented power for secular and religious leaders, by adding height to the figure, as well as denoting someone worth protecting. When the idea of a portable cover was transferred from North Africa and the East to Europe, the emphasis was more on protection from the rain – understandable, given the British climate.

When the cosmopolitan merchant Jonas Hanway first carried an umbrella in England in the 1750s he was jeered at, by people calling out, 'Why don't you get a coach?'[7] This was the initial problem for the umbrella, status-wise: anyone who had the money would surely pay for a sedan chair or coach, implying that an umbrella would only be carried by the impecunious. The prejudice remained at least until the 1850s. According to one Victorian visitor to Paris, 'In France, even urban workers preferred a cab to an umbrella – 'a milliner takes a cab when she brings home a bonnet, and a washerwoman, dressed out neatly with a pretty bonnet on her head, uses the same mode of conveyance to distribute clean shirts to her customers.'

Hanway's umbrella would have been an awkward contraption. Since the early 1700s inventors had been attempting to construct a model that wouldn't be too heavy to hold, for those who didn't have a lackey at hand. Hollow steel ribs supported a covering of oiled silk, gingham or alpaca.

Gradually umbrellas gained acceptance, and stands for

umbrellas – including gruesome hollowed-out elephants' feet – became a common item of furniture in hallways and public foyers. Lord Byron had a silk umbrella, which he wasn't too proud to have repaired when necessary; the exquisitely attired Beau Brummell used one while in exile from England in France. Thanks to Jonas Hanway's persistent public use of the umbrella over three decades, he has a memorial in Westminster Abbey, as an acknowledgement of his part in brolly history.

One slang term for umbrellas was *mushrooms* – because they sprang up quickly. And once the initial suspicion of them was overcome, they did indeed start to pop up in all sorts of contexts. Smart gentlemen carried them close-furled in town, like a walking stick; mourners huddled under them, open, at funerals. Late nineteenth-century cyclists could consider the option of having an umbrella attached to their bicycle. Politicians held them as a sign of prestige, although the black furled brolly carried by Prime Minister Neville Chamberlain for his meeting with Adolf Hitler in 1938 did not inspire respect from the Reich Chancellor, who reportedly said, 'If that silly old man comes interfering here again with his umbrella, I'll kick him downstairs and jump on him.'

Perhaps the most famous international incident involving an umbrella took place on 7th September 1978. The victim, Bulgarian political asylum-seeker Georgi Markov, was waiting for a bus near Waterloo Bridge in London when he was 'accidentally' stabbed in the leg with an umbrella that injected a micro-engineered pellet of deadly ricin.

In 2011 Nicolas Sarkozy, French president, ordered a Kevlar-coated umbrella for his bodyguards costing a staggering £10,000.

While the umbrella was appropriated by officers and gentlemen, the *parasol* took on a very feminine fashionable life for several centuries, for protection against the sun. Folding parasols were invented for portability in carriages. From the 1860s, parasols were available in the shocking new chemical colours, such as Perkin's Purple and Electric Blue. Fringed and frilled, they were an exquisite weapon in the accomplished flirt's arsenal. They could command very high prices.

Folding silk or cotton 'carriage' parasols were neat and attractive accessories.

8 In fiction, the green-parrot-handled umbrella belonging to super-nanny Mary Poppins – created by writer P. L. Travers – could transport her across the rooftops and chimney stacks of Edwardian London. Reality is more prosaic. The umbrella would be more likely to turn inside out on a windy day.

9 Thomas Brigg & Sons sold umbrellas and walking sticks in St James's Street, London, and were granted the first royal warrant to supply the Queen with umbrellas.

Parasols have even been designed with combat in mind: Queen Victoria was accosted by a mentally unstable man named Robert Francis Pate, who managed to get close enough to hit her with his heavy 'partridge' cane, bending her bonnet and smacking her forehead. To protect her from any other such attacks, an armoured parasol was designed for the Queen, purportedly by Prince Albert.[8] It was a stylish emerald-green with fringing – and a lining of close-lined chain mail between the silk layers, making it very heavy to hold. There is, sadly, no evidence of it actually being used, and it is now in the collection of the Museum of London.[9]

The twentieth-century cult of sun-worship put paid to the traditional notion that a sunburn was for the lower classes only. By the 1920s, although there were women to be seen guarding their complexion with stylish Japanese paper parasols, these were definitely on their way out. They are now more or less consigned to the mound of obsolete accessories.

On the other hand, the umbrella remains indispensable in wet weather – for men and women alike.

10 The girdle is essentially a belt – a cord or band around the waist or hips.

There is a very chilling scene in the children's book *Goodnight Mister Tom*, where a young wartime evacuee named Willie has his bag unpacked by his new host, Tom Oakley. Willie's mother has included a note with his few belongings: 'I've put the belt in for when he's bad.' At the sight of the belt, poor Willie faints, overcome by too many memories of buckle-bruises and beatings.

Another writer tells the story of a wife who was badly beaten by her husband, using his trouser strap. Finding his belt missing the next day, the husband said nothing, but fastened his trousers with string and sat down to a pie that his wife Queenie had baked for him. Curled up inside the pie was his leather belt. He never beat Queenie again.

A twentieth-century leather belt – simple, but almost indispensable for the modern trouser-wearer.

Clearly these tales do not describe the correct purpose of the belt, which is to hold clothes in place, and not hold family members in subjection. Twisted *girdles* of rope, hemp, silk and leather have featured among some of the earliest surviving clothing finds from the Viking era and the Middle Ages.[10] In later centuries girdles could be elaborately embellished with jewels and tassels, or else could be practical leather straps useful for hanging knives, keys, pens and money pouches from – the waistline's equivalent of a charm bracelet. A *troussoire* chain hanging from a sixteenth-century woman's belt might hold a silk purse, rosary, scent box, fan, mirror or seal. Later *chatelaine* chains included handy sewing kits.

Girdles and belts kept tunics and cloaks in order at the waist. Some had special significance, such as the Classical bridal girdle of wool, which only the husband was allowed to untie; brides sometimes chose the complex Herculean knot, perhaps to increase anticipation on the wedding night, or perhaps because of Hercules' legendary fertility. In Classical mythology, the girdle of Venus was so potent it could provoke ardent love. It had been made for her by her husband Vulcan, but fell off as she cavorted with Mars.

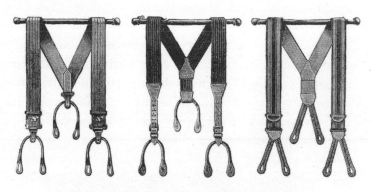

Braces replaced belts for a while, between the eighteenth and twentieth centuries.

Most importantly, girdles and belts kept trousers up, once these garments were no longer laced onto the torso's clothes. In the eighteenth century the belt for men was ousted for a long time by the introduction of braces, also known as *gallowses* or *suspenders*. These straps of silk, webbing or leather attached to the trousers and stretched over the shoulders to keep the newly fashionable pantaloons nicely taut. Although braces would have been hidden by a jacket, or at the very least a waistcoat, they soon came to be decorated with beautiful tapestry and embroidery designs. At first braces were fastened with buttons; by the 1930s they were usually clipped on. Rubber elastic helped with stretch and fit. However, by that time belts were once more appearing as a means of holding trousers up.[11] Belt buckles assumed special prominence. Braces enjoyed a resurgence during the economically confident years of the 1980s, as a bold feature of the City trader's professional apparel, or with loud novelty patterns as a more casual accessory.

Women in the nineteenth century rarely wore braces. They weren't permitted trousers, and their skirts were held onto the waist by metal hook-and-eye fastenings or drawstrings. Belts, on the other hand, provided ample opportunity for displaying craft skills – beading, embroidery and lace-making – or at least shopping skills. Belts could emphasise the narrowness of a waist already cinched in by a corset. Newly professional nurses at the end of the nineteenth century boasted elaborate silver buckles as a sign of their status. These, unfortunately, are no longer considered suitable in the supposedly antiseptic environment of the modern hospital.

Both braces and belts are now fashion accessories in their own right, in addition to their trouser-holding function. However, belts are by far the favoured item on both counts. Leather or leather-look plastics dominate menswear, with bolder designs and bigger buckles perhaps for jeans and other informal trousers. Modern women have functional belts for trousers, and highly decorative belts to accentuate the waist or to hang around the hips.

Strictly speaking, the *cummerbund* still in use in evening wear is more of a sash band than a belt. It originates from India, where British colonists preferred it to the warmer waistcoat. It is now popular in hire shops for formal wear. True dandies are wary of its use: 'Cummerbunds are not naff, but a cummerbund could *become* naff if you make the mistake of wearing the cummerbund with the pleats facing *downwards.*'

Until trousers are superseded by garments that don't require suspension from the waist, the belt will confidently keep its place in the modern clothes collection.

HANDKERCHIEFS

Do you own a handkerchief? Is there a pristine handkerchief in your suit front, showing a splash of colour? Or have you one crumpled in a pocket, ready to catch sneezes and sniffles? Handkerchiefs have a long and occasionally illustrious history, but they have recently been ousted from the ranks of indispensable items by the disposable paper tissue . . .

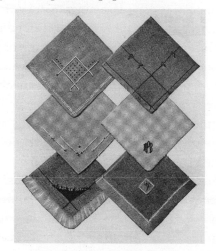

A selection of decorated women's hankies from 1925.

12 Among the many birthday presents gifted to Adolf Hitler was a hand-made handkerchief with the heads of Hitler, Hindenberg, Bismarck and Frederick the Great embroidered on it, one in each corner – 'all united to help you blow your nose!' joked his secretary.

Before the handkerchief was commonly used, nose-blowing involved a sleeve, apron or finger-on-the-nostril (the last method still favoured by male footballers on the pitch). Eighteenth-century theatre manager Tate Wilkinson deplored the habit of actors dressed in full court costume standing backstage and blowing noses with fingers, musing: 'How Adam and Eve managed such necessary business I cannot tell, but I imagine as Eve did make aprons of fig leaves, she might possibly make pocket handkerchiefs of a like commodity.'

In the sixteenth century handkerchiefs were expensive gifts and status symbols. Queen Elizabeth I was given embroidered sets as New Year's Day gifts. The practice continued for centuries, reaching its peak in the 1950s, when mass-produced presentation sets were widespread.[12] Once the technology had been mastered in the nineteenth century, printed handkerchiefs were sold to commemorate notable events, such as coronations and jubilees. They also made picturesque souvenirs of holiday visits. The very best handkerchiefs were stored in a *porte mouchoire* or handkerchief case, made of perfumed silk.

Handkerchiefs might boast the owner's initials – so beloved of crime writers, for furnishing clues – and other embroidery. In the Victorian detective novel *Mr Bazalgette's Agent*, the agent in question identifies her culprit via a handkerchief obtained by discreet flirting: 'It was of silk, and, as I had anticipated, it bore an embroidered monogram. Trembling with excitement I held the corner beneath the lamp; the initials were J. V. – I have found my man!'

Almost everyone could afford a pocket hanky. In the nineteenth century they ranged from fine lawn, French cambric or silk, to cotton handkerchiefs for the working classes, costing only a penny each.

Hankies historically had a multitude of functions beyond nose-blowing. An Indian visitor to London in the nineteenth century commented on the pollution: 'Wipe your face or furniture now and again, and in a couple of hours you will see your kerchief tinged with soot.' Handkerchiefs could also be used to wipe dusty seats, to mop fevered brows and to wave in farewell on a departing ship or train. With black edges, they were given as mourning gifts; with white lace edges, they made popular wedding presents. When Dick Whittington is shown setting off on his storybook journey to London, he carries his worldly goods wrapped in a handkerchief tied to the end of a stick. The Duke of Windsor noted that a red-and-white spotted cotton hanky was traditionally used to hold the British worker's lunch, though he preferred blowing his nose on one, since he found 'the cotton of which they were made was both strong, and, when washed, remarkably soft'.

Handkerchiefs were easy targets for both criminal and amorous pickpockets. An anecdote of 1772 describes a young lover in raptures over the thought of his beloved's silken lashes and the pallid roses of her lips. He reaches into his pocket to touch her handkerchief, which he stole at the previous night's assembly . . . and is immediately horror-stricken. 'It is gone!' he shrieks. 'I am undone! Undone for ever!' The gentleman in question later recovered the handkerchief and kept it safely hugged to his bosom.

No matter how useful or ornamental, some people simply couldn't keep track of their handkerchiefs. In the clean-up after the 1851 Great Exhibition, amongst the items of Lost Property catalogued in the Crystal Palace were 271 handkerchiefs.

Sadly, in Shakespeare's tragedy *Othello*, poor Desdemona loses her life not long after lamenting, 'Where should I lose that handkerchief, Emilia?' The handkerchief in question was a valued heirloom, given by Othello's father to his mother as a love-token. During the play Desdemona is unaware that the scheming Iago is using this particular handkerchief as a device to stir her husband to ultimately lethal jealousy.

All these stories are now firmly in the past. The handkerchief has just about survived for nose-blowing alone. At the South Pole, preventing the spread of the common cold is a very serious business. Any new arrival at the McMurdo research centre is given not one but *three* iodine-impregnated handkerchiefs: one to blow the nose on, one to wipe the nose and one to wipe the hands. Each hanky costs $1, making it a very expensive operation.

Modern handkerchiefs are almost always disposable. They are carried in compact plastic packets, and are available with soothing balsam or covered with novelty prints. Using paper for hankies is actually a little-lauded innovation of the First World War, when fabrics were in short supply and so train passengers availed themselves of the paper hand-towels in the carriage washroom. These were made 'of a nicely patterned absorbent paper which is an excellent substitute for linen', and were easily cut into dainty little handkerchief shapes. Fabric handkerchiefs were in general still very much the norm in the First World War, with nineteen-inch regulation service handkerchiefs of very soft mercerised khaki cotton on sale at two shillings for a half-dozen. From 1924 the Kleenex company marketed a commercial paper handkerchief, but it was for face-wiping at first. The idea of using it for nose-blowing took a few more years to catch on and some concerted advertising campaigns. When paper hankies eventually ousted fabric ones as the nose-blow of choice, it must have been a relief to laundry workers and housewives, who previously had the disagreeable task of boiling fabric handkerchiefs in a saucepan on the hob. *Mrs Lord's Laundry Work* – a household guide from the 1890s – gave instructions that pocket handkerchiefs should be washed separately, then ironed while damp. 'Iron first the right side, taking care to pull into shape whilst so doing, then iron in the middle. Fold in four and finish with the name uppermost.'

Fabric handkerchiefs were very much considered a decorative costume accessory. One dress guru of 1925 asserted:

In planning a costume that is to be correct to the smallest accessory, the handkerchief must be considered, because it may supply just that accenting colour note which will add the proper emphasis to the keynote colour of the ensemble.

Mods of the 1960s affected a silk hanky, speared with a pearl pin to stop it slipping into the pocket. Nowadays there are still chaps who like to display a folded handkerchief in their suit's outer breast pocket, but they are not considered true purists by the modern dandy set. One expert concedes, 'With a *country* suit, a coloured handkerchief *may* adorn the breast pocket,' but he goes on to admonish, 'Never ever sport a matching tie and handkerchief unless you manage an out-of-town superstore.'

Handkerchief-style squares of fabric were also worn as neckwear, in which case they were known as *neckerchiefs*. London costermongers took special pride in their neckerchiefs, the gaudier the better – fat flowers on a colourful background were particularly favoured in the 1860s, for example. In his 1851 picturesque survey of city life, *London Labour and London Poor*, Henry Mayhew gave vivid descriptions of everyday characters, remarking, 'Even if a costermonger has two or three silk handkerchiefs by him already, he seldom hesitates to buy another when tempted with a bright showy pattern.'

Large neckerchiefs were fashionable for females over many centuries, changing only their name and the number of frills. In the 1790s, for instance, they were puffed up over the bosom to create a pouter-pigeon chest; by the 1830s they fluted out over wide sleeves, like birds' wings. Lace kerchiefs were an excellent way to display wealth and taste while covering the shoulders.[13] More mundanely, nineteenth-century neck handkerchiefs were worn between the skin and the shirt collar, 'for those liable to be soon heated, or who are engaged in warm or dusty employment, especially if the dress is not of a washing material'. One of the fancy names for the female neckerchief was a *fichu* – as discussed in the Tie Rack chapter. There is no corresponding garment in the modern woman's wardrobe, unless we concede the plethora of neck scarves in vogue, which can be worn looped, twisted or knotted at the throat.

A lovely excerpt from Mary Braddon's 1879 novel *Vixen* sees Captain Winstanley, a mean-spirited husband, querying his vain wife's shopping bills:

> 'Fifteen guineas for a Honiton *fichu*!' he cried presently. 'What in mercy's name is a *fichu*? It sounds like a sneeze.'
>
> 'It is a little half-handkerchief I wear to brighten a velvet gown when we dine alone, Conrad. You know you have always said that lace harmonises a woman's dress, and gives a softness to the complexion and contour.'
>
> 'I shall be very careful what I say in future,' muttered the Captain.

APRON STRINGS

Aprons – of linen, leather, rubber, cotton and nylon – have been worn for both protective and decorative purposes for thousands of years. The modern home may own one or two, perhaps of wipe-clean PVC; perhaps with a comedy print.

13 In 1836 the *Ladies' Cabinet of Fashion* asserted, 'If you do not know the rank, or at least the fortune, of a lady whom you meet at an evening party, you may give something like a correct guess at the latter, by looking attentively at her fan, and her pocket handkerchief.'

A labourer of the 1840s in a protective apron.

Aprons were once an essential part of labouring life, and sometimes a symbol of the job. In Shakespeare's play *Julius Caesar* workers are berated for appearing in 'civvies' on a work day and not advertising their trade through their aprons and tools. A carpenter is asked, 'Where is / Thy leather apron and thy rule? What / dost thou with thy best apparel on?'

Agricultural workers from Classical times, through the Middle Ages and beyond, have been depicted with aprons holding seed for sowing or feeding chickens. Workers in the brewing industry had moleskin aprons; carpenters preferred leather, as did blacksmiths, who had theirs split so that they could grasp a horse's leg while shoeing it. In abattoirs and tanneries, rubber aprons were a welcome invention.

From the nineteenth century butchers had blue aprons made of Coventry cloth with a good-quality permanent dye, which wouldn't run in the wash. The expression 'True blue will never stain' refers to the fact that the butcher's blue apron won't show bloodstains. Modern butchers' aprons are often made of polyurethane-coated nylon with blue-and-white stripes, or cotton-backed rubber.

The Victorian butler had a large square-bibbed apron of linen. Household maids showed their roles and status through different apron styles, descending from the elegant frills of the lady's maid to the plain linen of the scullery maid. Even now waiters in certain classes of restaurants may wear a white or black waist-apron, while waitresses in tearooms may have *broderie-anglaise* frills. Female nurses had a long battle to be recognised as respectable professionals. The crackling white starched aprons of late nineteenth-century Nightingale nurses were hugely important in projecting both moral and medical cleanliness.

During the First World War the government issued guidelines for women entering industry for the first time. It recommended stout leather aprons for workers handling glass, asbestos cloth aprons for women welders and a rubber apron for chrome dyeing.

A pretty apron was supposed to make housework a pleasure, not a chore. Here, housewives of the 1920s.

When we speak of *cutting the apron strings* we refer to the idea of a child becoming more independent of home ties, and of the mother in particular. The apron here is thought of as a female, domestic garment. Throughout Western history the domestic apron was essential for household work such as cleaning, cooking, laundry and childcare. Clothes were simply too expensive to be carelessly stained.

Women of the leisured classes enjoyed the luxury of wearing aprons as a decorative novelty, mimicking the labour of their servants. In 1868 the *Ladies' Treasury* reported, 'Among the more useful fancies of the present fashions is the adoption of aprons, of every style and material, either short or long.' Black Victorian aprons of glossy silk advertised the wearer's sewing and embroidery skills. More unusually, in 1837 the Wakefield firm of Richard Baker & Sons invented a method for turning glass into cloth. Yorkshire ladies wore this pliable, yet potentially fragile fabric as headdresses. Some even made it into fine, artificial ringlets. In 1838 Queen Victoria was fortunate enough to be presented with a very elegant glass apron, as soft as silk. The Wakefield glass apron was, of course, a novelty; an example of the nineteenth-century craze for industrial lateral-thinking which would eventually lead to the development of man-made fibres.

By the early twentieth century labour-saving devices for the home were becoming increasingly affordable, putting subtle pressure on middle-class housewives to do their own chores rather than hiring cooks and maids, particularly when the upheaval of the First World War left many former domestic servants disillusioned with a life in service. Shopping catalogues advertised overalls from the Edwardian era onwards, then cotton-print *pinnies* as the twentieth century progressed. 'Pinny' comes from *pinafore*, referring to the old method of pinning an apron into place on the chest. Any maids in work between the 1920s and 1960s would have had plain aprons; their mistresses would have coloured and frilled ones.

Housewives were encouraged not to 'let themselves go' as they wielded vacuum cleaners and operated top-loader washing machines. It was bad manners to answer the door while wearing an apron, although gaily decorated cocktail aprons were popular in the 1950s. There were still cleaning ladies or 'dailies' for heavier work – known as 'chars' in Britain – who often wore floral wraparound aprons.

Nowadays the home cook can choose from a variety of

novelty-print aprons with humorous quotes, and house-cleaning is such a relatively light and easy series of tasks that for the most part it can be done in everyday clothes.

LANGUAGE OF THE FAN

The fan is an ancient accessory, with an impressive history of both use and craft. Fans from Classical Greece favoured peacock quills, as the peacock was the goddess Hera's bird and a symbol of refinement and luxury. For extra decadence there would be slaves to waft long-handled fans in hot climates – Egyptian palm fronds, for example. From the early thirteenth century, Crusaders returning from the Middle East brought fans home as souvenirs. Folding fans caused a sensation when they were introduced to Europe from the Far East in the seventeenth century.

As the fad for personal fans grew, so admiration for the craft of the fan-maker spread. In addition to imports from Japan and China, a London company of fan-makers and gilderers was set up in 1564 to create and garnish fans of sheepskin, silk and goatskin. Jewels and perfumes were added to gold, sandalwood or ivory sticks for extremely high-status fans, while delicate lace fans were carried in a satin bag for protection. Fans truly reached their zenith in the eighteenth century, and not just for cooling the owner. They displayed wealth, could carry notes and lists as an aide-memoire and even served as a basic communication device, through coded signals known as the *language of the fan*:

- Closed to the right cheek – *yes.*
- Closed to the left cheek – *no.*
- Open just below the eyes – *I love you.*
- Open just below the lips – *You may kiss me.*
- Open horizontally and slowly lowered before the body – *I despise you.*
- Closed and tapped to the temples – *You are mad.*

These are just a few of the words and phrases in the antique language of the fan, in use long before smartphones as a method of communicating across a crowded ballroom. Some fans had a code printed on their leaves to jog the memory (it is to be hoped that those using fan signals were sharing the same language).

A less-prescribed fan movement could still communicate a great deal of emotion and motive. The *Spectator* catalogued 'the angry flutter, the modern flutter, the modest flutter, the timorous flutter, the merry flutter, the amorous flutter'. According to the magazine, women in particular were adept with the fan: 'Women are armed with fans as men with swords and sometimes do more execution with them.' In Europe, both genders carried fans until the late eighteenth century, when changing aesthetics about masculinity pigeonholed the fan as a frivolous feminine accessory, unsuited to the new, plain tailoring of the 1790s gentleman. 'But the fan, what do these women not make it say!' observes the heroine of one Victorian detective novel. '"I like you," and "You bother me," "You may follow me" and "You are to wait here," are, I learn, among the commonest forms of expression in this most mysterious of tongues.'

Fans could also be printed with other helpful information, such as steps to the latest fashionable dances, calendars and almanacs, and contemporary song lyrics. For armchair travellers there were cartographic fans; for plant enthusiasts there were illustrations of botanical specimens. There were fans that acted as dance cards, and *Gunsen* fans used by Japanese battle commanders to send signals in war. Fans could hide blushes . . . and bad teeth. *Peeping fans* were for shielding faces and reputations at the theatre. *Dagger fans* were for stealthy assassinations. *Mourning fans* showed scenes of funeral urns and drooping willows; in contrast were pornographic fans with erotic scenes. Fans commemorated cricket matches and coronations. From the 1850s they were even given away free as promotional accessories.

A charming silk folding fan from the 1890s.

Sadly, fans have fallen out of favour, their last hoorah being the flamboyant ostrich-feather creations of the 1920s. Cigarettes took over from fans as the thing to fiddle with at social functions, and then handbags – and mobile phones – became the accessories of choice. In her *Dictionnaire des étiquettes*, the French savante Madame de Genlis equated fans with modesty:

> In the time when women blushed, when they wished to hide their timidity they sheltered themselves behind large fans; now that they blush no longer, that nothing intimidates them, they do not wish to screen their faces, and consequently they carry imperceptible fans.

Following this theory, perhaps the modern Western woman feels she has nothing to blush for, and consequently has no need to carry any fan at all.

PYJAMA CASE

He wore an ordinary grey flannel dressing-gown, no coloured ties, just ugly black socks and not even modern pyjamas. He lay in bed, well shaved and with his hair brushed, in the kind of plain white nightshirt that only the Wehrmacht could design.

DESCRIPTION OF ADOLF HITLER, ILL IN THE REICH
CHANCELLERY BUNKER, BERLIN 1945

DECENTLY COVERED UP

What we wear – or don't wear – in bed can reveal a great deal about cultural attitudes, particularly towards sex and privacy. Nightclothes come in a range of styles, on a spectrum between modest and debauched (though the idea of sensual sleepwear is relatively new). As late as the mid-twentieth century, nighties and pyjamas would be folded carefully after use and slipped out of sight into a cotton or satin case, nicely embroidered with the owner's initials. In homes with heightened sensibilities, even day clothes removed at bedtime might spend the night hidden from view under a discreet fabric cover.

A lot can happen in a bed – illness, idleness, copulation, procreation and expiration and, most pertinently, sleep. Clothes for this very busy place in the home reflect the moral ambiguity felt about those various activities, and show a mixture of practicality, prudishness and allure.

Until the sixteenth century tradition favoured sleeping naked. At most there were night-shifts and night-shirts, more voluminous than their daytime counterparts, for those who wanted an extra layer at night.[1] While these might have been a comparatively luxurious item, they came with a particular disadvantage – the proliferation of vermin in their seams; sewing a camphor bag to the nightwear was one way to ward off fleas and bugs.

The young Princess Victoria famously received news that she was to be Queen while still in her night-gown and dressing gown, June 1837.

The idea of specially created night attire only took hold in the nineteenth century, and at first these loose, long-sleeved gowns of white cotton, silk or linen were made at home. Male versions tended to be quite plain, reaching to the calves. Women's ballooned from neck to ankle. They were not sewn with seduction in mind, whatever actually went on between the sheets. As the century progressed these *night-gowns* – as they became known – became more elaborate, with embroidery, tucks and frills. Shops and department stores also sold ready-to-wear night-gowns, often as part of a prospective bride's trousseau;

the large, white garment therefore came to represent all the unspoken anticipation and anxiety about the wedding night.

For all the additions of ribbons and lace, modesty was still preserved by both width and length. The dawn of the twentieth century saw the notion of sensual lingerie-style nightwear slowly becoming acceptable to the middle classes, who were advised to buy night-gowns of thick silk – but still in 'good washing shades' such as pink or yellow. The adventurous Edwardian lady could order Indian gauze night-dresses from her Harrods shopping catalogue. Those with more common sense, or fewer servants to fill the hollow earthenware hot-water bottles in winter, could purchase flannel or alpine-wool night-dresses. By the momentous summer of 1914 night-dresses sported ruffles, bows, *broderie-anglaise* scallops, embroidery and lace, almost all machine-sewn and mass-produced.

WHAT TO WEAR IN AN AIR RAID

Evidence for nightwear can come from a variety of traditional sources, including art history, laundry lists, wardrobe inventories and shopping catalogues. However, to see the range of what people actually wore to bed requires an invasion of privacy – or an upset in proprieties of the sort caused by an emergency situation such as fire, earthquake, shipwreck or air raid. In fact, not only do such events enable us to glimpse the nightwear of others; some people actually created specially designed emergency nightwear. The first example of deliberately adapting nightwear for an emergency came in March 1750, when Londoners unsettled by two nocturnal earthquakes solved the problem of what to wear at night if forced to leave the house in a hurry by adopting warm 'earthquake gowns'. Sadly no images of these emergency fashions seem to have survived.

Most people caught up in a sudden disaster would not have time to don a specialist item of apparel, but disasters at night did create a dilemma between taking the time to dress properly, for respectability's sake, and prioritising speed and going out *in public* in nightwear. Notable among the eyewitness accounts of the *Titanic*'s sinking in 1912 are descriptions of the jumbled outfits thrown on by passengers: ladies with fur wraps thrown over their night-gowns, and men bundled into dressing gowns. One survivor said it was like 'a fancy dress ball in Dante's hell'. As the lights went out on the great ocean liner and it sank beneath the surface of the Atlantic ocean, in Lifeboat No. 1 couturier Lucy Duff Gordon joked to her maid, Miss Francatelli, 'Just fancy, you actually left your beautiful nightdress behind you.' One of the sailors in the lifeboat drily reminded them they were lucky to come away with their lives.

Three years on from this tragedy, Europe braced itself for night-time air raids during the frighteningly modern First World War. Fashion was quick to react.

A SLEEPING SUIT FOR AIR-RAID NIGHTS.

Fig. (4).

Cut out in white, pink, blue, or mauve nainsook, 8s., with trimmings, 10s. Made to order. 6s. extra.

A First World War 'onesie' – a sewing pattern on offer in 1918.

When Zeppelin raids began over Britain in 1915, fashion magazines such as *Tatler* promoted new all-in-one *sleeping suits* with flounces at the cuffs and ankles, designed for the style-conscious woman roused from her bed by searchlights and sirens. However, civilians also had a rather dashing alternative to night-gowns: *pyjamas*. That same year the fashion editor of *Patrician* magazine shared details of her newly purchased pyjamas, which were ultra-modern and rather stylish in a black crêpe-de-Chine sailor style. She gushed, 'I must confess that I do want a little Zep scare, so that I can wear them. Of course, I don't want anyone to be killed . . .' The same editor also acquired primrose-yellow pyjamas trimmed with fur:

> They were pretty but not very warm, and as a consequence it was quite impossible for me to resist a wild-rose pink dressing gown lined with primrose-leaf green silk, and finished with a pure white muslin collar, and cuffs edged with lace.

All very gorgeous, but not exactly practical when hiding from bombs under the stairs, or when rushing for shelter in a London Tube station. As the war dragged on and fuel shortages became dire, more rational women overcame their initial distrust of pyjamas – previously the domain of sleeping men – to wear striped flannel PJs in bed. There were also knitted sleeping vests for those who felt safest with wool next to the skin.

DOOM OF THE SLEEPING SHIRT

While they might have been a daring departure for women, pyjamas were fairly well established for men by 1915. They were introduced to Western Europe in the nineteenth century from India and Persia – the word 'pyjama' is derived from the Hindi for a *leg garment*. In Asian and Middle Eastern countries these loose trousers were worn by both women and men as day clothes. Western men matched them with a loose jacket and took to sleeping in them, from the 1880s onwards. They were made of cotton, flannel or silk – according to taste and budget – usually with neat stripes or a discreet paisley pattern. By 1897, the year of Queen Victoria's Golden Jubilee, *Tailor and Cutter* magazine was predicting the 'doom of the sleeping shirt' and suggesting it should be curated as a historic garment 'to show to succeeding generations the wonderfully and fearfully made garments their forefathers slept in'.

A traditional striped cotton-flannel pyjama set.

A chap on the Home Front during the First World War could choose from old-fashioned night-shirts of flannel, calico or 'unshrinkable' wool web or 'sleeping suits' (pyjamas) in flannel, silk or fancy striped taffeta – or even the new Viyella brand wool/cotton mix. Night-shirts became the preserve of the conservative common-sense sleeper who might, for example, browse the 1916 Oxendales shop catalogue for 'Gentleman's nightshirts, striped and double seamed, very warm, durable and comfortable'.

Male pyjamas were surprisingly flamboyant in the post-war years, with strong pinks, purples and blues, but by the 1930s they had settled to predictable block stripes in maroon, blue, brown and dark green, which have lasted in contemporary designs. Oblivious to the Youth Quake and Flower Power movements of the 1960s, modern men's pyjamas are still comfortable, well cut and rather dull, with an emphasis on being unobtrusive, hard-wearing and serviceable. One current alternative for men is sleeping sets of T-shirts and shorts.

However, it was the women of the post-war world who became the real peacocks after dark. They began the 1920s in so-called 'Oriental' pyjama suits, coloured in artistic pink, mauve, apple-green and heliotrope stripes. The decade ended with tailor-made pyjamas of pure peach silk or lemon crêpe de Chine, and Cossack-style pyjamas suits in flame-red and black. Giddy with the novelty of trousered ensembles, pyjama suits were worn by bohemian women and upper-class socialites as informal leisure wear – preferably teamed with a cocktail cigarette, a silk bandana, pearls and embellished high-heeled slippers. By the 1930s they were being flaunted as resort wear.

Silky PJs perfectly suited the bold palette of the Art Deco ethos. Their chic fluidity matched the new trend for figure-grazing fabrics cut on the bias. New synthetic fabrics were perfect for modern nightwear designs, so for those who could not afford pure silk there were a multitude of mixes and alternatives. Artificial silk, marketed as *art silk*, was a cellulose-based rayon fabric, a pre-First World War invention that now enlivened many a woman's nightwear collection. The textile firm of Courtaulds was at the forefront of the fabric revolution, investing significantly in researching new fibres and finishes, which also gave a new fluidity to night-gowns. Shoppers were seduced into buying artificial fabrics by exotic-sounding brand names such as Luvisca and Celanese.

A dainty and modest cotton gown from the 1920s.

It was a brave new world for nightwear, though not so futuristic as to fulfil the predictions of Aldous Huxley's 1932 novel *Brave New World*, in which the sexually liberated heroine Lenina Crowne strips out of zippicamiknicks and zips herself into 'pink one piece zippyjamas' at bedtime. This was taking the use of the zip fastener too far for real women's tastes. Women were more likely to follow actress Claudette Colbert's lead in the 1934 film *It Happened One Night*, where her character looks charmingly swamped in a pair of male pyjamas borrowed from co-star Clark Gable.

The increasingly overt sensuality of nightwear matched Western women's emerging sexual assurance and growing social freedoms in the 1930s. Nighties and pyjamas became acceptable Christmas gifts and a healthy boost to store profits over the festive season.

NAUGHTY, NICE, BUT NOT NEAR NAKED FLAMES

With ribbon-thin shoulder straps and delicate lace, bias-cut night-gowns of the 1930s eschewed the all-covering modesty of earlier styles. They were not so very different from the new generation of evening gowns being worn to dance halls and nightclubs across Europe. As war once again threw the world into tumult and populations shifted, there were women from remote rural areas who encountered seductive nightwear for the first time. A young Polish girl recalled how the communist wives of Russian soldiers occupying her home town of Zolkiew during the Second World War decked themselves out for theatre visits in newly acquired nighties. The Poles were too frightened to tell the Russians of their embarrassing mistake:

> These poor women, many from beyond the Urals, many from villages without a phone or even a road, assumed the stylish silk garments, decorated with lace décolletage, could be worn on the streets of Paris, Budapest or Berlin.

The Second World War did nothing to encourage nightwear innovation. During the 1940s *serviceable* and *durable* were the key selling points in most nightwear advertisements. Such hard-wearing cotton night-gowns endured in many a cold bedroom long after fashion had flagged up racier, more modern styles. Glamorous night-gowns were only worn by a lucky few on brief wartime honeymoons, or as an exceptional treat in otherwise austere times.

By the 1950s night-shirts were mostly the choice of old-fashioned men.

As with the First World War, the need to be dressed during air raids did impact on nightwear, this time with the advent of *siren suits*, of the sort that Winston Churchill filled so well. Siren suits were essentially glorified boiler suits, with integrated top and bottom. A snug home-made version of the siren suit called a *unity suit* was advertised in 1940, suitable for sleeping in, or else for zipping on in a hurry when the air-raid sirens sounded. The modern descendant of the sleeping suit and the siren suit is, of course, the fleecy *onesie*.

By the 1950s nylon night-dresses and pyjamas dazzled with their bold colours and modern feel. Bed became a fun, playful place. Pyjamas, for women at least, also became fun, as reflected in the zest of the 1954 musical *The Pajama Game*. They did not feel quite as fun when paired with nylon sheets. It wasn't so much the potential colour clash – the sheets came in lilac, apricot and ice-blue – as the intense static that was generated.[2]

2 This issue was addressed in the 1970s by nighties and negligees made of Celon anti-stat, which also promised to resist hunching, creasing and riding up.

Nylon nighties from the 1960s.

Nylon had another flaw: it could be highly flammable. Stories of people being burnt to death when their clothes caught fire are not mere urban myths. In fact the problem wasn't limited to artificial fabrics: *Fatal Flannelette* was the lugubrious nickname for cheap brushed-cotton fabrics in the late nineteenth and early twentieth centuries. Families on a budget were quick to clothe their children in flannelette, with devastating results, because cotton, too, can be highly flammable. In the decades before central heating became the norm, you could literally catch your death by catching a spark from the fireplace, or by catching a sleeve on the gas hob. When smoking became fully socially acceptable in the 1920s, nightwear was sold using images of mannequins with cigarettes, and movies showed people happily lighting up while under the covers. 'Do You Smoke in Bed?' questioned a 1930s advertisement, showing a dapper chap in smart pyjamas holding a smoking cigarette above the pillow. It was not a warning ad; the text continued: 'If so, smoke Will's Gold Flake . . .'

The British Fire Protection Association published information in popular magazines on 'Keeping Warm Safely', with parents urged to choose flame-resistant underwear and to remember that 'night-dresses cause about twenty-three times as many deaths as close-fitting pyjamas'. The fight to educate people of the dangers of smoking in bed has subsequently been allied with initiatives to make mattresses non-flammable. The fads of fashion have at least rejected bright Bri-nylon bedding, a victory for fire safety as well as good taste.

Cotton nightwear now vies for shop display-space with sophisticated acrylic mixes. The variety of colours, themes and styles means that nightwear is very much part of the modern cult of choice. The modern woman can opt for cute, elegant, cosy or come-hither – there are even oversized T-shirts that mimic historical night-chemises, although now they will have embellishments or will feature digital prints. For men the range is less exciting. The modern man's pyjamas – and he has not yet been brave enough to take up the night-shirt again – are not far removed from twentieth-century conservatism. T-shirt-and-shorts combinations often still come in muted 'manly' colours and patterns, though versions in silk permit an occasional hint of sensuality. Given the insulation of modern homes, high-tog duvets, central heating and electric blankets, it's not surprising that many people have reverted to the ancient mode of sleeping nude.

BATHROBES AND BED-JACKETS

There is more to bedroom wear than just what's worn in bed. Slippers, night-caps for pre-bed wear and dressing gowns all have their roles to play. The dressing gown's history, in particular, is entwined with fascinating changes in our concepts of privacy and informality.

Notwithstanding a modern trend for sharing bedtime spaces and activities on the Internet, bed is usually considered a private place. This was not the case in earlier centuries. From the Middle Ages to the nineteenth century beds were hung with curtains from four posts, partly to protect sleepers from draughts, partly to display textile wealth and partly because servants might well be sharing the bedroom, on roll-out truckle beds. Bed-sharing was also common until the mid-twentieth century, when relative affluence meant separate beds for siblings.

Nightwear was therefore part of the intricate see-but-don't-see ritual of sharing intimate spaces with family or servants. In the past, servants had ready access to all rooms, and knocking was not a prime requirement. In the seventeenth and eighteenth centuries, for example, friends and family might be received socially in the bedchamber or dressing room, along with the hairdresser, dressmaker and physician. Formal dressing required time and endurance, so there was a liminal period between bedtime and official house-leaving when *undress* was adopted – giving us *dressing jackets* and *dressing gowns*.

For women of these centuries *undress* meant gowns with less boning in the bodices and a looser cut around the torso, or easy-fitting dressing jackets that could be slipped on while the hair was being brushed or powdered. From the nineteenth century onwards, short coatees were worn as bed-jackets – often in pleasant pastel shades with matching satin ribbons and floral embroidery. Long versions of the dressing jacket became female dressing gowns as we know them – ankle-length, with buttons or girdle belts. By the end of the nineteenth century the well-dressed woman was advised to furnish her wardrobe with several kinds of *undress* garment: morning wrappers, breakfast jackets, tea gowns and bathrobes.

Flannel bathrobes were a welcome innovation. In 1899 *Ladies' World* lamented with mock-horror the need for bathrobes: 'Into what extravagances our civilisation leads us! Our great-grandmothers who knew not the bath intimately, were saved expenses which now fall upon every woman.' The magazine's fashion editor recommended a bathrobe not of cosy flannel, but of scarlet silk, with a hood to 'hide the ugly appearance of the head before it is dressed'.

Pastels and prettiness soon had to give way to fashion's surge of interest in more luxurious and exotic styles in the early years of the twentieth century. It was said to have been inspired by Diaghilev's touring Russian art exhibitions and his *Ballets Russes* productions, which brought Pavlova and Nijinsky to the West's attention. The colours of the sets and costumes for the ballets *Scheherazade* and *The Firebird* were vibrant, decadent and different. These designs, in striking jewel-coloured hues, were rapidly reproduced on avant-garde dressing gowns. From there, fashion went further east, to Japan, and kimono dressing gowns were suddenly all the rage.

Orientalism didn't always fare well when matched with British common sense. Middle-class dressing gowns were often still of sensible flannel, enlivened with so-called Oriental trims and colours – maroon, navy and strawberry-pink. Violet, Duchess of Rutland, apparently spent her mornings in bed, in state: 'Her silk-frilled nightdress was worn under a cream flannel kimono-shaped garment and her head was bound, seemingly in a knitted vest, the long sleeves of which wound round her chin.'

The 1930s dressing gown had, like the 1930s female, moved out of the seclusion of the home and into the wider world. Shop sales-pitches flagged up the fact that their dressing gowns were easy to pack, reflecting the ever-widening possibilities for travel and trips abroad, even for women of limited means. Rayon-made aspirations to luxury were displayed on board sleeper-trains or while queuing for the facilities at guest houses. For those still at home, a *housecoat* – a classier version of the dressing gown – could be worn informally between getting up and going to bed, just like the dressing jackets of the seventeenth and eighteenth centuries. It was fine to be seen in a housecoat if neighbours were popping in, or if the postie called, but only the most slovenly housewife would venture beyond the back yard in one.

In the early 1950s Italian designer Elsa Schiaparelli shook up the housecoat even further, producing quilted versions lined in her trademark shocking pink. These were tame compared to her dressing gowns, which featured mink and ermine collars. Women with smaller budgets risked being caught looking merely warm and comfortable in the dowdier quilted nylon housecoats of the 1950s and 1960s, or in cosy 'tiny-tuft' candlewick cotton. Eventually the dressing gown itself became a housecoat, though one designed to be truly informal, offering simple, almost childlike psychological comfort to the wearer.

DRESSING DOWN IN DRESSING GOWNS

The most iconic literary figure to have found fame dressed in nightwear is the notorious skinflint Ebenezer Scrooge, introduced to the reading public in Charles Dickens' December 1843 story, *A Christmas Carol*. His clothes at bedtime say a great deal about Victorian notions of male dress and undress. We read that after a busy Christmas Eve spreading ill-will, Scrooge prepares for his evening alone: 'he took off his cravat; put on his dressing-gown and slippers, and his nightcap; and sat down before the fire to take his gruel'.

In the original hand-coloured etchings by John Leech, Scrooge is shown in a night-gown, a white wrapped dressing gown, an upright cap and slippers. This memorable ensemble has since been copied countless times in stage plays, films and caricatures based on the novel. In fact this depiction owes a lot to artistic licence; in the actual text Scrooge is described as having a habit of putting his hands in his breeches pocket during thoughtful moments, and does just this when he is visited by the Ghost of Christmas Past. This demonstrates that he wasn't precisely ready for bed, merely relaxing informally, with a dressing gown on. For dramatic enhancement, directors and illustrators have preferred to show him looking vulnerable in a night-shirt – particularly effective when Scrooge dreams of falling into a gaping grave.

Tracing male dressing-gown styles backwards in time, we see limited variations in style and fabric, with synthetics preceded by cottons, silk foulards and camel hair. The Victorian gent's dressing gown could actually be rather flamboyant. One vain character from a novel of the 1860s was described as appearing on the balcony of his seaside hotel room in 'an elegant cerulean blue Turkish silk dressing-gown, with massive red tassels, and lily-of-the-valley worked slippers'. Mr Bunting, the wearer of the dressing gown, was also described as 'a hero or not in the eyes of his valet, accordingly perhaps as he paid him'.

The nineteenth-century gentleman's dressing gown had its origins as an informal robe borrowed from India in the early days of Western expansion into Asia. Known as a *banyan*, this loose gown was worn before dressing to leave the house, just as women might wear dressing gowns or housecoats. Its heyday was between the 1680s and 1780s. The declining career of Georgian dandy Beau Brummell could be charted through the state of his dressing gown. In 1829 he received visitors in a flowered chintz dressing gown, Turkish slippers and a gold-tasselled velvet night-cap. By 1836, in poverty and out of fashion, Brummell was reduced to living off the charity of his friends, one of whom unwisely sent him a towelling cotton dressing gown. It was so contrary to Brummell's notions of gentlemanly attire that he threw it from his third-floor window.

Some banyans were so smart they were wasted on the relative privacy of one's home. Londoners were reported to be wearing them as coats in 1785 – 'and if a sword is occasionally put on it sticks out of the middle of the slit behind'. The banyan embodied 'Oriental' indulgence long before women shed their white cottons for such exotic colours. Peter the Great of Russia had a particularly splendid green dressing gown covered with flowers and foliage; other wealthy Russians had patterned silk-damask gowns, padded with cotton wool or lined with fur.

Putting on a dressing gown and a night-cap was the Georgian or Victorian man's equivalent to retreating to his shed – his meta-phorical cave, where smoking and smutty talk were permitted. Carelessly dressed detective Sherlock Holmes was at his most relaxed when 'lounging upon the sofa in a purple dressing gown, a pipe-rack within his reach'. He also owned a large blue dressing gown, and one of mouse-brown. As late as 1907 dressing gowns were listed for sale in the same category as smoking jackets, lounge jackets and American dinner jackets, all items for informal relax-ation away from the demands of stiff collars and cuffs.

The modern male may enjoy hours of idleness in a dressing gown, usually calf-length and in subdued colours such as burgundy, navy and grey, or perhaps with a paisley pattern of equally muted shades. It is most certainly a private garment.

SLIP INTO SOMETHING COMFORTABLE

Another accessory that represented a transition from work to relaxation was the *slipper*. While Sherlock Holmes found unorthodox uses for his slippers – as a location to store his narcotics – most people prefer to keep feet in them. The term 'slipper' (from the Anglo-Saxon *slype-shoe*) originally referred to any kind of slip-on footwear. In the eighteenth and early nineteenth centuries 'slippers' was also used to describe ladies' light silk shoes worn in the house, and for dancing. Before the twentieth century, house-slippers, whether for men or women, were something of a luxury item, beyond the budget of working people. Embroidered slippers were a labour of love, crafted with pansies and roses by Georgian and Victorian women, then gifted to their menfolk. Moccasin-style slippers could be home-made from moleskin or felted wool and lined with rabbit fur for extra warmth.

Men's slippers haven't changed greatly since this style of a century ago.

Twentieth-century feet could enjoy slippers with cushioned soles, fleecy linings and, eventually, nylon-fur trims. There were silk quilted boudoir slippers with feather pom-poms and high heels, or comfy camel-hair slippers for the chaps. In 1943, as wartime austerity cleared shelves of many items, the Women's Institute was proud to report that its members had learnt how to make slippers out of old felt hats and odd remnants, which were 'not horrors of debased slovenliness, but block-heeled and well fitting, fit to catch the fancy of the most fastidious'.

Once the slippers are kicked off, feet can still be warmed under the covers by bedsocks, currently sold in all manner of materials including luxury cashmere, but, before the twentieth century, knitted in floss wool on whalebone or wooden pins. Bedsocks were easy to knit, having no turned heel and so requiring only two needles, as opposed to the four that were needed for regular sock-shaping. According to one 1940s Make-Do-and-Mend tip, an extra advantage was that they could be recycled as a snazzy hat. The author remains sceptical about such a hat's qualities, snazzy or otherwise.

THE NIGHT-CAP

On the subject of hats, we turn to something never worn in bed nowadays – the *night-cap*. The term 'night-cap' now refers to an alcoholic drink at bedtime, but from the fourteenth to the nine-teenth centuries it was an essential part of any clothing inventory for either sex. Even those who slept naked in bed would generally have their heads covered. Women made their own sleeping caps of fine cotton, silk or linen called *night-rails*, trimmed to excess.

Night-caps for sleeping in were made in a snug rib-stitch, sometimes plain, sometimes striped, and often finished with a tassel. In Victorian London professional knitters earnt a meagre living knitting and selling such caps on the streets.

Night-caps were a natural follow-on from the custom of keeping the head covered all day. Not all of them were meant for wearing in bed; some were informal at-home caps. Indoor caps were favoured by eighteenth-century men whose heads were shaved for ease of wig-wearing. Surviving examples are extraordinarily beautiful, with silk and silver-gilt embroidery.

For those men eschewing a night-cap proper, hair nets could be worn instead. Unfortunately these could become impreg-nated with hair powder and pomatum, attracting very unwelcome

An early Victorian men's night-cap with tassel.

bedfellows, as shown in the 1810 *Memoirs of a Georgian Rake*: William Hickey wakes at dawn to see 'not less than a dozen prodigious Bandicoot rats performing their antics about the room. Upon taking off a silk net I always wore over my hair when in bed, I found several holes gnawed by these animals.'

Edwardian gentlemen were the last generation to wear night-caps, with Harrods providing a choice of spun-silk, fancy striped, cardinal, navy, pear or brown types. Men in the trenches of the First World War bought knitted khaki sleeping helmets – very warm and comfortable and only one shilling and ninepence each – or were sent hand-made balaclava sleeping hats from home.

The night-cap now only survives in caricatures of Victorian sleepwear, such as images of the nursery-rhyme character Wee Willie Winkie, in night-gown, slippers and night-cap, holding a candle; and, indeed, in those portrayals of Ebenezer Scrooge.

ETERNAL SLEEP

Now that nights in pure white are long gone from our bedrooms, there will be fewer ghost stories with the famous 'Lady in White' spectre, evoking the ethereal image of a forlorn female in a pale night-gown. However, the tradition of keeping a 'best' night-dress in the drawer to be used as a *shroud* has not completely disappeared from Europe.

The shroud was sometimes bought at the same time as the wedding trousseau and the first-baby layette. 'Have you got your parcel ready?' was once the morbid question asked of sick or elderly ladies in Britain. The parcel comprised the best bed sheet, a night-dress and white stockings – ready for burial. One Yorkshire woman was greatly annoyed to find that her grand-mother had been buried in a long-coveted nightie. 'What a waste,' she said. Modern mourners may still request that the funeral director provides a night-dress for the deceased to wear in the coffin.

And so to bed . . .

BIBLIOGRAPHY

A Lady - *The Workwoman's Guide* (London, 1838)

A Lady of Distinction - *The Mirror of the Graces. Or, the English Lady's Costume* (Adam Black & Longman, 1830)

Acton, Harold - *Memoirs of an Aesthete* (Methuen, 1948; repr. Hamish Hamilton, 1984)

Adams, Carol and Paula Bartley, Judy Lown, Cathy Loxton - *Under Control, Life in a Nineteenth-century Silk Factory* (Cambridge University Press, 1983)

Adlington, Lucy - *Great War Fashion, Tales from the History Wardrobe* (The History Press, 2013)

Alcott, L. M. - *Little Women* (Roberts Brothers, 1869)

Alcott, L. M. - *Rose in Bloom* (Roberts Brothers, 1876)

Aldrin, Buzz, with Ken Abraham - *Magnificent Desolation: The Long Journey Home from the Moon* (Bloomsbury, 2009)

Allan, Maud - *My Life and Dancing* (Everett & Co., 1908)

Amies, Hardy - *Still Here, An Autobiography* (Weidenfeld & Nicolson, 1984)

Amphlett, Hilda - *Hats, a History of Fashion in Headwear* (Dover, 2003)

Andersen, Hans Christian - *Fairy Tales Told for Children* (C. A. Reitzel, 1838)

Andersen, Hans Christian - *The Little Mermaid* (1837)

Anon. - *The Whole Art of Dress, or the Road to Fashion and Elegance, by a Cavalry Officer* (London, 1830; repr. Carlton Books, 2012)

Armstrong, Nancy - *Fans* (Souvenir Press, 1984)

Arnold, Janet - *Patterns of Fashion: Englishwomen's dresses and their construction c.1660–1860* (Macmillan, 1984)

Ashenburg, Katherine - *Clean: An Unsanitised History of Washing* (North Point Press, 2008)

Austen, Jane - *Pride and Prejudice* (T. Egerton, 1813)

Avery, Victoria, Melissa Calaresu and Mary Laven (eds) - *Treasured Possessions from the Renaissance to the Enlightenment* (Philip Wilson, 2015)

Baclawski, Karen – *The Guide to Historic Costume* (Batsford, 1995)

Bailey, Catherine – *Secret Rooms* (Penguin, 2013)

Ballin, Ada S. – *The Science of Dress in Theory and Practice* (unknown publication, 1885; repr. Dodo Press, 2013)

Barnard, Mary – *The Sheepskin Book* (Brocklebank Publications, undated c.1940)

Bayle, John, *Purple Tints of Paris, Characters and Manners in the New Empire* (Chapman & Hall, 1854)

Baxter-Wright, Emma – *The Little Book of Schiaparelli* (Carlton Books, 2012)

Beaton, Cecil – *The Unexpurgated Beaton Diaries* (Weidenfeld & Nicolson, 2002)

Beattie, Owen and John Geiger – *Frozen in Time: The Fate of the Franklin Expedition* (Bloomsbury, 2004)

Bebb, Prudence – *Shopping in Regency York* (William Sessions, 1994)

Beckham, Victoria, with Hadley Freeman – *That Extra Half an Inch* (Penguin, 2009)

Belden, A. L. – *The Fur Trade of America* (c.1917)

Benson, Adolph B. (ed.) – *Peter Kalm's Travels in North America* (Dover, 1987)

Bierce, Ambrose – *The Enlarged Devil's Dictionary* (Doubleday, 1911; repr. Penguin, 1984)

Black, Sandy – *Knitting, Fashion, Industry, Craft* (V&A Publishing, 2012)

Blanch, Lesley (ed.) – *Harriet Wilson's Memoirs: The Greatest Courtesan of Her Age* (John Murray, 1957)

Bliss, Trudy (ed.) – *Jane Welsh Carlyle, A New Selection of her Letters* (Harvard University Press, 1950)

Braddon, M. E. – *Vixen* (1879; repr. Forgotten Books, 2015)

Brimley, Johnson – *Manners Makyth Man* (A. M. Philpot, 1932)

Braithwaite, Rodric – *Moscow 1941: A City and its People at War* (Profile Books, 2007)

Brewer, Rev. E. Cobham, *Brewer's Dictionary of Phrase and Fable* (1870; repr. Cassell, 1988)

Broad, Richard and Suzie Fleming (eds) – *Nella Last's War: The Second World War Diaries of 'Housewife, 49'* (Profile, 2006)

Brontë, Charlotte – *Jane Eyre* (Smith, Elder and Co., 1847)

Brooks Picken, Mary – *Corsets and Close-Fitting Patterns* (Woman's Institute of Domestic Arts & Sciences, 1920)

Bruna, Denis (ed.) – *Fashioning the Body, An Intimate History of the Silhouette* (Yale University Press, 2015)

Bullock, Dr Katherine – *Rethinking Muslim Women and the Veil* (International Institute of Islamic Thought, 2007)

Burney, Fanny – *Evelina, Or the History of a Young Lady's Entrance into the World* (Thomas Lowndes, 1778)

Buxbaum, Gerda (ed.) – *Icons of Fashion, the Twentieth Century* (Prestel, 1999)

Byng, John and C. Bruyn Andrews (ed.) – *The Torrington Diaries* (Eyre & Spottiswoode, 1954)

Byrde, Penelope – *Jane Austen Fashion: Fashion and Needlework in the Works of Jane Austen* (Excellent Press, 1999)

Cade Gall, W. – 'Future Dictates of Fashion', *Strand Magazine* (1893)

Cady Stanton, Elizabeth – *Eighty Years and More: Reminiscences 1815–1897* (Faber & Faber, 1945)

Calder, A. – *The People's War* (Jonathan Cape, 1969)

Carter, Howard – *The Tomb of Tutankhamen* (Sphere, 1972)

Cartland, Barbara – *We Danced All Night* (Arrow, 1970)

Cawthorne, Nigel – *The New Look: The Dior Revolution* (Reed International Books, 1996)

Chaucer, Geoffrey – *The Canterbury Tales* (c.1387)

Chosen, Francis (ed.) – *Kilvert's Diaries 1870–1879: Selections from the Diary of Francis Kilvert* (Jonathan Cape, 1946)

Christie, Agatha – *Autobiography* (William Collins, 1977)

Christie, Agatha – *Evil Under the Sun* (Collins Crime Club, 1941)

Christie, Agatha – *Poirot's Early Cases* (Collins Crime Club, 1974)

Clayton-Hutton, Christopher – *Official Secrets* (New English Library, 1962)

Cohen, Susan – *The Women's Institute* (Shire, 2011)

Coignet, Jean-Roche – *Soldier of the Empire: The Note-books of Captain Coignet* (Pen and Sword Military, 2002)

Coleman, Elizabeth Ann – *Changing Fashions 1800–1970* (The Brooklyn Museum, 1972)

Colquhoun, Kate – *Mr Briggs' Hat: A Sensational Account of Britain's First Railway Murder* (Little, Brown, 2011)

Clive, Mary (ed.) – *Caroline Clive, From the Diary and Family Papers of Mrs Archer Clive 1801–1873* (The Bodley Head, 1949)

Conan Doyle, Sir Arthur – *The Adventures of Sherlock Holmes* (1891)

Conan Doyle, Sir Arthur – *The Complete Adventures of Sherlock Holmes* (Penguin, 1984)

Conan Doyle, Sir Arthur – *The Memoirs of Sherlock Holmes* (1893)

Conan Doyle, Sir Arthur – *The Return of Sherlock Holmes* (1905)

Cooper, Lady Diana – *The Rainbow Comes and Goes* (Richard Clay & Co., 1958)

Cowan, Ruth (ed.) – *A Nurse at the Front: The First World War Diaries of Sister Edith Appleton* (Simon & Schuster, 2013)

Crompton, Frances E. – *The Gentle Heritage* (1893)

Cumming, Valerie – *Royal Dress* (Batsford, 1989)

Cumming, Valerie, C. W. Cunnington and P. E. Cunnington – *The Dictionary of Fashion History* (Berg, 2010)

Cunnington, C. Willet and Phillis Cunnington – *Handbook of English Costume in the 19th Century* (Faber & Faber, 1959)

Cunnington, C. Willet and Phillis Cunnington – *The History of Underclothes* (Michael Joseph, 1951)

Cunnington, Phillis – *Costume of Household Servants* (A. & C. Black, 1974)

Cunnington, Phillis and Catherine Lucas – *Occupational Costume in England from the 11th Century to 1914* (A. & C. Black, 1967)

Cunnington, Phillis and Alan Mansfield – *English Costume for Sports and Outdoor Recreation* (A. & C. Black, 1969)

David, Saul – *The Homicidal Earl: The Life of Lord Cardigan* (Endeavour Press, 2013)

Defoe, Daniel – *The Life and Surprising Adventures of Robinson Crusoe of York, Mariner* (1719)

de Genlis, Madame – *Dictionnaire critique et raisonné des étiquettes de la cour, des usages du monde, des amusements, des modes, des moeurs etc. depuis la mort de Louis XIII jusqu'à nos jours* (Mongie, 1818)

de la Haye, Amy (ed.) – *The Cutting Edge, 50 Years of British Fashion 1947-1997* (V&A Publications, 1997)

Delbo, Charlotte – *Auschwitz and After* (Yale University Press, 1995)

Devereux, G. R. M. – *Etiquette for Men: A Book of Modern Manners and Customs* (Arthur Pearson, 1902)

Dickens, Charles – *A Christmas Carol* (Chapman & Hall, 1843)

Dickens, Charles – *A Tale of Two Cities* (Chapman & Hall, 1859)

Dickens, Charles – *Great Expectations* (Chapman & Hall, 1861)

Dobbs, Brian – *The Last Shall be First: The Colourful Story of John Lobb the St James's Bootmaker* (Elm Tree Books, 1972)

Douglas, Mrs – *The Gentlewoman's Book of Dress*, ed. W. H. Davenport Adams (The Victoria Library for Gentlewomen, 1894)

Duff Gordon, Lady Lucy – *Discretions & Indiscretions* (Frederick A. Stokes, 1932); repr. as A *Woman of Temperament* (Atticus Books, 2012)

Duke of Windsor – *A Family Album* (Cassell & Company, 1960)

Edwards, Russell – *Naming Jack the Ripper* (Sidgwick & Jackson, 2014)

El Guindi, Fadwa – *Veil: Modesty, Privacy and Resistance* (Berg, 2003)

Ellis, S. M. (ed.), *A Mid-Victorian Pepys: The Letters and Memoirs of Sir William Hardman* (1923)

Ellison, Ralph – *The Invisible Man* (Random House, 1952)

Elms, Robert – *The Way We Wore* (Picador, 2005)

Etherington-Smith, Meredith and Jeremy Pilcher – *The IT Girls* (Hamish Hamilton, 1988)

Ewing, Thor – *Viking Clothes* (The History Press, 2009)

Fairfax Lucy, A. (ed.) – *Mistress of Charlecote: The Memoirs of Mary Elizabeth Lucy 1803–1889* (Orion, 2002)

Fields, Jill – *An Intimate Affair: Women, Lingerie and Sexuality* (University of California Press, 2007)

Fiennes, Sir Ranulph – *Cold* (Simon & Schuster, 2013)

Forrester, Andrew – *The Female Detective* (1864; repr. The British Library, 2013)

Friedel, Robert – *Zipper: An Exploration in Novelty* (W. W. Norton & Company, 1996)

Frister, Roman and Hillel Halkin – *The Cap* (Grove Press, 2001)

Fryer, Peter – *Staying Power: The History of Black People in Britain* (Pluto Press, 2010)

Gallico, Paul – *Mrs Harris Goes to Paris* (*Flowers for Mrs Harris*), (Penguin, 1958)

Gaskell, Elizabeth – *Cranford* (Chapman & Hall, 1853)

Gaskell, Elizabeth – *Ruth* (Chapman & Hall, 1853)

Gardiner, Juliet – *The Thirties* (HarperPress, 2011)

Gellar, Judith B. – *Women and Children First* (Avon, 2012)

George, Gertrude – *Eight Months with the Women's Royal Air Force* (Heath Cranton, 1920)

Gibbings, Sarah – *The Tie: Trends and Traditions* (Barrons Educational Series, 1990)

Gilroy, Paul – *Black Britain, A Photographic History* (Saqi, in association with Getty Images, 2007)

Ginzburg, Eugenia Semyonovna – *Journey Into the Whirlwind*, trans. Paul Stevenson and Max Hayward (Harcourt Brace Jovanovich, 1967)

Girotti, Eugenia – *Footwear: History and Customs / La Calzatura: Storia e Costume* (Itinerari d'Immagini, 1990)

Glenbervie, Baron Sylvester Douglas – *The Glenbervie Journals* (1811)

Glob, Peter V. – *The Bog People: Iron-Age Man Preserved*, trans. R. Dunce-Mitford (HarperCollins, 1971)

Glynn, Prudence and Madeleine Ginsburg – *In Fashion, Dress in the Twentieth Century* (Allen & Unwin, 1978)

Grant, Linda – *The Thoughtful Dresser* (Virago Press, 2009)

Gray, Mrs Edwin (ed.) – *The Papers and Diaries of a York Family 1764–1839* (London, 1927)

Grossmith, George and Weedon – *The Diary of a Nobody* (J. W. Arrowsmith, 1892)

Guenther, Irene – *Nazi Chic? Fashioning Women in the Third Reich* (Berg, 2004)

Gunn, Douglas, Roy Luckett and Josh Sims – *Vintage Menswear, A Collection from the Vintage Showroom* (Laurence King Publishing, 2012)

Hall, Rosalind – *Egyptian Textiles* (Shire Publications, 2001)

Halls, Zillah – *Women's Costume 1750–1800* (HMSO, 1972)

Ham, Elizabeth – *Elizabeth Ham, By Herself, 1783–1820* (Faber & Faber, 1945)

Hamilton, Peggy – *Three Years or the Duration* (Daedalus Press, 1978)

Hardy, Thomas – *Far From the Madding Crowd* (Smith & Elder & Co., 1874)

Harvey, Anthony and Richard Mortimer (eds) – *The Funeral Effigies of Westminster Abbey* (The Boydell Press, 1994)

Hawthorne, Nigel – *The New Look: The Dior Revolution* (Hamlyn, 1996)

Hayward, William Stephens – *Revelations of a Lady Detective* (George Vickers, 1864; repr. The British Library, 2013)

Hewitt, John – *The History of Wakefield and its Environs*, vol. 1 (1862)

Hickey, William – *Memoirs of a Georgian Rake*, ed. Roger Hudson (The Folio Society, 1995)

Hillard, G. S. (ed.) – *Life, Letters and Journals of George Ticknor* (1876)

Hoare, Philip – *Oscar Wilde's Last Stand* (Arcade Publishing, 1997)

Holdsworth, Angela – *Out of the Doll's House: The Story of Women in the Twentieth Century* (BBC Books, 1988)

Hollander, Anne – *Fabric of Vision: Dress and Drapery in Painting* (National Gallery Company, 2002)

Holme, Randle – *The Academy of Armory, Book III* (1688)

Horwood, Catherine – *Keeping Up Appearances: Fashion and Class Between the Wars* (Sutton Publishing, 2005)

Jaffé, Deborah – *Ingenious Women* (Sutton Publishing, 2003)

Jesse, Captain William – *The Life of Beau Brummell* (Saunders & Otley, 1844)

Jessop, Violet – *Titanic Survivor: The Memoirs of Violet Jessop, Stewardess* (The History Press, 2007)

Jonson, Ben – *Cynthia's Revels, or The Fountain of Self Love* (1600)

Jubb, Samuel – *The History of the Shoddy-Trade, Its Rise, Progress, and Present Position* (J. Fearnsides, 1860; repr. Forgotten Books, 2012)

Junge, Traudl with Melissa Müller – *Until the Final Hour* (Phoenix, 2005)

Kelly, Ian – *Beau Brummell, The Ultimate Dandy* (Hodder & Stoughton, 2005)
Kintz, Jarod – *$3.33* (2011)
Klabunde, Anna – *Magda Goebbels* (Sphere, 2007)
Klickmann, Flora – *The Girl's Own Annual* (1915)
Kramer, Clara – *Clara's War* (Ebury Press, 2008)

Lacy, Mary – *The Female Shipwright* (1773; repr. National Maritime Museum, 2008)
Langley, Susan – *Vintage Hats & Bonnets 1770–1970* (Collector Books, 2009)
Langley Moore, Dorothy – *Lord Byron: Accounts Rendered* (John Murray, 1974)
Lawrence, Dorothy – *Sapper Dorothy* (Leonaur, 2010)
Layard, C. S. – *Mrs Lynn Linton, Her Life, Letters and Opinions* (1901)
LeBlanc, Henri – *The Art of Tying the Cravat* (London, 1828)
Lee, Michelle – *Fashion Victim* (Broadway Books, 2003)
Lefebure, Molly – *Murder on the Home Front* (1954; repr. Sphere, 2013)
Lengyel, Olga – *Five Chimneys* (Academy Chicago, 1995)
Lester, Katherine and Bess Viola Oerke – *Accessories of Dress: An Illustrated History of the Frills and Furbelows of Fashion* (The Manual Arts Press, 1940)
Levi, Primo – *If This is A Man*, trans. Stuart Woolf (Orion Press, 1959)
Levi, Primo – *The Reawakening*, trans. Stuart Woolf (Collier Books, 1965)
Longford, Elizabeth – *Victoria RI* (Weidenfeld & Nicolson, 1998)
Lurie, Alison – *The Language of Clothes* (William Heinemann, 1982)
Lytton, Edward Bulwer – *Pelham* (1828)

McCall, Cicely – *Women's Institutes* (William Collins, 1943)
MacCarthy, Fiona – *The Last Curtsey: The End of the Debutantes* (Faber & Faber, 2007)
McDowell, A. G. – *Village Life in Ancient Egypt: Laundry Lists and Love Songs* (Clarendon Press, 2001)
Macintyre, Ben – *The Napoleon of Crime* (Flamingo, 1998)
Macintyre, Ben – *Operation Mincemeat* (Bloomsbury, 2010)
McKenzie, Julia – *Clothes Lines: Off-the-Peg Stories from the Closets of the Famous* (Robson Books, 1988)
MacLochlainn, Jason – *The Victorian Tailor* (St Martin's Griffin, 2011)
Magorian, Michelle – *Goodnight Mister Tom* (Kestrel Books, 1981)
Malcolmson, Patricia and Robert (eds) – *Nella Last's Peace: The Post-war Diaries of Housewife 49* (Profile Books, 2008)

Mansel, Philip – *Dressed to Rule* (Yale University Press, 2005)

Mansfield, Alan and Phillis Cunnington – *Handbook of English Costume in the 20th Century 1900–1950* (Faber & Faber, 1973)

Marchessini, Demetri – *Women in Trousers: A Rear View* (Ioni Illustrated Editions, 2003)

Markievicz, Constance – *Prison Letters of Constance Markievicz* (Virago, 1987)

Marsh, Gail – *Eighteenth Century Embroidery Techniques* (Guild of Master Craftsman Publications, 2012)

Marsh, Graham and Paul Trynka – *Denim: From Cowboys to Catwalks, a History of the World's Most Legendary Fabric* (Aurum Press, 2005)

Marshall, Peter A. and Jean K. Brown (eds) – *Swiss Notes by Five Ladies, An Account of Touring and Climbing in 1874* (Peter A. Marshall, 2003)

Marshall & Snelgrove Ltd – *Fashion and the Woman 4000 BC to 1930 AD* (unknown publisher, 1930)

Martin, Joanna (ed.) – *A Governess in the Age of Jane Austen* (Hambledon Press, 1998)

Mayhew, Henry – *London Labour and the London Poor*, the *Morning Chronicle* serialisation (1840s)

M'Donough, Captain Felix – *The Hermit in London* (1819)

Mendes, Valerie and Amy de la Haye – *Fashion Since 1900* (Thames & Hudson, 2010)

Meredith, Alan and Gillian – *Buttons* (Shire Publications, 2012)

Mermisi, Fatima – *The Veil and Male Elite: A Feminist Interpretation of Women's Rights in Islam* (Perseus Books, 1992)

Merrick, Leonard – *Mr Bazalgette's Agent* (George Routledge & Sons, 1888; repr. The British Library, 2013)

Merrifield, Mrs – *Dress as a Fine Art* (John P. Jewett and Company, 1854)

Mikhaila, Ninya and Jane Malcolm-Davies, *The Tudor Tailor, Reconstructing 16th-century Dress* (Batsford, 2006)

Miller, Alice Duer – *Are Women People? A Book of Rhymes for Suffrage Times* (George H. Doran, NY, 1915)

Miller, Judith – *Shoes* (Miller's, 2009)

Ministry of Education – *Make Do And Mend* (HMSO, 1940s)

Mitchiner, P. H. and E. E. P. MacManus – *Nursing in Time of War* (J. A. Churchill Ltd, 1943)

Mollo, John – *Military Fashion* (G. P. Putnam's & Sons, NY, 1972)

Molloy, John T. – *New Dress for Success* (Warner Books, NY, 1988)

Monsarrat, Ann – *And the Bride Wore...* (Dodd, Mead & Co., 1974)

Moore, Edward – *The World* (1755)

Morgan, Janet – *Agatha Christie, A Biography* (HarperCollins, 1997)

Morris, Christopher (ed.) – *Journeys of Celia Fiennes* (Cresset, 1947)

Morsch, Günther and Astrid Ley (eds) - *Sachsenhausen Concentration Camp 1936–1945: Events and Developments* (Metropole-Verlag, 2008)

Morton, H. V. - *Pageant of the Century* (Odhams Press, 1933)

Murphy, Paul Thomas - *Shooting Victoria: Madness, Mayhem and the Modernisation of the Monarchy* (Head of Zeus, 2012)

Murray, Margaret and Jane Koster - *Knitting for All* (Odhams Press, 1942)

Nadoolman Landis, Deborah (ed.) - *Hollywood Costume* (V&A Publishing, 2012)

Nahshon, Edna - *Jews and Shoes* (Berg, 2008)

Nevill, Ralph, *The Reminiscences of Lady Dorothy Nevill* (Edward Arnold, 1906)

Newark, Tim - *Camouflage* (Thames & Hudson, 2007)

Nicolson, N. - *Portrait of a Marriage* (Weidenfeld & Nicolson, 1973; repr. 1990)

Nightingale, Florence - *Notes on Nursing: What It Is and What It Is Not* (1860)

Noggle, Anna - *A Dance With Death* (Texas A&M University Press, 2002)

Norris, Herbert - *Tudor Costume and Fashion* (Dover, 1997)

Oakes, Alma and Margot Hamilton Hill - *Rural Costume, Its Origin and Development in Western Europe and the British Isles* (B. T. Batsford, 1970)

Opie, Iona and Peter, *The Classic Fairy Tales* (Book Club Associates / OUP, 1975)

Orczy, Baroness - *The Scarlet Pimpernel* (Hutchinson, 1905)

Østergaard, Jan Stubbe and Anne Marie Nielsen (eds) - *Transformations: Classical Sculpture in Colour* (Carlsberg Glyptotek, NY, 2014)

Owings, Alison - *Frauen: German Women Recall the Third Reich* (Penguin, 2001)

Page, Betty - *On Fair Vanity* (Convoy Publications, 1954)

Pankhurst, Sylvia - *The Suffragette Movement: An Intimate Account of Persons and Ideals* (London, 1931; repr. Wharton Press, 2010)

Panton, Reginald - *Memories of Burgh Le Marsh and District 1903–1936* (private publication, 2014)

Papworth, J. B., W. Wrangham and W. Combe - *Poetical Sketches of Scarborough* (1813)

Partridge, Eric, *Dictionary of the Underworld* (Routledge & Kegan Paul, 1950)

Pavitt, Jane - *Fear and Fashion in the Cold War* (V&A Publishing, 2008)

Pearce, Charles – *The Beloved Princess, Princess Charlotte of Wales, the Lonely Daughter of a Lonely Queen* (London, 1911)

Pearl, Cyril – *The Girl with the Swansdown Seat: Aspects of mid-Victorian Morality* (Frederick Muller, 1955)

Pearlman, Moshe – *The Capture and Trial of Adolf Eichmann* (Simon & Schuster, 1963)

Peel, Mrs C. S. – *How We Lived Then: A Sketch of Social and Domestic Life in England During the War* (The Bodley Head, 1929)

Pepys, Samuel – *The Diaries of Samuel Pepys* (Penguin Classics, 2003)

Perrault, Charles – *Perrault Fairy Tales; Histoires ou Contes du temps passé. Avec des Moralitez* (Paris, 1697; repr. The London Folio Society, 1998)

Picken, Mary Brooks – *Corsets and Close-Fitting Patterns* (Women's Institute of Domestic Arts & Sciences, Inc., 1920)

Pierrepoint, Albert – *Executioner: Pierrepoint* (Harrap, 1974)

Ping, Wang – *Aching for Beauty: Footbinding in China* (Anchor Books, 2002)

Plumb, J. H. – *Georgian Delights: The Pursuit of Happiness* (Little, Brown, 1980)

Pratchett, Terry – *Witches Abroad: A Discworld Novel* (Corgi, 1992)

Pressley, Alison – *The Best of Times: Growing up in Britain in the 1950s* (Michael O'Mara Books, 1999)

Preston, Diana – *A First Rate Tragedy: A Brief History of Captain Scott's Antarctic Expeditions* (Constable, 1997)

Priestley, J. B. – *Three Men in New Suits* (Hollen Street Press, 1945)

Protective Clothing for Women and Girl Workers Employed in the Factories and Workshops (HMSO, 1917)

Przybyszewski, Linda – *The Lost Art of Dress: The Women Who Once Made America Stylish* (Basic Books, 2014)

Quennell, Peter – *Victorian Panorama* (Batsford, 1937)

Quigley, Dorothy – *What Dress Makes of Us* (unknown publisher, 1897; repr. Dodo Press, 2008)

Quiller-Couch, Sir Arthur – *The Sleeping Beauty and Other Fairy Tales from the Old French* (1910)

Rajchman, Chil – *Treblinka, A Survivor's Memory* (MacLehose Press, 2011)

Rappaport, Helen – *No Place for Ladies* (Aurum Press, 2007)

Raverat, Gwen – *Period Piece: A Cambridge Childhood* (Faber & Faber, 1952)

Rémusat, Paul (ed.) – *Memoirs of Madame de Rémusat 1802–1808* (Appleton & Company, 1880)

Rhodes-James, R. (ed.) – *Chips: Diaries of Sir Henry Channon* (Weidenfeld & Nicolson, 1967)

Richardson, Samuel – *Pamela, or Virtue Rewarded* (Rimmington & Osborn, 1740)

Roach, Martin – *Dr Martens: The Story of an Icon* (Chrysalis Impact, 2003)

Robertshaw, Andrew and David Kenton – *Digging the Trenches: The Archaeology of the Western Front* (Pen & Sword Military, 2008)

Robinson, Jane – *Bluestockings* (Penguin, 2010)

Rodgers, Nigel – *The Umbrella Unfurled: Its Remarkable Life and Times* (Bene Factum Publishing, 2013)

Sandes, Flora – *An English-Woman Sergeant in the Serbian Army* (Hodder & Stoughton, 1916)

Schmiechen, James A. – *Sweated Industries and Sweated Labour: The London Clothing Trades, 1860–1914* (Croom Helm, 1984)

Sebesta, Judith Lynn and Larissa Bonfante (eds) – *The World of Roman Costume* (University of Wisconsin Press, 2011)

Shackleton, Sir Ernest – *South: The Story of Shackleton's 1914–17 expedition* (Century Publishing, 1919)

Shakespeare, William – *Antony and Cleopatra* (c.1607)

Shakespeare, William – *The Tragedy of Hamlet, Prince of Denmark* (c.1599–1602)

Shakespeare, William – *The Tragedy of Julius Caesar* (c.1599)

Shakespeare, William – *The Tragedy of Othello, The Moor* (1603)

Shakespeare, William – *Troilus and Cressida* (1609)

Shakespeare, William – *Twelfth Night, or What You Will* (1601–2)

Sharman, Helen and Christopher Priest – *Seize the Moment: The Autobiography of Britain's First Astronaut* (Victor Gollancz, 1993)

Shep, R. L. – *The Great War: Styles and Patterns of the 1910s* (Players Press, 2001)

Sheridan, Betsy – *Betsy Sheridan's Journal* (1789)

Sheridan, Richard Brinsley – *A Trip to Scarborough* (1777)

Sherriff, R. C. – *The Fortnight in September* (Victor Gollancz, 1931)

Shields, Jody – *Hats: A Stylish History and Collector's Guide* (Clarkson N. Potter, 1991)

Shipman, Pat – *Femme Fatale* (Phoenix, 2007)

Simons, Violet K. – *The Awful Dressmaker's Book* (Wolfe Publishing, 1965)

Skidelsky, Robert – *Oswald Mosley* (Macmillan, 1975)

Sladen, Christopher – *The Conscription of Fashion: Utility Cloth, Clothing and Footwear 1941–1952* (Scholar Press, 1995)

Smart, J. E. - *Clothes for the Job: Catalogue of the Science Museum Collection* (Science Museum, 1985)

Souhami, Diana - *Edith Cavell: Nurse, Martyr, Heroine* (Quercus, 2011)

Souhami, Diana - *Murder at Wrotham Hill* (Quercus, 2013)

Spanier, Ginette - *It Isn't All Mink* (Random House, 1960)

Spindler, Konrad - *The Man in the Ice* (Phoenix, 2011)

Stanhope, Philip Dormer (ed.) - *Lord Chesterfield: Letters to His Son* (Richard Bentley, 1847)

Staniland, Kay - *In Royal Fashion, the Clothes of Princess Charlotte of Wales and Queen Victoria* 1796-1901 (Museum of London, 1997)

Starkey, David - *Elizabeth: The Exhibition at the National Maritime Museum,* ed. Susan Doran (Chatto & Windus, 2003)

Steele, Valerie - *The Corset, a Cultural History* (V&A Publishing, 2007)

Stemp, Sinty - *The A to Z of Hollywood Style* (V&A Publishing, 2012)

Stoker, Bram - *Dracula* (Constable & Co., 1897)

Storey, Nicholas - *The History of Men's Fashion: What the Well-dressed Man is Wearing* (Remember When, 2008)

Streatfeild, Noel - *Party Frock* (William Collins, 1946)

Stubbes, Philip - *The Anatomie of Abuses* (Richard Jones, 1585; repr. W. Pickering, 1836)

Summers, Julie - *Jambusters, The Story of the Women's Institute in the Second World War* (Simon & Schuster, 2013)

Surtees, Robert Smith - *Ask Mama* (1850; repr. Quercus, 2013)

Surtees, Robert Smith - *Plain or Ringlets?* (1860; repr. Nonsuch Classics, 2006)

Tatar, Maria (ed.) - *The Classic Fairy Tales* (W. W. Norton & Company, 1999)

Taylor, Lou - *Mourning Dress* (Routledge, 1983)

Thackeray, William Makepeace - *Book of Snobs* (Punch Office, 1848)

Thomas, Rhys - *The Ruby Slippers of Oz* (Tale Weaver Publishing, 1989)

Thompson, Flora - *Lark Rise to Candleford, 1876-1947* (Penguin Classics, 2000), comprising *Lark Rise* (1939); *Over to Candleford* (1941); *Candleford Green* (1943)

Tolkien, J. R. R. - *The Hobbit, or There and Back Again* (George Allen & Unwin, 1937)

Tozer, Jane and Sarah Levitt - *The Fabric of Society, A Century of People and Their Clothes 1770-1870* (Manchester Art Gallery Trust, 2010)

Tranberg Hansen, Karen - *Salaula: The World of Secondhand Clothing in Zambia* (University of Chicago Press, 2000)

Turner Wilcox, R. - *The Mode in Footwear* (Charles Scribner's Sons, 1948; repr. Dover, 2008)

Tuvel Bernstein, Sara, with Louise Loots Thornton and Marlene Bernstein
    Samuels - *The Seamstress: A Memoir of Survival* (G. P. Putnam's Sons,
    1997)
Twain, Mark - *Adventures of Huckleberry Finn* (Chatto & Windus, 1884)

Veillon, Dominique - *Fashion under the Occupation* (Berg, 2002)
Veldmeijer, André J. - *Tutankhamun's Footwear: Studies of Ancient
    Egyptian Footwear* (Sidestone Press, 2012)
Vickery, Amanda - *The Gentleman's Daughter* (Yale University Press,
    2003)
Vincent, Susan J. - *The Anatomy of Fashion* (Berg, 2009)
Visram, Rozina - *Asians in Britain: 400 Years of History* (Pluto Press,
    2002)

Walford, Jonathon - *Forties Fashion* (Thames & Hudson, 2008)
Walford, Walter G. - *The Dangers in Neck-wear* (unknown publisher,
    1917)
Walton Rogers, Penelope - *Cloth and Clothing in Early Anglo-Saxon
    England AD 450-700* (Council for British Archaeology, 2007)
Warren, Geoffrey - *A Stitch in Time: Victorian and Edwardian
    Needlecraft* (David & Charles, 1976)
Waugh, Norah - *Corsets and Crinolines* (1954; repr. Routledge / Theatre
    Arts Books, 2004)
Weber, Caroline - *Queen of Fashion: What Marie Antoinette Wore to the
    Revolution* (Aurum Press, 2007)
Wilcox, Claire (ed.) - *The Golden Age of Couture: Paris & London 1947-57*
    (V&A Publishing, 2008)
Wilcox, Claire - *Vivienne Westwood* (V&A Publications, 2004)
Winocour, Jack (ed.) - *The Story of Titanic as told by its Survivors* (Dover,
    1960)
Wolf, Tony - *Edith Garrud* (Tony Wolf online publication, 2009)
Wood, Maggi - *We Wore What We'd Got: Women's Clothes in World War
    II* (Warwickshire Books, 1989)
Woolf, Virginia - *Three Guineas* (The Hogarth Press, 1938)
Worth, Rachel - *Discover Dorset: Dress and Textiles* (The Dovecote Press,
    2002)
Wortley Montagu, Lady Mary - *The Complete Letters of Lady Mary
    Wortley Montagu*, ed. Robert Halsband (Clarendon Press, 1967)

X, Malcolm with Alex Haley - *The Autobiography of Malcolm X* (Grove
    Press, 1965; repr. Penguin, 2007)

Yefimova, Luisa V. and Tatyana S. Aleshina – *Russian Elegance: Country and City Fashion from the 15th to the Early 20th Century* (Vivays Publishing, 2011)

Young, Lisa A. and Amanda J. – *Collections Care: The Preservation, Storage, and Display of Spacesuits* (Smithsonian National Air and Space Museum, Report Number 5, December 2001)

MAGAZINES AND NEWSPAPERS

Ackerman's Repository of Arts, Literature…
Bystander Illustrated
Cartwright's Ladies Companion
Civil Service Supply Association
Costume – The Journal of the Costume Society
Daily Herald
Daily Mirror
Daily Telegraph
Exchange and Mart – the Bazaar
Family Circle
Gentleman's Magazine
Harper's Bazaar
History Workshop Journal
Home Chat
Home Companion
Home Notes
Home Sewing
Journal des Demoiselles
La Belle Assemblée
Ladies' Gazette
Ladies' Treasury
Lady's World
Life
London Illustrated News
Oxendales home shopping

Pears Cyclopaedia
Pearson's Magazine
Picturegoer Magazine
Picture Post
Punch
Spectator
Tatler
The Children's Friend
The Lady's Magazine
The Ladies' Realm
The Lady's World Fancy Work Book
The Lancet
The Morning Chronicle
The Strand Magazine
The Textile Manufacturer trade journal
The Times
The Wakefield Kinsman
Time magazine
Vogue
Woman Beautiful
Woman's Life
Woman's Weekly
Woman's World
World of Fashion
York Courant

NOTES

KNICKER ELASTIC

p.2 **This solitary hunter:** *The Man in the Ice*, Konrad Spindler

p.2 **In the real world:** *Egyptian Textiles*, Rosalind Hall; *Village Life in Ancient Egypt: Laundry Lists and Love Songs*, A. G. McDowell; *The Tomb of Tutankhamen*, Howard Carter

p.3 **In 2008 archaeologists:** 'Medieval Lingerie', Beatrix Nux, *BBC History Magazine* (August 2012)

p.4 **Queen Elizabeth I's:** Noted in 'Accounts of the Great Wardrobe' (1558–1603)

p.5 **Surviving examples:** Photographed in *Patterns of Fashion 4*, Janet Arnold, and held in the collection of the Metropolitan Museum of Art, New York

p.5 **Even as late as the 1890s:** Discreet drying details from *Lark Rise to Candleford*, Flora Thompson

p.5 **later still, municipal flats:** Design critic Anthony Bertram, speaking on the BBC radio programme *Housing the Workers* in November 1937

p.5 **One *grande horizontale*:** Photographed in *Patterns of Fashion 4*, Janet Arnold, and held in the Museo del Tessuto, Prato, Italy

p.6 **He (unfairly) suspected her:** *The Diaries of Samuel Pepys*

p.8 **I lost one leg:** Quoted in *The History of Underclothes*, C. Willet and Phillis Cunnington

p.8 **She was sitting:** *The Glenbervie Journals*, Baron Sylvester Douglas Glenbervie

p.8 **Princess Charlotte was considered:** As described by Charles Pearce in *The Beloved Princess, Princess Charlotte of Wales, the Lonely Daughter of a Lonely Queen*

p.9 **'those comfortable garments':** From the unexpurgated *Letters of Lady Chesterfield to Her Daughter* (1860)

p.9 **'the other ladies hardly knew':** From the *Diary of Lady Eleanor Stanley* (1859)

p.10 **'cazimere pantaloons':** *Victoria RI*, Elizabeth Longford

p.12 **'The adoption of woollen undergarments':** Ibid.

p.13 **aviators of the First World War:** Descriptions of heated underwear are given in the Science Museum's catalogue, *Clothing for the Job*

p.14 **She also achieved notoriety:** *The IT Girls*, Meredith Etherington-Smith and Jeremy Pilcher

p.14 **'Picking them up':** *Discretions & Indiscretions*, Lady Lucy Duff Gordon

p.17 **'Always put on':** *Autobiography*, Agatha Christie

p.17 **The concern over being caught** Reported by Phyl Wood in the *Wakefield Kinsman* (November 2012) p.17 **One Yorkshire woman:** Anecdote recounted to the author at Washburn Heritage Centre in 2012

p.18 **'There was one garment':** *Murder on the Home Front*, Molly Lefebure

p.20 **A lady who made:** Incidents recounted to the author by Mrs Jean Elliot and Mrs Peggy Glassett of Cleckheaton in 2014

p.20 **'Oh no, I shall have':** *Fear and Fashion in the Cold War*, Jane Pavitt

SHIRTS AND SHIFTS

p.22 **'My father was always':** History Wardrobe oral-history survey, *My Life in Clothes*, courtesy of Alison Fleming

p.24 **While the pecking order:** From *Queen of Fashion*, Caroline Weber

p.25 **'Her modesty':** *Clean*, Katherine Ashenburg

p.26 **'You just cannot imagine':** 'Moscow *elegante* visits Paris 1790s', from *Notes* by S. P. Zhikharev, quoted in *Russian Elegance*, Luisa V. Yefimova and Tatyana S. Aleshina

p.27 **'The chemise is':** *The Science of Dress*, Ada S. Ballin

p.32 **'which swells out':** *Caroline Clive, From the Diary and Family Papers of Mrs Archer Clive 1801–1873*, Mary Clive (ed.)

p.33 **'I had a skirt':** History Wardrobe oral-history survey, *My Life in Clothes*, courtesy of Vera Clarke

p.33 **'It was a scene that made television history:** Andrew Davies was speaking at the Cheltenham Literature Festival about one of the most famous moments in TV history. Interview reported in the *Telegraph* online, Hannah Furness (9th October 2013)

p.36 **'These be goodly shirtes':** *Anatomie of Abuses*, Philip Stubbes

p.36 **'in snow-white smock-frocks':** *Far from the Madding Crowd*, Thomas Hardy

p.37 **'very fine linen':** *The Life of George Brummell*, Captain William Jesse

p.38 **Edward VII's grandson:** *A Family Album*, Duke of Windsor

p.38 **'put on a flannel shirt':** *The Science of Dress*, Ada Ballin

p.39 **Some Victorian dandies:** *The History of Underclothes*, C. Willet and Phillis Cunnington

p.39 **Possibly the most exotic:** *Book of Snobs*, William Makepeace Thackeray

p.40 **The black shirts:** *Dressed to Rule*, Philip Mansel

p.40 **'If you should join us':** Quoted in *The Thoughtful Dresser,* Linda Grant

p.40 **'In the Black Shirt':** *Oswald Mosley*, R. Skidelsky

p.41 **By then the shirts:** *Nazi Chic?*, Irene Guenther

p.42 **Smooth cuffs suitable for use:** 'The Naval Treaty' in *The Memoirs of Sherlock Holmes*, Sir Arthur Conan Doyle

p.44 **'Starched Eton collars':** *A Family Album,* Duke of Windsor

THE SOCK DRAWER

p.49 **When Howard Carter:** *Egyptian Textiles*, Rosalind Hall

p.49 **'I have sent you':** *The World of Roman Costume*, Judith Lynn Sebesta and Larissa Bonfante (eds)

p.50 **Moving forward:** *Viking Clothing*, Thor Ewing

p.50 **King Sigurd Syr:** Ibid.

p.50 **Henry VIII had:** *Tudor Costume and Fashion*, Herbert Norris

p.51 **'He will come to her':** *Twelfth Night, or What You Will*, William Shakespeare

p.51 **'They are not ashamed':** *The Anatomie of Abuses*, Philip Stubbes p.52 **Lord Foppington:** This is Richard Brinsley Sheridan's version of John Vanbrugh's 1696 comedy *The Relapse,* brought up to date as *A Trip to Scarborough*

p.52 **'They say he puts':** *Cynthia's Revels, or The Fountain of Self Love,* Ben Jonson

p.53 **'I felt mighty awkward':** *Soldier of the Empire,* Jean-Roche Coignet

p.53 **'stick pins in':** *Ask Mama,* Robert Smith Surtees

p.53 **'his calves revised':** *Plain or Ringlets?,* Robert Smith Surtees

p.54 **'wore enormously loud stockings':** Samuel Goldwyn, quoted in *Hollywood Costume,* Deborah Nadoolman Landis (ed.)

p.54 **'my favourite sport':** *A Family Album,* Duke of Windsor

p.56 **'Maybe it is something':** *The History of Men's Fashion,* Nicholas Storey

p.56 **'If the foot and ankle':** *The Gentlewoman's Book of Dress,* Mrs Douglas

p.57 **One member of:** *Bluestockings,* Jane Robinson

p.57 **'They call me':** *The Enlarged Devil's Dictionary,* Ambrose Bierce

p.58 **'In olden days':** Lyrics from the musical *Silk Stockings,* Cole Porter (1955)

p.59 **'Legs should be':** *On Fair Vanity,* Betty Page

p.59 **'the first thing I did':** *Frauen: German Women Recall the Third Reich,* Alison Owings, interview with Frau Marianne Karlsruhen

p.60 **'young females':** *Brewer's Dictionary of Phrase and Fable*

p.60 **'through which the outlines':** *The Girl's Own Annual,* Flora Klickmann

p.62 **'his stockings fouled':** *The Tragedy of Hamlet, Prince of Denmark,* William Shakespeare

p.63 **'I should feel quite tempted':** *Cranford,* Elizabeth Gaskell

p.64 **A multitude of variations:** *Ingenious Women,* Deborah Jaffé

p.65 **According to:** *Corsets and Close-Fitting Patterns,* Mary Brooks Picken

p.65 **Astronaut Helen Sharman:** *Seize the Moment, The Autobiography of Britain's First Astronaut,* Helen Sharman and Christopher Priest

p.66 **Gradually the ribbon garter:** *And the Bride Wore...* Ann Monsarrat

p.68 **'which they keep':** *Revelations of a Lady Detective,* William Stephens Hayward

p.68 **One very special:** *A First Rate Tragedy. A Brief History of Captain Scott's Antarctic Expeditions,* Diana Preston

p.68 **In 1915:** *Edith Cavell: Nurse, Martyr, Heroine,* Diana Souhami

p.70 **One of the punishments:** *Prison Letters of Constance Markievicz,* Constance Markievicz

p.70 **'when the foot':** *Elizabeth Ham, By Herself, 1783–1820,* Elizabeth Ham

p.70 **'as he was taking':** *The Fortnight in September,* R. C. Sherriff

STAY LACES

p.73 **Once, during a modern:** Conversation with the author at a Jane Austen Society (Northern Branch) meeting in 2005

p.74 **'When I took out':** *Eighty Years and More: Reminiscences 1815–1897,* Elizabeth Cady Stanton

p.75 **Elizabeth Ham remembered:** *Elizabeth Ham, By Herself, 1783–1820,* Elizabeth Ham

p.75 **'instrument of torture':** *Rose in Bloom,* Louisa May Alcott

p.75 **'Hush, hush!':** Quoted in *Dress as a Fine Art,* Mrs Merrifield

p.75 **'I had a bad figure':** *Period Piece: A Cambridge Childhood,* Gwen Raverat

p.76 **'Stretch, bend and touch':** *Home Chat* (1st April 1939) p.77   'in plain English': *The Complete Letters of Lady Mary Wortley Montagu*, Robert Halsband (ed.)

p.78   'a curious sort': *The Suffragette Movement: An Intimate Account of Persons and Ideals*, Sylvia Pankhurst

p.78   It did protect: *Ladies' World* (1899)

p.78   One young woman: Recounted to the author by Mrs Elsie Walton in October 2014

p.79   'to compress': *The Mirror of the Graces*, A Lady of Distinction

p.79   'Many ladies': *The Science of Dress*, Ada S. Ballin

p.80   ladies being rowed: Advertised in the *Bystander Illustrated* (1913)

p.80   'absurd willingness': Quoted in *An Intimate Affair*, Jill Fields

p.81   Viyella could still offer: *Home Chat* (1st April 1939)

p.81   'The ladies dressmaker': Quoted in *Costume* 36, Leigh Summers (2002), 'Yes, They Did Wear Them: Working-Class Women and Corsetry in the Nineteenth-Century'

p.82   'the too abundant mass': *The Mirror of the Graces*

p.82   An unwise amount: *Dress as a Fine Art*, Mrs Merrifield: the waist 'is rendered fuller at each end'

p.83   Tight-lacing was blamed: Ibid.

p.83   'Whenever I went': *Period Piece*, Gwen Raverat

p.83   'It is no rare thing': *The Science of Dress*, Ada S. Ballin

p.84   'It is impossible': *The Workwoman's Guide*, A Lady

p.84   'She was supposed': *Lark Rise to Candleford*, Flora Thompson

p.84   Tragically for: *Shooting Victoria: Madness, Mayhem and the Rebirth of the British Monarchy*, Paul Thomas Murphy

p.85   One very proactive: *Woman's Hour* interview, BBC Radio 2 (6th February 1968); www.bbc.co.uk/archive/suffragettes/8311.shtml

p.85   'ladies of the first distinction': Advertisement in *Ackerman's Repository of the Arts* (1817)

p.86   'entirely on Anatomical Principles': Advertisement for Madame W. G. Johnson's 'Improved *Specialité* Long Corset' in *Woman* magazine (July 1896)

p.87   'From the moment': Advertisement in *Woman's World* (February 1916)

p.89   'My Gran was': History Wardrobe oral-history survey, *My Life in Clothes*, courtesy of Lesley Murphy

p.89   'You see': *Murder on the Home Front*, Molly Lefebure

p.91   lightweight medieval bras: 'Medieval Lingerie', Beatrix Nux, *BBC History Magazine* (August 2012)

p.92   Brassieres were first referred: *The Guide to Historic Costume*, Karen Baclawski

p.93   'holes should be cut': *Before Baby Comes, A Talk to Expectant Mothers*, Glaxo Mother's Help Bureau (London, 1913)

p.94   'Darling, you'll never': Advertisement in *Vogue* (December 1950)

p.94   Examples of eighteenth-century stays: Musée des Arts Décoratifs, Paris

p.94   'any Thin Bust': Advertisement in *The Ladies' Gazette* (March 1896)

p.95   1940s tips: *Home Companion* magazine (November 1949)

p.95   A young lady: Recounted to the author by Helen Godson in 2013

p.98   'most useful': Wartime Oxendales catalogue

p.98   Advertisements for: Advertisement in the *Strand Magazine* (May 1940)

p.100   'Had Venus been compelled': *The Gentlewoman's Book of Dress*, Mrs Douglas p.105 One tight black satin: *Dictionary of Fashion*, Valerie Cumming, C. W. and P. E. Cunnington

p.105 'how to sit down': 'Paris Notes' by Zélie, *Ladies' World* (1898)

p.106 'I launched in Paris': *Discretions & Indiscretions*, Lady Lucy Duff Gordon

p.106 Fashion writer Edith Russell: BBC2 television interview, aired 18th April 1970; Edith was also interviewed in October 1953 for *Pageant* magazine

p.107 'There are too many': Quoted in *Forties Fashion*, Jonathan Walford

p.108 While it undeniably: *Out of the Doll's House*, Angela Holdsworth

p.109 'dowdy old grannies': *Nella Last's Peace*, Patricia and Robert Malcolmson (eds)

p.109 'The "new line"': Ibid.

p.110 'workmen on ladders': *On Fair Vanity*, Betty Page

p.110 'Can anyone imagine': Quoted in *The Conscription of Fashion: Utility Cloth, Clothing and Footwear 1941–1952*, Christopher Sladen

p.110 As a young girl: *Vivienne Westwood*, Claire Wilcox

p.110 'Our mothers freed us': *Picture Post* (27th September 1947)

p.113 'How did this happen?': *Elizabeth Ham, By Herself, 1783–1820*, Elizabeth Ham

p.114 'as if by accident': Reported in the *Ladies' Treasury* (1868)

p.114 Similarly, in 1896: Quoted in *The Lost Art of Dress*, Linda Przybyszewski

p.114 'quadrupedal tail': *The Gentlewoman's Book of Dress*, Mrs Douglas

p.114 By the end of: *Woman Beautiful* (1899)

p.115 'Madam if you don't': *On Fair Vanity*, Betty Page

p.116 'None so bold': *The Gentlewoman's Book of Dress*, Mrs Douglas

p.116 'Well, I don't know': *Woman's Life* (13th November 1926)

p.117 'Any power whatsoever': Quoted in *The New Look: The Dior Revolution*, Nigel Cawthorne

p.117 ' . . . when skirts shorten': *On Vanity Fair*, Betty Page

p.119 One girl: History Wardrobe oral-history survey, *My Life in Clothes*, courtesy of Jean (born 1960)

p.121 'She was towed': Quoted in *The Anatomy of Fashion*, Susan Vincent

p.121 Servant girls: *Jane Welsh Carlyle, A New Selection of her Letters*, Trudy Bliss (ed.); 1834 letter to her mother-in-law

p.121 In a daring attempt: *The Greatest Plague in Life, or the Adventures of a Lady in Search of a Servant 1847*, Augustus & Henry Mayhew, quoted in *The Fabric of Society*, Jane Tozer and Sarah Levitt

p.126 'It kept your petticoats': *Period Piece*, Gwen Raverat

p.126 'had at least prevented': *Victorian Panorama*, Peter Quennell

p.127 'Women getting into omnibuses': *A Mid-Victorian Pepys: The Letters and Memoirs of Sir William Hardman*, S. M. Ellis (ed.)

p.127 'The present ugly fashion': *Under Control, Life in a Nineteenth-century Silk Factory*, Carol Adams, Paula Bartley, Judy Lown and Cathy Loxton

p.128 'glamour and sweetness': *Home Chat* (18th February 1939)

p.131 Having survived: *Elizabeth Ham, By Herself, 1783–1820*, Elizabeth Ham

p.132 'of which fatal': *Woman Beautiful* (1899)

p.132 'not only repugnant': *The Mirror of the Graces*

p.132 Much of this: *Dress as a Fine Art*, Mrs Merrifield

p.132 There was one crucial: *Dressed to Rule*, Philip Mansel p.133 'in went a disgusting flower': Quotes from *Hollywood Costume*, Deborah Nadoolman Landis (ed.)

p.135 **When the Empress:** *Dressed to Rule*, Philip Mansel

p.136 'First I give': From the author's collection

p.136 'At breakfast': *The Gentlewoman's Book of Dress*, Mrs Douglas

p.137 'As a working lady': Interview quoted in *Clothes Lines: Off-the-Peg Stories from the Closets of the Famous*, Julia McKenzie

p.138 'Ladies entertaining': *Still Here, An Autobiography*, Hardy Amies

p.139 **Actress Dame Thora Hird:** *Clothes Lines*, Julia McKenzie

p.139 **More dramatically:** History Wardrobe oral-history survey, *My Life in Clothes*, courtesy of Patricia Payne

p.143 **Queen Victoria had:** *A Family Album*, Duke of Windsor

p.143 **The twenty-five battalions:** *The Great War: Styles and Patterns of the 1910s*, R. L. Shep

THE TROUSER PRESS

p.145 'Heigh! Ho!': Quoted in *Eighty Years and More*, Elizabeth Cady Stanton

p.146 **That said:** *Viking Clothing*, Thor Ewing

p.147 **Woollen examples:** *Cloth and Clothing in Early Anglo-Saxon England*, Penelope Walton Rogers

p.148 **Padded with bran:** From *Anthropometamorphosis: Man Transfor'd: or, the Artificiall Changeling Historically Presented*, John Bulwer (London, 1653), referring to the earlier century; quoted in *Anatomy of Fashion*, Susan Vincent

p.149 **In the sixteenth century:** *Historical Essay on the Dress of the Ancient and Modern Irish*, Joseph Cooper Walker (1787)

p.151 **Since the statues appeared:** *Transformations: Classical Sculpture in Colour*, Jan Stubbe Østergaard and Anne Marie Nielsen (eds)

p.152 'in a pair': *The World*, Edward Moore

p.152 **Lord Byron was:** *Lord Byron: Accounts Rendered*, Dorothy Langley Moore

p.153 **Sadly for Brummell:** *The Life of George Brummell*, Captain William Jesse

p.153 'A nether habiliment': *The Enlarged Devil's Dictionary*, Ambrose Bierce

p.153 **In Russia:** *Dressed to Rule*, Philip Mansel

p.155 'From such like excesses': *A Family Album*, Duke of Windsor

p.156 'There was talk': *The Way We Wore*, Robert Elms

p.157 'deliberately making themselves': *Women in Trousers: A Rear View*, Demetri Marchessini

p.157 **it is telling that:** *Ackerman's Repository* (1828)

p.158 **According to one:** *Viking Clothing*, Thor Ewing

p.159 **What incredible freedom:** *Eighty Years and More*, Elizabeth Cady Stanton

p.161 'wonderful sense': *The Science of Dress*, Ada Ballin

p.161 'unnecessary, and': *The Lancet* (1879), quoted in The *Anatomy of Fashion*, Susan Vincent

p.161 'the subject of': 'Practical Dressmaking', *Ladies' World* (1898)

p.161 **Cycling was a craze:** *Ladies' Realm* (September 1902)

p.162 **submitted a patent:** *Ingenious Women*, Deborah Jaffé

p.163 'in the unaccustomed freedom': *Portrait of a Marriage*, Nigel Nicolson

p.163 'I was left alone': *Sapper Dorothy*, Dorothy Lawrence

p.164 'It's a hard world': *An English-Woman Sergeant in the Serbian Army*, Flora Sandes

p.164 'I am sincere': *Hollywood Costume*, Deborah Nadoolman Landis (ed.)
p.165 'I suddenly thought': *Nella Last's War*, Richard Broad and Suzie Fleming (eds)
p.168 The first pair: *Denim*, Graham Marsh and Paul Trynka
p.169 'jeans have become': *That Extra Half an Inch*, Victoria Beckham

COAT HOOKS

p.170 this is no ordinary coat: Lincolnshire Aviation Centre; coat acquired from the RAF Escaping Society Collection
p.173 'it is a profound mystery': *The Fur Trade of America*, A. L. Belden
p.173 Novelist and Hollywood scriptwriter: *The IT Girls*, Meredith Etherington-Smith and Jeremy Pilcher
p.174 'Everywhere in the world': *It Isn't All Mink*, Ginette Spanier
p.175 As one middle-class lady: *Three Years or the Duration*, Peggy Hamilton
p.176 In 1962: *Fashion Victim*, Michelle Lee
p.178 one cloak found: *Rural Costume*, Alma Oakes and Margot Hamilton Hill
p.178 The basic Roman toga: *The World of Roman Costume*, Judith Lynn Sebesta and Larissa Bonfante (eds)
p.179 The story of Sir Walter Raleigh: *Tudor Costume and Fashion*, Herbert Norris
p.179 Monarchs and aristocrats: *Royal Dress*, Valerie Cumming; *In Royal Fashion*, Kay Staniland
p.180 'the English countrywoman': *Peter Kalm's Travels in North America*, Aldolph B. Benson (ed.)
p.180 'Bonaparte, who thought': *Memoirs of Madame de Rémusat 1802–1808*, Paul Rémusat (ed.)
p.182 In 1837: *Mistress of Charlecote*, A. Fairfax Lucy (ed.)
p.183 One particular shawl: *Naming Jack the Ripper*, Russell Edwards
p.183 'The one who can wear': *What Dress Makes of Us*, Dorothy Quigley
p.186 'I saw the whole man': *Dracula*, Bram Stoker
p.187 'suicide machines': www.wired.com/2012/07/batman-cape-physics/ – accessed January 2015
p.189 'There is at present': Quoted in *Costumes of Household Servants*, C. Willet and Phillis Cunnington
p.191 'A Mackintosh is now': Quoted in *Handbook of English Costume in the 19th Century*, C. Willet and Phillis Cunnington
p.197 'What impressed me': Vanessa Anderson of the University of Derby, 2005; UofD website Mallory Replica Project, accessed in 2014
p.197 'a 100-percent': *Magnificent Desolation*, Buzz Aldrin

SUITS YOU

p.200 Suits might shine: *Eighteenth Century Embroidery Techniques*, Gail Marsh
p.201 During the French Revolution: *Dressed to Rule*, Philip Mansel
p.202 'If John Bull': *Harriet Wilson's Memoirs*, Lesley Blanch (ed.)
p.203 One gentleman: Recorded by Grantley Berkeley, Coldstream Guards officer, quoted in *Beau Brummell*, Ian Kelly
p.204 In a *Punch* magazine: *Punch, or the London Charivari* (13th June 1863)
p.204 Victorian gentlemen: Recounted in Edward Giles, *The Art of Cutting and History of English Costume*, quoted in *The Victorian Tailor*, Jason MacLochlainn

p.204 'I went to a tailor': *Memoirs of a Georgian Rake*, William Hickey

p.205 'I have imbibed': 'Vagaries in the Life of a Single Gentleman', featured in *The Ladies' Cabinet of Fashion* (1836)

p.206 'We want a little assistance': *Pelham*, Edward Bulwer Lytton

p.206 'mere walking pincushions': *The Hermit in London*, Captain Felix M'Donough

p.206 'any good suit': *The History of Men's Fashion*, Nicholas Storey

p.207 'nobody would': *The Diaries of Samuel Pepys*, 12th June 1666

p.207 'the suggestiveness': 'Feminine Affectations', *Ladies' Treasury* (July 1869)

p.207 'just like two old men': *Mistress of Charlecote*, Alice Fairfax Lucy (ed.)

p.207 Hall was painted: 1918 oil portrait by Charles Buchel, National Portrait Gallery, London

p.209 'Did you make': Recounted to the author by Anne Perret at Strawberry Hill House, November 2014

p.210 As the Industrial Revolution: *Sweated Industries and Sweated Labour 1860-1914*, James A. Schmiechen

p.212 'where they will serve': *Handbook of English Costume in the 19th Century*, C. Willet and Phillis Cunnington

p.214 'You can't put': *Hollywood Costume*, Deborah Nadoolman Landis (ed.)

p.214 It was couturier Hardy Amies: *Still Here, An Autobiography*, Hardy Amies

p.215 'That is my son': *A Family Album*, Duke of Windsor

p.216 When he became: *Dressed to Rule*, Philip Mansel

p.217 'We are much more likely to believe': *New Dress For Success,* John T. Molloy

p.219 Survivors of the camps: *The Seamstress*, Sara Tuvel Bernstein

p.220 'and having two': 'Convict Life' article, *Pearson's Magazine* (1900)

p.220 'Recruits are not only': Quoted in *Military Fashion*, John Mollo

p.221 'I remember the time': *Pride and Prejudice*, Jane Austen

p.222 'Is there anyone': *Military Fashion*, John Mollo

p.223 'a ridiculous': *Three Guineas*, Virginia Woolf

p.223 'And now the days of uniform were over': *Eight Months with the Women's Royal Air Force*, Gertrude George

p.225 'I remember my first': *Clothes Lines*, Julia McKenzie

p.226 ' . . . walking slowly': *The Invisible Man*, Ralph Ellison

p.227 'I was measured': *The Autobiography of Malcolm X*, Malcolm X

p.228 The zoot suit: *Black Britain*, Paul Gilroy

p.230 'There are still little': *Clothes Lines*, Julia McKenzie

p.230 Buttons on military uniforms: *Digging the Trenches*, Andrew Robertshaw and David Kenton

p.231 One of the earliest: Museum of London collection notes ML:A.27050

p.232 One might have saved: *Bullets, Blades and Battle Bowlers* exhibition, Leeds Royal Armouries, autumn 2014

p.233 'a uniform for': *The Way We Wore*, Robert Elms

p.234 At the 1939 New York: *Fear and Fashion*, Jane Pavitt

TIE RACK

p.237 'goe flip flap': *The Anatomie of Abuses*, Philip Stubbes

p.238 In 1582 it was reported: Quoted in *The Anatomy of Fashion*, Susan Vincent

p.238 'the eyes almost': *The Art of Tying the Cravat*, Henri LeBlanc

p.239 'Oh, these, sir?': *Beau Brummell*, Ian Kelly
p.240 'it is requisite': *The Art of Tying the Cravat*, Henri LeBlanc
p.240 'This tie does not occasion': *Neckclothitania*, 1818
p.240 '*Swells of the fancy*': *Dictionary of the Underworld*, Eric Partridge
p.240 In 1885 a clothing expert: *The Science of Dress*, Ada S. Ballin
p.240 And as late as 1917: *The Dangers in Neck-wear*, Walter G. Walford
p.240 King William III: *Staying Power*, Peter Fryer
p.241 The laundry list: *The Tie: Trends and Traditions*, Sarah Gibbings
p.241 'speckeled and sparkeled': *Anatomie of Abuses*, Philip Stubbes
p.241 The most fashionable: *The Tie: Trends and Traditions*, Sarah Gibbings
p.241 Charles II spent: Ibid.; *The Funeral Effigies of Westminster Abbey*, Anthony Harvey and Richard Mortimer (eds); currency conversion via www.nationalarchives.gov.uk/currency
p.243 'the most luxurious form': *The Tie: Trends and Traditions*, Sarah Gibbings
p.245 'To hide the absence': *Diary of a Nobody*, George and Weedon Grossmith, 1892
p.245 'easily tied': Oxendales store catalogue 1916
p.248 Outré dancer Isadora Duncan: *Fashion Victim*, Michelle Lee
p.250 In reality: *Lord Byron: Accounts Rendered*, Doris Langley Moore
p.251 Those who still feel constricted: *The Torrington Diaries*, John Byng
p.251 'which duly floated': *Seize the Moment*, Helen Sharman

SHOE BOXES

p.252 'the sands of the sea': *The Anatomie of Abuses*, Philip Stubbes
p.253 'GAUNDRY & SON': Museum of London, 32.61/2a-b
p.253 a far more practical: Museum of London, 50.88/1201
p.253 'We were gripped': 'The Holocaust Shoe, Untying Memory: Shoes as Holocaust Memorial Experience', Jeffrey Feldman in *Jews and Shoes*, Edna Nahshon; *The Capture and Trial of Adolf Eichmann*, Moshe Pearlman
p.254 'High heels, low heels': 'Murder Inc.', Richard Lauterbach, *Time* magazine (11th September 1944)
p.254 Drivers may spot: *Murder at Wrotham Hill*, Diane Souhami
p.258 In 1852: *Treasured Possessions from the Renaissance to the Enlightenment*, Victoria Avery et al.
p.258 'We often see': *The Papers and Diaries of a York Family 1764–1839*, Mrs Edwin Gray (ed.)
p.259 'As he strutted': *The Life of Beau Brummell*, Captain Jesse
p.259 One girl of the 1920s: *It Isn't All Mink*, Ginette Spanier
p.260 leading to the advertisement: Quoted in the *Ladies' Newspaper* (1852)
p.262 Early hominids: *The Earliest Human Footprints Outside Africa*, Nicholas Ashton
p.263 'The manufacturer': *South*, Ernest Shackleton
p.264 'clogged with silke': *The Anatomie of Abuses*, Philip Stubbes
p.266 'Good God!': *The Last Shall be First*, Brian Dobbs
p.266 Christopher 'Clutty': *Official Secrets*, Christopher Clayton-Hutton
p.267 This is proven: *Jews and Shoes*, Edna Nahshon
p.268 The blurring of: *Dr Martens*, Martin Roach
p.269 'It is only at': *The Gentlewoman's Book of Dress*, Mrs Douglas
p.270 For centuries: *The Academy of Armory*, Randall Holme (1688)
p.272 It wasn't until: *Clothes for the Job*, J. E. Smart

p.272 'And handsome': *The Anatomie of Abuses*, Philip Stubbes

p.274 'Fashion to me': *Vivienne Westwood*, Claire Wilcox

p.274 'Because the heels': *Fashion Victim*, Michelle Lee

p.274 'I don't know who': Quoted in *Hollywood Costume*, Deborah Nadoolman Landis (ed.)

p.275 Peter the Great's: *Russian Elegance*, Luisa V. Yefimova and Tatyana S. Aleshina

p.275 In 1902 fashion guru: 'History of the Shoe', Mrs Eric Pritchard, *Ladies' Realm* (July 1902)

p.276 'Each step you take': *The Little Mermaid*, Hans Christian Andersen

p.276 'Maybe it's a Cinderella': *That Extra Half an Inch*, Victoria Beckham

p.277 'If you love your son': *Aching for Beauty*, Wang Ping

p.278 Hercule Poirot: 'The Veiled Lady', *Poirot's Early Cases*, Agatha Christie

p.278 'I had to bedeck her': *Viking Clothes*, Thor Ewing

p.278 'This drunken hound': 'Adventure of the Abbey Grange', from *The Return of Sherlock Holmes*, Sir Arthur Conan Doyle

p.279 By the 1760s: *La Calzatura*, Eugenia Girotti

p.279 'I peeled the leather': *It Isn't All Mink*, Ginette Spanier

p.281 In versions of the Cinderella story: *The Sleeping Beauty and Other Fairy Tales from the Old French*, retold by Sir Arthur Quiller-Couch; Perrault's original text was the 1697 *Histoire ou Contes du Temps Passé*

p.282 A Frankfurt fashion house: *Nazi Chic?*, Irene Guenther

p.282 Another set of shoes: *Hollywood Costume*, Deborah Nadoolman Landis (ed.); *The Ruby Slippers of Oz*, Rhys Thomas

p.284 'I can see the footprints': *Magnificent Desolation*, Buzz Aldrin

JUMPER COLLECTION

p.287 finely knitted jumper-style vest: Museum of London collection; the Victoria and Albert Museum owns a snug eighteenth-century cardigan-like jacket

p.288 'who sat beneath': *The Scarlet Pimpernel*, Baroness Orczy

p.288 In fact this gruesome: *Off With Their Heads (or not)*, Paul Friedland (OUP blog Oxford)

p.289 Guernsey sweaters: *Knitting for All*, Margaret Murray and Jane Koster

p.290 Aran sweaters: *Knitting, Fashion, Industry, Craft*, Sandy Black

p.290 Fair Isle sweaters: Ibid.

p.292 The seventh Earl: *The Homicidal Earl: The Life of Lord Cardigan*, Saul David

p.293 Even ladies of: *A Stitch in Time*, Geoffrey Warren

p.294 a 'servant of all work': *No Place for Ladies*, Helen Rappaport

p.294 'It had meant nothing': *The Rainbow Comes and Goes*, Lady Diana Cooper

p.294 'It was soothing': *How We Lived Then*, Mrs C. S. Peel

p.296 The most famous jumper: *The Little Book of Schiaparelli*, Emma Baxter-Wright

p.298 'When you think': *Knitting for All*, Margaret Murray and Jane Koster

p.300 'Double, triple woollies': *Fashion under the Occupation*, Dominique Veillon

p.301 Alas for the knitter: Oral-history interview, via Meridith Towne in 2014

p.307 One man who was: Recounted to the author in 2014

p.308 'Favourite garment ever': History Wardrobe oral-history survey, *My Life in Clothes*, courtesy of Liz Hamilton (born 1969)

p.308 'My favourite sweater': Ibid., courtesy of Jodie (born 1954)

p.308 'My grandma did': Ibid., courtesy of Madeleine Smith (born 1959)

p.308 'I gathered it up': *Nella Last's War*, Richard Broad and Suzie Fleming (eds)

POCKET FLAPS

p.309 'little Bags': *The Academy of Armory*, Randle Holme

p.310 One surviving pair: Museum of Fine Arts, Boston

p.311 'What', in the words: *The Hobbit*, J. R. R. Tolkien

p.311 'I took with me': *Pamela*, Samuel Richardson

p.311 'lying on the top': *Elizabeth Ham, By Herself*, Elizabeth Ham

p.311 'lovely hoards': *Period Piece*, Gwen Raverat

p.312 'clokes to sinne': *The Anatomie of Abuses*, Philip Stubbes

p.313 For security purposes: *Russian Elegance*, Luisa V. Yefimova and Tatyana S. Aleshina

p.313 Even more ingeniously: *Ingenious Women*, Deborah Jaffé

p.313 Canny female survivors: *Women and Children First*, Judith B. Gellar

p.314 'Instinctively my hand': *Magnificent Desolation*, Buzz Aldrin

p.315 'Dressmakers take': *The Gentlewoman's Book of Dress*, Mrs Douglas

p.315 'not a natural right': *Are Women People? A Book of Rhymes for Suffrage Times*, Alice Duer Miller

p.316 a reticule pattern: *The Workwoman's Guide*

p.316 Queen Victoria was: *A Stitch in Time*, Geoffrey Warren

p.320 'Why mayn't we': *Period Piece*, Gwen Raverat

IN THE SWIM

p.321 'The ladyes goes': *Journeys of Celia Fiennes*, Christopher Morris (ed.)

p.322 'the ladies, dress'd': *Poetical Sketches of Scarborough*, J. B. Papworth et al.

p.322 'carry their dresses': Quoted in *English Costume for Sport and Outdoor Recreation*, Phillis Cunnington and Alan Mansfield

p.322 'a chemise or shirt': 'Suitable Bathing Dresses as used in Biarritz with Instructions on Swimming', W. F. Taylor, quoted in *The Fabric of Society*, Jane Tozer and Sarah Levitt

p.322 'go down to the sea-bathing': *The Girl with the Swansdown Seat*, Cyril Pearl

p.323 'the detestable custom': *Kilvert's Diaries 1870–1879*, Francis Chosen (ed.)

p.323 'No person shall bathe': *English Costume for Sport*, Phillis Cunnington and Alan Mansfield

p.323 'each Lady unfurled': *Period Piece*, Gwen Raverat

p.325 'that a sack arrangement': *Woman Beautiful* (1896)

p.326 'Young ladies ought': 'Swimming Feats of Miss Beckwith and Miss Parker', *The Penny Illustrated Paper* (11th September 1875)

p.326 'Three or four': *We Danced All Night*, Barbara Cartland

p.326 'I had to swim': *A Nurse at the Front*, Ruth Cowan (ed.)

p.328 'It is deplorable': *Evil Under the Sun*, Agatha Christie (1941)

p.329 'Me mother worra': Recounted to the author in 2013

p.329 'We hired our': Recounted to the author by Marcia McCluckie in 2012

p.330   An unlucky RAF officer: Recounted to the author in 2012
p.330   One army engineer: Anecdote about the author's grandparents, Ella and Fred Pugh, recounted by their son Tony in 2014
p.333   The most humorous: *Borat, Cultural Learnings of America for Make Benefit Glorious Nation of Kazakhstan*, 20th Century Fox (2006)

THE HAT BOX

p.336   a bearskin cap: *The Man in the Ice*, Konrad Spindler
p.336   the sheepskin hat: *The Bog People: Iron-Age Man Preserved*, Peter V. Glob
p.338   'Our ears were muffled': *Cold*, Sir Ranulph Fiennes
p.339   Somewhat bizarrely: *Nursing in Time of War*, P. H. Mitchiner and E. E. P. MacManus
p.339   The idea of: Featured in the *London Illustrated News* (25th December 1920)
p.343   'We consider nurse': *The Gentle Heritage*, Frances E. Crompton
p.344   'with a breach of the peace': *St James's Gazette* (16th January 1797)
p.346   'Men of individuality': *Hats, a History of Fashion in Headwear*, Hilda Amphlett, quoting from the conservative *Tailor and Cutter* magazine
p.348   Holmes does, however: 'The Boscombe Valley Mystery', from *The Adventures of Sherlock Holmes*
p.348   He is also described: From *The Memoirs of Sherlock Holmes*
p.349   'fitted neither to': 'The Adventure of the Blue Carbuncle', from *The Adventures of Sherlock Holmes*
p.350   A century later: *Ingenious Women*, Deborah Jaffé
p.350   The idea was imitated: *Patrician* magazine (December 1915) – 'Sewn into the cap is a charming little fringe, so, no matter when the Zeps arrive, I can quickly don it.'
p.351   One dignified Highland lady: *Period Piece*, Gwen Raverat
p.352   'required a telescope': *Plain or Ringlets?*, R. S. Surtees
p.352   'I must own myself': *Evelina*, Fanny Burney
p.352   'A bonnet decorated': *What Dress Makes of Us*, Dorothy Quigley. Quigley deplored 'wisps of untidy hair, queer trimmings and limp hats'.
p.353   'Like the hood': 'August Fashion', *Ladies' Treasury* (1868)
p.353   Gainsborough's eye-catching painting: *The Napoleon of Crime*, Ben Macintyre
p.355   ' . . . and STOOD on it': *Period Piece*, Gwen Raverat
p.355   Frenchwoman Rose Bertin: *Queen of Fashion*, Caroline Weber
p.356   'Angles are attitude': *Hollywood Costume*, Deborah Nadoolman Landis (ed.)
p.357   In an informal poll: *Keeping Up Appearances*, Catherine Horwood
p.358   'if it be only to save': *Spectator* (9th November 1711)
p.358   'This is to give Notice': *Spectator* (15th September 1712)
p.358   'While there is': *Etiquette for Men*, G. R. M. Devereux
p.358   A woman going out: Quoted in *Hats: A Stylish History*, Jody Shields
p.360   'I'm afraid these hats': Ibid.
p.361   A craze for berets: *Hollywood Costume*, Deborah Nadoolman Landis (ed.)
p.361   'The distinctive sign': *Purple Tints of Paris*, John Bayle

p.363 'it removed my veil': *Jane Eyre*, Charlotte Brontë

p.365 Some saw potential: Edith Garrud, 'The World We Live In' (4th March 1910)

p.366 It was the interpretation: *My Life and Dancing*, Maud Allan

p.366 Ultimately Allan's downfall: *Oscar Wilde's Last Stand*, Philip Hoare

p.367 A particularly striking: Featured in *Mourning Dress*, Lou Taylor

p.367 Until veils went: Described in *The Female Detective*, Andrew Forrester

p.368 As with other veils: *Rethinking Muslim Women and the Veil*, Dr Katherine Bullock; *Veil: Modesty, Privacy and Resistance*, Fadwa El Guindi; *The Veil and Male Elite: A Feminist Interpretation of Women's Rights in Islam*, Fatima Mermisi

p.369 'One wore on his headpiece': Quoted in *Accessories of Dress*, Katherine Lester and Bess Viola Oerke

p.370 There is a pair: *Elizabeth*, David Starkey

p.371 At one burial: The burial of Colonel Edward Phelips, referenced in *The Anatomy of Fashion*, Susan Vincent

p.371 'Some of chicken-skin': 'Mundus Muliebris, The Ladies Dressing Room Unlock'd and Her Toilette Spread', John Evelyn (1690)

p.372 a salesgirl at: *It Isn't All Mink*, Ginette Spanier

p.374 'I wouldn't have': *Edith Garrud*, Tony Wolf

p.375 'A milliner takes': Ibid.

p.375 Gradually umbrellas: 'History of the Umbrella', in *Child's Friend* magazine (1906)

p.376 'If that silly old man': Quoted in *The Umbrella Unfurled*, Nigel Rodgers

p.377 Queen Victoria was: *Shooting Victoria*, Paul Thomas Murphy

p.378 There is a very chilling: *Goodnight Mister Tom*, Michelle Magorian

p.378 Another writer: *Lark Rise to Candleford*, Flora Thompson

p.380 'Cummerbunds are not': *The History of Men's Fashion*, Nicholas Storey

p.381 'How Adam and Eve': Quoted in *Georgian Delights*, J. H. Plumb

p.382 'It was of silk': *Mr Bazalgette's Agent*, Leonard Merrick

p.382 'Wipe your face': Quoted in *Asians in Britain*, Rozina Visram

p.382 'the cotton of which': *A Family Album*, Duke of Windsor

p.382 'It is gone!': *Lady's Magazine* (1772)

p.383 In the clean-up: *Changing Fashions 1800–1970*, Elizabeth Ann Coleman

p.383 'Where should I': *The Tragedy of Othello, The Moor*, William Shakespeare (1603)

p.383 At the South Pole: *Cold*, Sir Ranulph Fiennes

p.383 'of a nicely patterned': *Georgetown Gazette* (1918)

p.384 'In planning a costume': *Home Sewing Helps* magazine (1925)

p.384 'With a country suit': *The History of Men's Fashion*, Nicholas Storey

p.385 'for those liable': *Workwoman's Guide* (1838)

p.386 'Where is / Thy leather apron': *The Tragedy of Julius Caesar*, Act I, Scene I, William Shakespeare

p.386 'True blue will': *Brewer's Dictionary of Phrase and Fable*

p.387 It recommended: *Protective Clothing for Women and Girl Workers Employed in the Factories and Workshops*

p.388 More unusually: *The History of Wakefield and its Environs*, vol. 1, John Hewitt

p.390 'But the fan': *Mr Bazalgette's Agent*, Leonard Merrick p.391   'In the time when': *Dictionnaire des étiquettes de la cour,* Madame de Genlis

PYJAMA CASE

p.392   'He wore an ordinary': *Until the Final Hour,* Traudl Jung

p.394   'good washing shades': *Ladies' Realm* (July 1902)

p.394   'earthquake gowns': Horace Walpole, *Letters* (4th April 1750)

p.395   'a fancy dress ball': Helen Candee, quoted in *Women and Children First,* Judith B. Gellar

p.395   'Just fancy': *Discretions & Indiscretions,* Lady Lucy Duff Gordon

p.396   'doom of the sleeping shirt': Quoted in *The Dictionary of Fashion History,* Valerie Cumming

p.399   'These poor women': *Clara's War,* Clara Kramer

p.401   'night-dresses cause': *Family Circle* magazine (April 1974)

p.404   'Her silk-frilled nightdress': *Secret Rooms,* Catherine Bailey

p.405   'an elegant cerulean blue': *Plain or Ringlets?,* R. S. Surtees

p.406   The declining career: *Beau Brummell,* Ian Kelly

p.406   'and if a sword': *Town & Country* magazine (1785)

p.406   Peter the Great: *Russian Elegance,* Luisa V. Yefimova and Tatyana S. Aleshina

p.406   'lounging upon the sofa': 'The Adventure of the Empty House', *The Return of Sherlock Holmes,* Sir Arthur Conan Doyle

p.408   'not horrors': *Women's Institutes,* Cicely McCall

p.410   'What a waste': Recounted to the author by Mrs Elsie Walton in 2014

INDEX